How to LIVE 365 Days a Year

BY JOHN A. SCHINDLER, M.D.

FAWCETT CREST • NEW YORK

HOW TO LIVE 365 DAYS A YEAR

THIS BOOK CONTAINS THE COMPLETE TEXT OF THE
ORIGINAL HARDCOVER EDITION.

Published by Fawcett Crest Books, a unit of CBS Publications,
the Consumer Publishing Division of CBS Inc,
by arrangement with Prentice-Hall, Inc.

ISBN: 0-449-23922-5

Printed in the United States of America

33   32   31   30   29   28   27   26

IF YOU CAN ANSWER "YES" TO JUST ONE OF THESE QUESTIONS . . .

Do you feel you have given more to life than it has given you? ☐ No ☐ Yes

Do you see people with less "on the ball" getting ahead faster than you? ☐ No ☐ Yes

Do you have trouble adjusting to new situations and new people? ☐ No ☐ Yes

Do day-to-day problems cause you worry and trouble? ☐ No ☐ Yes

THEN THIS FAMOUS BEST SELLER WILL SHOW YOU HOW TO START LIVING LIFE TO THE FULL!

For many years research has been going on in the great medical centers of this country, to develop scientific techniques for helping people to live happier as well as healthier lives.

HOW TO LIVE 365 DAYS A YEAR shows you how these discoveries can help you.

READ THIS BOOK AND LEARN:

- how to make the present moment emotionally healthy!
- a cure for the jitters caused by your daily work!
- what to do when the going is rough!
- a prescription for family troubles—how to make the family the place where you get a lift instead of a headache!
- what to do when you "can't make up your mind"!
- how to avoid emotional stress in problems of marital relations!
- how to handle discouragement or adversity!
- what to do if you have lost your self-esteem!
- how to overcome fears about your health!
- how to achieve emotional control in the 12 important areas of living!

THIS BOOK IS DEDICATED
TO THE UNSUNG MAGNIFICENCE
OF ORDINARY PEOPLE

who, from paleolithic caves to modern assembly lines, have shown the *courage to endure* and the *determination to make the best of it.*

The courage to endure has helped people through woe piled on woe, defeat added to defeat, difficulty after difficulty. The determination to make the best of it has answered the dirges of ill winds with lilting, jigging tunes; has illuminated dark moments with cheerful, hopeful quips; has helped people grow better as situations grow worse.

To these two magnificent qualities in people this book is humbly dedicated, in the hope that it may be able to help, even a little, those who have forgotten that they, too, have these same qualities.

I WISH TO THANK . . .

I wish to thank the Editors of *The Progressive, The Reader's Digest, Science Digest, The Rotarian, The Wisconsin State Journal, The Milwaukee Journal,* and *The Chicago University Round Table* for permission to use portions of this book that they previously printed.

Especially do I wish to thank Professor H. B. McCarty, Rear Admiral Walter G. Schindler, U.S.N., Dr. Ben H. Brunkow, Professor Max Otto, Dr. Frederick Wellman, and Dr. Ralph D. Bennett, for giving of their time and valuable help in reading and suggesting changes in the manuscript.

Also I wish to thank the Honorable Alexander M. Wiley, United States Senate, Dr. Edgar S. Gordon, Dr. Burton Kintner, Dr. Millard Tufts, Mr. Henry Cox, Dr. Norman Vincent Peale, Dr. John Guy Fowlkes, and Mr. John English for their enthusiastic support and help in launching this book.

And most of all, I wish to thank my wife, Dorothea Schindler, for skillful editorial help, for never-failing inspiration and suggestion, and for an amazing understanding and patience over a period of three years during which the preparation of this book absorbed the few odd moments left over from a busy medical practice.

J.A.S.

CONTENTS

HOW WERE YOUR LAST 365 DAYS?

HOW WILL BE YOUR NEXT 365 DAYS?

FOR MOST PEOPLE, LIVING CONSISTS IN MUDDLING THROUGH A great many people have lived on this earth since the human race began—billions and billions of them. And over every head, just as over yours and mine, has dangled the tempting word and idea called "Happiness." Happiness connotes a state that most people touch only momentarily, if at all, and that the majority (including the high, as well as the low) never attain in any fundamental way.

One of the big failures of the human race has been the failure of its members to attain anything like enduring happiness here on earth.

HOW WERE YOUR LAST 365 DAYS?

To bring home what I mean, ask *yourself*, "How were *your* last 365 days?"

Were your last 365 days a thrilling series of gloriously alive moments? Were you running exhilaratingly and enthusiastically through a golden avenue of days, humming a happy tune, with never an apprehensive skip of a reluctant heart? How much of the time during your last 365 days were you occupied with cares (which is a mild term), or difficulties (which is a bit more severe), or troubles (which is frankly just what it means)?

Your last 365 days were probably not very different from anyone else's.

THE SAD REALITY IN MOST PEOPLE'S LIVES

Behind the front they put on for the public, most people are disturbed; many are perturbed; others are worried to the point of confusion; some are frankly frustrated. Most of them do not feel up to par; they have a tiredness, a pain, a disagreeable feeling, a misery. They have a dozen matters they are worried about. They are brimming with apprehensions, fears, irritations. They have never quite connected with good living. They have muddled through their last 365 days, trying to avoid but always managing to stumble over new, nagging troubles, never reaching healthy enthusiasms, but going along nibbling on constant cares, irritated more often than pleased, timorous more often than courageous, apprehensive more often than calm.

That is the sad failure of billions and billions of people who have passed across the earth.

The most important thing has not been learned: how to conduct ourselves so that we may *live*.

YOUR LIFE CAN BE GOOD

Human life—your life—need not be like that.

Your life *can* be an exhilarating and enthusiastic journey through a golden avenue of days, humming a happy tune. Actually, a life of that kind is just as easy, and infinitely better, than the old way of muddling through.

Living, instead of muddling through, is your reward for expending a very small amount of effort to attain know-how.

THE NECESSARY KNOW-HOW FOR LIVING CAN BE YOURS

In this Twentieth Century, for the first time in history, modern psychology and psychiatry have developed the know-how for *living.*

In this book, that new knowledge is presented in practical, usable terms. This book is specifically meant to teach people how to change their way of living from the way in which they conducted their last 365 days to a new way by which they can *live* during their next 365 days, and all their days thereafter.

THE METHOD USED IN THIS BOOK HAS HAD A LONG, SUCCESSFUL TRIAL

The method for *living* presented in this book has been gradually evolved through 20 years of effort, trial, error, and success, in a large midwestern medical clinic. It has proven very effective in helping thousands of people escape from the physical effects of muddled living and has given them a new know-how for going ahead on a new and better road.

THE CONNECTION BETWEEN MUDDLING THROUGH AND MOST OF OUR ILLNESS

It is in the doctor's office that the almost universal failure to handle living effectively stands out in all its unfortunate complications.

People come to the doctor still wearing the front they always put on that says, "Except for these aches and pains, I am doing all right, of course. I'm conducting my living as satisfactorily as anyone can!"

But as the interview and examination proceed, it is evident that the strain of poor living, of muddling through, is most usually the cause of the person's illness.

We Humans Are Used to Enduring Unhappiness

The patient doesn't come to the doctor about his *unhappiness*, which is actually the cause of his sickness. He makes no mention of his unhappiness until the doctor gains his confidence, and then he removes the front he is hiding behind.

The patient, even as you and I, has been toughened in a hard world. His is the attitude many people have always had: "Phooey! Happiness? This is a lovely word. But it's too bad! There isn't any! No one has ever really believed happiness exists, or ever will exist."

He accepts his unhappiness as an unfortunate, but normal, routine condition of life on earth.

But It Is Hard to Endure the Physical Symptoms of Unhappiness

The patient comes to the doctor because of the *physical symptoms* that the strain of of his muddling through has begun to produce, not because of unhappiness. He is, of course, unaware that his physical symptoms and unhappiness are both caused by the same muddling through.

He accepts the unhappiness as a matter of course.

But he doesn't accept the tiredness, the pain, and all manner of other symptoms. *They* are uncomfortable, and he is ready to do something about *them*.

He is amazed if he is told that the only effective thing he can do about them is to live differently, a concept that had not existed in his view of things. All of us think that the way we are living is the only way to live, under the circumstances.

But that is what the patient must learn to do—he must learn to live differently—to *live*. He must get rid of a lot of barnacles. He has only one alternative to continuing in his misery, and that is to quit producing emotional stress by muddling through and begin to make healthy emotions by knowing how to *live*.

Laymen have only the vaguest impression that emotional stress causes *physical* disturbances. Most people have a very hazy idea of how frequently, and how profoundly, emotional stress affects the body.

Occasionally a person can be objective enough to see that his life is a sea of troubles, but he usually remains unaware that he is having any such thing as emotional stress. Emotional stress is a pretty intangible sounding thing to most people, and when their physical distress begins, they haven't the faintest idea that it is coming from their emotional stress.

The physical effects of the emotions lie outside consciousness or volition. Consciousness can control the changes of emotions only by changing the emotion potential of thought.

Everyone, and that includes you and me, underestimates both the extent and the effects of his emotional stress. As he muddles through his sea of trouble, everyone half-consciously prides himself on some sort of a vague control over such supposedly ephemeral matters as emotional stress.

Everyone has the idea, "This thing they call emotional stress may cause illness in some people, but you can bet your boots I'm not going to let it get *me*!"

But you can bet your boots the goblin will get him just the same.

And it will get *you*, "if you don't watch out!"

Virtually everyone does get emotionally induced illness at some time or other. *Over 50 per cent of all the illness that doctors see is emotionally induced illness!* That, my friend, is not an ephemeral situation. Expressed in monetary terms, that situation costs the United States many times more every year than the damage that would result if every river in the country were to go on an all-time high flood.

A situation of that kind is a national catastrophe!

And when emotional illness hits *you*, it's a personal catastrophe!

THIS BOOK BEGINS WITH AN EXPLANATION OF EMOTIONALLY INDUCED ILLNESS

Most people, like yourself, are usually willing to go along unmindful of emotional stress until they learn, either the hard way or the smart way, that emotional stress eventually produces serious, disabling illness, and that *emotional stress is, today, our Number One cause of ill health.*

It is hard to shrug those facts off.

And so *How to Live 365 Days a Year* properly begins with an explanation of emotionally induced illness, because once you understand the miserable end results of emotional stress, you will understand the *necessity* of learning how to *live.*

PART I DESCRIBES EMOTIONALLY INDUCED ILLNESS

Part I of this book describes how the prevalent emotional currents in our lives cause the symptoms of the most remarkable, and by far the most common, physical disease we have.

This is a new field of knowledge, and as recently as 1936 the wildest imagination could not have surmised the tremendous effects that scientific research has since shown the emotions have upon our state of health.

In Part I the picture of emotional illness is painted with considerable completeness, in terms that do not bog the reader down in a morass of physiologic and medical jargon.

Chapter 1 is concerned with the question, "What, after all, is an emotion?"

You will be surprised to learn that an emotion, far from being an ephemeral sort of thing, is a very tangible affair that one can easily *observe* in the body. That's right! You can actually *see* an emotion.

The changes in the body that *are* the emotion are mediated partly through the stimulation of the *autonomic nervous system,* which is why emotionally induced illness has been called "It's your nerves."

But by far the most important emotional effects are produced through the action of the *endocrine glands,* of which the *pituitary gland,* situated at the base of the brain, is the most important. This role of the endocrine glands is a thrilling and almost unbelievable story that has been written since 1936, the year Dr. Hans Selye began his researches at Montreal University.

SO WHAT? WHAT ARE WE GOING TO DO ABOUT IT?

The question naturally arises, "What are we going to do about muddled living, emotional stress, unhappiness, emotionally induced illness?"

How, in this world, is one to live in any other way than the way one *is* living?

PART II PROVIDES THE ANSWER FOR EMOTIONAL STRESS FROM MUDDLING THROUGH

In Part II, this problem is reduced to the simple terms of a practical solution, a solution that is as easy to try as it is to understand.

The many varieties of help given us by modern psychiatry and psychology are leveled down to the common terms of daily life, and integrated into a one-two-three system for directing the course of your living from one minute to the next.

The method presented in Part II is essentially the same material my patients in the Monroe Clinic receive through private, illustrated talks and movies. As I said above, this method has gradually evolved out of many different approaches and attempts (varying all the way from group therapy to long ventilative sessions) to find a practical and successful way for patients to bring emotional *stasis* (that is, emotional tranquility; good adjustment) instead of emotional *stress* into their living. This method has proven to be very successful. Thousands of patients have found it a valuable guide to new heights in living they had never realized existed.

IMMATURITY IS THE CAUSE OF MUDDLING THROUGH

The problem boils down to this:

People conduct their lives so poorly, and have conducted their lives so poorly through all the ages, because no one has ever been taught how to grow up into fully rounded maturity. All of us, including the most dignified and responsible executive, fail to grow up in some important department of living or other; all of us continue to react to certain adult problems with childish reactions.

It is by trying to meet adult problems with childish reactions that we generate emotional stress.

THERE IS NO PLACE WHERE PEOPLE ARE TAUGHT MATURITY

People are not to be blamed for this universal failure to develop well-rounded maturity. Maturity does not come to a person naturally, like physical growth. Maturity is a cultural feature that must be learned.

There has been no organized attempt in our time, nor in any other time, to *teach* people the fundamentals of maturity.

THE FAMILY DOES NOT TEACH MATURITY

The average family has a negative influence on its members as far as developing maturity is concerned. Much of our emotional stress rises out of the common immaturities in family life. In fact, our families are our foremost cause of emotional stress, and, therefore, of ill health, in this country.

Chapter 10 reviews the common failures in families that cause stress in family members, and then presents a plan for successful family operation that will provide emotional maturity.

The Schools Do NOT Teach Maturity

The schools do not as yet teach the student maturity. But educators are strongly interested in the problem; not only are they talking about it, but they are beginning to do something about it.

A textbook for teenagers like the one written by Judson and Mary Landis, *Building Your Life,* is a promising and exciting development.* This is the sort of thing that we need; such efforts are going to grow and develop, and in another decade or two our public schools will, doubtless, be doing a good job of teaching this most important aspect of living— maturity.

This new enterprise in education—teaching and grounding youth in the attitudes of maturity—will bring to human life a quality never attained and never dreamed of before. It will be more than a mere milestone in human progress: it will deserve to be classed as a millennium.

But until education becomes maturity-minded, the influences in our society for developing maturity are entirely haphazard. Fortunate is the person who falls under the influence of someone who managed to acquire maturity and who can pass it on to others—perhaps a parent, a teacher, a minister, a friend. Such fortune, however, remains haphazard chance. Most people have no such good fortune and remain immature in essential fields of living and full of emotional stress.

Maturity Is a Matter of Attitudes

Maturity is not a matter of being crammed full of technical or classical knowledge; nor does it consist in the ability to make important judgments correctly.

Maturity is essentially a collection of attitudes, attitudes

---

* Judson T. and Mary G. Landis, *Building Your Life* (New York: Prentice-Hall, Inc., 1954).

that are more effective and helpful to the individual in meeting situations than are the attitudes a small child might have in the same situations. An attitude is an established way of reacting to certain classes of experiences.

The more mature a person is, the more complete is the stock of effective attitudes that he can bring to the great variety of experiences that arise in the course of living.

MATURITY INCLUDES MANY ATTITUDES

Throughout Part II the attitudes that comprise maturity are presented on the ground level of practical action, as obviously superior ways of handling the situations that are continually getting most people down.

There are several spots in life where the possession of maturity is particularly important.

One such spot is the competitive field of modern business and industry, which is the subject of Chapter 12.

Another such spot is the domain of sex; here mature attitudes are particularly rare. Maturity in matters of sex is the subject of Chapter 11.

One of the most difficult spots in life has become the period of old age. Mature attitudes for meeting old age gracefully are the subject of Chapter 13.

THERE IS A REVIEW AT THE END OF EACH CHAPTER

To help the reader to review, or to go back to pick up a thread, each chapter is concluded with a brief review.

There may be even an occasional reader who is in such a hurry, or who feels himself rushing into emotionally induced illness at such a speed (the two really go together), that he will care to read only the chapter reviews. That is perfectly all right. If he absorbs what is in the reviews, he will be soothed and calmed in his hectic flight, and will find himself about to read the whole book after all. *Following that*, he can begin *living*.

THE LAST CHAPTER IS A FULL BLUEPRINT

Chapter 15 is a blueprint of the chapter reviews in Part II, arranged in outline form so that the various items in the development of maturity can be correlated at a glance.

This outline will later serve the reader as a ready periodic review of the book's method for getting him out of the doldrums of muddling through and into the golden avenue of *living*.

You will find that *How to Live 365 Days a Year* is not merely another of the variety known as "self-uplift" or "inspirational" books. The information and techniques presented in this book are something that everyone needs and that no one can live well without.

Not only is this book a way out of emotional stress, but it is a prevention for, or a way out of, emotionally induced illness.

For you, and for every man, this book has been written, so that you may avoid emotionally induced illness and may see a way to turn emotional stress into emotional health.

PART I.

HOW AND WHY EMOTIONALLY
INDUCED ILLNESS OCCURS

1.

YOUR EMOTIONS PRODUCE MOST
OF YOUR PHYSICAL DISEASE

Probably no greater confusion exists in this confused world than the one in the minds of nonmedical people concerning the type of illness loosely and erroneously described as "It's your nerves." This confusion in the lay mind is not remarkable at all, since until recently confusion also existed in the medical mind. We began as recently as 1936 to understand the mechanism by which a set of emotions could produce physical disease. The medical profession's education in the matter is just under way. Between the time the profession is educated in a subject and the time the lay population generally understands it, there is usually a lapse of 20 years. Thus we see that the educative process is in its early stages.

Functional disease, or emotionally induced illness, as it had best be called, is, every way you look at it, a very, very remarkable disease.

THE REMARKABLE PREVALENCE OF FUNCTIONAL DISEASE

One of the outstanding things, for instance, about E. I. I. (emotionally induced illness) is that over 50 per cent of those seeking medical aid today have it.

Put it differently: If *you* become ill tomorrow, or if *you* are ill today, the chances are a little better than 50-50 that you are ill with E. I. I.

Or, still another way of putting it: A big textbook of medicine, such as medical students use, contains the account of roughly 1,000 different diseases that this human clay of ours

19

is subject to. One of these diseases, emotionally induced illness, is as common as all the other 999 put together!

Perhaps it is a little hard for you, a layman, to believe these figures. But actually they are probably on the conservative side. A few years ago the Ochsner Clinic in New Orleans published a paper which stated that 74 per cent of 500 consecutive patients admitted to the department handling gastrointestinal diseases were found to be suffering from E. I. I. And in 1951, a paper from the Yale University Out-Patient Medical Department indicated that 76 per cent of patients coming to that Clinic were suffering from E. I. I.!

One naturally asks, "If this disease is so prevalent, why doesn't one hear more about it?" What's the answer? The answer is as peculiar as the disease itself.

EMOTIONALLY INDUCED ILLNESS: THE DARK SPOT IN MODERN MEDICINE

Everyone, including you and me, has had emotionally induced illness at some time or other. If you saw a physician when you had it, the chances are that the physician did not tell you what you had. There are two good reasons why he didn't.

The first reason is that although physicians have always known about the disease, and have been able to diagnose it for many years, it has been only in the last ten years that we have understood it well enough to begin to talk about it.

The second and most important reason the doctor did not tell you what you had arises from the peculiar method by which this disease has been treated.

A doctor does not have to be in practice long to learn that merely telling a patient "You have nothing wrong with you; your trouble is being produced by your emotions," or "It's your nerves," is very poor therapy. It not only does the patient little or no good, but often angers him, sets him on the defensive, and sends him to another doctor. This one, with greater understanding of the patient's needs (not his condition), gives the patient the kind of a diagnosis he is willing to accept.

If a physician insists on using the frontal attack, and tells the patient that his trouble comes from his emotions, he must be prepared to follow up with an explanation of how the disease works to produce the patient's symptoms, what emotions are responsible for the patient's illness, and how the patient is to substitute better emotions for those he has been having. We call all this *adequate psychotherapy*. It is the only rational way we have had of treating E. I. I.

Drawbacks of adequate psychotherapy. But adequate psychotherapy, as it is understood today, is impossible—impossible because of TIME. The great obstacle to "adequate psychotherapy" is that it requires 20 hours per patient.

Using it, a doctor could, by working 20 hours a day, treat the equivalent of one patient a day. But the average doctor in this country sees 23 patients a day! Suppose the general doctor were to send these patients to psychiatric specialists. (I can hear some of you suggest that.) Giving adequate psychotherapy to the tremendous number of patients with E. I. I. would require several hundred thousand psychiatrists. There are only 5,000 at the present time in the United States. The problem of treating functional disease by "adequate" methods is thus, obviously, overwhelming. Less than 1 per cent of the patients with E. I. I. receive adequate psychotherapy by present standards.

Substitution therapy. The other 99 per cent of the patients with E. I. I. received what might be termed "substitution therapy." This consists of giving the patient a substitute diagnosis that he can readily understand to be a cause of his illness, and then carrying on the treatment ostensibly for that cause. This is psychotherapy, too, but of a bastard variety.

Such substitution therapy has been the accepted treatment for thousands of years. The primitive witch doctor told his functional patient he was possessed with evil spirits. The treatment consisted in driving out the evil spirits by very dramatic and suggestive methods. I sometimes wish, when I have a tough patient, that I had a method of therapy half as suggestive as the one the witch doctor used.

The medieval doctor told his patient that he had an unbalance of the four humors and then proceeded to remove one—usually blood, because that was the easiest to remove.

The cultist of today tells his patient, "You have a vertebra out of place" and then makes passes purporting to put it back into place.

The modern physician uses modern substitute diagnoses such as *high or low basal metabolic rate, high or low blood pressure*, or *adrenal cortical insufficiency*. The last would make a hit in Park Avenue practice; but out in the grass roots country, a homely "sluggish liver" would get across much better and with much less fuss. Any *good* substitute diagnosis must be less severe than the disease the patient is afraid he had; otherwise, the diagnosis merely makes the patient sicker.

Substitution therapy has been possible through the ages because 60 per cent of the patients treated by almost *any* variety of substitution therapy feel improved for a period of two months. A patient improved for two months is a good advertisement for the substitution therapist. New patients are "sold" by the temporary improvement. It has made possible such substitution-therapeutic successes as the nostrums and quackeries for which the public annually spends billions of dollars. It is the functionally ill who buy these items, along with the billions of dollars of vitamin preparations that swamp the national market.

If the medical profession treated emotionally induced illness as effectively as it does lobar pneumonia, the quacks would be out of business overnight. This disease is the bread and butter of both the physician and the irregular healer. If adequate methods of treatment were to banish it altogether, the cults and the marginal, lower-grade physician would vanish from the scene.

The worst feature of substitution therapy is that, in the long run, it makes the emotionally-ill person worse, and serves to cement the chronicity of the illness. Of the people treated by this method, only 8 per cent are any better at the end of one year. The others have added the name of another disease to their fear that they are not well. And where the doctor is not wise and careful in his substitute diagnosis, he may give the patient a very severe phobia of a serious illness. This kind of doctor-started disease is known in the profession as an *iatrogenic illness,* meaning, in Greek, an illness started by a doctor. Three out of every five emotionally-ill patients I see in my office have an appreciable amount of iatrogenic illness, which makes treatment more difficult.

Large-scale efforts are under way to develop more rapid and more adequate methods of treating this disease that can be used by the general physician. It is safe to say that another 20 years will see a complete revolution in the treatment of this, our most common disease. This present dark spot of modern medicine will become as brightly illuminated as the rest of the medical map.

EMOTIONALLY INDUCED ILLNESS IS A PHYSICAL DISEASE

Let us distinctly understand that patients with this disease present themselves with *physical* symptoms, not *mental* symptoms. This is a difficult point for the uninitiated to grasp.

22

The following is a partial list of the hundreds of symptoms this disease can produce. The percentage number after each symptom indicates how often its occurrence is due to emotionally induced illness.

From this partial list, you can get the idea that the common things people complain of are emotionally induced. But anyone in medical practice can tell you that most of the uncommon, bizarre symptoms are also usually caused by emotional troubles.

Complaint	Percentage
Pain in the back of the neck	75
Lump in the throat	90
Ulcer-like pain	50
Gall bladder-like pain	50
Gas	99 44/100
Dizziness	80
Headaches	80
Constipation	70
Tiredness	90

THE MORE INTELLIGENT YOU ARE, THE MORE YOU ARE PRONE TO E. I. I.

Many people who do not understand the nature of the illness are apt to think that because of their own superior intelligence they are immune to emotionally induced illness. As a matter of fact, E. I. I. becomes more prevalent as one goes up the ladder of human responsibility, mental alertness and capacity.

This is probably because the alert mind can find ten things to be worried and concerned about in the time the unalert mind can think of only one. The person with greater mental capacity also takes on greater responsibilities, which means, usually, more tense emotions.

If "Intelligence" actually consisted of being intelligent, it would include, before anything else, the intelligent orientation and handling of the emotions. But apparently up to the present day this ability has been pretty generally left out of being intelligent, and the so-styled intelligent people are usually the ones least capable of guiding their emotions through the maze of everyday living.

The group in my part of the country who have emotionally induced illness least often are the farmers' wives with families of nine or ten who, in addition to their housework, also help out on the farm. Their minds are too busy with work to "think," and they are too busy taking care of other people to think of themselves.

One of these wonderful human beings told me one time when I asked her whether she ever got tired (one of the most common functional symptoms), "Son, 25 years ago, I taught myself never to ask myself that question." And that, incidentally, is the best cure for that kind of tiredness.

WILLIAM JAMES' DEFINITION OF AN EMOTION

To understand emotionally induced illness one must, of course, understand what an emotion is. In 1884, emotion was defined by William James as "a state of mind that manifests itself by sensible changes in the body." With every emotion (and we are having some kind of an emotion every minute) changes are taking place in muscles, in blood vessels, in the viscera, in the endocrine glands. These changes and the perceptive mental state that accompanies them *are* the emotion. Without these bodily changes, there would be no emotion.

TWO GENERAL KINDS OF EMOTIONS

Although there are some minor exceptions, all emotions belong in one of two groups as far as the changes they produce in the body are concerned.

The first large group of emotions includes those whose changes consist in *overstimulation* of various parts of the body: an overstimulation, via the nervous system, of any organ or any muscle; overstimulation of one or more of the endocrine glands.

Because these emotions overstimulate organs and muscles, they produce a feeling that is unpleasant. People for thousands of years have naturally called these the "unpleasant emotions." These include such well-known ones as anger, anxiety, fear, apprehension, discouragement, grief, and dissatisfaction. Actually, there is no limit to the variety and nuance of emotions; one could make a list of unpleasant emotions a mile long.

The second large group of emotions are those whose manifestations in the body are an *optimal stimulation*, one neither too extreme nor too weak. These are the emotions that we can lump together under the long-used term of "pleasant emotions." We call them pleasant because the changes they produce give us a pleasant feeling. These are the emotions like hope, courage, joy, equanimity, affection, and agreeableness. Here again the possible list is endless; there is no limit to their variety.

SOME OF THE MANIFESTATIONS OF THE EMOTION OF ANGER

Let us see what the actual manifestations of a specific emotion are. We will take an emotion that you and I, of course, have never had, but that we have seen other people have—the emotion of *anger*.

In any emotion, there are external manifestations—that is, changes one can see exhibited externally on the surface of the body. These external manifestations make acting possible, for acting consists in duplicating the external manifestations of as many emotions as possible. A good actor can command many more than a poor actor. We can tell simply by looking at him whether he is portraying happiness, dissatisfaction, fear, and so on.

The manifestations of the emotion of anger are so numerous that Dr. W. B. Cannon, of Harvard University, who studied them in detail, required an entire printed page to merely list them.

The chief external manifestations in the emotion of anger are: a reddening of the skin of the face, a widening of the eyelids, bloodshot whites of the eyes, contraction and tightening of the lips, a setting of the jaw, clenching of the fists, a tremor in the arms, and very often a tremor in the voice. You know immediately on seeing anyone with such manifestations that he is in a state of anger.

But the internal manifestations, that is, the changes that are occurring inside the body, are much more profound and remarkable. For example, when you become angry, your blood immediately clots quicker than normal—not just a little quicker, but a whole lot quicker. An emotion is a very fundamental biological change and most of the manifestations are of some biological significance. Obviously, the blood-clotting change in anger serves a biological purpose. In the emotion of anger one is very apt to have a fight, to receive a wound, and to bleed; it is then beneficial to have the blood clot quickly.

Another similar biologically valuable manifestation is that the moment you become angry the number of blood cells in the circulating blood increases by as much as a half a million per cubic millimeter. When a person becomes angry, the muscles at the outlet of the stomach squeeze down so tightly that nothing leaves the stomach during anger, and the entire digestive tract becomes so spastic that many people have severe abdominal pains either during or after a fit of anger.

The heart rate goes up markedly during anger, often to 180 or 220, or higher, and stays there until the anger has passed. The blood pressure rises markedly and steeply from a normal of 130 or so to 230 or more. This is a manifestation that often produces dire results. You have possibly known of a person who developed a stroke during a fit of anger because his blood pressure rose so high he "blew" a blood vessel in his brain.

Also, in anger, the coronary arteries in the heart squeeze down, hard enough to produce angina pectoris, or even a fatal coronary occlusion. This happens fairly frequently.

John Hunter, one of the greatest physiologists England ever had, had the uncomfortable combination of a ready temper and a bad set of coronary arteries. Hunter always said that the first rascal who really got him mad would kill him. His wife came close to finishing him a couple of times, but the rascal finally appeared at a medical meeting and made him so angry he dropped dead of a coronary occlusion.

You can readily see how, if a man were angry enough at the time, the manifestations of his emotions might produce physical symptoms—such as abdominal pain, exhausted heart, apoplexy, or a coronary occlusion.

Fortunately there are not very many men who are angry continually, although there are some. But we do find people, and many of them, who have some of the other unpleasant emotions continually.

Examples of Single Emotions Producing Single Symptoms

Let me give you two further examples (that you have doubtless seen yourself) of how a single emotion can produce a single symptom.

You have seen, or heard of, a person who faints when he looks at blood. He doesn't faint because he has a weak heart or a high blood pressure. He faints because the sight of blood produces the emotion of fear, and part of the manifestation of the emotion of fear is a squeezing down of some of the blood vessels supplying the brain—this produces the faint.

In other people, the sight of blood may cause vomiting, not because they have a disease of the stomach, but because, in them, the sight of blood produces the emotion of disgust.

Part of the manifestation of the emotion of disgust is a contraction of the stomach violent enough to cause vomiting.

A Single Violent Emotion May Cause Sudden, Severe Illness

Occasionally, a severe emotionally induced illness may follow one single severe emotion.

A man was carried into our clinic one morning at nine o'clock. He was carried in because he couldn't possibly have walked; he was too weak and too dizzy to stand. His heart was going 180 beats a minute. He was vomiting. He couldn't control his bowels; he couldn't control his urine. He stayed in that condition in the hospital for three months, during which time there were moments when we thought he couldn't live any longer.

Until eight o'clock that morning, this man had been a perfectly healthy and unusually strong man. At about eight o'clock, he walked into his wife's bedroom and discovered that his wife had killed their only daughter and then committed suicide. From the time he made that discovery, he was a very sick man. It was not that he had acquired cancer, or tuberculosis, or heart trouble, although he was as ill as though he had developed all three. What he had developed was powerfully unpleasant emotions.

Let's not forget this: Any one of the rest of us, with that man's mental background, in that man's situation, would have developed the same sort of violent illness. No one is immune to emotionally induced illness.

Most E. I. I. Comes from Relatively Small, Unpleasant Emotions

Most of the emotionally induced illness we physicians see in our offices does not come as the result of one large, terrific emotion, nor even from any series of catastrophes. Instead, most cases of emotionally induced illness are the result of a monotonous drip, drip of seemingly unimportant yet nevertheless unpleasant emotions, the everyday run of anxieties, fears, discouragements and longings. Clinically, we've known this to be true for years. But a peculiar thing in medicine is that we never believe anything unless it can be demonstrated in animals.

Monotonous repetition of unpleasant emotions. A few years ago two Cornell psychologists, H. S. Liddell and A. V. Moore, demonstrated that the monotonous repetition of rather minor unpleasant emotions can produce E. I. I., at least in sheep.[1]

These two investigators tied a light wire around one of the legs of one of the sheep, a wire so light that the sheep could carry it all about the field. At the end of a week of such wire pulling, the sheep was perfectly healthy and normal in every way.

For the next week, small electric shocks were sent through the wire; not hard shocks, just light shocks, so that the sheep twitched its leg slightly with each shock. Drs. Liddell and Moore could repeat this light shock as often as they pleased during the week. The sheep went right on eating in a perfectly normal fashion.

Then the two investigators tried varying the stimuli and they finally found that by introducing two other elements into the light shocks, they could produce a severe illness in any sheep in the field.

The first element was the introduction of *apprehension* into the shocks. This they did by ringing a bell ten seconds before they gave the shock. It was the same shock as before, not a bit stronger, but now when the sheep heard the bell, it stopped eating, or whatever it was doing, and waited apprehensively for the shock it soon learned was coming. But this new element alone was not enough to produce the disease.

The second element was monotonous repetition of the bell-shock apprehension. The interval of repetition did not make much difference as long as it was monotonously repeated. With this kind of treatment, every sheep it was tried upon soon showed signs of illness. It would first quit eating. Then it would stop following its companions around the field. Next it quit walking. Then it failed to stay on its feet. Finally it began to have difficulty in breathing. Then the experiment had to be stopped or the sheep would have died. Once the monotonous repetition of apprehension was stopped, the sheep soon returned to normal.

The effect of interrupting monotonous apprehension. A most interesting and important secondary finding made by Drs. Liddell and Moore in their experiments on the sheep was that if the monotonous repetition of apprehension was interrupted for a period of two hours in every 24, none of

[1] H. S. Liddell, "The Neurotic Animals of Ithaca, N.Y.," *Science Illustrated*, February, 1949; 4:2, p. 26.

the sheep would develop functional illness. A rest period less than two hours was ineffective.

It is thus apparent that to get E. I. I., the monotonous repetition of unpleasant emotions must be almost constant. To interrupt the stream completely each day would effectively prevent the disease. However, we do meet exceptional cases where an emotionally induced illness arises from a single precipitating event; these are always interesting and valuable in understanding and appreciating the profound nature of the illness. In addition to the case of the man whose wife committed suicide, another interesting example comes to mind.

The superintendent of schools in a neighboring city was a level-headed, well-adjusted individual who seemed as little likely to develop emotionally induced illness as anyone you could name. Then one day he developed a severe dizziness that could be relieved only by lying down. Just as soon as he attempted to sit upright, he became intensely dizzy and had to vomit. He was taken home and put to bed. There he stayed for many days, not improving. Nothing his physician gave him made him the lest bit better. Then one day, as if by magic, he was better, and returned to school.

Some days afterward he went to his physician and said, "I wouldn't have thought that I could have emotions that would make me sick, but I am absolutely certain the illness I had was caused by a distressing series of emotions."

"What makes you say that?" asked his doctor.

"Some time ago, one of my best friends in this city asked me to back him up on a loan of a considerable sum of money. It was such a large loan that I hesitated signing his note, since I knew that if the man failed to pay the note it would completely wipe me out of house and savings. Yet it seemed safe enough, and since the man was a good friend, I could not refuse. So I signed.

"It wasn't long after that the man was seriously hurt in an accident and spent months in the hospital, during which time it looked more and more as though his business venture was going to the wall. Worrying about that brought on my dizziness."

"But how can you be sure about that?" asked the doctor.

"Well, sir," went on the superintendent, "when I was in bed, feeling my sickest, this friend of mine for whom I had signed the note came to visit me, and told me that he had just been over to the bank and had paid off the note in full.

From that moment, I started to recover. The next day I went back to school."

THE PRODUCTION OF SYMPTOMS IN EMOTIONALLY INDUCED ILLNESS

Emotions manifest themselves through two different systems in the body. Some of the manifestations are mediated through the nervous system, others through the endocrine glands. Some of the symptoms can be produced *either* by way of the nervous system or by way of the endocrine system.

CHAPTER 1 IN A NUTSHELL

When you, or I, or any one of us, has a physical illness, the chances are better than 50 per cent that our illness is emotionally induced.

Emotionally induced illness is a *physical*, not a *mental* disease. It produces thousands of symptoms, varying from such homely ones as "pain in the neck" and "gas," to such complicated ones as "nephrosclerosis" and "peptic ulcer."

An emotion consists of chemical and physical changes *in the body* (either on the face, where they may be seen by others, or internally, where they are felt by us)—changes that are the *feeling* of every thought we think.

In the emotion of *anger*, the physical changes on the face *spell anger*. One of the internal changes in anger is an increase of blood pressure that sometimes breaks a cerebral blood vessel and produces a stroke. Another internal change that takes place in anger is a narrowing of the coronary blood vessels of the heart. This sometimes produces a coronary death.

The so-called "unpleasant" emotions are the ones whose internal changes produce the symptoms of disease.

The "pleasant" emotions produce changes that make us feel *good;* that is to say, they are optional changes.

The chemical and physical changes in the body, which *are* the emotions, are mediated from the brain through the (1) autonomic nervous system, and through the (2) endocrine glands.

HOW YOUR EMOTIONS PRODUCE ILLNESS THROUGH YOUR NERVOUS SYSTEM

THE MANIFESTATIONS OF EMOTIONS MEDIATED THROUGH THE NERVOUS SYSTEM

The portion of the nervous system concerned with the emotions is the part called the *autonomic nervous system*. It is outside the control of the will. The brain center of the autonomic nervous system is the *hypothalamus,* which is also the center for pituitary gland stimulation. We shall see later that the pituitary gland is a more powerful agent for manifesting emotions than even the autonomic nervous system.

MUSCLE TENSION AND THE PRODUCTION OF PAIN

Tense muscles are one of the most common sources of the general aches and pains we experience more or less constantly. The intense pain produced by a cramp illustrates very well how very severe muscle pains can be. If you will make a fist of your hand, not tightly, but firmly, you will find that it produces no pain at first. After a while, however, the muscle tension involved in making a fist begins to hurt more and more intensely.

The unpleasant emotions are commonly manifested by tightness both in the skeletal muscles and the muscles of the internal organs. If these muscle-tensing emotions are continued long enough, or if they are monotonously repeated, the muscles involved begin to hurt.

"SO-AND-SO GIVES ME A PAIN IN THE NECK"

The muscle groups most commonly involved in emotional manifestation are the muscles most commonly used. The muscles at the back of the neck, which are used more than any other set of skeletal muscles, are such a group. These same neck muscles are common sites of tense emotional manifestation. Eighty-five per cent of the patients complaining of a pain in the back of the head, radiating down the neck, have their pain as a result of *emotional* tightness in these muscles. This tension origin of neck pain was recognized years ago by that wise practical physiologist who first remarked that "So-and-so gives me a pain in the neck." Such a statement is literally true.

To demonstrate to yourself how emotions can tighten the muscles at the back of the neck, seat yourself in an easy chair tonight, and then worry hard about something for an hour. When you get up you will twist and stretch your neck because it feels tight, and the chances are that it will hurt.

THE COMMON LUMP IN THE THROAT

Another folk-saying is "I was so scared that my heart came up into my throat."

More commonly, patients complain of a lump in the throat. All the while, naturally, they are afraid they have some sort of a growth. Actually what 95 per cent of these patients have is an emotional tightness of the muscles at the upper end of the esophagus; this tightness feels like a lump. If the individual tries to swallow when these muscles are tight, there is a moment's hesitancy before the muscles loosen up, and the person feels as though he is choking. Then he becomes doubly sure there is something dreadfully wrong in his throat, and the lump becomes twice as bothersome.

CARDIOSPASM, OR EMOTIONAL TIGHTNESS OF THE LOWER END OF THE ESOPHAGUS

The muscles at the lower end of the esophagus enter into emotional manifestation much less commonly than do the muscles at the upper end, and fortunately so. For when the lower esophageal muscles squeeze down, they are apt to stay "squoze" for days or even weeks, during which time nothing will run into the stomach, not even water. Such an individual would slowly starve if something were not done for him.

EMOTIONAL MANIFESTATION IN THE MUSCLES OF THE STOMACH

The stomach is one of the organs *par excellence* for the manifestation of emotions. The emotional activities of the stomach are felt by everyone every day. When our worlds are going along well, we have a good appetite because the stomach is manifesting pleasant emotions. However, when things do not go well, we suddenly find that we have entirely lost our appetites. If then something good should happen, if an unknown uncle should leave us a cool million (whoopee) right away our appetite is back.

When the muscles of our stomachs tighten because of a certain variety of emotions, the resulting feeling is that of a lump in our upper abdomen; some people describe it as a "stone."

When the stomach muscles squeeze down *really hard,* a pain is produced, sometimes a very severe one. This pain oftens bears a considerable resemblance to the pain produced by an ulcer. We will see, in the next chapter, how ulcers are produced by the emotions, but we are speaking now of a muscle pain, not an ulcer pain.

Fully 50 per cent of the patients who complain of an ulcer-like pain are found not to have an ulcer but merely an emotional muscle pain of the stomach.

That the two pains resemble one another can be understood when one knows that even if one *has* an ulcer, it is not the ulcer that hurts, but the contraction of muscles next to the ulcer. A painfully-contracting muscle will feel the same whether an ulcer or an emotion is producing the spasm.

Some time ago, I had as a patient a grocer who had an emotionally induced pain in his stomach. Being in competition with chain stores is a source of trouble sufficient to give one an emotional stomach pain. But that wasn't all the trouble this poor fellow had. I am sure that if I had had the man's wife, I would have had all his pain. And even that wasn't all—he also had a son who was always getting into trouble; not just a little trouble, but a whole lot of trouble. And between his grocery, his wife, and his son, this poor grocer had a pain in his stomach most of the time. And, of course, every once in a while some consultant would tell him that he had an ulcer. Then the thing really hurt. Whenever he went to doctors who knew what they were talking about, he was told that he had no ulcer. That didn't help his pain much because he was only made more confused, and that gave him pain.

But finally he began to believe that he had no ulcer. Every time he went to Northern Wisconsin for fishing, which he did twice a year, all he had to do was to get to Belleville, a town 25 miles north of his home, and there, on the main street of Belleville, his pain stopped. It did not return again until two weeks later when, on his way home, he came to Round Grove Hill and caught sight of the courthouse tower in his home town. There his pain started again.

At the Mayo Clinic, there used to be a famous doctor who had the same kind of pain. He knew what his pain was, but he said that as long as he was in Rochester with patients pushing and pulling him, and with many things on his mind, he would have his pain almost all the time. To get rid of the pain all he had to do was to get on the train, and when the train came to Winona—no, when the train came to the center of the bridge crossing the Mississippi—the pain left, not to return until the train again pulled into the Rochester station and he looked out to see the Clinic tower.

The doctor's analysis of why the pain left in the center of the bridge was this: that was where the train left Minnesota, and he never had liked Minnesota.

My grocer patient said that he had always admired Belleville—in fact, he had always wanted to live there—and when he reached its main street, he had a feeling of well-being for the first time in weeks. That was where his pain stopped.

THE COLON IS THE MIRROR OF THE MIND

The same kind of painful spasm can occur, and does occur, in the 28 feet of intestine that lie beyond the stomach, but most especially in the part known as the colon. The colon, *more than any other organ*, is a manifestor of the emotions. So much so that a wise doctor in Philadelphia remarked some years ago that "the colon is the mirror of the mind, and when the mind gets tight, the colon gets tight."

One of the most remarkable things about emotional manifestation is illustrated by the colon, and I wish to call your attention to it here. In any given individual the same emotion will be manifested in the same way every time it occurs. If, in one individual, the muscles at the back of the neck squeeze down every time he gets anxious, these same muscles will always act the same with the same emotion.

In some other individual it may be a three-inch segment of the colon that squeezes down hard with a similar emotion, and it will always be the same three-inch segment that responds to the emotion.

If this spasm happens to be in the colon in the upper right-hand portion of the abdomen, it will produce a pain very similar to a gallstone colic. Fifty per cent of the people we see with fairly typical "gall bladder attacks" turn out to have normal gall bladders. They are having their attacks from emotional spasm of their colon, or some other adjacent muscle. Dr. Andrew C. Ivy, Chicago physiologist, showed that an emotional spasm of the small sphincter muscle at the bile duct outlet can also produce a pain as severe as any gall bladder attack.

EMOTIONALLY INDUCED GALL-BLADDER-LIKE PAIN

Probably every doctor has at some time mistaken an emotional colon spasm for a gall bladder attack. I admit I have. I was called to see a patient who had all the symptoms and findings of a very severe gall-bladder colic. Any other doctor seeing her that day would have made the same diagnosis. I had to give her three "hypos" before the pain finally abated. I paid too little attention to the fact that the patient's only son had received notice of the draft only two days before.

Two days after her son had left for an army camp, the lady had a second and similar attack, which again had all the earmarks of gall bladder disease. Again, three "hypos."

The third and most severe attack occurred three months later, two days after the patient had received word that her son had left New York City for overseas, destination not announced. On that occasion, the patient was so very ill that I had to move her to the hospital. When gall bladder X-rays were taken, I was surprised to find a normal gall bladder. Nevertheless, I felt so certain that the gall bladder contained stones invisible to X-rays, that I advised operative removal of the gall bladder. This the patient agreed to, and the gall bladder was removed.

Following this, the patient did well for many months. I was about ready to regard myself as a remarkably clever fellow when the lady had her fourth severe attack of right-upper-quadrant pain, this time without benefit of the gall bladder. This attack occurred two days after she had received word that her son had landed in North Africa, and the papers carried the news that fighting had started with the Germans. A fifth attack occurred when she learned that her son had been wounded. Following this, the boy returned home and the lady has had no spells since.

EMOTIONAL "APPENDICITIS"

If the emotional spasm of the colon occurs in the right lower quadrant of the abdomen, it will look for all the world like an attack of appendicitis. Even a very smart doctor may be unable to make a positive diagnosis, especially in children in whom this kind of thing is especially apt to occur. Very often, to be safe, the surgeon will open the abdomen, only to find a normal appendix and a bowel squeezed down so tight that it is blanched white.

In other people, painful spasms may occur throughout the entire length of the colon, and believe me, these people are intensely uncomfortable.

There are so many emotional disturbances of the colon that all sort of terms have been evolved for them like "spastic colon," "irritable colon," "nonspecific ulcerative colitis," and many other terms, all of them merely synonyms for "emotional colon."

"GAS"

One of the commonest complaints people have is of "gas" and "bloating." "Doctor," they will say, "everything I eat goes to gas." "Doctor, I bloat up something terrible," or, "When this gas forms, it crowds my heart." One patient even said that her gas, which "came from her food, went up through her chest, through her neck and whistled out through her ear."

It always surprises these patients, as it did me when I first heard it, to hear that not even a little bit of gas is formed in the process of our digestion. All the gas that we get in our stomachs and intestines is swallowed when we eat our food or swallow our saliva.

The thing that is happening when we have "gas," or "bloating," is that one or more of the three-inch segments of the small bowel is squeezing down tightly. These spasms are so tight that they produce temporary obstructions through which nothing can pass. These spastic obstructions may last from five to 60 minutes, or even longer. The liquid and gaseous content of the intestine is carried up against this obstruction by the normal peristalsis of the bowel, and the intestine, consequently, balloons up. The victim feels this ballooning, or bloating, along with the spasm, as a very disagreeable feeling. When the spasm is finally rather suddenly relieved, the contents of the ballooned bowel shoots ahead with an angry gurgle which one can feel and often hear. With this relief of pressure the individual says to himself, "There goes my gas."

That, my dyspeptic friend, is what gas is. Under the X-ray fluoroscope, I have viewed as many as 18 or 20 such spasms occurring at the same time in the same person. Believe me, he was an uncomfortable human, *and he wasn't imagining it*.

To our patients suffering with "gas," we show colored photographs of an opened abdomen on an operating table. The patient photographed was a young man with a considerable police record. For certain medical reasons, his abdominal operation was performed under local anesthesia so that only his abdominal wall was anesthetized. When the abdomen had been opened, the small intestines and colon were in full view and appeared normal.

The first picture was made. Then the surgeon said to the patient, "Have you had any encounters with the police lately?" knowing full well that the police were waiting for the fellow at the front door as soon as he was dismissed from the hospital. Within a minute, several visible spasms formed in the small bowel with typical ballooning behind the spasm.

Then the second picture was taken. The surgeon asked, "How do you feel now?" The young man answered, "I'm all bloated."

FROM THE EMOTIONS, TOO, STEM MOST BELCHES

Belching is very much the same thing, except that it occurs in the stomach. I don't, of course, mean the lusty animal belch that escapes after a big meal or a glass of beer, but the more embarrassing belching you see many people struggle with whenever they become disturbed or under pressure. I know a very good public speaker, who, during his first ten minutes of feeling out his audience, struggles with himself, often unsuccessfully, to hold down the belches. Once he finds himself and hits his stride, he leaves his belches behind.

I'll never forget a patient I saw in 1942. The poor miserable man was belching at a constant rate of once every 30 seconds! He did this whether he was at home, at church, or in my office. And it had been going on for a week. Believe me, he wanted to get rid of it! Nothing he had tried had helped in the least. One surgeon had advised cutting the phrenic nerves to immobilize the diaphragm.

Here is how his belching started: In the spring of 1942, he had sold his farm and bought a bakery, a business entirely new to him. In 1942, you will remember, sugar, flour, lard, all the ingredients he needed in his bakery, were strictly rationed. The poor chap was as poor at arithmetic as he was at the bakery business, and very soon he was in

37

such difficulties with the local rationing board that the Federal agents were being called in. Just at this time his consternation became abysmal because his baker, on whom he absolutely depended, was called by the draft. The poor owner started to do what you and I would probably also have done under the circumstances—he started to belch.

There was obviously only one treatment. That was to sell his bakery and get out. When this was suggested, the poor man smiled for the first time in our acquaintance. Twelve hours after the sale was consummated, the man quit belching, to his infinite relief.

BE CHOOSY, IF YOU MUST HAVE BAD EMOTIONS

You see what problems the emotions that manifest themselves in the digestive tract can produce. If you must have them, therefore, try to pick out an emotion which manifests itself in the left side of your colon; there are fewer emergency operations possible on that side.

EMOTIONAL MANIFESTATIONS IN THE MUSCLES OF THE BLOOD VESSELS

So far we have dealt with symptoms produced by emotional manifestation in the muscles of the digestive tract. But all the other muscles of the body are influenced by the emotions, especially the muscles that are to be found in the walls of all but the very smallest blood vessels. One of the more obvious and common emotional responses of the blood vessels is blushing. But there are many others.

The moderate-sized blood vessels, lying inside or outside the skull, are highly sensitive to emotional stimuli. As these vessels contract, emotionally, headache is produced, both the common type of headache, or the more severe type we know as migraine. Fully 85 per cent of all headaches are emotionally induced. In some individuals the casual connection between the emotional disturbance and the headache is clearly evident. But sometimes it is not so apparent.

The emotional excitant may be some deeply-seated trouble which the person may try to hide even from himself, one he certainly would not tell anyone else even if he could. But the emotions behind most headaches are easy enough to spot.

For example, one of my patients developed a terrific migraine, that kept her in bed for a day, every time she went to town. She was a fastidious housekeeper, living on a farm. Going to town meant getting her house in spic-and-span condition, getting the children cleaned and dressed, thinking of what she had to do in town, and becoming apprehensive about meeting people, because she was very shy. By the time she started for town, her headache had started, and when she returned home, she would have to go to bed. The cure for her headaches was obvious—not to go to town. She does, of course, occasionally—sometimes it is to see her doctor. She goes home with her headache.

Emotionally induced skin trouble. But blood vessels manifesting emotions can do even more remarkable things. Fully 30 per cent of the skin trouble in these United States is what the dermatologists call *neurodermatitis*. A neurodermatitis can occur anywhere on the body. In the skin involved, the small blood vessels in the second layer are constantly squeezing down in emotional manifestation. Every time they do so a small amount of serum is extruded through the thin layer of the vessel. As this continues, an appreciable amount of serum accumulates in the tissues. First, the skin gets slightly brawny, then red. Soon there is enough serum under pressure to force its way to the surface, and one has the weeping, scaling, crusting, and itching of a full-blown case of neurodermatitis.

One of my patients was a man of 73 with a terrific generalized neurodermatitis, which he had had for some years. He had never had any skin disease until he was 68. At 67, his first wife died, and at 68, he married his second wife, a lady of his own age. It was on their honeymoon that he first developed his dermatitis, and when they got home, it was so severe that he soon had to be hospitalized. After a week in the hospital, the skin would be very much better and he would return home, only to have the whole thing recur a short time later.

In the course of time he had to go to a town several hundred miles away on business. After being there a week, his neurodermatitis cleared up. The next time it became bad again at home, he returned to Moline because it was cheaper than going to the hospital. Some time later he went to another distant town on business, and found that there, too, his dermatitis cleared up in a week. Finally, his wife had to leave home to care for a sick relative, and our patient stayed home alone, and lo and behold, after a week, his skin was clear. The connection had become obvious enough.

We asked him, "What did you discover about your wife during your honeymoon?" He had the answer ready immediately: "I found out that she was domineering and dominating, and I just can't stand it!" We then took his wife aside and explained to her that she was causing her husband's dermatitis. She didn't like to believe it, but she promised that she would lean over backwards trying not to be domineering. She performed admirably, and the man's neurodermatitis left completely. Occasionally, there is a hint of return, and then we simply talk to the wife once more.

EMOTIONAL MANIFESTATION IN SKELETAL MUSCLES

We saw earlier in this chapter how tightening of the neck muscles caused our most common neck pain.

It was learned by careful study during World War II that the thing we have called *muscular rheumatism*, or *myofibrositis*, or *fibrositis*, is almost invariably produced by emotional tension. During the first World War, a certain percentage of the boys in the trenches developed fibrositis. It was thought to be due to the wet, miserable, and exposed living conditions in the trenches. But in the second World War, almost exactly the same percentage of the boys in the battle line developed fibrositis. The percentage was the same whether they were fighting in the cold, wet Aleutian Islands, or in hot, dry North Africa.

It was found, furthermore, that the incidence of fibrositis increased steadily as the boys moved forward from the base camps toward the fighting front. And it was eventually determined that an emotion was responsible—the emotion a person has when he is called upon to do something he would not do if compulsion were not upon him.

In this situation he involuntarily steels himself and tightens certain muscles—very often those of the shoulder girdle. This also occurs, of course, in individuals in civilian life who must constantly meet situations they would rather avoid. If such situations are acute enough, or if they are of long enough duration, pain is eventually produced.

One of the common sites of such pain is the pectoral muscle of the left chest. The same thing, of course, can occur in the pectoral muscle of the right chest. But a person pays much more attention to a pain in the left chest than one in the right, and becomes much more alarmed, because he fears, more and more, as the pain goes on, that he has heart disease. All he needs then is for some uncertain doctor to murmur that "You might have a little heart trouble," and he is off on a long emotionally induced and physician-augmented illness.

Fibrositis is an exceedingly common cause of pain in human beings. Most people will get a fibrositis at some time or other, and *some* people are subject to fibrositis all the time. I happen to be one of the latter; I have a fibrositis most of the time. And, of course, it is emotionally induced. Every day I am compelled to see more people in my office than a doctor ought to see—so many, that seeing them thoroughly constitutes severe physical and emotional pressure. So I am hurting somewhere most of the time, especially if the irate relatives of a particularly sick patient camp on my trail.

When I leave on a vacation, my fibrositis stays behind in my office; when I get back to my office, I put it on again. Right now, for instance, I have a fibrositis in my right shoulder area so severe that I can't push a screen door open. The important thing is that I recognize properly what my pain is, and what its source is. Then I don't worry about it.

Many other people, who do not have the fortune to be doctors, worry about their fibrositis. They fear, perhaps, they are filled to the brim with cancer, or they believe they have crippling rheumatism, and apprehensively expect to be crippled and incapacitated. Nothing could be further from the truth.

Fibrositis never becomes crippling; it becomes incapacitating only if you let it. It is not serious; it merely belongs in the class of confounded nuisances.

MOST OF US HURT SOMEWHERE ALMOST ALL THE TIME

I must deviate here just a moment to call attention to a very important point that, when it is unrealized, is apt to start many people on the long, hard road of bellyaching.

If at any time on a busy day we stop and ask ourselves, "Where do I hurt?" we can usually find a pain somewhere, perhaps in a foot, perhaps in the lower abdomen. Sometimes, out of nowhere, there will come a very severe momentary pain: perhaps in the thigh, perhaps in the chest, a pain severe enough to make us pause a moment in our hectic flight. Such pains are part of the normal processes of living. For no explainable reason, a pain-nerve-ending is being stimulated, or a blood vessel is contracting painfully, or a muscle bundle is cramping. Some people feel these pains more readily than others because their threshold to pain sensations is lower than other people's.

The late Dr. E. Libman, of New York City, one of America's great physicians, some years ago, called attention to the fact that some people are more susceptible to pain than other people, not because they are bigger babies, but simply because they feel pain more readily. He devised a simple clinical test to tell how sensitive to pain a person is. It consists in pressing against the *styloid process*, which lies just below the lobe of the ear, behind the angle of the jaw. A nonsensitive person will not wince when the styloid process is pressed, whereas a person who is sensitive to pain will draw away and make an awful grimace.

A person who is very sensitive to pain *will feel the normal peristaltic contractions of his intestines as a pain*. I am italicizing that sentence because it explains why some people have a *continual* discomfort or pain in their abdomens. Unless they appreciate their sensitiveness to pain, and realize the cause of their abdominal pain, these people will be chronically ill all their lives, and the victims of all the organically-minded physicians in the country.

Anyone feeling one of the common pains all of us experience every day can work it up into quite a major experience if he puts all his attention and awareness into it. To make such a minimal pain worse, all one needs to do is to center one's awareness upon it. It will begin to perform for him, growing bolder and more magnificent until it can be worked up into quite a thing.

Another factor that will magnify and aggravate any minimal pain is the development of any tension state. It has been shown in a number of different ways that an anxiety state lowers the threshold of pain. Sensations that we would term mildly painful, or that we would overlook altogether when we are in a happy state, will become very painful at times when we are emotionally distressed.

It is partly for this reason that so many people develop low backaches when they are under emotional tension. Everyone experiences a low backache at some time or other. Usually, after a bit of muscle strain, it may be so mild that one pays no attention to it; but during emotional stress, the threshold of pain becomes so lowered that the painful stimuli in the back are highly magnified.

You Have Read Only a Very Partial List of Emotional Muscular Symptoms

In this chapter, I have listed a few of the commoner and the more interesting symptoms produced by emotional manifestation in the muscles. There are as many more as there are muscles in the body and organs that contain muscles. It would be too time-consuming and too boring for you if I listed them all.

I simply wish to give you an idea of how our emotions, *your* emotions, work to produce illness.

If we realize that this is true, that it is true in ourselves, then we do not need to feel apprehensive over most of the discomforts we feel in ourselves. By realizing this, we will have made the first great step (and the most important one) in avoiding the disease that is causing more morbidity, more disability, more misery, more absenteeism, and more accidents than all the other diseases this human clay can contract.

Certainly this is important, primarily important, to every one of us.

BRIEF SUMMARY OF CHAPTER 2

The emotional effects produced through the autonomic nervous system are less severe than those produced through the endocrine glands, but they are more common and just as disagreeable. A common nerve effect is a tight muscle; a tight muscle is painful, whether it is in a leg, in a blood vessel wall, or in the stomach.

Thus emotionally tight muscles produce pain in the back of the neck, in the stomach, in the colon, in the scalp, in blood vessels, in skeletal muscles. Emotionally tight muscles produce ulcer-like pains, gall bladder-like pains, common headaches, migraine headaches, and a great host of clinical pictures. Another blood vessel effect is neurodermatitis, which constitutes 30 per cent of all skin disease.

The phenomenon that we ordinarily term "gas" is in reality an emotional spasm of muscles in the small intestines. Most belches are emotional muscle effects in the stomach.

3

HOW EMOTIONAL OVERBREATHING
AFFECTS YOU

WE ALL HYPERVENTILATE AT TIMES

There is one set of symptoms, emotionally induced, that is especially common, and that produces severe apprehension in the people who experience it. This set of symptoms is known medically as *the hyperventilation syndrome*. It is of interest historically, since it was the first syndrome known to be emotionally induced in which a chemical factor plays a leading role.

The chance is that you too have experienced the hyperventilation syndrome at some time or other.

By *hyperventilation* we simply mean breathing too deeply, or too fast, or both. You have noticed that if you become acutely disturbed, you will breathe faster than usual. Actors, whose art consists mainly in portraying the external manifestations of emotions, do the same on the stage. Normally, most of us breathe between 16 and 18 times a minute at rest. If we were to increase our rate to 22 or 23 times a minute, we ourselves, or those near us, would probably not notice the difference, but our bodies would soon notice the increase, in ways we will describe in a moment.

WHAT HAPPENS WHEN YOU HYPERVENTILATE

When we breathe faster than normal, more carbon dioxide is being lost from the blood through the lungs than is being formed in the body. Consequently, the level of carbon dioxide in the blood gradually drops to a point at which things begin to happen.

About the first thing that happens is a crawling sensation under the skin. Next, there is a perceptible numbness of the fingers, hands, and other parts of the body, gradually becoming more pronounced, until finally there is a sensation of needles pricking the skin all over. But long before the numbness becomes as acute as that, other symptoms appear. The heart starts to race; there is a trembling feeling, at first inside, and later all over the body. Lightheadedness, or even fainting, occurs. Finally, cramps appear increasingly hard until it seems that every skeletal muscle is cramping; the legs and arms draw up in a painful spastic position known as *tetany*. We have patients who, when they are upset, will go through the entire gamut of hyperventilation and end up in tetany.

A farmer, for instance, called up excitedly one day because his son had just fallen out of the haymow. I hurried out to his farm, and, on arriving there, I found the father lying on the floor in tetany, because he had hyperventilated so hard in his excitement. He needed attention more than did the son who had fallen out of the haymow. This man had these hyperventilation episodes ever so often.

One day a dentist in town called me to come immediately to his office because this same farmer was having (the dentist said) a fit. But I found him lying on the floor in tetany. He had been so apprehensive all day about going to the dentist that he had been hyperventilating. The pay-off came in the dentist's chair.

In other patients, some of the other symptoms of hyperventilation stand our more prominently than the cramps. It is quite common to find a terrified patient with the sensation of a thousand needles all over him, and his heart beating wildly. He is naturally terrified, because if he ever felt as though he were going to die, it is at that moment. Other patients will become very lightheaded, or may faint, during or after hyperventilation. One young lady had not been able to get out of bed for two months because she hyperventilated so constantly that she fainted as soon as she tried to stand.

HYPERVENTILATION IS COMMON DURING SLEEP

One of the most interesting things about hyperventilation is that it occurs most commonly in our sleep. If you will watch a sleeping person, especially someone who is in a troublesome life situation, you will see him breathe more rapidly and deeply for a time, and then lapse into quiet breathing, only to repeat the whole cycle over again.

Our minds are never at rest; we are dreaming every minute of the night; and at night in our sleep, the usual censor—common sense—is not around.

If someone on our street says something nasty to disturb us during the day, at night in our dreams that person, at the head of a band of Indians, is probably chasing us toward a precipitous cliff. In our sleep, we react emotionally as though we really were being driven toward catastrophe. We roll and toss—and we hyperventilate.

About once every week during my 20 years of medical practice, I have had to see someone about 2:00 A. M. who awoke during hyperventilation—probably just at the point where he was about to be hurled over the cliff. When he awakens, the stage of hyperventilation is usually at the point where his heart is racing and his hands are numb. Naturally, he thinks he is dying of heart trouble. One such call came from a distance of 15 miles. The husband yelled into the phone, "My wife is dying of a heart attack. Come quick!"

I knew them both, and I would have given odds of ten to one that she was hyperventilating. When I arrived I was glad I had gone, because both husband and wife had hyperventilated to the point of tetany, and needed medical relief in the worst sort of way.

This is what had happened: The wife had awakened from sleep to find her hands numb and her heart beating wildly. Her first thought was, "I am having a stroke like my mother had." She awakened her husband and told him how she felt. His first thought was, "My wife is having a heart attack like my father had." They then both got more excited, and continued to hyperventilate. To their surprise, they lived.

At other times a person may not awaken until hyperventilation has produced cramps in the legs. This is a common cause of leg cramps at night, a condition which can be prevented rather simply by an inexpensive pill.

THE GIST OF CHAPTER 3

A person under stress is likely to hyperventilate, that is, breathe more rapidly than normal, without being aware of it. In doing so, he breathes out enough carbon dioxide to lower the level of carbon dioxide in the blood. As this blood level of carbon dioxide drops, the person experiences numbness, tingling, rapid heart action, internal quivering, fainting, weakness and cramps. He may experience all of them, or some more prominently than others.

Since hyperventilation is apt to occur with the emotions produced by the dreams in our sleep, we often awaken feeling some of the symptoms of hyperventilation, and, if we don't know what they are, we are apt to fear impending disaster.

4

HOW YOUR EMOTIONS PRODUCE
DISEASE THROUGH YOUR GLANDS

IT'S NOT YOUR NERVES

Doctors and people knew for a long time that the nervous system had, in some way, a great deal to do with emotionally induced illness. Remarks such as these are common:

"It's your nerves."

"I'm all nerves."

"If I could only do something about my nerves."

"My nerves are in a terrible condition."

"I'm just a bundle of nerves."

"If my nerves were only better."

Actually, there is nothing wrong with the nerves in E. I. I. They are just as organically normal as the rest of the body. All the nerves have to do with it is that they act as a messenger telling the colon to contract or telling the heart to speed up.

As I say, we've known for a long time that the nervous system was in some vague sort of way tied up in E. I. I. Then doctors like Lange, Cannon, Dunbar, Wolf, and Wolff, and many others began to show us more precisely just how the thing works. We reviewed a few of these mechanisms that are mediated by the nervous system in the last two chapters.

Dr. Hans Selye. Then along came Dr. Hans Selye of Montreal.[1] He started his work as recently as 1936. Many others have joined him, or have followed the leads Dr. Selye pioneered. And today a tremendous and amazing new chapter —a new understanding—is being written on emotionally induced illness. The wildest things we imagined before 1936,

[1] An excellent summary of Dr. Hans Selye's monumental work can be found in his book, *The Story of the Adaptation Syndrome,* 1952, Acta, Montreal, Canada.

or could have imagined about the mechanism of E. I. I. are a tame understatement compared to the things which have become known. And the accumulation of the new knowledge has barely started.

We do know today that the group of organs in the body we call the endocrine glands have as much to do with emotional manifestation as the nervous system has. What is more important, the endocrine effects of the emotions far outweigh the nerve effects in magnitude and importance. So much so that it would be closer to the truth to say, "It's my endocrines," rather than, "It's my nerves."

THE PITUITARY GLAND

Dr. Selye started with investigations of the pituitary gland.

Merely from the pituitary gland's location in the most inaccessible part of the body, one might surmise that the pituitary gland must be of vital importance. Located inside the cranium, on the underside of the brain, the pituitary is nestled and cradled in a complete bowl of bone, protected against almost any conceivable injury. One might surmise, from this protected position, the pituitary is about the most important organ we have. And it is.

The pituitary is only about the size and shape of an overgrown pea. Yet despite this insignificant size, the pituitary is the master regulator of the entire body. It produces an amazing variety of hormones (hormones are substances carried in the blood, which act on other parts of the body) some of which are known, one of which has been secured in *pure* form, and several others that are suspected but not yet demonstrated.

We know there is one hormone of the pituitary that raises blood pressure, another that makes smooth muscles contract, one that inhibits the kidneys from producing urine, one that stimulates the kidneys to make more urine. Then there is a whole group of hormones that regulate the other endocrine glands of the body. These other glands produce many more hormones to regulate just about everything that goes on in our bodies.

Your pituitary is always on the job. The pituitary is like a key industry that works quietly but efficiently night and day making certain commodities that are absolutely essential to the well-being of our body. The well-being of the entire body is dependent on its smooth operation.

But this factory—the pituitary—is more important than that. Not only does it control our physiology in time of peace and quiet, but it becomes the key defense plant if the body is threatened in any way, shape, or form. With *any kind* of a threat to the safety of the body, this key industry puts out the commodity necessary to mobilize the defenses against that threat.

Stress and stressors. These threats to the body Dr. Hans Selye called "stressors," and the action of a "stressor" a "stress." The pituitary reacts to a vast variety of stressors that threaten our well-being in any way. The pituitary is not only the master regulator of the body under normal conditions, but also the organ that adapts the body to meet threatening conditions.

Stressors that threaten the well-being of the body are extremely numerous. One stressor will stimulate the pituitary to produce one hormone in excess, or a combination of hormones in excess. Another stressor will stimulate the production of another hormone.

Two such stressors are bacterial invasion and virus infection, in response to which the pituitary puts out a hormone that mobilizes the body defenses. Other stressors are exposure to heat or to cold, exposure to excessive moisture or dryness, severe muscular exertion, drug effects, injuries, operations, and many others.

Dr. Selye learned from his experiments that the greatest stressors are the psychic stressors, the unpleasant emotions. The unpleasant emotions can stimulate any or all of the many hormones. *What is more, a very acute emotion will produce immediate, profound effects to a much greater degree than will any other type of stressor.*

Witness the man we told about, in Chapter Two, who became violently ill when his wife killed their only daughter and then took her own life. But, what is even more important, it is characteristic of emotional stress to act over a longer period of time than do the other stressors, often for months, or years, whereas the stress of an infection usually lasts only a week or two and exposure to physical effects of muscular overexertion even less long. We shall see in a moment how important this long-time effect is.

THE DIURETIC HORMONE

The *diuretic hormone* is relatively unimportant, but it illustrates how stressors, including emotional stress, act.

The diuretic hormone makes the kidneys excrete an increased amount of urine. I'm sure you remember having had somewhat the same experience with the diuretic hormone that a boy in our local school did the other day. The boy was about to take a final examination in geography, for which he felt himself utterly unprepared. He was tense, anxious, and apprehensive. Two minutes before the examination was about to start, the boy suddenly realized that he must, that he simply *must*, leave the room. He didn't merely imagine that he must, he really and truly had to.

His emotions had stimulated the pituitary to produce the diuretic hormone which, in turn, stimulated the kidneys to excrete an increased amount of urine. Not to have left the room would have ended in acute misery, and probably in disaster. Actually the latter happened, because the teacher was not wise in the ways of hormones and emotions, and refused to let him leave the room. The parents called me in as a sort of a medical-legal advisor. The upshot was that the boy was given credit for passing the geography exam that the accident prevented him from taking. The boy can thank his stars that there are emotions and hormones.

THE SOMATOTROPHIC HORMONE

STH. One of the most important hormones made by the pituitary is the *somatotrophic hormone*, known for short as STH. STH acts directly on the body, but it also induces the adrenal glands to produce DOCA (desoxycorticosterone), which also acts like STH. STH mobilizes the body's defenses (antibodies, white blood cells, and so forth) against any kind of an infection. But in addition, STH, and not the bacteria, produces the picture we know simply as "being sick."

We used to think that the picture of "being sick" was directly due to the toxins of the bacteria or virus. Dr. Selye has shown beyond question that STH is responsible for our "being sick." *Any* infecting agent produces the same general initial picture.

If the infection is mild, as with a cold, or light flu, the picture of sickness is very mild—perhaps a headache, tiredness, loss of appetite, and an increase in temperature of a few tenths of a degree. But if the infection is more severe, the production of STH is greater, and the picture is much more severe. Locally, at the site of the infection, there is an inflammation with redness, swelling, and heat; the temperature may rapidly climb to 105°, as in pneumonia; there are general aches and pains, headaches, gastrointestinal upsets, loss of appetite, loss of weight, albumin in the urine, an increased elimination of nitrogen, potassium and phosphates, and often a skin rash. All these effects, and many more, are produced by STH. As we shall see later, they disappear very rapidly if one injects ACTH, which opposes STH.

But the main importance of STH is that it mobilizes the defenses of the body against infection at the same time that it produces the symptoms of being sick. It mobilizes the antibodies and the phagocytic cells. In fact, the symptoms of being sick are in themselves a defensive and beneficial reaction to an invading germ. If it were not for STH, we would die with the first cold.

STH is also stressed by dark, dismal, futile, despairing emotions. One will see patients like Mrs. G——, who, when she gets an ordinary cold that produces a mild STH stress, becomes morbidly despondent and despairing at the idea of having a cold. Consequently, she adds the emotional stress of STH to that of the infection. As a result, Mrs. G—— is always as sick with a very mild cold as she would be with a severe pneumonia. Actually her resistance to infection is superb because of the splendid STH output. But even after every sign of the infection has disappeared, she continues to be sick for a long time because her emotions are continuing the STH output.

Her attitude at the beginning of a cold is, "Oh, dear, dear me; here is one of these awful colds again; and now, woe is me, I'll be dreadfully sick all winter and into the summer. These colds are always so terrible and they get me down so hard. My back aches terribly; this headache is killing me; I know this will end up with kidney infection," and so forth.

It is not exaggerating a bit to say that Mrs. G——frequently goes through all the agony of one of her long drawn-out colds without ever actually having a cold infection. I have seen her several times when she *thought* she was getting a cold. Actually there wasn't the least evidence of an infection present, but her emotional stimulation of STH was sufficient to produce a severe picture of being sick. The funny and truthful thing is that Mrs. G——is just as sick as she says she is.

ACTH counteracts STH. A very opposite type of thing happens in a person who has an infection, but who has also the aggressively disagreeable type of emotions which stress ACTH. As we shall see in a moment, ACTH counteracts all the effects of STH, *including the defensive action against infection.* This person will have a severe infection which at first does not seem serious because ACTH is toning down the picture of being sick. This person will go on to develop all the complications in the book. We shall give a picture of such a person later.

PROLONGED STH STRESS—STH STRESS DISEASE

Prolonged, low-grade STH stress can be produced by a low-grade, chronic infection, such as one might have in the tonsils or in the infected root of a tooth; but prolonged STH stress is more apt to be produced by prolonged bad emotions. Whether it be a prolonged infection, or prolonged emotions, the final effect will be the same.

Under such low-grade STH stress, a person is tired, possibly has many aches and pains and other symptoms of the acute STH picture. With prolonged STH stress, new disease processes are started.

Dr. Selye became acquainted with these STH stress diseases by injecting STH into animals over a considerable period of time. Later he showed that these many changes could also be produced in animals by chronic infection, *or by prolonged emotions*. If he injected STH, and *conditioned* the animal with a high salt diet, the animal developed a malignent type of high blood pressure. If he *conditioned* the animal with a high protein diet, STH injection would then produce nephrosclerosis, a very severe type of kidney disease. If the conditioning factor were cold and wet to the joints, STH would produce rheumatoid arthritis, one of the worst varieties of arthritis. If conditioned by inhalations of mildly irritating bronchial inhalants (which by themselves had no bad aftereffects, the animals would develop asthma from the STH. If the conditioning were a spastic colon, STH would produce severe ulcerative colitis.

Other conditions, as well, are produced by STH, all of them diseases of which we previously did not know the cause, such as periarteritis nodosa, lupus erythematosus disseminatus, and some others with high-sounding names. What is known as the "allergic state" is in some way (as yet undetermined) tied up with STH.

ASTHMA, AN STH STRESS DISEASE

We begin to understand the role of emotions in asthma through the work of Dr. Selye. Time was, not too long ago, when we thought that all asthma was a sensitization to some protein outside the body. It was discouraging that in very few cases of asthma could such a connection be proven.

A few years ago we began to accept the obvious evidence that many cases of asthma definitely took their onset from a bronchial infection, and became worse with every renewed infection. And now we are seeing how, due to STH production, just as in the case of an infection, *asthma can be generated by the emotions, and be made worse by emotional tension.*

Mrs. D——— seemed to be a reasonably happy woman who was very active socially and civically in the medium-sized city in which she lived. Her children grew up. One of the daughters married badly and became a problem. Mrs. D———'s husband, at the foolish and experimental age of 53, had a perfectly foolish affair, which nearly prostrated Mrs. D———. Finally, as an outlet or escape, Mrs. D——— went into office work, worked long hours at the job, and then worked into the wee hours at home, only to have her boss in the office tell her how perfectly awful her work was. After such a day, at her wits' end for recognition, feeling completely isolated and alone, and thoroughly tired, Mrs. D——— developed her first attack of asthma. The next day the asthma was bad enough to necessitate hospitalization. For the next six months Mrs. D——— was in the hospital, or hospitals (she went all over), without finding more than temporary relief.

On the surface she was a smiling, agreeable individual, seemingly with no great trouble, but fundamentally she was tense, discouraged, forlorn, and futile. The bottom had dropped out of her life. The office job was a last attempt to establish her usefulness and that failed. She tried hard to be jolly; it was a laudable effort. Her asthma then became her greatest apprehension. Her fears increased with each attack, and consequently, each attack became more severe and more difficult to control.

Infection stress versus emotional stress. It is easily possible to distinguish between the patients who have their asthma on an infectious basis and those who have it on an emotional basis. The latter are usually the more serious cases and the more difficult to control. It is very infrequent that a patient dies of infectious asthma, but I have seen a number die of emotionally-induced asthma.

It is also possible to separate patients whose rheumatoid arthritis is developed on an infection-stress basis from those whose malady is developed on an emotional-stress basis. Here again, the latter are the more severe.

SAM AND HIS CHRONIC STH STRESS DISEASE

Sam, a farmer who has had a lifetime of dismal, discouraged, futile emotions—just the kind to stress STH—has had a long picture of STH stress disease. When Sam was comparatively young, he developed rheumatoid arthritis, not very severe, not crippling, but painful. Later he developed asthma, again not so severely that he couldn't go on working. Later he developed high blood pressure, and now he has nephrosclerosis. One can say, and with truth, that all these illnesses must have helped to produce Sam's morose outlook. But the most important truth is that Sam's outlook was responsible for the illness.

THE ADRENOCORTICOTROPHIC HORMONE

ACTH. The ACTH (*adrenocorticotrophic hormone*) of the pituitary does not act directly on the body, but on the adrenal glands, stimulating the latter to produce cortisone which acts on the body in many remarkable ways. However, since cortisone is produced under the stimulation of ACTH, we will refer to its action as being that of ACTH.

The chief effect of ACTH is to oppose the action of STH. By giving ACTH in large enough amounts, one can completely counteract the effect of STH—the inflammatory effect, the defense against infection, the picture of "being sick." This action is one of the most dramatic things that has ever been demonstrated in medicine. One has to see it to believe it.

For instance, a patient may be sick with a *severe* lobar pneumonia. His temperature is 105°F., his face is flushed, his lips are blue, his respiration is rapid, he has a stabbing pain in the chest, he is tired and exhausted and aches all over; the skin is dry, the tongue furred, the eyes glassy.

If the doctor gives him sufficient ACTH intravenously, within a matter of a four hours, the temperature is normal, the flush is gone, the pain is gone, the tiredness is gone, he breathes easily, he feels strong, he can walk around with ease, and eat a good meal. He looks as though he had never been sick. One would say, looking at him, that he is cured.

But all that has actually happened is that the STH effects have been cancelled out—*the infection is still there,* now unopposed by the defensive action of STH. If one kept giving ACTH, the infection would go on like a prairie fire. *Even though the individual felt well,* lung abscesses would develop, or empyema, and the patient would certainly have a fatal termination.

ACTH would have the same symptom-relieving effect in any infection and would produce a fatal outcome. That is

54

why one is careful not to give ACTH to a person who has ever had tuberculosis for fear of lighting up the old infection.

However, it is quite a different thing if one gives ACTH to a person who has STH stress disease. In that case, there is no infection. For example, if one gives ACTH to a person who has rheumatoid arthritis or bronchial asthma, the asthma or the arthritis will completely disappear—as long as the administration of ACTH is continued. But the asthma and arthritis reappear again when the ACTH is stopped, because nothing has been done to stop the STH stress.

ACTH has been used, and successfully, in all the STH stress diseases. However, there is one very great limitation to its use in the present state of our knowledge—that is, that the continued use of ACTH leads to ACTH stress disease just as STH did.

ACTH stress disease. The only two ways that we know a person can get ACTH stress disease is either by prolonged injection of ACTH in one of the STH stress diseases or through prolonged emotional stress. The type of emotions that stimulate ACTH are the aggressively unpleasant emotions, the emotions one gets by driving oneself relentlessly toward a goal, or the emotion of militant dissatisfaction.

A common ACTH stress effect is peptic ulcer. Practically every animal receiving ACTH for any length of time develops an ulcer, and the same is true in humans. Ulcer is an executive's disease because the emotions that stress ACTH are the emotions an executive is apt to have. However, executives are not the only ones who have the particular brand of emotions necessary to get an ulcer.

Anyone who is aggressively dissatisfied is a candidate. In some very noisy occupations, such as a body-grinding department in an automobile body plant, a high percentage of workers develop an ulcer. Ulcers can easily be produced in rats by subjecting them to irritating high-pitched noises.

But let's look at a surprising chemical effect of ACTH overproduction, remembering that there is no chemical activity in the body (which is a tremendously complicated chemical plant) that is not in some way under the direction of the endocrine system, and realizing that the effect of emotional endocrine stress on chemical actions is both terrific and manifold.

An important ACTH stress experiment. Dr. Selye and his co-workers selected two groups of Montreal children. One group was chosen from homes in which there was a terrific amount of trouble and in which everyone was unhappy, including the children. The other group of children were chosen from homes that were happy and in which the children were happy.

These two groups were fed in the university mess hall on the same diet, a very excellent, well-prepared diet. Dieticians were present to see that the children ate their meals and liked their food. Excepting for their meals in the mess hall, all the children went their usual ways and lived as they were accustomed to live.

At the end of a given time, it was found that the children from the happy homes had gained weight well above the normal average for the age, whereas the group of children from the unhappy homes, although they were on the same diet, had not kept their weight gain up to normal for their age. During the period of the experiment, it was determined by actual assay that the unhappy children were stressing their pituitaries to produce an excessive amount of ACTH, this in turn produced cortisone, and cortisone affected the metabolism of protein in an interesting way. The amino acids, which is the form in which protein is absorbed from the intestine into the blood, were changed in increasing amounts into glucose by the ACTH, and less than the usual amount into protein for body building. Many of the unhappy children were at times in a negative nitrogen balance, that is, they were losing more protein from their bodies than they were making, in spite of their excellent diet.

The reverse was true of the children from the happy homes. They were stimulating their pituitaries optimally. Their amino acids were being changed into protein in optimal amounts. The stressed children also had a greater number of infections during the time of the observation because ACTH overproduction was also lowering the resistance to infection, which is, you remember, dependent on STH.

THE PICTURE OF CHRONIC ACTH STRESS DISEASE

One sees people who are chronically dissatisfied all their lives. They are aggressively resentful—quick to be upset—quick to be hurt—long to hold a grudge—always struggling to change something or somebody the way *they* want.

Mrs. V———— was exactly such a person. Her life was a chain of illnesses, each a new ACTH stress disease. In her girlhood she had a succession of boils, colds, and abscesses. No one could understand why she had no resistance to infection. She didn't like her teachers, or the way they ran the school. She often became angry at her schoolmates. She became a store clerk, but contracted tuberculosis.

After a period in the sanatorium, she married. Her husband then became the central object of her dissatisfaction, principally because his earning power cramped her possibilities. When I first saw her, she had an ulcer and a tremendously irritable colon. The ulcer refused to heal over a period of years, even under the most meticulous medical care. She was in such a continual emotional dither that even the usually willing surgeons refused to perform an ulcer operation. But over the years the cicatrix produced by the ulcer gradually closed the outlet of the stomach, and surgery finally became an emergency.

She did poorly after surgery, healed slowly, and never really pulled herself back together. Immediately after surgery she had an infection of the lung, which gradually became worse until she had multiple lung abscesses. A portion of the lung finally had to be removed. Next she had rectal fistulas. At the age of 50, she had a painful and well-developed osteoporosis. One cannot predict what this poor woman will develop next. Her illness, of course, has roughened her disposition, but the important relationship is the other way around.

The thing which immediately strikes us about people like Mrs. V——— is their personality, in which emotional stress stands out like the nose on their face. Not infrequently these people take to alcohol to give themselves temporary relief from the effects of their emotions. They readily become chronic alcoholics, and develop cirrhosis of the liver because, with alcohol as a conditioning factor, cirrhosis occurs as the result of ACTH over-production.

THE FUTURE OF ENDOCRINE RESEARCH

In this chapter, we have considered emotional stress as it affects only two of the hormones of the pituitary gland, and the effects of these two hormones only in a very sketchy way. What happens when combinations of hormones are relatively stressed in differing amounts is still a subject for future investigation. In fact, the subject of endocrine stress has been barely opened. But already a new era is imminent in the treatment of stress disease.

THE HIGHSPOTS OF CHAPTER 4

The endocrine glands (pituitary, adrenals, thyroid, parathyroids, thymus, pancreas, and gonads) govern and regulate the normal functions of our bodies. But they also start and regulate the body's reaction to stressing, threatening forces. The pituitary is the master endocrine that controls all the others.

The pituitary responds to stress by producing one or more of its twelve hormones in increased amounts. Common stresses are bacterial or viral infection, exposure to heat, cold, moisture, dryness, or high altitudes, muscular overexertion, starvation, and many others. But the most important stress of all is that of the stressing emotions. Emotional stress can be greater than any other stress. Emotions usually act for a longer time than do other stressors, and they can produce the same effects as *any* other type of stress.

An infection stresses the pituitary to overproduce *STH*. The emotions of defeat, futility, and discouragement have exactly the same action. The immediate effects of *STH* are tiredness, general aching, nausea, weakness, as well as inflammations and defense against bacteria. Small increases of *STH* over a long period of time produce a variety of conditions: asthma, rheumatoid arthritis, high blood pressure, nephrosclerosis, periarteritis, lupis erythematosis, and others.

The aggressively unpleasant type of emotions, such as an executive must often have to be an executive, or that a crusader or reformer might have, stress the pituitary's production of *ACTH*. *ACTH* stops all the effects of *STH*, including the defense against infection. *ACTH* also produces peptic ulcers, a variety of diabetes, a diminution of the available protein in the body, and other changes.

In short, consider what you're doing to yourself before you give vent to an emotion.

5

GOOD EMOTIONS ARE YOUR
BEST MEDICINE

GOOD EMOTIONS ARE THE BEST MEDICINE

In the few years since medical men began to understand
the mechanism of functional disease, they have been so occupied with telling the bad effects of the wrong emotions that
they have neglected to stress the effects of the good emotions.
These last are just as beneficial to the person having them as
the wrong emotions are detrimental.

As a matter of fact, the good emotions are *the greatest
power for your good health* that we know anything about.
The only medicines we have whose power is comparable to
the power of good emotions are the antibiotics (such as
penicillin), on the one hand, and ACTH and cortisone, on the
other. The usefulness of ACTH and cortisone are limited
by their possible bad effects. We have not learned to give
ACTH or cortisone without producing the ill effects of
ACTH stress disease.

The body knows the secret of optimal hormone balance.
We do not. *But there is one way you have of achieving optimal hormone balance. That is to provide your body with
the stimulus of the pleasant and cheerful group of emotions.*

The physiologic effects of the good emotions are just as
great in the right direction as the effects of the bad emotions
are in the wrong direction. The "medicinal" value of the
good emotions cannot be overestimated.

Dr. Paul White of Boston, one of the country's leading
heart specialists, was one of the first men to call attention to
this fact.

THE POWERFUL EFFECT OF GOOD EMOTIONS

Dr. White, in *The Annals of Internal Medicine* for De-
cember, 1951, gave examples to illustrate his point. In the
days before we knew anything about ACTH, he had a patient,
a young mother with two children and a drunken, worthless
husband, who developed a serious case of rheumatic fever.

She had been in bed three years, and her doctors gave her, at most, another year to live.

Rheumatic fever is another disease which Dr. Hans Selye has produced in animals with STH and the proper conditioning; and today this young woman would receive ACTH or cortisone, with resultant amelioration of her illness. But at the time of this story it was, of course, not available.

The young woman's emotional state was at a terrifically low ebb. Even her will to get well had left. Then a blessing in disguise occurred; her husband pulled out for parts unknown, leaving the mother and two children without even the meagre support he had been giving. The patient rose to the occasion, and the occasion pulled her out of the doldrums.

When Dr. White came to see her, she said firmly, "Dr. White, I'm going to get out of bed and support my two children."

Dr. White answered, "My dear lady, I wish you could, but your heart wouldn't stand it."

Now, it wasn't, mind you, that Dr. White was underestimating her heart. A man like Dr. Paul White knows a heart when he examines one, and knows what can be expected of it. But Dr. White was underestimating the physiologic effects of ACTH (which were unknown at the time) and the possibility that certain emotions could stimulate the production of ACTH and produce a normal hormonal spectrum. Despite Dr. White's advice, the young woman, with courage, determination, enthusiasm, and cheerfulness, got out of bed and went to work. She supported and reared her two children for eight years.

Any observant physician can tell you similar stories out of his own practice. One commonly sees such examples after surgery. One of the surgeons in our clinic did a very extensive and difficult piece of surgery to save a man's life from a malignancy. Three days after surgery the surgeon asked me to see the patient, saying, "The man is going to die."

I looked at his hospital chart, and from the record it certainly did look as though he were going to die. I went into his room. The man was conscious, but that was about all.

I said, "Henry, how are you today?"

Henry pulled a generous smile, put a glow of determined enthusiasm into his eyes (I don't know where he got the strength to do it) and answered with a genuine sincere feeling: "Fine! I'm going to be out of here in a few days."

And that remained Henry's attitude. He got well. If he

had accepted the emotions of despair and defeat that his condition warranted, I am sure Henry would have died.

Another remarkable individual I will never forget was a middle-aged lady who was in the hospital because of an uncontrollable hemorrhagic disease. Every day her condition grew seemingly worse. Every time I came on the wards I no longer expected to find her alive. But whenever I asked her how she felt—"I feel fine and I want to sit up today. I'm going home soon." She maintained that cheerfulness and courage. She got well; not because of any treatment I gave her, but because of the treatment her emotions gave her.

The Good Emotions Produce an Optimal Hormone Balance

These people stimulate their pituitaries in just the proper optimal way to produce a balance of hormones such as we cannot achieve by giving the hormones artificially. Don't forget, these are the same hormones, just as powerful and just as effective, as those we were talking about in the last chapter. But the right kind of emotions produce these hormones in the right amounts, just as the wrong kind of emtions produce them in harmful amounts.

Good Emotions Work Miracles

Our knowledge of hormones, incomplete and fragmentary though it still is, sheds light on many seemingly miraculous cures. As we understand it better, our natural world becomes increasingly wonderful, and thousands and thousands of times more amazing than the ancients thought it to be.

Let's take a case for illustration. Before the days of antimicrobials, a colored man had a kidney infection. Of course, the antimicrobials would now clear this up in 24 hours. But in 1934 it was a serious affair. The man had always been irritable and aggressively disagreeable. He gradually grew worse. He had the type of emotions which stimulate ACTH; he was counteracting any defensive action STH might have. He was providing no resistance to the infection.

Then a voodoo healer got hold of the man. He changed the man's emotions to the cheerful ones, gave him enthusiasm, hope, and a terrific courage (all of which, mind you, I had been unable to do). What happened in the man was that an optimal balance of hormones allowed the maximum defensive mobilization of STH. The body's own immunity reactions were all the treatment we had at that time. The man got better.

The same effect would have occurred had his emotions been changed to the good by any other means—for example, a romantic love affair. The important thing was not the means, but the right kind of emotions.

This kind of thing has been going on ever since the human race started. We are only beginning to appreciate its true significance.

THE GOOD EMOTIONS WORK IN TWO WAYS

Don't forget that the good emotions have two general effects. First, they replace the bad emotions which were producing stress effects; and secondly, they produce their own pituitary effect which is an optimal balance of endocrine function. It is this optimal balance which produces the state which we human beings have always called, "Gee, I feel good!" But the first effect, that of replacing the bad emotions and their stress effects, is equally important.

WHY NOT LIVE?

Once we appreciate that healthful living is more a matter of having the right kind of emotions than anything else, it becomes apparent that the most important aspect of living consists in training and handling our emotions.

So far, education has consisted largely in educating our intelligence, which is quite necessary also. But one can have a very high intelligence, and very bad emotions, and live perfectly miserably. If it were a matter of one *or* the other, life would be sweeter with good emotions and low intelligence.

As a matter of fact, if one goes about it right, it is *easier* to acquire good emotions than a good intelligence. And there is actually no need for anyone to have bad emotions. So many people do have bad emotions because, for so many thousands of years, we have neglected to train people in emotional control.

THIS CHAPTER IN A NUTSHELL

The healthy emotions have just as great an effect on the pituitary as the stressing emotions do. Their effect is just as powerful in the direction of good health as the effect of the stressing emotions is toward bad health.

The healthy emotions, such as equanimity, resignation, courage, determination, and cheerfulness, stimulate the pituitary to produce an optimal hormone spectrum, an effect with far greater power for good health than any drug, or set of drugs, that we know anything about.

6

YOUR FUNDAMENTAL AND YOUR
SUPERFICIAL EMOTIONS

YOU HAVE TWO EMOTIONAL LEVELS AT ALL TIMES

There is one more important point to understand about emotions if we are to understand their effect on us.

We all are always having emotions on two different levels at the same moment. Or you might say that we have two layers of emotions, an outside layer that everyone sees, and an inside deep layer that no one sees unless he has learned to spy beneath the surface. The emotions in the deep underlying layer we may call the FUNDAMENTAL emotions.[1] Those in the outside layer we may call the SUPERFICIAL emotions. We can best understand these two varieties by an example.

Let us suppose that this morning you committed a misdeed or a crime. Let us also suppose it is your first crime, and you are obviously not a hardened criminal. You are afraid. You have a feeling of guilt. You wish mightily that the moment of your dreadful deed might be blotted away, or relived without crime. Most of all, of course, you are expecting to be apprehended by the police, who are on your trail. For the next hours, for the next days, perhaps, you will constantly have a FUNDAMENTAL emotion of fear-anxiety-remorse.

The emotion *is* the manifestation; without the bodily changes, there would be no emotion. And so, every minute of those waitful, apprehensive hours or days, the emotion will be tightening muscles, overstimulating the endocrine glands. Because of these manifestations you will, doubtless, feel unwell.

There may be moments during those hours when your mind will necessarily have to be on other subjects, and there may be a play of SUPERFICIAL emotions, some of which may

---

[1] These are what the psychiatrist terms the *affect.*

63

be seemingly cheerful and pleasant, even though the FUNDA-MENTAL emotion is continuing its manifestations unchecked. There are moments when to an outsider you *seem* happy, your joking sincere, and your heart light. But inside, all the time, you know the real state of affairs, because you can feel that dreadful sensation in your stomach even when you are laughing at someone's joke.

The FUNDAMENTAL emotion continues through your day like a backdrop on a stage; the SUPERFICIAL emotions flit about before the backdrop, and hold the stage for their little time; but before them, and during them, and after them, the backdrop of FUNDAMENTAL emotions continues.

FUNDAMENTAL EMOTIONS HAVE THE GREATEST EFFECT

Such FUNDAMENTAL emotions have more to do with bringing on functional disease than do the SUPERFICIAL emotions, because they are constant, because they are often very basically unhappy, and because they often continue for a very long time, longer than the event or situation that started them.

FUNDAMENTAL emotions may last an entire lifetime, constantly producing symptoms of disease, without the person being precisely aware that the FUNDAMENTAL emotion exists, and without those near and with him sensing its presence.

For example, Walter, age 27, was a friendly young man, likable and pleasant, and generally regarded by the people who patronized his gas station as a happy fellow. To those who knew him better, like his wife, he had moments when he looked apprehensive, became pensive with a serious look in his eyes as though he were looking for something to happen. Not even his friends knew he had a chronic diarrhea which had grown steadily worse ever since he was six years old.

At age five, Walter was riding with his father on a wagon. Suddenly, (there was a storm coming), a bolt of lightning killed his father and the two horses. From then on, Walter was never without a FUNDAMENTAL emotion of fear and anxiety, which manifested itself in part in the colon. The FUNDAMENTAL emotion was present regardless of what his SUPERFICIAL emotions might be.

BATTLE EMOTIONS

Battles or other dreadful frightening events, may produce emotions which carry on for years, even though the person's surface may often appear smooth, cheerful, and unruffled.

FUNDAMENTAL EMOTIONS FROM UNFILLED BASIC NEEDS

One of the commonest causes of a prolonged, severely unhappy FUNDAMENTAL emotion is an unfilled basic psychological need, six of which—love, security, recognition, creative expression, new experiences, self-esteem—we discuss in Chapter 14.

FUNDAMENTAL EMOTIONS FROM IMMATURITY

Another common cause of unfavorable FUNDAMENTAL emotions is immaturity and the consequent problems which an immature personality manufactures for itself. Some of these we discuss in Chapter 7.

CHEERFUL FUNDAMENTAL EMOTIONS

Fortunate is the person who has a layer of FUNDAMENTAL emotions that are habitually cheerful. He has what we call a cheerful disposition, and it is worth more to him than wealth of all the world. In fact, it is hardly ever found where there is wealth.

A cheerful and pleasant disposition, that is to say, happy FUNDAMENTAL emotions, should be the central aim in the raising of children. Give them this, and they will have more than they can ever get in any other way. If you've grown up without a naturally happy disposition, it is not too late to cultivate one. It calls for the constant practice of a few principles that are simple, and which we will present in Part II of this book.

POINTS TO REMEMBER IN THIS CHAPTER

Each of us has, at all times, two different sets of emotions. Each set is making its own physical and chemical changes in our bodies.

The SUPERFICIAL emotions are the set we have out on the surface from minute to minute, such as our radiant pleasantness when someone gives us a box of candy.

The FUNDAMENTAL, or deeper emotions, are the ones that are the background of the world we are living in—the feeling that persists inside us when our son is a prisoner in the enemy's hands, or a feeling of the dark dismal view of the world our parents may have given us, or the general tone of apprehension we have when a loved one is sick.

A person may have an outwardly genial manner and yet

have a set of FUNDAMENTAL emotions which are doing him no good. Sometimes the FUNDAMENTAL emotions may be the result of unfulfilled psychological needs, sometimes they may result from the effects of immaturity, and sometimes they may be due to factors which the person does not admit to exist.

The only satisfactory FUNDAMENTAL emotions are those that go with the person who has acquired a truly happy disposition, who has learned to maintain emotions of equanimity, resignation, courage, determination, and cheerfulness.

PART II.

HOW TO CURE YOUR
EMOTIONALLY
INDUCED ILLNESS

7.

YOU CAN ACHIEVE
EMOTIONAL STASIS

THERE HAS ALWAYS BEEN E. I. I.

There is probably no more emotionally induced illness today, nor any greater amount of emotional stress, than there
was in days gone by. The world has always been full of it.
People in bygone days didn't meet the ups-and-downs of
living with any less emotional stress than people do today.
And although we of the mid-20th Century have such stresses
today as the world political situation, practically every age
had its world situations and its wars, in some ages much
more constantly than we have had. Although we have the
stress of an excessive amount of publicity on diseases of all
varieties, past ages had the greater stress of smallpox, tuberculosis, diphtheria, plague, typhoid, dysentery, osteomye-
litis, and many other miserable conditions which today are
rare indeed.

No age ever "had it as good" as ours; no age has ever
been as free from want, or as free from the effects of just
plain weather, as we are. Every age has had emotional stress.

We, in the United States, probably have less emotional
stress today than any people ever before in the history of the
world. That isn't the way you usually hear it. We pay more
attention to the stress people are under today because we
are beginning to learn about its importance. We are going
to be able to reduce people's emotional stress in the future
just as we have reduced contagious disease. We are just beginning to learn how.

EMOTIONAL STASIS VERSUS TROUBLE

The most surprising thing about people who have E. I. I.

is that usually they do not have a great amount of trouble. You'd think they would, wouldn't you? You would think the rule might be expressed in equations something like these:

Much trouble in life=emotionally induced illness.
Little trouble=No E. I. I.

But this is not true. A large amount of trouble may, of course, help bring on E. I. I. but *the majority* of patients with E. I. I. actually have very little real trouble.

The chief factor that brings on E. I. I. is that the patient has never learned to maintain good healthy emotions in just plain, ordinary, everyday living—in those situations where there are only the usual daily varieties of trouble every one of us has all the time. That factor is responsible for the disease in 90 per cent of E. I. I. patients.

They have never learned to produce a good, healthy stream of emotions in the face of the changing situations they meet in ordinary living. By ordinary living I mean having to make a living, having to meet problems of income and expenditure, having to discipline a family, having to iron out an occasional altercation. Death in the family must be faced, too, since that is a part of all ordinary living.

These patients have never learned the art of *emotional stasis;* they meet living with emotional stress. *Emotional stasis* is the ability to meet a wide variety of life situations, the bad with the good, with emotions like equanimity, resignation, courage, determination, cheerfulness, and pleasantness. The person who lacks emotional stasis meets most of his situations, good with bad, with emotions like anxiety, fear, apprehension, discouragement, disappointment, and frustration.

But, of course, what we are saying about the E. I. I. patient who doesn't have a good healthy stream of emotions applies to almost all of us, since practically everyone, at some time or other (including you and me, dear reader), has E. I. I.

EMOTIONAL STRESS IS DUE TO AN EDUCATIONAL FAILURE

So many of us today, as well as most everyone in the past, has lacked emotional stasis because man leaves to chance a quality that must be learned. The only way a person can develop emotional stasis is through the right kind of education. But the right kind of education *does not exist.*

There is no place you can go to learn emotional stasis. There should be, but there isn't. And there isn't because it has taken mankind until the middle of the 20th Century to learn what emotional stasis is. Education in emotional stasis is coming, and some day our descendants will learn it in school. But that doesn't help you and me right now, does it?

The family influence. A person's total education, of course, includes much, much more than what he learns in the schools he attends. Our *most important* educational influence is the family we are brought up in. And there are many, many families whose effect on their children is a terrible and ruinous one. Most families develop strong emotional stress. There are many exceptions, certainly, but by and large, our families are educational flops of the first water.

Influence of our friends. The second most important educational factor each of us has is the people who live within our circle, those with whom we play, talk, visit, work, fight, love. This circle includes authors who enter our private worlds through their books, even though they may be dead. If we are lucky, some strong enlightened individual enters our circle and influences us in the development of a healthy attitude or two. But most of the people who stream through our lives are mediocre and full of educational stress.

Influence of our schools. Our schools are our third most important educational influence. The schools do not even pretend to do anything about emotional stasis. I think they will before long. There are several forward-looking educators who are beginning to plan for it and think about it. The central goal in our education should be to fit people for living full, enjoyable lives, instead of having them run a marathon of seventy years of emotional stress.*

Influence of the church. The churches are our fourth most important educational influence. Like the schools they, too, do not have a conscious program for developing emotional stasis. Religion, as it is conceived by the churches, does not provide its members, or its clergy, with the type of emotions which save them from E. I. I. The clergy, in my experience, have functional disease as much as any other group. Only among the Quakers and the Christian Scientists

* A recent book, *Building Your Life,* by Judson T. and Mary G. Landis, published by Prentice-Hall, Inc., New York, is a valuable aid for adolescents in the development of a mature life. It is an important book for all who are interested in this subject.

is there an appreciable lack of E. I. I. I say this without prejudice; I belong to neither denomination.

"MATURITY" IS ANOTHER NAME FOR EMOTIONAL STASIS

The same educational influences which make for emotional stasis also make for the thing we call "maturity." An education that would provide a person with emotional stasis would also provide him with maturity. Emotional stasis is the emotional counterpart of being mature.

It has been only recently that psychologists have come to understand, and to be able to state, just what maturity consists of. *Maturity* is just what it sounds like—the ability to react to life situations in ways that are more beneficial than the ways in which a child would react. *Emotional stasis* is exactly the same thing. *Emotional stress* is what a child produces when faced with a menacing situation; a mature person has *emotional stasis* in the same situations.

Psychologists have also become aware that few or no people are fully mature—there is some place in their personality where they still react like children, with childish stress emotions. There are only a very few people that even approximate full maturity simply because there is no organized educational effort to make us mature. It is left to chance. A few people are fortunate enough to fall into the hands of very sensible individuals who can show them how to achieve some degree of maturity, but even so, it is never the complete course.

A man in the forefront of his profession or industry will display to the public a fairly well-rounded maturity in the sense we are going to describe. But somewhere in his makeup, there is apt to be a very immature spot; in regard to some things that he meets in his living he will have reactions characteristic and worthy of a child.

Some public office holders, men in the headlines every day, are extremely immature in very fundamental ways. Once the public learns what maturity and immaturity are, men like these will no longer reach high office. They will be spotted for what they are—immature fakes—and society will be spared the nonsense and nuisance they produce.

Once our society makes it a point to train people to reach maturity and emotional stasis, there will be many, many more people reaching fairly well-rounded maturity. The entire complexion of public as well as private life will be changed for our great good.

70

A Common Misconception of Maturity

I would like first of all to invite your attention to a common variety of immaturity which a certain group of men regard as maturity. This particular variety of immaturity causes a great deal of trouble to society, to the man who has it, and to the woman unlucky enough to have married the big stiff.

The most typical example of this immature hero is the rough don't-give-a-damn-for-anything he-man-bravado individual who plays a kind of a four-year-old cowboy-badman game all his life. These are the gangsters, the bad men whom radio and television play up to their youthful audiences, and to whose activities the newspapers devote reams of copy.

This typical bad-man immaturity occurs much more frequently, in watered-down form, in the he-man who keeps his family at home while he participates in fishing, hunting, small gambling—the man forever going out with the fellows for this and that, and a drink.

I mention this group particularly because it is surprising how frequently their immaturity figures in the emotional stress of their wives and children. There are many variations of the immaturity represented by these two types. Every town has many of them around.

The tougher they are, and the tougher they act, the more immature and childish they actually are. Their babyhood crops out terrifically whenever one of them has to be stuck with a needle, or has to submit to some form of minor surgery without an anesthesia. They just can't take it. I've seen some of the "toughest guys" in St. Louis, men who were in the headlines of gangsterism, carry on like babies when they were faced with an intravenous needle.

Their toughness is, of course, a front they kid themselves with. They simply can't take it. They can't stand stress of any kind, and they turn easily to drink, which is an ineffective way of easing tension. And so their concept of maturity comes to contain the idea of hard, regular drinking, just as it contained the idea of smoking when they were ten or eleven. Their concept of maturity, furthermore, contains the idea of "handling their women rough," or with indifference. It's a pity the law lets them marry.

These fellows come into the clinic when their concepts of maturity are beginning to show the strain—that is, in their forties or fifties. At that age, most of them are pretty poor physical specimens; they are children in every department of living. They have been children so long and so thoroughly they cannot conceive of any other state.

Their poor wives come to the clinic a little earlier—in their thirties and early forties. Their children come to the clinic still earlier. There are no problem children, only problem parents.

The Qualities that make for Maturity *

1. *Responsible independence, the first criterion of maturity.* A necessary step in growing up is the development of the ability to assume responsibility independently of father, mother, and other protective agencies. Long years of childhood, especially in families where protective concern is carried to an extreme, develop the tendency to keep depending on someone else. Many parents, especially mothers, strongly foster dependence when they should be molding independence.

Those who grow up with a *dependent attitude* sooner or later have a hard time. A wife runs to mother with every squall, and with every responsibility of marriage. This running to mother, and her consequent intervention, irritates the husband more and more. The marriage gradually falls apart at the seams, and everybody in the play, wife, husband, and mother-in-law, have emotionally induced illness.

Then there is the well-known boy who is made to depend on his mother. As he grows into his teens the boys make fun of him, and he feels that his dependency on his mother is a weakness. To prove his strength to himself and to his fellows he becomes a super kind of a regular guy, which is only a step away from gangsterism. After that there is petty crime, and trouble all over the landscape, with emotionally induced illness in mother, father, son.

Other people start out leaning heavily on parents, friends, relatives. When these supports are removed, they look for support in alcohol. They always have E. I. I.

2. *Maturity means a giving, rather than a receiving, attitude.* A characteristically childhood attitude is to want to receive, to be given desired things. In this immaturity, the person does things with the attitude, "What is this going to get me?" This is a springboard into mean, crabby emotions.

* For the qualities of maturity discussed in this chapter I am indebted to Dr. Leon J. Saul, *Emotional Maturity*. Philadelphia: J. B. Lippincott Company, 1947.

72

As they get older they no longer receive as they did when they were children, although they still think in terms of what they can get. They are in a dead-end alley that leads to intense desire, and finally to intense frustration.

Two unmarried sisters had always lived together, supported by a fair competence left them by their father. Then an old uncle, who had always been a troublemaker, died, and left his farm to the older (by two years), with the provision that it would pass to the younger when the older died. But the younger sister wanted to get her share at once, and demanded that the farm be sold and divided equally. But the older sister had the farm, and she wanted to keep it. Over this, they quarreled. They left each other to live alone.

Today, they are both miserable with emotionally induced illness, and will continue to be until they both mature enough to want to give rather than to get. So far, after ten years, neither has matured. They are both slightly under fifty and have many years of ill health to look forward to. Furthermore, both have lawyers, and the litigation they are in may well cost them the farm the troublemaking uncle hung around their necks.

Maturity brings with it a rich concern: how to make the living of others more enjoyable. With this concern, horizons, vision, and sympathy broaden. The person with such maturity is not living in a little closet, grasping and pulling everything possible into its dark confines. He is roaming the sunshine and the great wide world, finding other people interesting and worth the effort of knowing and giving.

Actually, in his mean position, the constant receiver never learns what great enjoyment giving can bring; he does learn how his cramped, grasping, tight emotions produce almost constant ill health.

3. *Maturity means leaving egotism and competitiveness behind.* The childish attitude is, "I've got something you haven't got," or "I can do something you can't do," or "My father can lick your father." There are many people who never lose this childish constellation of egoism and competitiveness. They are always hard to get along with because they are always pitting themselves against everybody else. They never develop a kindly cooperativeness. They are obnoxious as partners in a business, they are irritative in a gathering, they are quarrelsome in a twosome.

The over-competitive person. The person who constantly compares himself (in jealous competition) with everyone else is destined to be a miserable human being. He constantly generates envy, hurt pride, and hostility in himself and in others.

The irascible, headline-seeking politicians who are constantly imposing their will on everyone else are of this breed. If you watch their movements in Washington, they are frequently over in Bethesda Medical Center (which Congress built for the Navy and Congressmen) being "checked-over" or being treated for "sinus trouble" or having an operation for a substitution diagnosis of E. I. I.

These men consider themselves leaders, and highly mature. If their voting public only knew it, they are highly immature—immature in the category we are speaking of, as well as in most of the other categories of maturity. The continual blustering of this class of politicians produces anxiety in themselves, as well as in those they bluster against. In their innate childishness, they are striving to be something that isn't in them—mature men.

Competition can be valuable. Competition, to a degree, has its place in living. But when it becomes too strong and all pervasive, it defeats its own purpose. It produces anxiety, strain, stress, and remorse, and effectively precludes enjoyment even in those who are successful.

One of the elements in modern business and industry that produces a great amount of E. I. I. is the competition between those striving to get to the top. The managers of local stores in large chain systems are frequently seeking medical attention because they are pitted against each other on the sales sheet in their effort to rise above the local store. The same is true in banks and industries. Those who manage to go up in their system suffer from the strained aggression, and often have ulcers. Those who fail, suffer frustration and is resulting fatigue and prolonged headache. Who wins? I don't know; I haven't as yet seen any of them win.

The system is at fault. We can say without exaggeration that a system of this kind is childish and immature. We may hope that with the passage of time it will perhaps grow up and develop a kindlier and more cooperative feeling for human beings. Today it is the ruin of many of the lives of those who serve under it. IsBig business, big industry, pursued solely for its own sake, worth the hyman price? I am inclined to think it is not.

The building of a mature human being, that is to say, a happy human being, is the only honest and worthy business

74

and industry that any of us has a right to have. Any form of industry and business that provides its human beings with an unhealthy set of emotions is as immature and socially undesirable as the childishly egotistical and competitive individual.

Dick was the manager of a local chain store. The store he was running was in competition with the other stores in other towns. To get to be district manager, Dick had to outsell the other managers of the competing stores. For a rather poor salary, he worked night and day. He developed an ulcer, but he became district manager. There were some other fellows in other stores who developed the same kind of ulcers without becoming district manager. In every competition, someone has to lose. Then they develop something beside an ulcer. But Dick became district manager. His pay was then a little bigger, but he had much bigger worries, and much bigger competition. He worked and stewed harder than ever, but his district fell behind someone else's district, and he didn't make the next promotion he was hoping for. So came the frustration of defeat with fatigue, constipation, headache, insomnia.

Then there are people like Mrs. B—— who has an ego as big and rough as the Tetons. Every contact she makes with anyone else is a competition in which she demonstrates that she is just a little smarter. She has outrun and outpunted her husband so long that the poor fellow drags around with a pitiful inferiority complex. At any meeting in which the chairman is silly enough to open the discussion, she rises militantly to her feet and starts out to change something, or someone. She is a frightful power in the woman's club, a caution in the P.T.A., and a terrific headache in her bridge club. The city hall shudders every time she passes through. But nature is a balance of compensations. She pays dearly for her immaturity. Every so often at night, she privately develops a most disabling spell, which lasts until morning, and which leaves her deflated for a couple of days. The trouble with Mrs. B—— is that she hasn't matured enough to become kindly cooperative with other human beings. She is a child in that respect. "My mamma can lick your mamma" is about where this aspect of her education stopped. Watch them sometime—the people who chronically run things are themselves run by the chronic effects of their own emotions.

4. *Maturity in sex.* The childhood sexual attitude is one of genital satisfaction in the interests of self-love without

the realization that sex is part of the larger experience of mating. This, like every other experience involving two human beings, becomes mature only when kindliness, sympathy, and mutual cooperativeness enter into it.

Sexual immaturity is so very common largely because of the fears and inhibitions that block rational efforts at sex education. The schools, the families, the churches give the individual no organized instruction for handling sex in the course of his living. Most of the instruction is left to disreputable sources, and is of a disreputable flavor. Little wonder that so few grow up into sexual maturity.

Two types of sexual immaturity. One type of sexual immaturity is a hysterical fear of sex and all it connotes.

Rose was an extremely pretty girl who lived in a very rough neighborhood. Endeavoring to help Rose survive the tough neighborhood, her mother put a tremendous fear of sex into the girl. When Rose was married, years later, she was incapable of mating. Her husband tried every possible approach with infinite patience. But Rose withdrew more and more, physically and mentally. Knowing she was not a successful wife made her feel very guilty and inadequate. She developed a nonspecific ulcerative colitis and at one time she was hospitalized for an entire year.

Quite the opposite variety of sexual immaturity consists of making sexuality the most important thing in living.

Darlene grew up in a family that, in a vulgar sort of way, made a fetish of being uninhibited. The only kind of humor Darlene ever heard was the very broad, sexy variety. There was no restriction put on sexy movies; there were always mother's sexy magazines around the house. The visitors who came to the house were of the sophisticated variety whose sophistication runs to sex.

Before Darlene was old enough to date, her mother thought it cute for her to go to dances and shows with boys. Darlene became pregnant before her time, and dragged the family through one affair after another. So far, and she is still only 35, Darlene has made herself enough trouble for a lifetime, and she is capable of filling up three more. She is complaining of one thing and another all the time, and has practically leased a chair in a doctor's waiting room.

5. *Maturity means living higher than the level of hostile aggressiveness.* There are some who regard hostile aggressiveness—anger, hate, cruelty, and belligerency—as strength. Quite the opposite is true. These are childish arrests, gross

forms of immaturity, signs of weakness, evidences of fear and frustration.

Childishly aggressive men. Children, living in a world in which they are relatively impotent, feel weak, dependent, and insecure. When they are frustrated in their desires by discipline, they react with anger, hate, belligerency, and, if they can, with cruelty. Many people grow into adulthood without growing out of this form of hostile aggressiveness. They remain cruel and belligerent because they still feel weak, dependent, and insecure. They *are* weak; they haven't learned how to be strong. Only the strong can be gentle. The men who usurp power in the governments of the world, who rise to the top by cruel, aggressive, belligerent methods, are wrongly regarded as strong men, and, by common standards, as mature.

If it were generally realized that such men are, in fact, extremely childish and basically incompetent to guide human affairs, the people of their nation would vote them out or overthrow them before they could do much damage. Much of the damage the 20th Century has suffered has come from men of this variety. We have them also in America. Fortunately in this country they have not been able to usurp government, but their very presence is a threat we cannot afford. It is because so many people grow up without outgrowing their hostile aggressiveness that *the only real danger of our time is man's inhumanity to man.*

Sometimes the immaturities of hostility and cruelty are displayed in full view on the surface, as they are in the gangster of the Dillinger type. That these men have their immaturity out on the surface is a fortunate thing for society, because society can and does react to it in a way appropriate to its danger. However, there are many who have the same type of immaturity but manage to keep it pretty well concealed; they are able to bring trouble to those unfortunate enough to get in their way.

The childish troublemaker. Bert, for instance, is a pleasant looking chap who would appear to be 100 per cent harmless. One of Bert's employers told me that after Bert came to his department many of his employees gradually began showing dissatisfaction and began making trouble in the department. There was a constant irritation and agitation for one thing and another. The problem became so bad that a quiet search was made for the agitator.

It turned out to be Bert, who in a quiet, pleasant, conversational sort of way dropped barbed suggestions and remarks to the other employes. Bert would put these barbs across in such a cunningly clever way that the employees themselves did not suspect that Bert was putting hostile thoughts into their heads. After Bert was fired, the department soon settled down into its old smooth ways. Bert never feels well and I suspect he never will.

Many are the women who have thrown themselves away by marrying one of these children with hair on his chest and more muscles in his arms than maturity in his head. Hell cannot hold anything worse than what these women go through on earth. Very often these husbands will have an outward bearing, appearance, and manner that make the rest of the world think well of them.

The wife will say, "Other people simply cannot appreciate how mean and cruel he is every hour he is at home."

Such fellows inevitably develop emotionally induced illness. They rightfully deserve it. But their wives do not deserve the emotional illness they get.

6. *Maturity is able to distinguish fact from fancy.* It is characteristic of a child to accept a fancy as a fact, and not to try to differentiate between them. A child can afford to do this almost without limit because there is usually no practical disadvantage, or advantage, in doing otherwise. However, if the child grows into responsible adulthood and still cannot distinguish between fancy and fact, the results are a terrific amount of trouble that means misery and wrong emotions.

A widespread type of childishness. It is appalling how much of this kind of immaturity exists. Someone develops an idle fancy about someone else and starts a harmful rumor which becomes accepted as a fact.

A selfish, dishonest and in-every-way-despicable politician builds up a fancy concerning his value to the republic as an enemy of totalitarianism, and a great number of honest but immature voters accept the fancy as a fact. A man takes a fancy that he hears messages from God, and persuades other people that this is a fact. Religious wars and divisive hatreds among men are started on the basis of what is actually pure nonsense. Every person I have ever known who claimed to be receiving messages from God turned out to be a schizophrenic. A childish man fancies that all human illness is due to displaced vertebrae, and gets people to accept this as fact. The communists start the fancy that their system is a heaven for the farmer and the laborer; a certain number of people accept it as fact.

With each instance of such immaturity, the world, or a

part of it, must suffer. There is no immaturity that we pay for so dearly as this. It is expensive on a personal or a community level.

People who feel the world is against them. There is a common variety of this type of immaturity which especially merits attention. It is found in the individual who accepts as facts, *and worries over,* things that have never happened. Such a person lives in a terrible world of fancy, a terrible calamitous world where everything is bad, but yet a world which isn't real because it doesn't exist.

Actually, the everyday world we are in is a very enjoyable and highly interesting affair, in which the things which happen to us can be turned into some sort of a good feeling. But these immature people fancy that it is a terrible world which holds for them only the worst possible conclusions. They are afraid to stay alone in broad daylight because they accept as fact the fancy that something (they do not know what) is going to happen to them. Like the children they were and still are, they haven't grown up, and they accept as fact the fancy of their unreal fears. Such people are common patients in the doctor's office.

One patient, for instance, while working in the hay barn unloading hay, suddenly had the fancy, "Supposing there might be a snake in the hay." Now there had never been a single snake on the farm; but the fancy came; and the woman allowed her imagination to develop the fancy with many thrilling and horrible ramifications until it assumed the status of a fact in her thinking, and it became impossible for her to go to the barn.

Another lady, in her sixties, came to my office with the complaint, "I know you'll laugh at this, but I have a snake in my stomach; it's been there many months and, whenever it is irritated, it bites me and makes me miserable."

In every other respect she was perfectly sane, and, in the matter of this fancy, she was no more insane than anyone else who accepts any fancy as a fact.

You might like to hear the sequel to her snake story. No amount of examination, which included looking into her stomach with a gastroscope, could persuade the lady she had no snake. Finally one of our doctors, who was a slight-of-hand artist, contrived, while putting in and drawing out a stomach tube, to bring a garter snake out of his sleeve saying as he did so, "Well, by Jove, you did have a snake in there, and here it is."

"See," the lady said triumphantly, "I told you so all the

time." She was much relieved and felt fine. Then, three months later, she came back and said, "I've got another snake in my stomach." This was in winter, and the clever slight-of-hand doctor could find no snake for his act. The patient went to another clinic with her snake before summer came. I do not know whether she still has it or not. Perhaps by this time there have been eggs and hatchings and her entire digestive tract may be full of them.

7. *Flexibility and adaptability are most important parts of maturity.* A person who does not learn to bend, unbroken, before a wind, and to adapt himself readily to changing conditions, cannot possibly be happy in a world where disaster can fall at any time with great rapidity and where the things we hold valuable one day entirely cease to exist the next.

Flexibility and adaptability are probably the most valuable kinds of maturity to possess. When circumstances are cruel, as they often are, when the ground we were standing on is taken from under our feet, the only quality that can stave off an illness-precipitating and misery-producing set of emotions is the ability to be flexible enough before the blows of fate to remain unbroken, and adaptable enough to carry on valiantly under the new set of conditions.

It is only by possessing this kind of maturity that a person can avoid being upset if some of his basic needs (discussed in Chapter 14) are left unfilled. Without this maturity a person is forever finding himself in trouble. One simple form of flexibility and adaptability is Pollyanna's, whose system is so good it has gone for 15 or 16 commercially-successful volumes. Her system consists in finding four good things hidden away in every bad thing that happens.

Another simple system is that of the woman who had a constantly drunken husband. She decided not to allow her situation to make her miserable, and strove to make life as pleasant as possible for herself and her children.

Another simple system is not to look back, reviewing the last catastrophe, but to look ahead, determining how much good can be introduced into the future.

MATURITIES AND CERTAIN DEFINITE ATTITUDES

Maturities are, after all, nothing more than certain definite attitudes we develop in regard to ourselves and our relation to our world. But they are attitudes which are not developed without learning processes. They do not come naturally to people. They are part of the things we must learn.

These attitudes determine whether we live happily or unhappily, whether we live healthily, or whether we wallow in ill health.

Every person can profitably ask himself, "How mature am I? In what respects am I still immature and how can I outgrow it?" A great many people find it possible to mature after they are 30, 40, 50, or even 60. All one needs is to be shown what he needs to learn, and to have the desire to learn it.

With maturity comes emotional stasis.

IMPORTANT POINTS OF CHAPTER 7

People have emotional stress and emotionally induced illness not because of overwhelming amounts of trouble, but because they haven't learned to handle the ordinary amount of trouble which is the rule of everyone's living.

The ability to handle the various phases of ordinary human life in an effective way, that is to say, in a way that produces a maximum amount of enjoyment and a minimum amount of stress, is what is known as *maturity*.

Being *mature* means having *emotional stasis*, which is the ability to maintain equanimity, resignation, courage, determination, and cheerfulness when a situation might lead an immature person to apprehension, fear, anxiety, or frustration.

Becoming mature is a learning process. Unfortunately, there is no place today where people can learn to become mature. Our three educational institutions, the school, the church, and the family, all fall down in this essential part of our education.

> *Maturity consists of the following qualities:*
> 1. *A well grounded feeling of* responsibility *and* independence.
> 2. *A giving rather than a receiving attitude.*
> 3. *Graduating from egoism and competitiveness to* cooperativeness *and the* feeling for the human enterprise.
> 4. *Recognizing and accepting the social restrictions on sex, and making sexuality one item of many in a happy marital life.*
> 5. *Realizing that hostile aggressiveness, anger, hate, cruelty, and belligerency are weakness, and that* gentleness, kindness, *and* good will *are strength.*
> 6. *Being able to distinguish* fact *from fancy.*
> 7. *Being* flexible *and* adaptable *to the changes dictated by fate and fortune.*

81

8

HOW TO DEVELOP
EMOTIONAL STASIS

BECOMING MATURE IS A GRAND EXPERIENCE

So we are caught, you, I, and just about everyone else, with many immaturities and emotional stress.

Really, *we* are not to blame; *we* are the victims of circumstance. The development of our maturity and our emotional stasis was educationally neglected. We have our emotional stress because of the things we didn't have a chance to learn, rather than because of the things we did learn.

This, at least, is certain: we can't go back and start constructing ourselves all over again. If we are going to improve, we'll have to start right here, in all this mess we're in, in this state of emotional confusion which to some of us seems so utterly big and heavy. There is no other way.

We've got to start improving ourselves even with all these barnacles of emotional stress hanging to us and holding us down. A fellow like me says to you, "Come on, old boy, let's improve our emotions." You look around at what looks to you like an insuperable amount of whirling, swirling, madly dashing—a tremendous amount of trouble. The invitation to develop emotional stasis in this state of affairs may look to you like an invitation to take a first swimming lesson in the lower rapids of Niagara River!

But, actually, changing over to emotional stasis and getting rid of emotional stress is simple, and what's more, *it's an exhilarating, refreshing experience*. You can begin turning immaturities into maturities almost at once.

As a matter of fact, you start today!

CONSCIOUS THOUGHT-CONTROL

Stop just a moment to consider this interesting angle. Suppose that the right kind of education has given lucky

Henry Smith emotional stasis and maturity. Just what has this education done to Henry Smith? Principally this:

The right kind of education has trained Henry Smith to *think in certain definite ways*, and *to hold certain definite attitudes*, in the face of situations that would, in Sam Jones, who was not so trained, give rise to thoughts and attitudes producing fear, apprehension, discouragement, and similar unhealthy emotions.

In Henry Smith, who was properly trained by the right kind of education, healthy ways of thinking and healthy attitudes pop into his mind without conscious control. They just find themselves there at the right time because of the training he received.

Now here is the nubbin of the trick you and I must practice: If you and I knew just what Henry Smith's ways of thinking are, and what his attitudes are, we might, even without any educational training, bring them into our minds through conscious thought control, that is to say, *by just making them be there*.

GETTING ON THE RIGHT TRACK

In other words, you are going to have to watch your thinking, just as if your Mind's Eye were standing in a little balcony from which it can look over everything that comes into your mind. Your Mind's Eye must watch what goes on, and report immediately when your mind is becoming occupied with thinking that will generate stress.

When the report comes from your Mind's Eye that your mind is engaged in such skulduggery, you *consciously* start *the way of thinking* and *the attitude* that you might have had if you had emotional stasis and maturity like Henry Smith.

This is a trick called *conscious thought-control*. Anyone can do it. You can, for instance, sitting there in your chair, direct your thoughts to your last summer's vacation or to the vacation you are planning this summer. You can turn your thinking in any direction you wish. Of course you can!

Now, try it. Think of something you are planning that is really very agreeable. There, see? It's no trick at all.

The important point to know then is just *how* and *in what direction* thought is to be controlled if we are to approximate Henry Smith's maturity and emotional stasis. This would, at first glance, seem like a very complex process, and it *would* be if we had to come to a decision first as to just what Henry Smith has that we haven't. But, fortunately, psychologists and psychiatrists have this already prepared, cut-and-dried for us. As a matter of fact, it has been reduced to beautifully simple terms, readily understandable and very practical to follow.

Now don't let me mislead you: I said *simple;* but, admittedly, following these simple directives is not always *easy,* and there will be many times when you have to put considerable pressure behind your efforts. But since it concerns the most important part of your personality (your maturity and emotional stasis), and since it concerns the most important element in your living (your happiness), and since it directly concerns your health, *the required effort is decidedly worth ten thousand times what it takes.*

So, let's get going. *What track is our thought control to take?*

HERE'S WHERE YOU START: THE KEY THOUGHT

The thought that you must carry all the time, like a big sign hanging over the stage of your living, is this:

> *I am going to keep my thinking and my attitude calm and cheerful right now.*

That thought you are to have always with you, repeating it over and over to yourself until it sticks there without conscious effort. Just as the present moment is always with you, so is the thought, "I am going to keep my thinking calm and cheerful—right now."

Whatever happens, whatever situation arises as the day goes along, keep that *one* thought active and alive.

And, of course, situations will arise, every day, to which you have gotten in the habit of reacting with one of the unhealthy emotions. Then you will say to yourself, "Whoa, there, old fella, here's where we need calmness and cheerfulness."

Then you must substitute a healthy emotion—one containing equanimity, courage, resignation, determination, cheerfulness and pleasantness—for that unhealthy stress emotion you might otherwise have—the one containing fear, apprehension, remorse, disappointment, anxiety, or frustration.

SUBSTITUTING HEALTHY EMOTIONS FOR STRESS EMOTIONS

At first you'll find that you have usually *started* stewing over something, or you've already become irritated and upset before you remember to say to yourself, "I am going to keep my thinking and my attitude calm and cheerful—right now." As you practice, you'll be *ahead* of stress with the key thought, and be able to stop your descent into stressing emotions.

Either way, the moment you remember, "I am going to keep my thinking and attitude calm and cheerful—right now," you stop the thinking that generates the stress emotion and start a train of thought that will generate healthy emotions. Everybody develops his own tricks for substituting a healthy emotion for a stressing one—RIGHT NOW, when it is needed.

On the occasions that are just "nasty little situations" of minor importance, one of my patients learned to begin whistling, and soon he trilled himself into complacency, equanimity and cheerfulness. Another patient, who had a good voice and liked to sing, learned that if she sang she could change her emotions for the better at once. Another patient has learned to find beauty in the little things about her when she needs the lift. And a man told me that he keeps planning a new experience ahead that he can turn to and think about whenever he finds his emotions are running toward the stressing side.

Many people find prayer a ready way for starting a pleasant stream of emotion. But it is important to get into the prayer the same attitude of calm and cheerfulness. For instance, it would not do to pray like this: "Oh, Lord, I feel miserable, and the situation I am in is terrible. Won't you help me, God?"

The supplication should run more like this: "Thou hast created a wonderful, wonderful world for our enjoyment, O Lord. Give me the courage, the resignation, the determination, the equanimity, the cheerfulness, the pleasantness to enjoy this wonderful life Thou hast given me from Thy bounty."

These are all useful methods of substitution. They will help you out of those numerous little snarls that come along every day—the sum total of which can get you down.

MASTERING THAT NASTY LITTLE MOMENT

These nasty little situations are easy to handle by remembering, "I am going to keep my thinking and my attitude calm and cheerful—*right now*," and then deliberately calling up and tossing in a healthy emotion instead of allowing the stressing one to go ahead. It is very important in developing emotional stasis that you do handle stresses in this way. For although each of these minor stresses may seem trivial, yet these seemingly trivial episodes, if allowed each time to

85

run a stressing course, will by themselves be enough to produce chronic emotional stress and E. I. I. Eighty per cent of the average patient's stress arises from these poorly-controlled and relatively minor situations.

IF THE GOING IS SMOOTH

If you happen to be traveling through a good, smooth period of living, then, for heaven's sake, allow yourself *to feel* happy. Fill the hopper with equanimity, cheerfulness, and pleasantness. Go the limit to enjoy the delightful magnificence of your world. Life is wonderful if you allow it to be.

FOUR THINGS TO DO IF THE GOING IS ROUGH

The big situations that may arise in your living, (you and I have had them, and will continue to) are not as readily dealt with as are "the nasty little moments." Suppose your wife is sick, you can't get (in fact, you can't afford) help, the children are at loose ends, and it looks as though your plant was about to shut down; you already are working only three days a week. Creditors are after you. That, my dear fellow, is not a spot where simply substituting an emotion is going to do the trick.

There is a general mode of procedure to keep in mind:

1. First, stay outwardly as cheerful and calm as you possibly can. Lighten an awkward situation with a bit of humor, wry though it may be. (Wry humor is, after all, the best variety.)

2. Avoid running your misfortune through your mind like a repeating phonograph record. Do not let yourself get irritated, upset, or hysterical. Above all, don't start pitying yourself.

3. Lay your plans always to turn every defeat into some kind of a victory, remembering that the best victory is to have kept your courage, your equanimity and pleasantness. Everyone will admire you for that.

4. Run these flags up on your masthead and *keep them flying:*

    Equanimity ("Let's stay calm.")

    Resignation ("Let's accept this setback gracefully.")

    Courage ("I can take this, and more.")

    Determination ("I'll turn this defeat into victory.")

    Cheerfulness ("Bowed but not broken.")

    Pleasantness ("Still good will toward men.")

THE STORY OF TWO MEN

You should know about these two men, and remember them as you deal with your problems. They are as different as night and day. One of them, Sam, is the perfect example of emotional stress. The other, William, is the epitome of emotional stasis.

SAM, KING OF HIS OWN STEW

Sam's world, if someone other than Sam inhabited it, would be a dreamland. The *only* bad feature in Sam's life is his own condition of emotional stress, which, mind you, Sam is not accountable for, since he got it through bad family education.

Sam is a well-to-do farmer and a director of a bank in a neighboring town. Sam has a wonderful farm which he inherited from his father. From his father, too, he received a grouch of the kind fairly common among "successful men." I don't think a grouch like that is inherited; it's acquired by living in the shadow of someone else's grouch. His mother was grouchy too; I imagine she got it living with Sam's father; or, perhaps, his father married the woman because she had the type of grouch he felt went with a solid citizen.

In spite of the fact that Sam had never had any hardships, no financial losses, no extraordinary family catastrophes, no blows beneath the belt from unkind fate, he, nevertheless, walked through life as though utter and complete ruin were just around the corner.

On Sam's side of the street, the sun never shone. Sam was like the man walking in a park telling a friend how unfortunate was his every move, saying, "Some people buy bonds —they go up. Some people marry—she is a princess. For me —everything goes wrong." Just then a bird flew overhead; the complaining man took out a handkerchief and carefully cleaned a fresh spot from his lapel. "See?" he explained. "For some people they sing."

I have asked Sam's family, and Sam's neighbors, whether they have ever heard Sam say a hopeful, pleasant word, but none of them ever have. Oh, yes, I almost forgot. His wife thinks that Sam did say something pleasant the first year they were married, but that was so long ago she is no longer sure.

To illustrate how Sam's disposition operates, I drove into his farm one day in July just about the time the oats were ready to be cut. Sam had 60 acres of the nicest oats you'd ever want to see. I said, "Sam, that's a wonderful field of oats you have there." Sam answered mournfully, "Yeah, but the wind'll blow it down before I get it cut."

I watched the oats. Sam got it cut before it blew down. He got it threshed before it burned up. And I knew he received a good high price for the oats. So the next time I saw Sam I said,

"Sam, how did the oats turn out?"

"Oh, I suppose good enough," he replied. "But a crop of oats like that sure takes a lot out of the soil."

Another year he had corn that ran 165 bushels to the acre. Before it was harvested, Sam was in my office and I said, (conversationally, as well as to see whether Sam was running true to form), "How's the corn this year, Sam?"

And Sam said, "Terrible! It's so heavy I don't know how we're going to get it in."

At another time in October, I met him on the street. It was one of those beautiful dreams of an October day that we so often have in Wisconsin. With what I thought was contagious enthusiasm, I said,

"Hello, Sam. Wonderful day, isn't it?"

Sam's answer was, "Yeah, but when we get it, we'll get it hard."

These outlooks are typical of Sam.

You will remember in Chapter 4 we talked about the type of emotionally induced illness that Sam has. People with Sam's emotional color *always* develop emotionally induced illness, certainly by their middle fifties. And when they get it, they get it, like Sam's weather, *hard*. Very often they are invalids for the rest of their lives.

WILLIAM, KING OF LIVING

The other man to contrast with Sam is a man still to be seen on the streets of our town. His hat is respectable but old. His coat is clean but worn. His smile is sincere; the look in his eyes is glad. He is called William.

William, too, inherited a good round sum from his father, just as Sam did. And in an adventurous sort of way he tripled it and quadrupled it, and enjoyed it, as only William knew how to enjoy.

Then came 1929 and 1930. The bankers (and one was particularly bad) set upon William gleefully, and cleaned him out. I am told, on good authority, that with a little lenience William could have come through the depression in good condition. But this one banker snapped up what William had, while the snapping was good. William went on W.P.A.

I stopped one day when I saw him digging in a ditch with a string of other men. William was 60, and he hadn't worked at manual labor for years, if ever. When he saw me he smiled a great big smile and rested on his shovel.

"You might almost say," he laughed, "that you are watching an honest man earn an honest dollar. But it isn't quite true. I earn only 79 cents of it. The rest of the time I lean on my shovel and talk. But then that's what the Government wants—it's not so much to get this ditch dug as it is to help the public's morale, and so the 21 cents I don't earn shoveling, I make up for by boosting the general morale of these fellows working here with me."

All the fellows down in the ditch laughed with him. They had been feeling good ever since he joined them. He always made everybody feel good.

William still had a few irons in the fire and he made a little money over and above his W.P.A. intake. But then both he and his wife, whom he adored, developed an abdominal malignancy at the same time.

Each had an operation. He lived and was cured. But he lost his wife. And it took all his recent savings to pay the hospital. Through the whole thing, William never changed; he never talked about himself, nor complained.

He had a pleasant story, an interesting anecdote, cheerful greetings, whenever anyone came to see him in his hospital room. His wife's death must have made a great hole in his life, but he never let on. He filled it with the old smile which shone now beneath the battered hat that was all he could afford. Here and there, he made a little to live on, one way and another, but always happy.

Then he developed a malignancy of the larynx. More operations. I'd see him in the office, and he had so many interesting things to tell me I had difficulty finding out how *he* was. And, miraculously, he was cured of the malignancy in his larynx. He still goes around the town, smiling, interested in everything, and interesting everyone in something.

Probably the most remarkable thing about William is this: The banker who cleaned William out in the depression has never had a friend. I have never heard anyone say a good or kind word about him—except William.

William thinks the banker is a man of great capacity, and told me once, "People think the man has no heart, but he is kind, really. Nobody seems to pay any attention when he is kind, but they sure talk about it when he does the kind of thing a banker necessarily has to do."

One of William's neighbors, having admired the manner in which Will kept his head up, the cheerful smile on his lips, and the friendly, unwhining greeting through all his misfortune, stopped Will one morning and said, "William, if you'll excuse me, I want to say simply that I admire the way you come through misfortune after misfortune. I'd sure like to know your recipe. Would you mind giving it to me?"

William smiled warmly. Like everyone else, he liked a pat on the back.

"Well, I'll tell you. A long time ago I sat down to try to figure out my next move. It didn't look as though there was another move. I thought a long time. And then the answer came to me. I got up and repeated it to myself, 'William, you might just as well cooperate with the inevitable.' And that's what I've been doing ever since—cooperating with the inevitable."

THE IMPORTANCE OF HANDLING THE AVERAGE MOMENT

Let me give you one more example of the general procedure for you to follow, this time an example of how to handle, and how not to handle, the "nasty little moment."

Some time ago, I chanced to go Christmas shopping with two ladies in the department stores of Chicago. These two ladies were twin sisters.

The first of these sisters had left a chronically-ill husband at home, and had a boy fighting in the Far East. The second sister had nothing in her life to cause a ripple.

The first sister knew the art of enjoyment, that is to say, she knew how to attain emotional stasis. She made herself enjoy the entire day.

When we went into a department store, she would look around at the holiday decorations in genuine pleasure and say something like, "I just love to shop at Christmas, the stores are all so gay."

If we stopped at a counter looking for some particular article, she would exclaim with pleasure, "My, they have such a wonderfully rich selection of everything. I've got a better choice of better things right here than any Roman Empress ever had," or, "Oh, wouldn't Charles just be thrilled to death with this? Why it just suits him to a T."

We had lunch in a department store restaurant. She said as we entered, "I always like to eat in here, it's so nice and big, and the meals are always so delicious." She enjoyed the whole meal, and we started out again with a neat tip to the waitress.

Her sister, on the other hand, had no reason for acting differently, except her acquired habit.

As we entered a store—the very same store—she looked around in horror, "Just look at all the crowds. I just hate to do Christmas shopping."

At a counter she would say, "They have so much you just don't know what to choose. They simply have too much. Last year the thing I got Charley he didn't like, and I know he wouldn't like this either. And look at the prices. It's positively robbery, that's what it is."

In the department store restaurant, nothing was right or satisfactory. She complained to the waiter of every bit of food that came before her, and finally she became irritated because the waitress reached in front of her. She made a scene with the manager that I thought would never be over. She entirely spoiled her own meal, and she could have spoiled her sister's and mine if we had not (knowing her) found her intensely amusing.

The next day the pleasant twin felt fine and chipper, and was about her usual work. But the self-made battle-ax was sick abed with a migraine headache, as I knew she would be. "Why in the world," she grumbled belligerently, "do I get these headaches? Oh, oh, I'm so sick."

A SUMMARY OF THE AIDS FOR DEVELOPING EMOTIONAL STASIS PRESENTED IN CHAPTER 8

I. Practice thought control. When you catch yourself starting a stressing emotion like worry, anxiety, fear, apprehension, or discouragement, *STOP IT*. Substitute a healthy emotion like equanimity, courage, determination, resignation, or cheerfulness.

II. Carry this idea every minute of every day: *I am going to keep my attitude and thinking calm and cheerful—right now.*

III. When the going is good and smooth, allow yourself the delightful feeling of being happy.

IV. When the going gets rough:

    1. Stay outwardly as cheerful and as pleasant as you possibly can. Lighten an awkward situation with a bit of humor, wry though it may be.

    2. Avoid running your misfortune through your mind like a repeating phonograph record. Above all, do not let yourself get irritated, upset, or hysterical.

    3. Try to turn every defeat into a moral victory.

4. Run these flags up on your masthead and *keep them flying:*

>*Equanimity* ("Let's stay calm.")
>*Resignation* ("Lets accept this setback gracefully.")
>*Courage* ("I can take all this and more.")
>*Determination* ("I'll turn this defeat into victory.")
>*Cheerfulness* ("Really, I'm holding my own," or "Bowed but not broken.")
>*Pleasantness* ("I'll still have good will toward men.")

9

TWELVE IMPORTANT PRINCIPLES
TO MAKE YOUR LIFE RICHER

Your maturity and emotional stasis will take a great step forward if you can maintain certain attitudes toward several of the important broad aspects of living. These all involve departments of living that seem to give many people considerable trouble, departments of living in which people are apt to react with typical immaturity and develop much emotional stress.

It is best to formulate a definite mature plan of action in handling these aspects of life that cause people so much stress. Let us examine such guiding principles. They will save you an immeasurable amount of stress.

1. KEEP LIFE SIMPLE

Keep yourself responsive to the simple things that are always near at hand and readily accessible. Don't get in the habit of requiring the *unusual* for your pleasure, a failing one is very likely to find in people having more than a little money or education.

Life becomes a tremendously interesting adventure if you learn how to get your pleasures from the world that lies immediately before your five senses.

How easy and simple it is to live enjoyably when the simple, interminable blue of the sky, with its long wisps of white cloud, becomes a pleasant thing to behold, a thing of beauty that thrills you every time you care to look skyward. How easy to live when the grain in the panelling of the door arouses your admiration, or a scrambled egg satisfies, or plain Mrs. What's-her-name down the street becomes an object of keen interest because of her absorbing preoccupation with her lawn.

How simple and how nice to live like Gilbert White of Selbourne, like W. C. English, John Muir, or Thoreau, occupied with the constant, wonderful world of color, sound, smell, and sight that is available every single instant. If you tune yourself to it as Walt Whitman did, your every moment is a walk down an avenue of ready-made enjoyment.

W. C. English, a remarkable man. One of the finest men it has been my great fortune to know was a man who made himself entirely happy in the world that lies at the tips of our fingers, visible to our immediate sight, and always within hearing. His name was W. C. English.

I met him when I was in college; he was already in his sixties. W. C. English was John Burroughs, John Muir, and Gilbert White of Selbourne all rolled into one. He enjoyed everything around him. His life was simple, his only needs were eyes to see, ears to hear, nose to smell, and fingers to feel.

He needed no automobile to travel. He could see more afoot. And in a mile afoot, he found infinitely more wonder than most people find in ten thousand miles on wheels. He knew every plant, every bush, every tree, by its scientific name, as well as its common name. He knew the places where the pink lady's-slipper grew, where to find the fringed avens. He knew what plants the Indians used for food, for paint, for other purposes; he knew how to prepare them. The few people who have eaten one of his meals of wild Indian vegetables beside an oak fire on the bluffs of the Wisconsin River have had one of the rare experiences men can have.

He knew the insects. They astounded him. Through personal observation he knew the life histories of some insects that were known to no other man. He enjoyed the birds and could spot and name them from far off. The Wisconsin River Valley he knew as no other man has known it. He thoroughly knew his world, and was entirely at home in it. At night he was at home with the stars and the sounds of the forest.

He showed me how to catch sight of a wild deer, where to find the badger, how to trick a fox into showing where he lived, where to expect a rattlesnake and how to pick him up. He knew about geology, fossils, and caves.

In all this, he was not a pedant, but just a smiling, pleasant man with his hat tipped back on his head, striding along easily with long strides, enjoying a world in which *everything* interested him.

I have seen him spend a whole afternoon watching a jumping spider. He lectured when he needed money, or wrote an article. But he had no great need for money, because he was richer than Henry Ford and John D. Rockefeller combined. He would chuckle when he heard of other people's misfortunes, asking why people should be foolish enough to cause themselves so much trouble. For him the people he met were as interesting as the plants and birds, and he treated them with the same solicitude.

He was one man who was truly loved and respected by all who knew him. His wife always said that she adored him more every year. They lived 60 years together.

We can't, of course, be W. C. English's, or live like him. But the point is, we should cultivate the ability to find our major and constant enjoyments in the common things which are always at hand. To be able to do so gives living a most tremendous lift whose value cannot be overestimated. Developing a capacity for enjoying what is at hand, of course, carries with it simplicity in living.

Now, mind you, it doesn't preclude soaring into the heights, but it makes soaring what it is, namely, a *soaring,* after which one again returns to set one's feet on the terra firma of the world of our five senses, rather than making soaring a permanently insecure detachment from which there is no return because there is no place to return to.

2. Avoid Watching for a Knock in Your Motor

Among the world's most miserable people are those who cannot get over the idea that they have something terribly and intrinsically wrong somewhere—something very rotten in the state of their constitutions. They are forever miserable, listening for a possible knock in their motors, a grinding in their differentials. They belong to a tremendously large organization—the "Symptom-a-Day-Club," in which it is required that the members start the day by waking up and immediately asking themselves, "Where am I sick today?"

Bellyachers are miserable people deserving our greatest sympathy and help. They have gotten the way they are because of:

(1) *Parents who were chronic bellyachers,* and who gave their poor miserable children the idea that our bodies are hellholes of aches, pains, and agues.

(2) *Doctors who gave them an organic substitute explanation for their E. I. I.* These doctors were either inexperienced or were thinking more of their fee or their time, than they were of the patient.

(3) *An interesting physiological fact*: if any of us stop and ask ourselves, "Where do I hurt?" we can by self-

examination find some place where we hurt. The bellyacher by habitual self-examination is constantly finding these places and playing them for all they are worth. All one needs to do to turn one of these insignificant, unimportant pains into something genuinely severe is to keep one's attention on the pain. It soon grows ten times as severe.

A common fuel for the bellyacher's fire is a common type of muscle-sheath and tendon pain known as fibrositis. Fibrositis *never* turns into anything serious. Although it is primarily an emotionally induced symptom, it is aggravated by muscular exertion, and by temperature and moisture changes. It is exceedingly common, and there are few people who do not have it.

Some people, like myself, have fibrositis somewhere practically all the time. The bellyachers manage to squeeze every ounce of pain out of their fibrositis. Not knowing that it is *merely* fibrositis, they add apprehension to it; if the fibrositis is in the chest, they are sure they have heart trouble; if it is in their scalp, they have a brain tumor; if it is in the abdomen, they have the cancer that is the beginning of the end.

Sometime when you haven't anything else to do (God help you), center your awareness for an hour on the sensations that arise in your throat. At the end of the hour you will understand how a person who has allowed himself the apprehension that there is something wrong with his throat can feel so sure that his throat is plugged, swollen, inflamed, dripping, abscessed, cancerous—in short, fulminatingly catastrophic—beyond anything the medical profession has ever witnessed before. What a sneering look of contempt the M.D. receives who assures such a throat searcher that he has nothing wrong with his throat!

There are a terrific number of people, physiologically sound but emotionally unsound, who have developed the idea they are unwell, and who no more expect to be well in the future than you and I expect to grow younger. Sad to say, in the development of this idea they have often been ably abetted by some lazy physician who offered them an easy organic explanation for feeling the way they do.

For instance, I had as a patient a lady who was sure she had some unusual fluid trickling about in odd ways in her abdomen. She had already had three major operations. She had a small myoma of the uterus that actually amounted to exactly nothing.

She had been told by a surgically-minded physician that

the myoma was the cause of her trouble and should be taken out. I thought I was doing pretty well in allaying her fears and explaining her feelings. Then, in a moment of doubt, she returned to the surgically-minded individual of the first part.

He operated, assuring her afterward that not only had he removed the offending uterus, but that, through his magnanimity, her ovaries, too, would never after cause her any trouble. She felt well and was fairly happy for two months. Then she had a new set of complaints.

Now her thinking was, "If my former trouble was caused by *something* that had to be removed, this one is, too." Now rational treatment is even more difficult than it was before. I am trying again, but I'm afraid the idea is pretty well fixed in her mind that she has a diseased organ again, and is never to be well. *She never expects to be well.* She is a sitting duck for the next physician who suggests an operation.

But it isn't always the doctor's fault. Josephine was a pretty maiden lady who was sacrificing herself to take care of her mother and father. The plans she had once made for her own adventure in living had been laid aside. On the surface she appeared pleasant enough, but, fundamentally, she rebelled secretly against her lot.

She had an ulcer, and she centered all her complaints around that. Her complaints, and her parents' complaints, became so wearing that her physician consented to an operation for her ulcer. Now, several years later, she is just as miserable abdominally as she was before, this time without an ulcer. The physician was literally pushed into an operation. He knew he could remove her ulcer, but he also knew he couldn't remove the situation that would produce new abdominal difficulties after the ulcer was removed.

Never before in history have people been bombarded by so many warnings of ill health as we are today. The radio and television are constantly suggesting symptoms in order to sell a remedy which even the truly sick do not need. Anyone in a properly receptive mental state can feel the necessary symptoms and buy a bottle of the stuff the commercial on the radio or television makes so alluringly curative. Daily papers and magazines whoop up a disease and recite enough average feelings as symptoms, so that anyone can imagine he has the disease, or that he soon will have it. Never before in history has a public been made so aware and so afraid of the diseases which our clay is heir

97

to. This constitutes a tremendous factor in the onset of emotionally induced illness.

A person may have symptoms from wrong emotions. If he pays no attention to these symptoms, either because he knows what they are, or because he has other more important things to think about, he cannot be said to have emotionally induced illness. But the moment he gets apprehensive, and concerned, about the symptoms he feels, and allows them to make him miserable, he has emotionally induced illness.

One of my patients was an executive of a large concern. He was always under terrific pressure, with large responsibilities. As he went about his work, he frequently felt a tightness in his chest, and because it was not actually uncomfortable, and because he was intent on his job, he paid no attention to it but went on his way.

During a routine physical examination he mentioned the tightness to the company doctor, who told the executive that he probably had early coronary heart disease. From then on the poor fellow was licked; he thought of his heart all the time, and became extremely apprehensive whenever the tightness appeared. He became unable to work and was a complete invalid for a year. It took numerous examinations by the best heart specialists in the country, and very intensive assurative therapy, to get the man back to his work. Finally, he could again evaluate the tightness for what it was—a manifestation of the harrying and worrying, anxiety and hurrying, that was a part of his job.

But be sure you are organically sound. Here is the way to take care of your health. Have a good thorough physical examination every year by a sensible doctor, to assure yourself that you are sound, or practically sound. Between the yearly examinations *believe* you *are* sound. If something turns up to cast any doubt in your mind as to your condition, go to the same doctor. If your fear turns out to be groundless (as fears usually do) make nothing further of it. It is so much more enjoyable to know that you are well than to believe there must be something morbidly wrong with you in spite of what the doctor says.

We saw in Part I how a constant, morbid fear that there must be something wrong will eventually produce E. I. I.

3. LEARN TO LIKE WORK

The chances are that you, like most of the rest of us, have to work for a living. As with every other necessary factor in your life, you might just as well like it and avoid making trouble for yourself by not liking it.

A person who has convinced himself that he doesn't like work has a monotonous repetition of unpleasant emotions while he is working, and he is well on the way to an E. I. I. There was a time when I used to suggest to a person who didn't like the type of work he was doing that he find himself a job he did like. But I found that usually such a person didn't like the second job any better than the first. The root of the matter was that he just didn't like WORK—period.

It is perfectly obvious that anyone not liking work will have a dreadful set of emotions while he is working. And, as is usual with such people, they intermittently find an excuse for not working. Then the economic pressures that go with no income produce an even more dreadful set of emotions.

The loafer is not the happy man. There has long been a myth, half-believed in every generation for centuries, to the effect that the lazy loafer is a happy person. A happy, lazy loafer is such an outstanding envy to the folks who slave for a living that he draws a great deal more comment than most human beings do, and more than he is entitled to. But he is, nevertheless, a very definite exception to the rule. The rule is that most lazy loafers are miserable people. Of 25 lazy loafers I know personally, only one is outstandingly care-free and happy. And he happens to be a very energetic man; he is merely energetic in unproductive ways.

Unless, then, you expect to end up either in prison or on relief, you had better persuade yourself that you like work. Dislike for work carries with it unpleasant emotions in more ways than one.

We have our likes and dislikes because they were suggested to us, sometimes boldly and outright, sometimes insidiously and slyly. It is very easy, especially if you are still young and not too strongly set in your ways, to keep suggesting to yourself that you *like* work. The stronger and more frequent the suggestion, the better the "take." After a little practice, you can get up in the morning, pound your fists on your chest, like Tarzan, and yell, "Come on, work! Bring on the work!"

A young person in high school or in college is often desperately troubled and bothered about what kind of work he should choose, or what kind he is most adapted to. Actually what choice he makes is not very important. Any person can do a number of things equally well; some people could succeed in any kind of work. The important ingredient is that the individual *wants* to work. With that one quality, he will make a good doctor, a good plumber, or a good teacher. Without it, he won't be worth having around at any kind of a job. What's more, he will be a drug to himself.

If a person likes to work, and has learned the simple joy of doing something well, if he feels pleased at producing something of value to society, he will be generating pleasant emotions for himself all the time he is working, as well as for the chap who hires him.

A person who has more than enough work to keep himself occupied, and who likes work, seldom develops E. I. I. He does not have time to "think." "Thinking" usually means thumbing mentally over troubles. I mentioned earlier in this book that the group in my local society who have E. I. I. least often are the farmers' wives who have eight or nine children, who take care of their homes, and also work on the farm. They don't have time to "think" or to get sick. As one patient, who had too little to do, put it, "I'm all right until I start to think."

Work is therapy. Liking to work is a wonderful prophylaxis against E. I. I.

4. Have a Good Hobby

A fascinating and creative interest apart from your work is an absolute essential for happy living. Two of our basic needs are the needs for new experiences and for creative effort. A good hobby supplies them both.

Without a hobby, spare time becomes a boring span of time during which our minds are more and more apt to cogitate upon our troubles.

There are any number of interesting and creative hobbies; I do not have to name them for you. On the whole, I would say that the creative hobbies are more satisfactory than the collecting hobbies. But collecting hobbies are not bad.

I remember one patient, a lady in her early seventies, who for 40 years had carried on a monologue of how miserable her abdomen felt. She could occupy hours telling the miserable stories of her visits to the country's greatest doctors; what each did, what each said, what each tried, and how her abdomen emerged victorious each time and continued unimproved or even worse than it had been. There were embellishments and details which varied a bit with each recounting, but even these became old and worn to the immediate family, who were tired of the tale and probably tired of seeing the raconteur live on to tell it yet again. Her children avoided her to avoid hearing the story *ad nauseam*. She added their alienation to the current chapters of her miserable saga.

On one visit, as I listened to her extended story, as I had listened many times before, I managed to get a word in edgewise, saying, "Why don't you get yourself a hobby?"

I received no answer at the time—she went right on into her transverse colon and all the mischief that lay therein. But to my surprise, she called up two weeks later on the telephone and said, "I've got a hobby."

"Good," I answered, "what is it?"

"Button collecting," she replied.

My immediate feeling was, "Oh, pshaw—button collecting!" But since then, I have watched her collect buttons, and I think I'll take it up myself sometime. It has done the intestinal lady a world of good. In fact, it has made a likeable lady out of her.

Now when she hears about a certain button, she will go out searching for it—perhaps, the search may take many days. When she finds the button, she puts it on a card with similar buttons and puts the card up on the living room wall. Now when visitors come to see her, she actually finds it more to her liking to tell them the stories of the buttons than the story of her miserable bowel. Her family is drifting back, interested, also, in the buttons.

One day the lady went to Madison to see the Governor of Wisconsin, at that time Governor Goodland. He was 84 years old, she 74. When she had been admitted to the Governor's presence, she said, "I've come, Governor, to ask you for a button from your vest to put in my button collection."

"I'll be glad to give you one," the Governor replied. "But I haven't anything to cut a button off with."

The lady had foreseen that difficulty. She promptly extracted a pair of scissors from her handbag and handed it to the Governor. That worthy man proceeded to cut all the buttons from his vest and all the buttons from his coat.

As he handed them to the lady he said, "There you are, madam. I'd give you more, but I have to get home."

5. LEARN TO BE SATISFIED

There is one understandable excuse for being dissatisfied: when there is obvious negligence, dishonesty, carelessness, or incompetence on someone's part, for example, your Congressman's. But it is obviously *useless* to be dissatisfied when a situation cannot be altered, or when dissatisfaction can be seen to be entirely useless.

For instance, you meet people who are obviously disturbed by the weather and, just as easily, by everything else. Living in chronic dissatisfaction is about as close to living in Hell as anything the world has to offer. The real tragedy is that it is so useless and unnecessary.

You remember the twin sisters I went Christmas shopping with. The one found it just as easy, and much more pleasant, to be satisfied with all the things her sister found it necessary to be dissatisfied with.

This habit of dissatisfaction is often acquired innocently by a child living in a family where one or both parents are continually at odds with everyone and everything else.

Other people acquire the habit of dissatisfaction in a different way. Albert was a boy who was awkward and "queer." The other children loved to use him as a scapegoat for their cruelty. Albert gradually came to suspect and dislike all other people. He came to dislike things other people liked or thought important. Today he registers dissatisfaction with everything and everyone, excepting himself, whom he is unconsciously defending in everything he does and thinks.

A few others become habitually dissatisfied because a series of misfortunes has soured them on everything, and they weren't originally equipped with the fortitude to rise above it. This kind of thing is apt to happen to the man or woman who picks a lemon in marriage and then has to live with it. There are so many people attached, really tragically attached, to marital lemons that it is a great credit to *homo sapiens* that so few murders are actually committed. Henry once told me the secret, and Henry knew, for he was irrevocably riveted to about the sourest lemon I ever saw. Well, the secret, Henry said, was to cultivate a taste for lemons.

If I ever have enough money to erect a statue to anyone, it will be a statue for Henry. Henry, through 33 horrible years, took a terrible, unmerciful beating; while he took it, he maintained a cheerful disposition, a warm, friendly outlook on the world and an unusual degree of good will toward men. There have been saints who were not half so deserving. And many men like Henry are flowers born to blush unseen, and waste their sweetness on the desert air. I hope someday I can raise enough money for a statue, or a sculptured group to praise them all.

A classic example of dissatisfaction. A young lady patient of mine had to be hospitalized with emotionally induced illness. She was a mess. Her underlying trouble was that she had become thoroughly dissatisfied with *everything* in her life. She had been educated in an excellent eastern school to be a secretary and had a wonderful position in Washington, D. C., when World War II came along and brought a certain young, handsome army captain in and out of the office in which she worked.

One and one add up to four—I mean two, at first—they were married and had two children by the time the war was over, over, that is, for everyone but Ellen. Then she found herself living in a trailer, bringing up her children in a trailer (soon there were three).

The first time I was called to see her, she was in bed at one end of the trailer, and the captain stood wringing his hands at the other end. She told me then, in no uncertain terms, and in a voice that made the captain's fingers white, that she didn't like housekeeping "A-tall," AND she didn't like living in a TRAILER, OR keeping house in a TRAILER, AND bringing up children in a TRAILER was TERRIBLE, AND (this she didn't say, but implied) she wasn't sure she liked her husband in a TRAILER—AND she CERTAINLY wished she had stuck to her secretary's job in Washington.

I was sure, from other remarks, she was dissatisfied with her physician since he wasn't getting her over her nausea and dizziness. She welcomed the idea of the hospital for the simple reason it took her out of that so-and-so trailer. Without giving her a diagnosis, I *ordered* her (we were past the suggesting stage) to send to the library for the four Polly-anna books they had.

Now, many people may consider them silly books, but usually the people who call them silly are on the defensive because of a rotten disposition, and they half-way know it. Anyway, the young lady read the books. I didn't say a thing; at the moment, she was enjoying the hospital.

One morning she volunteered her own diagnosis. I had known all along she was bright enough. She said, "I've been thinking, or trying to think. Good Lord, what a little fool I am. I've been dissatisfied with keeping house; I've been dissatisfied at having to bring up children in a trailer; I've been dissatisfied with my husband because he couldn't provide something better; I've been dissatisfied because I'm not a secretary with a good job.

"All right, Doc, I've been thinking—I'm a damn fool. I can't change this, at least not right away. You and Polly-anna win; what am I making myself miserable for? Here's

103

the answer: Keeping house in a trailer is, after all, very easy and no trick at all. If Jud and I don't like the view out of our living room window, we can move the trailer and get a better view.

"As for bringing up children in a trailer, there is a great expanse of outdoors for them to run around in, and you don't get that on 33d Street. I'm going to make a go of it, and I'm going to start planning a little house, the kind Jud and I want some day. AND—bless me—I wouldn't trade this for the best secretarial job in the world."

You see, *she had the idea, the simple idea, that it's easier to be satisfied than dissatisfied, and much healthier.* She read all the Pollyanna books—I guess there must be about 16. She quickly learned the art of being satisfied. She evolved her own little mental tricks and had a lot of fun doing it. It wasn't long before she was perfectly well.

As I say, she really had a great deal of good sense. She soon found happiness in her family. Finally they moved into the house she and Jud had dreamed of. I like to visit them to see how pleasant and cheerful a family can be when they understand how important it is to stay that way.

It's not hard to feel good. In regard to satisfaction and dissatisfaction, remember two things:

First, it is as easy, and much pleasanter, to find elements of satisfaction instead of dissatisfaction in the daily run of events. All that is required is *the will* to feel satisfied. The wise individual knows that life is one damned frustration after another if you allow yourself to be frustrated, but it is also one satisfaction after another if you are determined to be satisfied. *Trouble is where you make it.*

Don't want what you can't have. Secondly, another trick for dispelling dissatisfaction is to quit *wanting*, wanting this, wanting that. This, of course, goes back to our first aid, which was cultivating the simple and the things at hand. I knew a man of moderate means with a large family, who made himself miserable wanting things he couldn't afford. First, he longed for an expensive camera. He worked himself into such an irritation of desire that he finally bought it, although he could ill afford it, and his family could afford it even less. When he had that, he began to fairly itch for a power saw and could think of little else until he had that; next, he had to have a drill press. And so it went on. He was always dissatisfied with what he had and thought he needed more. His family, meanwhile, were deprived of much they really needed.

It would have been just as easy for this man to have found pleasure in things that it was easier for him to have. His education had been faulty; there had been no one to show him how to find enjoyment without expense. With a little help he might have learned to enjoy the beauties and wonders which surround us on all sides. Had he invested a dollar for a copy of Gilbert White's *The Natural History of Selbourne*, he would have found there is more in a simple walk than in a houseful of gadgets.

Learning the trick of being satisfied goes a long way toward making us well-adjusted, efficient, happy, and the possessors of a rich and rewarding life.

6. LIKE PEOPLE AND JOIN THE HUMAN ENTERPRISE

In a world where people live next door to each other, rub elbows in the subway, and meet bumper-to-bumper on the highways, it is disastrous to emotional stasis to take a dislike to the race and to the individuals who comprise it. Letting people get in your hair is far, far worse than getting bats in it. There are many more people than bats.

Some people dislike everybody. It is surprising in meeting people with E. I. I. how many people there are in the world who dislike practically everyone, from the president, whom they have never met, to their next-door neighbor, whom they wish they had never met! They have nothing complimentary to say about a single soul, and are very derogatory toward everyone. Their immaturity has isolated them in a shell. Yet they *have* to live in the world of people. The extent of their cooperation in the affairs of people consists in getting what *they* require out of society.

One of my patients was a man who had risen to be the superintendent of a manufacturing plant employing six thousand people. He was sick. In the beginning of his illness, he would suddenly be overcome by a spell of weakness, trembling, dizziness, and vomiting. This occurred whenever he went to his office, which he shared with the other assistant manager. These spells became more and more frequent, and, before long, he began having them at home whenever he merely thought about his office. Naturally he lost weight, and both he and his wife were quite certain that he had some serious malignancy and his days were numbered.

The root of his trouble was that he didn't like the other assistant manager who occupied the same office with him. He said, "The first time I saw him, I didn't like him. I didn't like the way he combed his hair. I didn't like the way he whistled through his teeth, and the way he always started every sentence with the word 'listen,' and ended every paragraph with 'don't you know.'"

On questioning him further, I learned that he had never liked anyone. He hadn't liked his father, his mother, his brothers and sisters. He couldn't say that he cared for his wife. In short, he had never liked anyone.

He was a surprised man to find that he recovered from his illness when he began to suggest to himself the things he could find likeable about the man he had to work with, to assure himself that this man had likeable qualities, and to take the trouble to cultivate him and take him out for a round of beers.

Most people's peeves are an expression of their dislike for other people. I asked one of my patients to write down a list of his peeves, since he seemed to have so many. He filled out both sides of a sheet of typewriter-sized paper.

The first peeve he listed was "people chewing gum." "I can't stand anybody chewing gum," he said. "It just makes me grit my teeth." His second peeve was, "My wife rocking in a rocking chair. I just want to jump up and down and scream when she does that." His third peeve was, "My daughter playing the piano." And so on, and on. You can imagine how miserable his peeves must have made his family.

These dislikes are essentially childish. Dislikes like this are childish arrests in the selfish, self-centered attitude typical of childhood. Because people so afflicted are in their shell, they either never make friends or they drop the friends they start to make. This they blame not on themselves (Heaven forbid) but on the other people, whom they regard as being incapable of friendship. Next, on finding themselves isolated, they begin to pity themselves and to feel persecuted. They become hypochondriacal and develop deepseated inferiorities. In all these ways, in addition to the plain irritations which other people cause them, these individuals lead a miserable life.

One of the finest sides to living is liking people and wanting to share actively in the human enterprise, the sum total of the effort the human race is making to get out of the jungle state and frame of mind. The greatest pleasures come by giving pleasure, to the fellow who works with us, to the chap who lives next door, or to those who live under the same roof.

There is no such thing as an "individual" in our society. Each one of us is an "individual-community." If everyone in the United States were to begin today to live entirely as an individual without the materials and services he receives from the community (the people around him) there wouldn't be more than a couple of hundred people alive at the end of a year.

Entering consciously into this human enterprise, feeling one's self a part of the community, and looking upon one's self as an "individual-community" is an important element in maturity.

7. GET THE HABIT OF SAYING THE CHEERFUL, PLEASANT THING

There are some people, like Sam, who have never been heard to utter anything but a jarring note. Such a note ruins the present moment; a steady steam of them turns the whole day into a junk pile. Some people do it regularly; usually one hears it from the very high and the very low. The very low think they ought to gripe, so they gripe. The very high think they should sound worthy of their position, so they gripe at the taxes and the political opposition; they lambaste everyone under them.

Hardly a moment arises during an entire lifetime that wouldn't benefit more by a sally of humor or a cheerful lift than by a mean barb or a sharp gripe. I know executives who carry on under tremendous pressure as affably and kindly as a girl skipping down the street. They are the boys who get along and stay out of the hospitals.

On the other hand, there is the great-tycoon variety. They snarl and hiss and backfire, slugging everybody verbally—in short, making constant, ugly asses of themselves. You do not have to envy this great tycoon type, gentle reader, this constantly enraged bull who paws and bellows. You may be sure he is feeling just as miserable as he sounds. In his climb up the ladder of success, he is just as miserable on the top rung as he was on the bottom rung. The added difference is that on the top rung he is dizzy with his own eminence, and that starts another immature rush of emotions that gives him, as well as those around him, a pain in the neck.

Get up on the right side of the bed. Get the habit of starting out the day right. A neat little trick is to look at your husband, or your wife, when you are both awake, and, even if it is an overstatement, say, "Good-morning, dear; you look fine this morning."

The next neat little trick is to go to the window, look out, and in a beautiful baritone, or soprano, that reaches to the end of the avenue, sing, "Oh, What a Beautiful Morning." Should it be raining, you say enthusiastically, "Ah, what a fine rain. Certainly good for the soil."

Sounds a bit silly, of course, but it pays off. Positively the easiest way to lift your mind out of the mud is to dash off a series of pleasant remarks, or still better, a good funny story. The more adept you become in pleasantries, cheerios, and humor, the easier it is to stay out of despondency, frustration, and E. I. I. Incidentally, good humor is a quality which endears you to other people. No one loves a crepehanger. Everyone likes to have someone around who has a sense of pleasantness and humor.

Be pleasant to your family. It is particularly important in family life to develop the habit of pleasant conversation when the family is together. Do not, for your own, your children's, or your digestion's sake, make the family meal a recitation of troubles, anxieties, fears, warnings, and accusations. And what is more important, don't let the feeling pervade your family that everyone is so taken for granted that a pleasantness or kind word is unnecessary. The crabbed note that clangs daily in so many families is a good foundation for many of the neurotic characteristics of later life.

A sense of humor is a wonderful adjunct to common sense. There are various degrees and varieties. Practically everyone can develop a sense of humor if he goes after it.

One of our town's clergymen was about as humorless as a dried apricot. Moreover, it was very difficult for him to engage people in a conversation. He gradually overcame both defeats in this way: every day he read a good story and memorized it. The next day he would tell his story to everyone he met. Every day he would do the same. Usually the person to whom he told his story gave one in return. Gradually he came to recognize a good story when he heard one, and gradually he could pull a story out of his bag for almost any occasion. He became known around the country as the clergyman with the good story. People were happy to see him approach.

8. MEET ADVERSITY BY TURNING DEFEAT INTO VICTORY

Many people are precipitated into E. I. I. by some adversity. Everything they had appears at one moment to have vanished, and they are completely at a loss to go on. Futility and frustration are piled on disaster. The underlying crack in most of the people who give way beneath adversity is the immaturity of selfishness and egocentricity. The death of a person near to them is calculated in terms of what it means to them, personally, in the way of services lost.

One poor woman who had always been highly selfish and self-centered became hysterical after her husband died, to the point where she insisted that her son withdraw permanently from college to keep her company. "Otherwise, I'll be alone here! I can't be all alone! I've got to have someone here!" and so on. No real thought or kindness for the man who had passed away, or for the son whose life she was continuing to ruin.

Do you remember William—King of Living—we talked about in Chapter 8? At the time his wife died of a malignant disease of the intestines, he was in the hospital convalescing from an operation for the same thing. No married couple had ever been more firmly attached to one another, nor more appreciative of each other's company than Mr. and Mrs. William had been.

He took the news of his wife's death thoughtfully. He considered it silently for a few minutes. Then in a very appreciative, straightforward tone, he began to tell of incidents which illustrated what a remarkable and fine person his wife had been. After that he never referred to her or her death. He never bemoaned the fact that now he would be all alone. When he left the hospital to return to his two rooms, in which he was now to be alone, he did so without a mention that it would be changed or that the rooms they had called "home" would be without the presence of his wife.

When I called on him there, he was just the same as before; he was just as cheerful, he was just as interested in the great wide world as he had ever been. He never dropped a note to indicate that his life was different now, or empty. Soon he was out and around, talking to old friends (and everyone is his friend), apparently unperturbed.

A few years later I met him on the street outside my office. "Well, howdy, Doctor," he said. "You look as though you had to get somewhere fast."

"No," I replied, "no hurry, just a habit. I'm on my way to see a type of patient one always hates to see—a woman who has been upset and in bed ever since her husband died four months ago." Then I added that few people were able to handle adversity the way he could.

"It isn't hard to do," he said, "if you keep your feet where they belong—on the ground. When you can't change something—you'd better accept it, and figure out how you can keep living the best possible way. When a man loses his wife, or a wife her husband, what is mourning but just plain feeling sorry for *one's self?* There are long philosophical arguments leading up to that last statement, Doctor, but you're too busy to hear them right now. I'll give them to you later." He laughed, and walked on.

9. MEET YOUR PROBLEMS WITH DECISION

In the multitude of practical problems you are obliged to meet in the course of living, you cannot possibly always be right, or make precisely the move that would be to your greatest advantage. But if, by and large, you can act using the principles and aids you are reading about in this chapter, your mistakes will not loom large or be very important.

Furthermore, *it is better to adjust your thinking to allowing and admitting a few mistakes than it is to keep milling and turning every little problem over and over in your mind.* Doing that results in a troubled, apprehensive outlook that will certainly produce E. I. I.

Of the total number of decisions we have to make, only a very small percentage will be improved as the result of long continued study and consideration. Also, a great many of the decisions fall into the same category as deciding whether one wants to buy the pink-flowered set of dishes, or the dishes with the gold design. These are decisions in which the issue is usually of a minor nature; either of two actions will do perfectly well.

The best rule to follow, therefore, is to make your decisions without a long huffing, puffing rumpus and fuss. Decide what you are going to do about a problem, then quit thinking about it.

One of my patients had a severe recurrent fibrositis, so severe that she would be in bed with it at times for weeks. No type of therapy would do the least bit of good. She was a very vigorous and self-assured individual, and I knew she would resent my telling her that her fibrositis was due to a wrong set of emotions. However, seeing her in a few of these attacks, I was certain that there was a recurring factor in her life that was responsible for her attacks.

I was planning on how I could most diplomatically bring this to her attention, when (to my relief), she offered her diagnosis of her own accord. "I think I know what is bringing these attacks on, Doctor. You may disagree with me, but I am sure by this time that there is some sort of a connection. My idea may be all wrong, but I've noticed that every time my husband gets into one of his terrible scrapes,

I get an attack of my pain and have to go to bed."

"You are perfectly right," I assured her. "I was just getting ready to suggest the same thing."

"Well, Doctor," the poor woman asked, "how am I possibly going to handle it?"

"You must, of course, continue doing your best to help your husband, and get the best help for him. On the other hand, he has gotten himself into a particular rut which he is likely to stay in for some time. Every time he precipitates himself into a mess, and you know he will continue to do so, *decide at that time what you are going to do about it, then make yourself quit thinking about it.* It is turning the thing uselessly over and over in your mind, even after you know what course you will take, that is the thing that brings on your fibrositis."

She practiced this simple instruction with understandable difficultly at first. But it gradually became easier as she practiced, and the husband gave her plenty of practice. Finally, when the tremendous decisions came, which she always had feared would eventually come, she was well enough practiced that she could pass through them with a minimal amount of somatic disturbance, and had nothing nearly as severe as her old fibrositis.

Some decisions just can't be made. In our living we are apt to come upon a piece of trouble (and it is usually a tough, large piece) to which there is no apparent solution. The important thing in handling this variety of trouble is to tell ourselves that *there is no solution other than to* QUIT THINKING ABOUT THEM.

Mrs. K—— had a family of three children and a husband who had been drunk just about every day for fifteen years. The depths of misery to which that woman and that family descended are beyond simple description. Every possible treatment and approach had been tried to break the man of his drinking habit. None had more than a very short beneficial effect. For certain reasons, the woman did not wish to divorce him. Her misery, and the children's misery, grew deeper and deeper.

Then one day she came to an important decision.

She said to herself, "We had better give up the idea that Albert ever can, or ever will, stop drinking. From here on in, I'm not going to torture my mind any more over Albert or his drinking. We'll take care of him, of course, but we'll quit worrying about him. Instead, I am going to devote every energy I have toward making the rest of my life, and my

111

children's lives, as happy as they can possibly be under the circumstances."

She realigned herself in relation to her problem.

She was admitting that her problem was insoluble, and that there was no use expending any further worry or thinking upon it.

Her realigned efforts worked wonders. She was like a new woman. The children began to take on a new dignity in place of the beaten looks they had worn so long.

10. MAKE THE PRESENT MOMENT AN EMOTIONAL SUCCESS

Getting rid of lousy emotional habits should not and need not be a complicated procedure Above all, keep it simple. Reduce it to the terms of a common denominator—*keep your attitude and thinking as cheerful and pleasant as possible*—RIGHT NOW.

The only moment we ever live is the present moment. It is the only time *we ever have* to be happy.

Some people live on an expectancy basis, always looking for something in the future, completely losing the only value they have—that which is in the present moment.

The boy in high school anticipates college; in college, he anticipates the joy that will be his when he gets an engineering job. When he gets his engineering job, he believes that joy will come when he marries Mary and has a home; and so he goes on . . . anticipating.

There finally comes a time in his life when further anticipation is no longer rosy. That point is accompanied by a tremendous reorientation of thinking, values, and emotions. That is the point where the individual begins, visibly, to look old, licked, and beaten. At that point, too, anticipation is metamorphosed into thinking about the wonders and glories of the past (which are past).

Plan for the future, but don't brood on it. Naturally, we have to plan for the future, but we shouldn't make our present moment a constant thinking about it. Beyond the necessity of providentially planning the future, constant thinking of it and living in it entail fear, concern, and apprehension.

It is utterly silly to be constantly worrying about what the future may do to our affairs, cattle, health, children, yes, even our life after death. Being upset over the future isn't going to alter it a great deal. Most of our worries are interest we pay ahead of time on things that never happen.

The best insurance for a satisfactory future is to handle

the present hour properly, do a good job of living now, be effective in your work, your thinking, your pleasantness, your helpfulness to other people, RIGHT NOW. Yes, RIGHT NOW. The future will turn out to be as good as your present if you keep on handling THE PRESENT MOMENT correctly. That's an important trick.

11. ALWAYS BE PLANNING SOMETHING

A basic psychological need in every person is the need for new experiences. Without new experience, life sags down into a rut of interminable drudgery.

To have *the expectation* of a new experience coming up is always a lift to the present moment, and you should always be planning an experience. It may be only a day's outing, or a half day of something on a Sunday, or merely a new feather in your hat. Your planning needn't be anything elaborate, except on rare occasions. The important thing is that it be *new experiences you are looking forward to.*

The planning is just as beneficial in supplying the right kind of emotions as is the new experience itself. Barney Olds, whom I could just as well have used instead of William as an example of the King of Living in Chapter 8, was a man who had met one catastrophe after another with superb equanimity, resignation, determination, courage, and cheerfulness. He finally had an illness that kept him in bed for three months; then a recurrence kept him in bed for a solid year. He never complained.

I said to him once, "Barney, don't you get tired of being in bed?"

Barney laughed heartily, "No. I have a good appetite; that's half of living. *And every day I have a good cigar;* that's the other half."

Barney enjoyed life more, confined to bed, than most people do on a holiday. He loved to plan trips to distant parts of the world, to Tibet, Manga Reva, to Tasmania, and so forth. He would write to travel agencies and steamship companies for information. He would get books and literature from the library about the place he was "going to." At the end of each "trip" he knew as much about the land of his destination as though he had actually been there. One travel agency was afraid it was missing Barney's business, and sent a representative to see him. After that, the travel agency helped Barney play his game by sending him copies of official tickets to the places he was "visiting." Barney enjoyed himself all the more.

113

12. Don't Let Irritating Things Get Your Goat

In almost every moment there are worries or irritations that would get under your skin IF YOU LET THEM. It is hard to conceive of a single irritation, at least in the usual run of things, that *ever needs* to get under one's skin.

Whenever you are confronted with an irritation that is knocking and trying to get in, try the trick of forming the "magic circle" with your forefinger and thumb, holding it out before you, and say, "Nuts to that. I'm not going to let it get under my skin." A little practice with this magic circle and you will soon be able to say "Nuts" very agreeably and pleasantly to most of the potential irritations that come along.

The Best Part of Being Human Is That You Can Learn

By including these twelve items in your general attitude, you will make a big stride toward emotional stasis and maturity. Living will begin to take on a general glow of enjoyability. You'll find yourself changing in very fundamental and effective ways; you'll begin to feel the grand feeling of "Boy, I feel good!" and life will become enjoyable.

The really best quality of human beings is that they can always learn something new, once they see the necessity for learning it. In my practice, I have seen hundreds of people rise to that capacity and turn themselves from a state of emotional stress to a creditable state of emotional stasis. If that hope and that possibility did not exist, I would long ago have left the practice of medicine for other fields, because more than half of the practice of medicine is curing E. I. I.

Before leaving this chapter, I wish to anticipate a question that is frequently brought up. "Why don't you include religion as one of your aids?"

Religion and Emotionally Induced Illness

The answer is in no way a disparagement of religion.

It is true that many people are relieved of emotional stress when religious faith comes into their lives to occupy the vacuum that was made by the lack of one of the basic psychologic needs that are discussed in Chapter 14. These are people in whom there is a deep sense of insecurity, or people in whose lives there has been a great lack of affection or a minimum of recognition, or people who have a deep feeling of complete personal incompetence.

But it is equally true that religion, per se, neither increases nor decreases the individual's chances of getting E. I. I.

The clergy and strongly religious people have E. I. I. just as often as non-religious people.

One excellent minister, for instance, developed a very bothersome colon because of the terrific pressure of work that the great charge under his care entailed. Another good churchman had marked dizziness, weakness, and headache as a result of a prolonged and tough campaign to raise money for a new church. These, of course, are stresses of the type anyone might have. But sometimes the stress arises out of religion itself as in the case of the militant and crusading minister who was greatly concerned and disturbed over the wickedness of his small town congregation and who succeeded, after a violent campaign, in bringing them to do as he wished. The physical effect was a prolonged dyspepsia, which finally became a frank ulcer.

It is evident in medical practice that a religious person needs the attitudes we are presenting in this book just as much as the non-religious. As a matter of fact, the attitudes presented in this book will beautifully augment and complete religious living, because the attitudes that comprise maturity are exactly the things the great teachers of ethics have always been driving at.

KEY POINTS IN CHAPTER 9
IMPORTANT POINTS TO WATCH IN LIVING

1. *Keep life simple.*
2. *Avoid watching for a knock in your motor.*
3. *Learn to like work.*
4. *Have a good hobby.*
5. *Learn to be satisfied.*
6. *Like people.*
7. *Say the cheerful, pleasant thing.*
8. *Turn the defeat of adversity into victory.*
9. *Meet your problems with decision.*
10. *Make the present moment a success.*
11. *Always be planning something.*
12. *Say "Nuts" to irritations.*

ACHIEVING EMOTIONAL
STASIS IN THE FAMILY

THE FAMILY IS OUR NUMBER-ONE CAUSE OF DISEASE

The most important single educational factor to which most people are subjected is the family in which they grow up. Because of the amount of time a person spends in the family and the authoritative nature of the control which the family has over our early thinking the family has more to do with molding our personalities and our ability to handle living than any other factor.

In view of this tremendous effect the family has upon its charges, it is very sad that such a tremendous number of families are muffing their opportunities, and are doing a poor job.

It is very obvious, in seeing patients in the office, that our families are by far the greatest cause of wrong emotions our society has. Not only in their childhood families do so many people contract emotional stress, but equally in the families of which they have themselves become a head. The family—our past family, and our present family—is by far the most common cause of E. I. I., by far our most prevalent disease.

The saddest part of this family failure is that with a small amount of steering the families that have been off-center for generations might be guided into the proper channel, where they would become an effective educational factor for good. But, as in other fields of emotional guidance, there are no organized programs for accomplishing such an improvement.

First, let us review the family atmospheres that produce immaturity and emotional stress.

FAMILY ATMOSPHERES THAT PRODUCE STRESS

1. *A kill-joy atmosphere in the family.*. One of the common family atmospheres productive of the wrong kind of

emotions is the KILL-JOY ATMOSPHERE. In such families a dismal, pessimistic attitude toward everything prevails. "Oh, what do we want a picnic for anyway? It will probably rain; if it doesn't, the ants will eat everything up." In families like this, joy is nipped in the bud before it ever starts to bloom.

Betty came from a family like this, a family of constant gloom. Like the rest of her family, Betty had no sparkle or lustre; nor did any of her known ancestors. Her family life provided her with none of the qualities that would make her popular at school. Betty was passed over by the students and by the teachers; it wasn't a dislike they had for her, but she was so negative that she always faded out of consideration. She was just never invited to other children's homes because a gloomy atmosphere always attended her presence. Betty's mother never invited other children over to play with Betty because her mother was gloomy and didn't like fun. And, of course, Betty developed a gloomy attitude toward her own physiology, the same attitude her mother had regarding her own health.

By the time Betty was 13, she was a confirmed hypochondriac. She was apprehensive of every manifestation that her gloomy emotions produced, until her health, or her supposed lack of it, became her major concern. She joined the great and numerous Symptom-a-Day Club. When she awakened in the morning, her first thought would be, "How am I sick today?" After she was 13, Betty was not without medical attention any year of her life. Her apprehension concerning her health was strongly augmented by her mother's insistent concern. By the time she was 40, she had had four operations and a surgical menopause.

Betty's father, as well as her mother, was a glum pessimist, entirely taciturn and humorless. He was that way because of the family *he* was brought up in. The line of such families probably went back to neolithic times. He was the Sam, King of His Own Stew you read about in Chapter 8 whose wife said that possibly he had said something pleasant the first year they were married, but that it was so long ago she could no longer be sure.

2. *The critical atmosphere in the family.* Another family atmosphere that breeds the wrong kind of emotions is the CRITICAL ATMOSPHERE, In such families, the atmosphere is charged with criticism of everybody. Usually the father starts it originally, but it becomes so universally prevalent among all the members of the family that all a visitor can say is,

117

"Who flang that last brick?" An argument in the family is frequently this, "I'm not either losing my temper. You're the one who is losing your temper." As a matter of fact, all of them have permanently lost their tempers.

Barbara had the misfortune to have been born into a family like that. As she grew up she became, of course, the mirror of the family, and carried the atmosphere of criticism to school with her. In school she had a great deal of trouble because of her critical attitude toward the teacher and children. And at home her life consisted in running a critical gauntlet in which all the other members of the family were arraigned against her. At ten, Barbara had emotionally induced illness.

Cold war in the home. There are some families in which the critical atmosphere is maintained in the form of cold warfare instead of more or less open flinging of bricks. The criticism here is in the nature of sharp, cutting insinuations, often delivered in dulcet tones. Clifford was a master at this sort of thing; when he and his wife Betty had guests in of an evening, Clifford would get in a cutting criticism of Betty by saying at the bridge table, "Better not let Betty keep score, she'll just get our accounts hopelessly balled up," insinuating that Betty couldn't keep her household accounts straight. Or he might say conversationally, "At our house we never know when or where we're going to eat until the can is opened."

This sort of thing, which went on year after year, always hurt Betty a great deal, and as time went on, Betty was sick a great part of the time with emotionally induced illness. Notice that Clifford, who was responsible, was hit by the boomerang of having to pay the medical bills.

Critical influences from outside the family. Sometimes an illness-producing stream of criticism may issue from an odd source in an otherwise normal family. Jane was a fine girl and married George, a fine boy, who was deeply in love with her, and who, in a very understanding way, took good care of Jane. Jane's life was going along splendidly until she brought her first-born home from the hospital. George secured the services of a practical nurse to help Jane with the housework and with the baby.

This practical nurse was an old-timer who knew everything better than Jane did, or the doctor did, for that matter, and she openly criticized the way in which Jane was handling the baby. She would criticize everything, including the formula the pediatrician had given the baby. She would

118

make remarks, "I don't think the baby is getting along well. There is something wrong with it; it just doesn't act like a baby should." Then Jane would cart the baby off to the pediatrician who would assure Jane that the baby was perfectly all right. Whereupon, back home, Old Battle-ax would remark, "Well, you know sometimes these doctors don't tell you everything."

As this sort of thing continued, Jane began to feel poorly without knowing why. George and the doctor, at first, did not know what was wrong, either. Then they both caught on. Jane was a capable girl, intelligent and alert. Her baby was a great event to her, a great challenge and opportunity for intelligent, creative motherhood. But the Old Battle-ax had completely deflated Jane's confidence in herself and had sent her into a state of constant worry and deep-seated concern. When the doctor and George found Jane's trouble, the remedy was simple and George applied it promptly. He fired the Old Battle-ax. Jane was soon getting along fine.

The remedy isn't always that simple. Barbara, for instance, couldn't fire her father and mother.

3. *The atmosphere of dislike.* Another common family atmosphere which produces the wrong kind of emotions is the ATMOSPHERE OF DISLIKE, or the atmosphere of lack of affection, an atmosphere that is fatal to anything good that the family as an institution stands for.

Usually this atmosphere of dislike stems from the basic fact that father and mother do not like each other, and the only reason they hang together is "for the children's sake." In the atmosphere of such a home, the children quickly learn not to like each other. Love, or dislike, comes to children largely by example. The parents have no genuine affection for the children, and the children reciprocate with even less.

In this kind of family nobody wants any of the other members. No one is necessary to anyone else, and when a person feels he isn't necessary, he never develops full mature individuality. No one in a family like this is made to feel important or desirable for himself. No one ever gives or receives any appreciation. Life is like eating dried, tasteless prunes.

Ellen was the youngest of seven children in a home where no one really cared about anyone else. Being the youngest, she was the target of everyone else's ill will. Every member of the family was criticizing Ellen as soon as she was old enough to understand. "Oh, she's dumb." "She isn't going to be able to get through school." No one ever helped Ellen.

By the time she got into school, she had a deeply grounded inferiority complex. She looked past her teachers because everyone told her she was stupid. When Ellen, after a hectic childhood, at last grew up, she married a boy who had had the same kind of a past and the same kind of an inferiority complex. When she had children, she was sure she lacked the ability to rear them; she had no confidence in her ability as a housewife. Hers was a constant life of worry.

Ellen has been sick most of the time since childhood and is still sick today. It is not so easy to correct the factors in her illness as it was in the case of Jane, George, and the Old Battle-ax.

4. *The atmosphere of selfish egoism.* Another family atmosphere that breeds the wrong kind of emotions is the ATMOSPHERE OF SELFISH EGOISM, which is a little different from the atmosphere of criticism, although it, too, usually starts with the father.

Virginia, who had been doing all right alone, married a boy who was a pathological egoist of the kind whose only concern is himself. This was not immediately apparent in Roger because he was the kind of an egoist who doesn't talk about himself. But every thought he had was for himself. When Virginia married him, of course, she didn't know what she was getting into.

Roger was decent enough, but he used Virginia solely for his own purposes. Roger was addicted to hunting and fishing; and that's what he was forever doing—without taking Virginia along. Outside of that, he liked to play cards, and bowl; so he did that. Virginia was alone at home most of the time. Roger liked only a few foods, so they were what the family ate. Roger's work took him on the road much of the time, and Virginia was alone at home bringing up one, two, three, and four children. When Virginia began to complain about not feeling well, Roger had no sympathy and no patience.

Today, Virginia is a very sick girl and her health will not readily be brought back to normal. Roger does not see what *he* has to do with her health, and he now regards Virginia as an obstruction to his pleasure. Virginia's children are maladjusted and are functionally ill too.

5. *The complaining atmosphere.* Another bad atmosphere in a family is the COMPLAINING ATMOSPHERE. No family is more miserable than the one that has in it a perennial and perpetual bellyacher. Most often the bellyacher is the mother, although I have seen families in which it is the father.

When a family contains someone who is constantly complaining, there is no possible enjoyment for anyone. These complainers awaken in the morning and start analyzing themselves for symptoms. It's usually easy to find a symptom somewhere, especially in the morning before you've had breakfast. Every one of us has a pain somewhere or other most of the time, if we wish to make something of it. If you ask yourself, as you sit there, "Where do I hurt?" you can find a place that hurts. These complainers are forever looking for those places and allowing their minds to play over the painful areas all day long. The most pitiful part is that they paddle the rest of the family with their miseries.

In 99 cases out of 100, these complainers have nothing more wrong with them than an emotionally induced illness, but to hear them expound on their health, you would think they were fully equipped pathological museums. In the family they succeeded in producing an atmosphere of gloom and anxiety, and these are the elements the children acquire. Gloom, anxiety, and hypochondriasis is the educational influence such families give their children.

In addition to making the family miserable, these complainers are poison to the bank account. One lady had, during the course of her miserable life, seen fifteen doctors, four cultists, two spiritualists, and had eight operations, had been in three sanitaria, and had spent a total of $32,000.

6. *The atmosphere of fear and anxiety in the family.* One businessman I know gets up in the morning with an anxiety, and jumps anxiously from one anxiety to the next until he goes to bed, and then keeps himself awake with more anxieties.

For instance, *every morning* he hesitates and debates what particular tie he will wear, and sometimes goes into a dither over it. At breakfast he worries whether he is using too much sugar on his cereal and immediately wonders whether he has diabetes. Driving downtown to work he will debate with himself whether to take one street or another and, having taken one, worries that he should have taken the other, lest fate decree that he have an accident on the street he is on. Coming to his store he worries about the show windows and about the whistling of one of his clerks.

His family has caught the same worrying habit—it's very contagious. His wife picked it up; his children have grown up in it. To them, it is the normal, natural way to live. They just haven't experienced any other way.

Some day, if they are lucky, they may be released from

the habit sufficiently to realize they are unhappy, that they are personally maladjusted, and that they have emotionally induced illness.

7. *The atmosphere of in-law domination.* Another atmosphere that can be very bad for the family's emotions is the ATMOSPHERE OF IN-LAW DOMINATION. In-law domination may be very obvious and yet not easy to deal with.

Helen was a fine young lady who hailed from Philadelphia. She married a young man and went to live in his home town, a small village of 250, loaded with his relatives, some of whom were banshees. Some of these relatives saw Helen settled in a new, modern house and felt that Helen was getting the deal *they* deserved but didn't get. They made good every opportunity to pick on Helen, to hurt her in little underhanded ways. Helen became ill, and after a while she was too sick to work. Then the banshee relatives really swooped down on her like vultures, and finished her up. After that, the only time Helen ever felt well was when she returned to Philadelphia for a month's visit. In the course of a few years she became practically incapacitated by functional disease. She was finally carried off the battlefield by the divorce court, and within a year she was back to her normal self. Ever since then she has been well.

Young people should live by themselves. With few exceptions, it is best for young people, just starting out, to live independently and far enough removed from their elders to have complete control and command of their own families. In close proximity, parents are always finding it easy to offer suggestions, if not orders, a thing which neighbors do only when asked, but a thing which parents are apt to do when not asked. In one family where the newlyweds lived in the same house with the parents, the mother-in-law was well-meaning and only wished to be helpful. The daughter-in-law, too, wished, above all, to get along with the mother-in-law. They did get along, seemingly very nicely, but with the mother in the lead and guiding position, which frustrated the daughter-in-law's need for independent, creative living. In-laws, grandmothers, and grandfathers had best live apart from the children and allow the children an independent life.

A FAMILY DOESN'T NEED TO BE A BAD INFLUENCE

Those we have reviewed are, of course, only a few of the bad atmospheres that make our families our most important breeding ground for disease. In a physician's office, it becomes apparent that a great many families are doing a perfectly rotten job and are providing their members with the wrong kind of emotions. Many other families are not doing as good a job as they might.

The pitfalls that a family can fall into are so numerous that it might seem discouraging to the well-intentioned homemaker or the intelligent newlywed.

However, there is no need for discouragement.

If you introduce into the family atmosphere the same rules that bring emotional stasis to the individual, you will have a family whose influence on its members is a healthy one. You will have an atmosphere which develops maturity. You will have a family that is a unit of enjoyable life for everyone in it.

HOME IS THE PLACE WHERE—

Robert Frost once said, "Home is the place where, when you have to go there, they have to let you in."

We can paraphrase that to define what a home *should be*: "A good home is the place where, when you desperately need a lift, you'll be sure to find one." *A lift,* you understand, not more irritation, not nagging, not arguments, not a scathing look, not a lack of sympathy, but a LIFT.

Your first job, as a member of your family, is to keep your attitude and your thinking calm and cheerful—RIGHT NOW.

Your second job is to help the other members of your family keep their attitudes and thinking calm and cheerful RIGHT NOW.

Here are a few ingredients to work into the daily living of your family:

FAMILY ATMOSPHERES THAT PRODUCE EMOTIONAL STASIS AND MATURITY

1. *Emphasize simplicity in living and simplicity in enjoyment.* As the American standard of living has increased, a greater and greater array of mechanisms have been dangled invitingly before the consumers' eyes. The trend in American living has been to put so much emphasis on the means for enjoyment—fine houses, automobiles, better television sets, cameras, electric ranges—that in the process of getting the means, we provide ourselves with frustration and anxieties. Yearning, longing, and then paying the installments become so constant we never learn how, indeed, we never have the opportunity to learn how, just simply to *enjoy.*

The way to proceed is to learn the art of enjoyment first. Minimize the need, or the longing in the family, for new installments. RIGHT NOW enjoy what there *is*: the green of the trees, the blue of the skies, your own whistling, having fun with each other. Leave out conversation of yearning for what you haven't.

The idea is to utilize the little, ever-present opportunities for pleasantry, the immediately available chances for a humorous sally, the RIGHT NOW moment for being nice to each other.

2. *Get the idea of the family enterprise.* As soon as the children are old enough to understand, indoctrinate them with the idea that the family is meant to be a wonderful place for everybody in it; it's everybody's job to make it a wonderful place for everybody else; it's an enterprise for everybody, by *everybody*. The family enterprise is a cooperative effort in which father, mother, sister, brother, all have an active interest and a personal responsibility. The family enterprise is the primary and most important activity and responsibility that father, mother, brother and sister have.

Don't forget this; the children will acquire and carry on the family enterprise if mother and *father* do their share. Usually it's the father who is just a boarding and bored member, always off to business, the races, and Heaven knows where. If the top brass takes the proper initiative, the children will invariably follow.

The family enterprise becomes a continual round of mutual projects, of things done together, games played together, stories told around the fire, group studies of interesting things and places, Sunday afternoon nature jaunts, yearly family trips to the fair, laughter, conversation, and gaiety *that everyone* (and that includes father) engages in and which everyone helps everyone else to enjoy.

3. *Attach the family to the human enterprise.* An important idea to get into family living is that the family is in tune with the wide community which surrounds it. Beside the responsibility the members have to one another in the family enterprise, they have a similar responsibility to the HUMAN ENTERPRISE. This is quite a necessary step in the development of the children's maturity. It is part of that aspect of maturity which consists in turning our ego away from purely selfish considerations out toward the welfare of others. Never to develop this sense of the human enterprise is to bury ourselves for life in a pit of very stinky little emotions. If the children get the idea that the most important thing for

anyone is the welfare and the happiness of the other people in our individual-community, they will have the instrument for producing a highly satisfactory emotional color, and they will find that life is filled with the highest kind of enjoyment.

Furthermore, the idea of the human enterprise in the family brings to the members of the family a kindliness, a sympathy, and an understanding for other people, *which you cannot live happily without*.

Part of the family enterprise consists in projects directed toward meeting, knowing, and helping the great wide world outside: parties, "get to know your neighbors" picnics, family trips through industrial plants, family trips into the great wide world, adopting a war orphan, other projects that the family can, as they go about them, specifically label "Human Enterprise." Getting to use the name "Family Enterprise" for one type of activity and the name "Human Enterprise" for another, in itself teaches maturity and awareness of purpose in the children. Whatever helps the children is sure to help father and mother.

4. *Develop a family ability for turning defeat into victory*. Whatever happens, when events occur that might disappoint or frustrate, the attitude in the family should always be, "We are not going to let that get us down; we are going to make the best of it, and the best is going to be pretty good!" This gets easier and easier to do, and as the family becomes competent in its use, there will be very little that can sour the family's day.

The particular maturity that is taught to the children by the tactic of turning defeat into victory is *flexibility and adaptability*.

The family is all set to go to Parfrey's Glen on a picnic when the rain begins to pour; so what?—yipee—it's just as much fun playing games in the living room with the picnic later on the living room floor.

Handling the lesser upsets in that way makes it easier to meet the tougher assignments. Mother gets sick and goes to the hospital; everyone pitches in, not only on the work, but in holding up the family morale and mother's morale. It's doubly important, then, that every member keep the family clicking with heads up and chins out.

The trick of turning defeat into victory can become a game, with everyone trying to see who has the best solution for licking the upset, and then all cooperating on the best suggestion.

5. *Without affection, the family is a failure*. General af-

fection is easily generated in a family if there is affection between father and mother. Affection must include everyone equally and must not be partial. Everyone is made to feel necessary and indispensable to the general family operations. Animosities between the children need never exist if they are nipped in the early bud, and if no animosities ever exist between father and mother. If there is bickering, strife, and verbal warfare in the top brass section of the family, the children will almost surely grow up to be bickering and disagreeable. They in turn get married and start another cycle of foolish disagreement and bickering.

A doctor gets tired of seeing these silly nincompoops who lose most of their affection for each other before the first year of marriage is over. It is so completely childish and unnecessary. The answer to any marriage is that you should be mature enough to rise above the problems it entails. With ten cents' worth of good intentions, a nickel's worth of sympathy, and a quarter's worth of understanding, affection would grow through the years.

If the parents have affection, one of the rules in the family can be that no one is *ever* to quarrel or bicker with anyone else. That rule is not hard to maintain if the example comes from the top.

6. *The general tone should be kindly cheerfulness.* There is no such thing as the "dumps" in families where everyone pitches in to help the one who, because of some outside factor, needs a lift. Such a home is the place where, when you need a lift, you'll find it.

Here again the example is set by the top brass. If the parents never get crabby at one another, or allow themselves the misery of feeling lousy and mean, a rule in the family can be that no one is to engage in this nefarious activity.

7. *Discipline should be reasonable, firm, yet pleasant.* Parents in unhappy families probably will not believe this, but in a happy family there isn't much call for discipline. Misbehaving children are unhappy children. If the children are provided with a happy, pleasant atmosphere, two-thirds of your disciplinary problems disappear.

Children must be taught certain fundamentals, like respect for others' rights and for others as individuals. They should be taught to respect their elders; they should be taught the advisability of not flouting convention and living well within the law. Honesty and integrity are absolute requisites.

There will be times, of course, when discipline will be

necessary. Then discipline should be based on the reasonable ground that we act thus and so because that way of acting is for our own good, and we do not act otherwise because it is bad for us and bad for those around us. This basis for action can be explained just as well in a pleasant, well-meaning manner; it adds nothing to do it in a fit of splenic anger. For a wrong action there should be corrective explanation, and then a disciplinary measure carried forward without wavering or retracting. Punishment twice for the same offense will hardly ever be necessary.

8. *The family should instill confidence into its members.* It is important that the family should give the child a feeling of confidence—not only confidence in financial security, even if it isn't there, but confidence in his place in the family as someone who is respected for himself and as someone who has an important responsibility in contributing to the welfare and enjoyment of the family. No child, however awkward or backward he may be, must be made to feel that he is any less useful or important to the family.

Thus a basic psychological need is satisfied and a step in the development of an important aspect of maturity is made.

9. *Mutual enjoyment in the family—right now.* An indispensable idea in the family is that family living is a series of mutual enjoyments—every moment and RIGHT NOW. It *means* mutual enjoyment to its members, a pleasant quip or a jolly phrase when father passes son in the hall, or when Mary comes into the kitchen with mother. The family means mutual enjoyment, the glad word, the bit of fun, the happy smile—RIGHT NOW.

RIGHT NOW, of course; "What are we waiting for—why wait—this is the time—right now—right now is the time to show affection—now is the time to operate the Family Enterprise—*this* is the moment—why wait any longer?" It is perfectly all right to plan for the future, but don't spend your present in the future.

How Does Your Family Rate?

Stop right now and ask yourself, "What kind of a family do I belong to?" Is it the kind of an enterprise that is producing the wrong kind of emotions, functional disease, personal maladjustments, and unhappiness? If it is, be fair to yourself and admit it.

Then take the next step: Set an example.

And the next step: Hold a get-together with your wife or your husband, include the children if they are old enough, and talk this over, lay plans to have the kind of a family where, when your spirits are low, you will be sure to find a lift.

THE IMPORTANT POINTS TO REMEMBER IN CHAPTER 10

Your family will become a center of good, happy living, and an influence for maturity and emotional stasis in its members, if you introduce into the family these things:

1. *Simplicity in living, and simplicity in enjoyment.*
2. *The idea of the family enterprise.*
3. *The idea that the family is part of the human enterprise.*
4. *A family attitude for turning defeat into victory.*
5. *An atmosphere of affection, mutual respect, and regard.*
6. *A general tone of kindly cheerfulness.*
7. *Reasonable, firm, yet pleasant discipline.*
8. *A feeling of mutual confidence and security.*
9. *An atmosphere of enjoyment—RIGHT NOW.*

11

HOW TO ATTAIN
SEXUAL MATURITY

There is one *very* important spot in human living in which people's education has been either *nothing at all* or *worse* than nothing at all. That spot, of course, is sex.

More people show immaturity in their sexual life than in any other field of human activity. That is why doctors see so many people whose emotional stress is intimately related to immaturity in sex and sexual matters. There are a tremendous number of people who have made a mess of sex, or sex has made a mess of them.

Maturity in any field has to be learned. How can you possibly blame anyone for an immaturity in sex when no sensible effort is made to show him how to become mature? Where but on society and its institutions responsible for education—the family, the school, the church—does the blame rest for sexual delinquency, sexual stress, sexual mess?

BIOLOGY AND CIVILIZATION

The sex instinct is a relatively weak instinct compared to some of the others. The biological urge for food is *much* stronger, and so is the desire for security. A person can go for a long time, even for a lifetime, without satisfying the sex urge, but no one can stand food and security deprivation very long.

The relative insignificance of the sex instinct is further apparent in the fact that the cooperative effort we call "civilization" is mainly an attempt to supply food and security, *not sexual satisfaction*. Had the sex instinct been the strongest and most demanding of our biological urges, civilization would, doubtless, have been patterned to supply sexual satisfaction.

The biological urges being what they are, and civilization

129

being the kind of thing it is, everyone can be allowed to be promiscuous in eating, or promiscuous in developing security, but it became apparent thousands of years ago that the very basis of civilized society would be destroyed if everyone were to be allowed to be promiscuous sexually. The social and economic consequences of complete sexual promiscuity would be simply catastrophic.

The restraints are necessary. Granting that we want the economic benefits of a cooperative enterprise like civilization, we have taken the only course in regard to the sexual instinct that we possibly could have taken. That course has been to put the sexual instinct into well defined shackles of restraint. And *that* is what provides our sex problem.

The only way to shackle a thing as fundamental as a biological instinct, without upsetting the individual, is to develop a good educational process for showing the individual how he can possibly manage the instinct within its shackles. *But civilization had to curb the instinct long before it developed wisdom enough to devise an educational process.*

Is it any wonder we have the trouble with sex we do? You've got to be careful to put a cork in a bottle of highly charged liquid. Either the cork will blow out or the bottle will burst.

The more you study a tough problem like sex, the more you become amazed that we human beings get along as well as we do, and the more you become convinced that the bunch of us are pretty remarkable little people. The whole race muddles through.

THE SEX URGE IS NOT THE MAINSPRING OF THE HUMAN BEING

Sigmund Freud and the psychoanalysts have developed the idea that sex is the mainspring of the human personality. It is true that sex causes a great deal of trouble for people for the reasons set forth above, but not because it is the mainspring. It isn't. Sex is, as human biological urges go, a relatively little spring that has been jumping all over the box. It is a spring that has been jumping all over the box because of these factors:

1. Every person is equipped with the sex urge.
2. The structure of our civilization makes it imperative to curb this urge to a very considerable extent, so that it still serves the purpose of reproducing our kind without upsetting social and economic structures.
3. Although society makes such a curb necessary, society

makes no organized effort to show people how they can handle their urge without trouble to themselves.

4. There are numerous agencies, within society, deliberately fanning up people's sexual desires, largely because they find it profitable to do so.

Many commercial enterprises capitalize on shaking up the fizz in the charged bottle. These efforts to shake up the fizz have never been as prevalent as they have been in the last fifty years, and are one of the chief reasons why one out of three marriages is ending in divorce.

Commercial advertising, newspapers, magazines, movies, television, find "cheesecake" attractive to the unrequited yearnings and earnings of a sexually-uneducated public. It helps roll the dollars in, but is hard on those whose excited sexual desires get them into emotional or legal trouble.

Some youth (or immature adult) who is having trouble trying to adjust his sexual inclinations opens a magazine (any of our better weekly magazines) and he finds stimulating "cheesecake" on every other page. The sexual longings that he has been trying to stifle are freshly stimulated, his imagination is stimulated, and a fresh set of stressing emotions are stimulated. If he stops there, the youth (or the immature adult) is just plain lucky. He may go on to get into trouble.

The Popular Brand of So-Called Sophistication Is Immature

"Sophistication" has become a popular concept in the mid-20th-century United States. A person is not in the mode if he is not "sophisticated," by which is meant a varying degree of looseness concerning sexual taboos. There are, of course, various levels, or depths, of sophistication, beginning with sexy stories in open mixed society (the more shriekingly daring, obviously the more sophisticated) and progressing in ten easy lessons to situations of grossly illegal intimacy, in which the intimacy gradually becomes rancid and the illegality ever more bitter.

The philosophy underlying sophistication assumes that sophistication *is* sexual maturity—maturity in the same sense we defined it in Chapter 7, namely, that *maturity is the capacity to handle human living with a minimum of trouble and a maximum of enjoyment*.

There are two distinct parts to the philosophy of sophistication. Some people subscribe only to the first part; others go along with both parts.

The first part states that treating sex as an unmentionable human misfortune, to be regarded definitely as a sordid affair to be admitted reluctantly even into marriage, is merely to increase the amount of misery that the tromped-upon sex urge can produce. This first part of the philosophy of sophistication is, doubtless, correct. I am in full accord with it.

The second part of the philosophy of sophistication is that sex constitutes a major sport that is always in season, that licenses are free, and the game is to be pursued through all the byways of so-called romance.

This second part is a gross error, as most of those discover who have to learn the hard way. Almost without exception, the apple that is picked turns out to be much less of a pippin than it seemed to be on the tree; and worse still, it contains a large worm of discomfiture. The miscreant realizes too late that it is much easier to stay out of trouble than to get out of it once he is in it.

THE TROUBLE WITH SO-CALLED SOPHISTICATION

A person who has strong sexual urges that he represses and denies can develop a severe and serious, acute and chronic, anxiety state. But the person who resorts to the liberation of "sophistication" will suffer equally severe anxiety states. He can bring himself, as I shall show you in a moment, to the brink of considering and committing suicide. There is no anxiety state more advanced than that.

Even short of the state in which suicide becomes a consideration, the devotee of "sophistication" has other anxiety backgrounds. Being apprehended by the law, or being dragged before a court is neither the major trouble nor its culmination. There is the personal degrading effect of lying, the constant fear of apprehension, the feeling of guilt. Then there is the broken home; or worse, a home in which things are not going smoothly; or still worse, a home in which growing children are being brought up in a poor atmosphere.

What a silly, foolish, "sophisticated" adult does to himself is to a considerable extent his business. But it leaves the realm of private affairs when children are ruined for life because their family gave them wrong emotional patterns and habits.

Even the sophisticate acknowledges the futility of "sophistication" when he has arrived at the point where he is ready to jump from a bridge or reach for a pistol. No system of action is mature or good that can possibly bring a person to the brink of suicide. And "sophistication" can.

Let me give you a couple of examples.

ANYTHING THAT CAN LEAD TO SUICIDE IS BEST OMITTED

Richard Roe was a smart, quiet fellow. At least *he* thought he was. He meant no harm to anyone. He was a good husband, and a good father. Also, he didn't intend to be exactly mid-Victorian. Well, you know—it wasn't infatuation for another woman—not that kind of "triangle" thing, just an arrangement with a person of the other sex who, too, wasn't exactly mid-Victorian, but, shall we say, merely modern or advanced.

Richard carried on for a long time without anyone being the wiser (not even Richard). He thought, "This isn't hurting anyone else. I wouldn't want it to." He met the girl in various ways, at various places.

Then one night they were at a motel they had often frequented. The manager suspected an irregularity and intercepted the couple in the midst of a tryst. Richard had registered under an assumed name as husband of the lady. He was in a legal "spot." In fact, he was in a hot spot. He and the lady left before the police could be called, but the manager had secured his right name and address.

For two days Richard sweated. He came to see me because of indigestion—and told me his trouble. In addition to a physician, he had gone to a lawyer, too.

Believe me, *there was a miserable man.* He was trying to stave off utter and complete disaster. Mind you—UTTER AND COMPLETE DISASTER. For two days, Richard was as miserable as any human being could be. Physically *he felt terrible,* and he needed medical aid.

On the third day the hotel manager filed his complaint; at ten-thirty, Richard was given the summons; at ten-forty-five Richard had put a bullet through his head.

The newspapers did not print news of the summons. They printed news of Richard's death. The reason why Richard died never got out. The family honor was saved. Richard was not. Richard was dead.

Doctor Mac, let us call him, was a nice sort of a guy, until he decided to give in to the urge and look at life in a broad, serene way. (Without any malice, you understand, but why shouldn't there be a little fun? After all, there are the Kinsey reports.)

So he made advances and the affair went on, until his accomplice became pregnant. Seeing the commercial value of her situation, she refused to let the doctor perform an illegal abortion (she would have had him there, too) but threatened him with suit.

The woman had come to me for examination when she thought she was pregnant, and told me the story in a boastful sort of way. Doctor Mac faced complete ruin—the suit would have thrown things wide open, of course. But more than that, in the state in which Mac lived, immoral conduct would cost him his medical license to practice. Knowing that the woman was just as responsible for the affair as was the doctor, I tried to talk her out of her intended law suit. She was too silly to listen.

On the first inkling that she had seen a lawyer to start a suit, Doctor Mac committed suicide by taking arsenic. Everyone thought he died a natural death. I never saw the woman any more, but I read of her drowning a month later.

MORE OFTEN, THE TROUBLE WITH SOPHISTICATION LIES THIS SIDE OF SUICIDE

Alwin had been a pretty stable fellow and an astute businessman. Then he came to my office with something obviously functional. He tried to act his usual self. He swore he had nothing to upset him or worry him. His trouble became more acute and gradually took a new course. He was apprehensive and worried, which was unusual for him. I told him he wasn't fooling anyone by playing anxious-free, and jokingly suggested he was having an affair. Whereupon, he unfolded a lurid tale. He hadn't met any legal noose, like Richard or Mac had, but he was worried just the same.

IT IS EASIER TO STAY OUT OF TROUBLE THAN TO GET OUT

The point in all this is, why start out on a track that can lead to a spot where suicide becomes a serious consideration, or short of that, a course that can result in serious emotional illness?

There are communities in which sexual irregularity has become so accepted that discovery is not often attended by anything as drastic as suicide. But I know from personal conversations with the doctors in such areas that functional illness holds a terrifically large place in the lives of the people in these communities.

OTHER FORMS OF SEXUAL IMMATURITY BESIDES "SOPHISTICATION"

I have talked about "sophistication" first because so many people mistakenly consider it to be sexual maturity. But there are other forms of sexual immaturity that produce much more emotional stress than does "sophistication."

A doctor's office during the course of a year sees many people with emotionally induced illness because they have brought sexual immaturity into marriage. Less often we see young people, or unmarried people, to whom sexual immaturity is also a source of emotional stress.

SEXUAL DIFFICULTIES BEFORE MARRIAGE

Youth is as innocent in the awakening of his sex curiosity as he was in his desire to eat, but the attitude of his elders makes the whole business seem at once bad and yet darkly inviting and mysterious. He is ordered to abstain, and then subjected to numerous varieties of sexual suggestion. Finally, the intimacy and privacy necessary for experimentation are only as far away as the car in the family garage. It, of course, isn't, and wasn't even in the horse and buggy days, anything like a good or a healthy set-up.

Then we add the final spice, which is that, owing to economic circumstances, marriage must be delayed ten or fifteen years beyond the awakening of the urge.

Here is a spot where a little planning by society, or the development of an educational method, would be an excellent thing. As it is, the advice these young people get is pretty poor and misleading stuff.

Youth's sexual urge leads them in one of three directions. First, the youth may be lucky enough to have someone with the necessary amount of good sense steer him, or her, in the less troublesome direction.

Secondly, they may break down the barriers and experiment with sex; possibly they may break down the barriers forcibly and come up for assault or murder. If they cross the barriers amiably, they precipitate themselves into the types of trouble we spoke of above. Thirdly, they may take masturbation as a way out.

MASTURBATION IS OFTEN THE SOURCE OF POOR EMOTIONS

Many people come to the doctor with emotionally induced illness because they are worried and apprehensive over a strong, unconquerable habit of masturbating.

For instance, a twenty-eight-year-old single woman had tiredness, headaches, a long string of symptoms because she was sure that her habit of masturbating was wrecking the foundations of her health. Her symptoms had become more severe after she found and read an old family health

135

guide in which the writer stated that masturbation is invariably followed by such dire physical consequences as sterility, tumors, heart disease, cancer, and insanity. The author of that article was a far more enthusiastic moralizer than scientist, a fact which the poor lady did not know. She felt that she had all the physical degeneration described by the author, and she was certain that her mind was going too. She had arrived at the point where she was unable to do her usual work.

There is another variety of poor emotions that results from masturbating, that is even more prone to produce E. I. I. These emotions arise because masturbating causes the individual to withdraw into himself and into a dream world of his own making. He develops introvert tendencies, lives in social isolation, and prefers to live in his world of dreams and fantasies. As a consequence, he lacks effectiveness in the real world; he lacks decisiveness; he staggers along through life, unproductive, unhappy, and alone. His emotions are predominantly brooding, regretful, and generally unhappy. He or she presents a sad regressing picture.

To put it simply—masturbation is immaturity. It is a childish way of satisfying one of the basic needs. Just as with other forms of immaturity, it is bound to be unsuccessful in a world which calls for maturity.

SEXUAL PERVERSION AS A SOURCE OF POOR EMOTIONS

There are, of course, people made miserable by the guilt, the difficulties, or the stigmata encountered by following one of the many types of sexual perversion, of which there are 14 or 15 different varieties, the most common being homosexuality. Sex perversions are evidence of deeply-seated personality difficulties that require individualized treatment.

Consequently, we will dismiss further discussion of the perversions in this book, except to offer assurances to the reader that boys and girls whose lives are rich with outside interests, who have had good training at home in thinking and acting carefully and critically, do not develop sexual perversions.

Nor need parents be afraid about the danger of their sons and daughters coming in contact with homoerotics and thus being misled into unnatural sexual relations. Careful investigations disclose that the individuals who take up homosexuality were definitely homosexuals before they met their seducer.

Another misconception that requires correction is that it

is the man who is markedly feminine, or the woman who is markedly masculine, who is most apt to be homoerotic. There is not the slightest connection. The male homoerotic is just as apt to be the athletic masculine type, and the female homoerotic a perfect feminine type. The unfortunate feminine man and the unfortunate masculine woman have enough of a handicap without adding this misconception.

SEXUAL IMMATURITY IN MARRIAGE

Sexual difficulties in marriage are extremely frequent, extremely provocative of emotional stress, extremely apt to start the schism that leads to divorce, and are always caused by sexual immaturity on the part of one or (usually) both the partners. There are many varieties, of course, of sexual difficulties in marriage, and we can mention only the most frequent here.

The difficulties start most often on the honeymoon, which to most newlyweds is the end of the dream world youth paints of the marital state. The *usual* experience on the honeymoon is that the boy and the girl find that it isn't as wonderful as they thought it would be, and they blame each other. If the boy and the girl can overlook the first years in which their experiences are vaguely somewhere between success and failure, they may find at the end of 30 years that the experience *can* be the rainbow they found it wasn't on their honeymoon.

Most young men, when first married, have the imagination of rabbits, the romantic capacity of sloths, and the sexual technique of oysters. When you mix this combination with the fears, the discomforts, and the misinformation which the girl has accumulated, you end up with nights filled with horrible experiences.

If a fair amount of maturity exists in the couple, such as sympathy, understanding, comradeship, and good will, all may not yet be lost and the marital craft may yet be rescued before it founders. But with many couples, who have no maturity in other directions to save their sexual immaturity, the disillusionment of the beginning grows into the final break of the end.

When sexual immaturity brings one, or both, of the partners into the doctor's office with E. I. I., it is very apt to center around frigidity in the woman. Over 40 per cent of the married women I see in my practice get no sexual enjoyment out of their marriage, and provide little enjoyment

137

for their husbands. Wife happy? No—miserable. Husband happy? No—just as miserable.

Frigidity is most often the husband's fault. Much of this frigidity on the part of the wife is not her fault, but is due primarily to the clumsy, selfish technique of the husband, not merely in the first delicate experiences of marriage, but forever after.

As many women put it, "He has not thought of anything but his own wishes. He leaves me cold and disgusted. Now it only makes me nervous. I hate the whole thing."

You will always find that these husbands are immature children in other aspects of living as well as in sex. Mentally, their maturity stopped at age eight; physically, they went on to develop hair on their chests. Many an otherwise excellent girl has been precipitated into chronic illness and chronic unhappiness by this common variety of inept and immature husband. Even though she may try to meet the situation philosophically, the situation proves to be too difficult.

Frigidity may be the result of faulty education. In a relatively smaller number of women, such frigidity is sometimes the result of poor sex education in their childhood. Rose, for instance, was the unusually attractive daughter of a family that lived in a tough part of town. Because of the bad influences of the neighborhood, the mother stringently indoctrinated the young Rose against the entire matter of sex, scaring her on the entire subject until Rose had the idea that sexual intercourse was far and away the worst experience that could ever befall a woman, that it was, in fact, worse than death. Rose never did know why or just how she ever became married. Marriage for her was a hateful, hideous experience. After bearing two children, conceived in utter agony, Rose added the fear of another pregnancy to her already unwholesome sex outlook. She developed an intractable ulcerative colitis and has spent years in and out of hospitals.

Frigidity in the wife is an important cause of yet another grave marital difficulty—unfaithfulness in the husband. As one English Earl remarked, he greatly preferred to have his romantic efforts returned by the appreciative and enthusiastic embraces of the chambermaid than to suffer the reluctant frigidity of the Countess. Every man, earl or no earl, is made of the same material.

Appetite is not the same in both partners. Another common source of difficulty in marriage is a failure on the part of the partners to recognize the *usual* difference in sexual appetites in man and woman. In general, men are moved by the sexual instinct more frequently than are women. Unless this difference is appreciated by the partners, and each tries to meet the difference at least half way, irritation, disgruntlement, and deep displeasure are bound to result. This common situation can be avoided only if each has enough maturity to appreciate the individual needs and desires of the other.

There are many other varieties of difficulties arising in the complex relations of marriage. We are not going to review them, but deal with them merely by saying that they all, without exception, result from immaturity, and are all to be corrected by developing maturity.

SEXUAL MATURITY

Sexual maturity begins with the attitude that sex is not bad in itself, and, when rightly used, will enrich life and add materially to the pattern of enjoyment.

The phrase, "rightly used," is the key to the whole business.

First, "rightly used," means acknowledging the existing restrictions on sexual activity as a necessary and a good thing so long as people are trying to continue the social and economic projects we call civilization. Obviously, to keep out of trouble, sex had best be used within the legal limits, *that is to say, only in the married state.* This is the one side to maturity—minimizing trouble.

Secondly, "rightly used," means developing the capacity to make the sexual aspect of marriage a satisfactory, complete, and constantly finer experience for husband and wife. This is the other side of maturity—developing the capacity to handle living for maximum enjoyment.

The first meaning of "rightly used" concerns chiefly the person out of wedlock, and the second concerns those who are married.

HANDLING SEX BEFORE MARRIAGE

As far as a sex program for youth is concerned, an excellent, or even a good, solution does not exist. The best that can be done to help youth is to mobilize a few factors in their behalf that will help tide them over.

The first thing we can do for youth is to be frank about the whole business. It doesn't do to tell these young people they have no problem, or to imply that if they have, it is of their own making. It is best to lay the cards on the table, and admit their elders had the same problem—and for them, as for youth now, the fact is that before marriage, there is no altogether satisfactory answer. Then we should try to make it clear that marriage is a satisfactory answer only if personal qualities of maturity can be developed before they get married.

The second help is not to insist, or even to imply, that the sexual urge should be forced out of mind. Instead, the youth's mind should be given interests and urges, important and lively enough to take up a good portion of his time, interests worthy in their own right of demanding the best the youth has.

Ways to help control the urge. Such urges are the urge to become proficient in a sport, adept and skilled in a handicraft, socially accepted and liked, capable of adding a desirable skill to the community enterprise. Not only will a wealth of such pursuits serve to enable the youth to forget much of the time that he is a sexual animal, but it will also develop the maturities so necessary to his future.

General mental maturity, the capacity to think, is the best step toward sexual maturity. A family which gives the youth a sense of belonging to the family enterprise, an education that gives the youth a keen sense of being a part of the human enterprise, a good mind with generally sound ideas —these are the best measures for sublimating the sex urge to a distinctly secondary level. Such a sublimation of interest and such a development of new urges must be provided, principally by *the family,* and also by the schools, churches, and by youth centers.

The need for youth centers is usually underestimated by our communities, and when the youth centers *are* provided, it is often in too niggardly a fashion. A good youth center in a community, designed to give youth high interests in their off-hours, is the most important organization outside the family. Any community with the interests of its young people truly at heart can much less afford to be without a youth center than it can afford to be without paved streets or a municipal water supply.

A youth center is in the nature of a necessary public utility which only the municipality can provide.

The third help is for adult society to fan the sexual flames of youth as little as possible. It is entirely laudable to lift sexuality out of 19th-century prudery, but it is still necessary that parents, teachers, psychologists, and psychiatrists take pains to point out to adolescents the dangers of "petting"—the danger of excessive sex stimulation under conditions which do not provide for its proper gratification.

One sees high school teenagers, either regrettably pregnant, or what is almost worse, with wrong emotional habits resulting from petting, which will give them lifelong nervous difficulties. If young people are to be overstimulated by sexy literature, sexy movies, sexy stories from their elders, plus the opportunity provided by the family automobile, their elders should not be surprised when they seek a natural outlet for their sexual tension. By and large, our society is dealing youth a wretched hand, and then asking them to play a good game. The pay-off is apparent in present-day divorce rates and marital difficulties. For the foolish things people do all the people pay.

SEXUAL MATURITY IN MARRIAGE

Lamentable as poor handling of sex may be in the premarital individual, it is even more lamentable when sex produces clouds of wrong emotions to a married couple, as it does with great frequency.

In marriage, as in adolescence, general maturity is the best guarantee of sexual maturity. The same sympathy, understanding, and willingness to cooperate that stamp maturity in general are absolutely essential if marital sexuality is to be something other than a source of trouble and internecine strife. The golden rule of sympathy, understanding, and kindliness must be the basis of marital sexuality, just as it must be the basis of mature social ethics. Most people at the time of marriage have for each other the feeling we call affection. Affection is entirely essential, but unless it is augmented by the golden qualities of sympathy, understanding, and kindliness on the part of both marital partners, it will soon be replaced by remorse, disillusionment, bickering, and dissatisfaction.

Sex must be a mutual delight. The sexual relationship in marriage should be a truly cooperative enterprise in which neither wishes to derive pleasure at the expense of the other, and each is more intent in providing the maximum enjoyment for the other rather than for himself. They learn that finding pleasure in each other is a much wider thing than sex, and includes many more things than sex, but in which sex is an important factor.

Creating a mutually enjoyable experience becomes the object of each, and no rules apply except that whatever is done be good and pleasant to both, and enjoyed by both.

When two married people are personally mature together, sexual married life consists of mutual appeal and response, offer and acceptance, enticement, surprise, suspense—all achieved by constantly shifting aggressiveness and passivity, activity and relaxation on the part of each partner.

To two such people the pleasure to each from pleasing the other becomes so intermingled with the pleasure of being pleased and of knowing that the partner is pleased and wants to return the pleasure, that their two personalities become indistinguishable and become truly one through the years.

Each shared pleasure reinforces and builds up a long series of potentially limitless shared experiences of ecstasy. The physical and mental components of pleasure react and enforce each other. Such married partners become more and more indispensable to each other. No marriage can be a successful enterprise in which there is not such a sexual unity.

Egocentricity and selfishness are the childhood arrests that most commonly make a mess of marriage. The only person capable of true affection is the person who can forget himself and his own immediate interest while he places the welfare and interest of someone else foremost. When both husband and wife can do that, they will have no domestic nor sexual trouble.

Assuming now that both marital partners are capable of working for the other's welfare, the stage is set for marital success.

The next quality to maintain in the family between husband and wife, and later between parents and children, is the idea that TODAY, RIGHT/NOW, *we are going to be cheerful and pleasant and make living enjoyable*. Quarreling and fighting and bickering are permanently and completely out of the picture because they accomplish exactly nothing. Under *no circumstances* are they justified.

The "value" of "blowing your top." There is a school of psychiatrists who think that "blowing one's top" is a good way to work off something bad. This view is held mostly by psychiatrists who cannot control their own tops. There is nothing to it. Blowing one's top serves no good purpose; one blowing more firmly sets the habit for the next blowing. If both husband and wife are given to blowing their tops, something usually cracks sooner or later, such as patience, affection, or the standing invitation to cooperate. Children blow their tops; it is a childish adult who finds it necessary to do so.

Marriage should and can be based on this fundamental assumption: *"We can make life more enjoyable for each other by living together; neither of us has any right to make any moment miserable for the other."* That becomes a perfectly simple, satisfactory, and practical formula if husband and wife each have about a dime's worth of sympathy, understanding and good will.

In such an atmosphere, the sexual side of marriage becomes a growing experience that constantly makes each more indispensable to the other; sexually their experiences are as cooperative, sympathetic, and understanding as are the other aspects of their life together.

Young married couples should know something about the anatomy and physiology of sex. Ignorance is the only deterrent to human possibilities. When I see young couples going afoul in marriage because their sex life is going sour, along with their other marital enterprises, I refer them to a sensible and concise discussion of sexual relations such as *Sex Manual* by G. Lombard Kelly, M.D.*, which I advise them to read together. Sometimes it is sex that goes sour first in marriage, sometimes it goes sour because everything else has gone sour.

When a marriage gets sour, the first thing for wife and husband to do is for *each of them* to bring cheerfulness and pleasantness back into their attitude toward the other.

KEY POINTS TO REMEMBER IN CHAPTER 11

The individual's sex problem consists in adapting his biological urge to the restrictions imposed by society. Society has imposed the restrictions, but hasn't taken the trouble to teach the individual how to make a mature adjustment. Maturity and emotional stasis in sexual matters boils down to three rules:

> *1. Tell yourself, in no uncertain terms, that in matters of sex you are going to play the game according to the rules. It is easier to keep out of trouble than to get out of it once you are in it. For all-important reasons—legal, moral, social, economic—sex must be confined to marriage.*

* Published by *The Southern Medical Supply Company*, Augusta, Georgia. This book cannot be secured without a prescription from a doctor.

2. *The successful sublimation of sex in the unmarried person (or in the married wolf) consists in providing the individual with interesting, absorbing, and vigorous activities, and in helping him mature in as many other departments of living as possible.*

3. *Sexual maturity in marriage is dependent on developing the qualities of general maturity, especially sympathy, understanding, unselfishness, cooperativeness and affection.*

12

WHAT TO DO WHEN YOUR
WORK IS GIVING YOU
THE JITTERS

THE EMOTIONAL STRESS OF OUR INDUSTRIAL SYSTEM

Never has the civilized world had the wealth of useful goods and materials that our present-day industrial system provides. That, of course, is a wonderful benefit and help to all the people.

But never has a method of production inflicted on its personnel such a flood of disagreeable emotions as does our present-day industrial system. This, of course, is a primary source of unhappiness and emotionally induced illness for a great many people.

When the industrial system began in England, it was the laborer in the sweat shops who had most of the bad emotions provided by the system. But today it isn't primarily the common laborer, or the white-collar man at the foot of the ladder, who suffers most emotionally because of the system. The greatest victim is the man at the top, or near the top, who masterminds and manages the system. We see here the operation of nature's balance of compensations.

The businessman or the craftsman, before the industrial age, experienced *few* of the conditions that in today's world produce tense emotional states in corporation executives, vice-presidents, store managers, sales force, assembly line workers and so forth. The incessant competitive business growth, departmental growth, and the pressure of piece work, competitive striving, angling for advancement, low-interest, repetitive jobs, are at once the elements that make the industrial system great, and the elements that give men the emotional jitters and emotionally induced illness.

THE EXECUTIVE HAS STRESS

Werner had come up the hard way in the sales division

of a company that makes several well-known, nationally advertised products. The company was old, and didn't amount to much, until one of its new products made a national hit far above anything even the company heads ever expected. From then on, the board of directors wanted to continue putting out "hits."

Werner, by working around the clock for the company, on a small salary, and having no fun for himself or his family, had achieved a good position in the sales division. Then he was placed in charge of sales for a new product that the board hoped would outdo the original "hit." What an opportunity! Werner thought; and there *were* opportunities, including the opportunity never to feel physically well again. The board would call Werner in and show him a comparative chart silhouetting him against some more successful department. The board would ask him for a progress report before the expected time. The board would ask for an explanation of a lower-than-expected sales curve. The board would pound its fist upon the table.

With every new pressure from the board, Werner developed a new pressure in his upper abdomen and chest. After one board meeting he checked his lungs, after another his heart, once his stomach, again his gall bladder.

He was an organ on which the board was playing a dismal tune. Even before Werner was made head of sales, he could never brag that he felt fit as a fiddle. But after his climb to sales manager, with the heat of the board upon him, he became a symphony of complaints, which included a completely equipped indigestion, finally centering around a perennial full-blown ulcer.

I met him the first time on a train. The poor fellow told me of his symptoms, ending with, "And the doctors don't seem to understand it." That last statement usually means the patient doesn't understand it.

Werner worked up a tremendous tension and a diabolical indigestion, trying to bring his product before a reluctant public. Actually, the product he was given by the board to promote was developed 20 years too late. It died a slow, expensive death, and with it, Werner went down in the company, a functional wreck. The effect of the system was exactly the same as if the board had inoculated Werner with tuberculosis. Yet the members of the board considered themselves kindly human beings; they were playing the part of good businessmen, as far as Werner was concerned.

Now take a top-flight success from one of the boards—

as a matter of fact, he has been on 22 boards at the same time—Old H——. He worked, he pushed, he pulled, he got there. But getting there meant holding on; holding on meant advancing with a bunch of enterprising young fellows yelping at his heels. There came a steady competitive fight to stem off a reorganization, sleepless nights on which he'd gotten out of bed and walked for blocks, jittery spells when he tried to rest a minute on plane trips he took to secure stockholders' votes; finally a blackout when he hemorrhaged from an ulcer that he had, in his frenzy, tried to ignore. He was a great success—he beat the reorganization —he controlled the stock—he was really a great financier. But as a man he was jumpy, jittery, restless, constantly nursing an ulcer—himself a financial success, and also a financial success for the doctors.

THE HALF-WAY MAN HAS STRESS

Now let us look at some of the lower rungs on the ladder. There is no form of modern business management that is more competitive than being the manager of a chain store. I've known many of these managers—fine fellows, every one of them, smart, honest, hard workers. They had to be to survive the rigid screening process they went through to ascend from clerk to manager. But I have not seen a single one who did not have, in the course of his managership, some form of functional disease.

Bill went farther than any of the others I ever knew; he finally ended as a manager over ten large districts. We X-rayed Bill four times from stem to stern while he was store manager in our town, to assure him that his abdominal pain and constipation were no more serious than his sour stomach and frequent belching. Every advancement, every move to a new city, was punctuated with more X-rays. The last time I saw him in his plush office in Chicago, he was still belching, still eating antacid tablets by the handful, and I could tell from the occasional wince that strolled across his face that he was still having abdominal pain.

Then take Joe. Joe had been a good man in the brass foundry; so good he was made foreman of 27 men. Then his headaches began, and the pain in his neck and in his chest. The men above him wanted output; the men below him wanted to loaf. Between them, Joe was in a vise.

THE LABORER'S JOB GIVES HIM STRESS

Take a look at the lowly assembly lines. Henry left the

farm for the glamour of the factory. There he was given the thrill of putting the spark plugs into the engine block as it came down the line. The company speeded up the line. Incidentally, Henry had to speed up too. Then the engineers added two more cylinders; they weren't thinking of Henry. Henry became more and more ailing. After a necessary leave of absence, he was put on a punch press doing piece work. After two years he broke down again. Now he's back on the farm. He wonders why he ever went to the factory.

A very interesting thing happened in another plant—in one division a dozen men run grinders over sheet metal, producing a terrific piercing noise. I've seen four men from that division with ulcers in the last two years; how many more quit because of stomach trouble, I do not know. You remember that Dr. Hans Selye produced ulcers in dogs by subjecting them to a constant piercing disagreeable noise!

WORRY AND ACCIDENTS

It's the worried man in industry who has most of the accidents. Attention to the job is interrupted by a train of thought about a disagreeable problem—possibly trouble with the wife at home—possibly worry over the house mortgage —possibly anxiety over a dozen different things—then zingo! zip! he loses his hand in a press, or a moving rod pierces his arm. Seventy-five per cent of the accidents happen to repeaters.

THE PRESSURE IS THE SAME IN ALL INDUSTRY

In every line of modern industry and business, the competitive pressures are the same, probably nowhere greater than in the newspaper game. An editor friend of mine says there is no one on his paper from the editor (himself) on down who doesn't have a few physical complaints. And he adds, "In addition to feeling punk physically, these fellows are fundamentally unhappy, because the pace and the pressures are so great."

PERHAPS INDUSTRIAL CIVILIZATION IS WORTH IT

What price modern productive methods? What good is wealth acquired with a raw stomach? Far better a sweet stomach and a modest living. But where, in modern business-industry, can you find a sweet living without a sour stomach? The tension of bigger and better commercialism ruins almost every job you can pick up.

Modern business and industry is one of the great reasons for the terrific prevalence of the emotionally induced illness of our time. In certain respects the system is a childhood arrest—it is psychologically immature. At a certain age the child is constantly competitive, pitting and matching himself against all comers, striving to beat his fellows, constantly endeavoring to excel. As a person matures, this competitive spirit melts into a cooperative willingess to share with the other fellow, to give rather than to take. Such maturity is frightened off by our present economic Frankenstein.

To be mature in this sense, to act with mature decency when competitive striving calls for selfish pushing ahead, means inevitable failure in the kind of system we have. Anyone who follows such mature principles as noncompetitive cooperation, a desire to be of benefit to human beings as human beings, a feeling for helping people out of difficulties, can be a financial success only by a most miraculous series of accidents.

I know several financial failures, that is to say, men who never succeeded in any business or in any commercial endeavor they ever undertook. Almost without exception, they are among the finest human beings I have ever met.

STILL, WE'VE GOT TO EAT

Nevertheless, we do have to make a living. Maybe you've gotten your functional illness as a direct result of our business-industrial system. You are going to have to continue living in it and being a part of it.

Then (to yourself) play it as a game, something that's a great big lark, something done because it's ENJOYABLE, not a duty. Play it cheerfully and pleasantly, and don't let the trap of competitive striving catch you.

It's barely possible that following this advice, you may never drive a Cadillac, but you'll enjoy eating peanuts and watermelon at a picnic you get to in a rattling good 1937 Chevvy. You may even end up in the poorhouse, but you'll have a good time getting there, and you'll live to sing at the funerals of the poor devils who beat you up the ladder.

A BRIEF SUMMARY OF CHAPTER 12

The industrial system, as we know it in this country, is a wonderful provider of human needs. But unfortunately it is also a great provider of stressing emotions to the people who make it run. Great responsibilities, the constant demand for great effort, and the fight to maintain his gains are common stresses of the top executive. The competitive fight for advancement, with its overshadowing insecurity, is the lot of the man on the way up. Non-creative and low-interest jobs with monotonous repetitions bring a deep form of stress to the laborer.

The only good, long-range answer is that industry must gradually humanize itself, as some portions of industry are already trying to do.

For the individual who is caught in his job, the only answer is to try to sneak enjoyment in through the back door; to make himself as cheerful as possible; and to be upset by the irritations of the job as little as possible. He himself must dictate the level of his emotions, not allow the job to dictate them for him.

In short, the man who is being crushed by industrialism can put the methods you are reading about in this book to good use.

13

MEETING THE AGING YEARS

EMOTIONAL STRESS INCREASES WITH YEARS

E. I. I. is prevalent at all ages, but it grows more and more prevalent in the declining years of life—the very time an individual should be gliding into a calm, easy harbor, instead of back into the storm. This is true partly because of the conditions and situations that the aging person must try to cope with; on the other hand many people handle age poorly simply because they never handled any part of their lives well. The inability grows larger like a giant snowball toward the end.

This increase with age in the incidence of E. I. I. is a new development in our century. It has come about because aging today is attended by far more stress than ever before in history. For several thousand years the social and economic status of the aged did not change at all; the conditions of the aged in the 4th century, B.C., were practically identical with those of the 19th century, A.D. Today, the status of the aged is very different from what it was 100 years ago, and, in another 50 years, the changes will be even greater.

The important change in our time has been *a tremendous increase in the absolute and relative number of people over 65*. In 1900, one person in 20 was over 65. Today one in 11 is over 65, and by 1980, it will be one in seven.

"SENILITY" IS OFTEN E. I. I.

The functional illnesses of age may be any of those of earlier years, but they tend to assume one similar pattern because the prevalent emotional picture in old age is insecurity (of finances, of health, of the future), apprehension, disappointment, discouragement, and so on.

These emotions, you will remember (Chapter 3), are the ones that stress the pituitary to produce the somatotrophic hormone (STH) with its attending joint, arterial, and kidney effects. In other words, STH effects *are* degenerative effects.

We have no way of judging, as yet, just how much of the degenerative disease of the aged is emotionally induced, but probably a large part of it is. Without the degenerative diseases, which are so chronic and slow and debilitating, the aged person would go along smoothly and fairly vigorously to a happier and more kindly end.

It is important to note that the group of people over 65 is the *only* group whose life expectancy has not increased since 1900. At any age up to 65, you can expect to live longer than an individual of the same age in 1900. But after 65, you cannot expect to live longer than a person of the same age did a hundred years ago. This holds in spite of the fact that practically no old person today dies of pneumonia or other infection, and in spite of the fact that people even with some of the degenerative diseases, such as heart disease, can be carried on for years longer than might have been possible even 20 years ago. It can mean only that degenerative disease has been accelerated in our time, and the cause of the acceleration is an increase in emotional stress.

At first sight, it is hard to believe that much of what we regard in the aged as natural deterioration is actually E. I. I. But let me give you an example that will illustrate the truth of such a statement.

George W—— illustrated perfectly the way in which the emotions characteristic of old age produce degenerative disease, *and how a change toward the right kind of emotions will produce a reversal of the degenerative changes*. You have to see this sort of thing to believe it.

I was introduced to George by his physician, Dr. K. M. Bowman, a well-known San Francisco psychiatrist. George, at 83, was working on the stage of the theater in the San Francisco Municipal Home for the Aged. He was the stage manager, and he was getting ready for a production the people of the Home were putting on that night. George was as active as a good man of 60, and you could tell he was greatly enjoying his work.

"George," Dr. Bowman said, "hold out both your hands."

George did. There was a slight tremor in them, especially in the right, but it didn't amount to much.

"How bad did you shake two years ago?" Dr. Bowman asked.

George demonstrated with a terrific wobbling of both hands.

"He isn't exaggerating," Dr. Bowman said.

Then he told me the story. When he had first seen George two years before, George was living with his son and daughter-in-law. He had been bedridden for six months; he shook so hard he had to have help in eating; he was so weak he couldn't take care of his own toilet.

George had been a stage manager on Broadway in his prime. He was a master at his work, one of the best in the business. He had one child, a boy, who moved to the West Coast when he became of age. When George was 48, his wife died. The theater business was declining; some of his shows went sour. For a number of reasons, George began to drink, and he lost the job he had had for 23 years. From then on, he went from job to job, occasionally managing a small, obscure stage, but usually as just a common stagehand.

At 72 he was destitute, and his son sent him enough money to come to San Francisco. There George lived with his son, to whom he had become almost a stranger. His habits were not too tidy; his ways were not those of his hosts. I suppose at first his son and daughter-in-law had intended to make the old man happy. But the relationship, especially on the part of the daughter-in-law, became one of belligerent and bare tolerance. George knew he wasn't wanted. The city was new to him, he had no friends there; there was no one around the few legitimate theaters who cared to talk to him. So George began to ail; his degeneration became more and more rapid, and it was not too long before he was in bed. They had a doctor once or twice. The doctor called it hardening of the arteries and senile debility.

Then Dr. Bowman chanced to see him. He examined George and said, "We're just finishing a new theater with a fine stage up at the Municipal Home for the Aged, and we need a stage manager from Broadway. I'm going to take you up there."

George was excited, but he didn't think he could ever get out of bed again. His son and daughter-in-law were even more dubious, but secretly they were happy to have him move out of their care.

He was moved in an ambulance, and carted out to the theater stage in a wheelchair. In two weeks he was walking out, and, in another two, he was as active as an old tomcat. He improved rapidly after that.

Around the Home, Dr. Bowman showed me at least eight other people we just chanced to meet who had stories of a reversal of their degenerative disease just as remarkable as George's.

The demonstration that degenerative processes in the aging *can be* the result of *emotional stress* as well as "natural senility" requires a laboratory—like the San Francisco Municipal Home for the Aged. In the average community there is usually little chance to reverse the stressing situation which is producing the degeneration of the aging person.

The San Francisco Municipal Home for the Aged has that *necessary* difference most homes for the aged do not have. One of the best contrasts is afforded by the unimaginative, expensive depositories being built in so many counties for the aged. The central idea of the San Francisco Home is that it is a COMMUNITY of elderly people, run by elderly people. The bookkeeper, the vegetable purchaser, the engineer, the plumber, the stage manager are residents who are old hands at their trade. The Home aims to be self-supporting in a financial way, in a recreational way, and in an essential-service way.

What Getting Old Today Means

Don't think that getting old today is the same kind of thing that getting old was 50 years ago. Times change, and so do the factors that the aging have to contend with.

Financial insecurity. First is the matter of financial security. How well off are you, or how well off are you going to be at the age of 65? With the depreciation of the dollar, which means lower annuities, with the high tax level, with the hesitancy to employ people older than 45, more people than you think are not going to be self-sufficient at the age of 65. The average family today, maintaining the standard of living that everyone has become accustomed to, is just barely able to scrape along, let alone save. We always think that next year we will start to save. The only person who doesn't procrastinate with saving is the financier, or the banker, or the insurance salesman. Don't envy them. They have other problems that give most of them severe functional disease.

One third of the people over 65 have no income whatever of their own, and 75 per cent have an income of less than $1000, including old age assistance. At least there's the Federal old age assistance, you say (if you're under 50). Thank somebody for that. That, at least, is the difference between eating *something* and eating nothing; between sleeping in a bed *somewhere* and sleeping out in the park. Would you

154

(supposing you are 40) like the idea of having to go on "relief?" You can bet your last dollar you won't like it any better when you are 65.

Job insecurity. The last resort of the scoundrel is to suggest, "Why doesn't the old fellow get a job?" The scoundrel doesn't appreciate that in the present labor market it's getting hard for the fellow over 45 to pick up a fresh job.

Here is a man of 60. He is a skilled tool maker, his accident liability is considerably less than a younger man's, his absenteeism will be definitely less, his dependability in a pinch will be greater, he will be less aggressive in fomenting labor trouble. Yet he can't get a job, even though a doctor would pronounce him physically fit. Why can't he, why can't the others of 60 or over—no, let's say 50 or over—get a job so that they might support themselves?

Because, being a vigorous young nation, we worship youth and *slight* (that's a mild term) old age. Old age is regarded as a regrettable incident, necessary (God forbid) for others; an incident which we hope will not be prolonged beyond reason (which isn't long); an incident which will be as troubleless to the younger members of the family as possible (somehow *they* cannot see *themselves* at 65).

The older man doesn't get a job. Some efficiency expert found the younger man more dextrous, turning out more parts for the company. He didn't stop to think that the older man was putting something human into the company; he didn't know that something human in a company would be worth more than lucre. He didn't find out that the company would be still making enough for everyone (including the stockholders and management) to live.

Not being able to make a living or having enough to live on isn't all—it's just the beginning of the troubles which the aging have to take on.

The insecurity of children's indifference. There's the matter, for instance, of changing family sentiment regarding the aged. I can remember the time when "Honor thy father and mother" was taken seriously. If it was the last thing they were able to do, the children felt obliged to see that their aging parents were well cared-for.

Today it is *usual* for children to stand by without emotion (except a sigh of relief) and see their parents placed upon Federal aid; or if the presence of their elders becomes irksome, it is quite satisfactory to see them placed in a nursing home. This has gradually become the attitude that is acceptable to the society in which we live. It is not going to be changed for decades, if ever.

But the truth is that it's terribly hard on the old folks. They remember when these same children had to be fed, had to be protected, required long hours of their time and care. And the compensation is to be set aside as though they had never mattered. For these children they lived. What has it brought them? These children they loved. Now who returns any love? There are plenty of people, don't you fear, who have broken hearts (that is to say, severe pituitary stress) because they have been so damnably let down in their needy years.

More than just the children are at fault. But it isn't only the children. It's *everybody*. Everybody around them regards the aging person as someone who is just in the way impeding progress. Slow on the street; slow getting off of buses; yes, slow to die. Actually and truthfully, the old folks aren't wanted by society. The best indication of that is that we call them a "problem." A problem and the makings of it are not wanted. The kind of county homes we throw them into as a last resort is an indication that we don't really care a great deal for the aged.

Don't think the aged don't sense these attitudes; don't think for a moment that these factors do not have a great deal to do with the health of the aging. That is the point I'm trying to get across. The social solution is evident enough—either children should become old-fashioned enough to care, or society become interested enough to provide adequate community life for those it is now throwing out of society. But that still isn't all that stresses the pituitary to produce STH in the aged.

Fear of ill-health. There's the matter that they don't feel well (suppose it *is* functional) always, always, they fear that complete disability may be just around the corner. The ordinary young person goes into a tailspin when he is told that he needs to be incapacitated for two years. As a matter of fact, it is very seldom that we doctors dare to put it to a patient so simply. Well, now, suppose you have to be afraid, as an elderly patient always has to be afraid, that your age may bring you to your bed tomorrow of a wasting disease you can never be rid of!

It takes a lot of courage in the aged just to act cheerful and never say anything about these fears!

Fear of death. And, too,—you youngsters to whom death is still something that never happens—to the aged (and they think of it, never fear) death is closer at hand than it has ever

156

been. Most every living thing, unless it is very, very miserable, wants to keep on living. And so they think, during those long nights (many are the aged who don't sleep well) of the experience that lies threateningly just ahead. They feel like the Irishman, "If I knew where I was going to die, I'd sure stay away from that damn place." But for them the situation has lost its humor. It's the BIG THING that's just ahead; HOW and WHEN is it going to be?

Loss of friends. But there are all kinds of other sad things for the older person. Their friends who once dropped a cheerful word, their spouse, who once offered a helping hand, their dog, who once wagged his tail, have all gone. Have you ever in the deepening twilight stood out on a lonely sweep of the earth—have you ever felt an awful lonesomeness pulling you down into the soil—a lonesomeness so deep as if to say, "This and only this is all, there is no more?" If you have, you have just a little inkling of how the aged person feels who is *really* alone in the twilight, without a soul to care, or show the least parting affection.

You'd think that after 70, 80, 90 years, one would at least deserve—if not a band and a celebration—some appreciative recognition from society for having accomplished his feat—staying out of jail, bringing up a family, and just generally carrying on through all the difficulties of the years. But a posthumous text is the best the children and society can wring from hearts that (never fear), too, will grow old.

Poor housing for the aging. Then take another social cause of distress to the aged—the matter of housing. Fifty years ago, two-thirds of our elderly people lived in rural areas. Today, two-thirds live in cities. With this change they have lost the sympathies, friendliness, and neighborliness of the small communities. Today, 50 per cent of our aged have unsatisfactory housing and living arrangements, and a large portion of the other 50 per cent are realizing with dismay that their industrial pensions or other income that had, heretofore, been adequate, no longer cover increased rentals and increased food costs. A person on a Federal pension is expected to feed and house himself on seventy-five dollars a month. Housing on such an income can be only the very worst available, a dreary inhospitable room where one must be ashamed to have visitors.

An age that is dark when it should be golden. And so, old age is for most of the aging in our society the dark age instead of the golden age. For more and more people, the last years mean more and more misery. Those who are now under 55 may think they have their troubles; but when they are 65, they will really know what trouble is.

The troubles of the aging are so acute and so fundamentally devastating, that the miseries of the older people are frequently sending them beyond emotionally induced illness into frank mental derangement. Twenty years ago most of the people in mental institutions were young or middle-aged. The old stayed sane. Today four out of every ten admissions to mental institutions are over 65! The cause? Simple! The conditions our aged are asked to meet are enough to break men's minds. These patients are often labeled "senile dementias." But don't forget, they are degenerative dementias, emotionally induced. The proportional admissions of the aged to mental institutions has increased considerably faster than the increase in the total number of the aged.

IT'S YOUR PROBLEM, TOO

Practically every adult living today will live to be 65 and over. In 1925 there were 20 younger people for every person over 65. Today there are only 11 younger for everyone over 65, and in 1975, there will be only 8 younger for everyone older than 65. You see, you are going to get there too! The problem of the aged is not like the problem of India. You will probably never have to live in India, but you will most certainly live to be older than 65. What is to be done about the problems of oldsters?

You are 20 or 25 or 30:

What are you doing about your old age? Now is the best time to start planning.

You are 40 or 45 or into the 50's:

You cannot afford to waste time when time is so precious.

You are 60 or 65:

There is still time to do much—you have a long time to live.

You are in the 70's or 80's:

Contentment, which is something inside and not outside, can still be yours for the trying.

WHAT WILL WE DO ABOUT OLD AGE?

This:

Whether you are 20 or whether you are 60, the sooner you develop a mature idea of what your program will have to be after you are 65, the happier your old age is going to be.

Maturity in old age means essentially what maturity at any

age means—it means that as an individual lives, he enjoys what there is to enjoy, his friends, family, work, spare time, and the wonderful world, and he develops a great kindness and thoughtfulness which enables him to be a giver to all, but especially to those weaker and less fortunate. Finally he is able to compromise and see the other fellow's point of view instead of disagreeing and rearing up into a fight.

PRACTICALLY, MATURITY IN OLD AGE MEANS THIS—

If you are young:

1. Develop emotional stasis now. We talked about the tough situations our oldsters are faced with. But the most important source of trouble is not any of these. By far the greatest trouble oldsters have—I should say about 75 per cent of their trouble—is that in their upper years their emotional states have at last caught up to them, as emotional states always do by the time we are 65. The reactions a person allowed himself to have when he was 20 become more obvious as a person grows older. Nine times out of ten, the old man "who is just as sweet as he can be" was always a kindly, understanding person. The old lady with an acid tongue and a battle-ax approach to the ordinary incidents of life, was that way when she was 40, and also, though possibly less obviously so, when she was 20. Unless we work on them with conscious thought control, our emotional states in old age are the quintessence of our earlier dispositions with most of the masking flavors filtered off.

So, whether you are 20 or 60 you can still learn kindliness, love for your fellows, cheerfulness, and an eye for the thousands of little enjoyable things about us that cost nothing.

All through life we have a choice—we have the same choice whether we are 20, or 40, or 60, or 80, except that, at 80, we have more strongly established the habit of making the choice in one certain direction. But even at 80 a resolute person can change the habit in his choice. We have the choice between reacting with *equanimity, resignation, courage, determination, and cheerfulness* on the one hand, or with *crabbiness, grumbling, worry, and apprehension* on the other.

The choice is yours—RIGHT NOW.

If a person *realized* that he had a conscious choice between the two ways or reacting to his world, *and he knew the consequences of taking one or the other path,* he would not hesitate in choosing equanimity, resignation, determination, courage, and cheerfulness. As in many simple truths, the better choice is so obvious it is missed. Somewhere our education should have made it crystal clear that the choice was ours, and that with a flip of our mind a good emotional state was ours, with all the trimmings.

2. *Plan future finances.* Save something regularly to add to retirement income. Cut your present scale of living if you need to. Remember what Thoreau once said, that any event that requires a new outfit is not worth the trouble.

3. *Plan a place to live* when you are advanced in years. Will you have your home or will you have money to pay rent?

4. *Expand your interests* by developing hobbies—gardening, farming, or anything that you can use later when you are done in the office or the shop.

Instead of retiring, start a little trade or a little business, be it ever so small. Get your mind active in new fields; go to night school, take a correspondence course in some new subject. Get acquainted with books.

5. Since you are going to be old some day, *start making people see the problems of the aged* as realistically as you do —they are going to get there too. Above all, help turn sentiment against the type of county old-age homes that are being built in so many states. These are poor solutions to the problems of the aged and the very fact of their existence will, in years to come, forestall a better answer. Throw your opinion and your efforts toward the establishment of the San Francisco-type of home for the aged, which is a community plan on a community scope. These obviously cannot be built by most counties. They will have to be built at the state or Federal level.

If you are already aged:

1. Cooperate with the inevitable and accept gratefully whatever fate may bring.

2. Whenever an old friend departs, seek a new one; life is as empty or full as you make it.

3. Try to be flexible and adaptable in your thinking; avoid prejudice; don't criticize youth for being as they are.

4. Dress neatly; sew up the holes in the old garments very carefully. Retain good, clean manners.

5. Do not dawdle; pursue interests as though you meant business.

6. Above all, keep the disposition pleasant and cheerful. Greet people with a smile and a kind word. Don't gripe except when no one else can hear you, and when you can't hear yourself.

7. Never let yourself know how tired you are. Just sit down for a while, telling yourself that doing so was what you had in mind, anyway.

8. Don't worry about dying. Everyone who lived before you stood it.

A SUMMARY OF CHAPTER 13

Instead of being a Golden Age, the sixties, the seventies, and eighties are an age of increased emotional stress owing to financial insecurity, job insecurity, children's indifference, the fear of ill health, fear of death, the loss of friends, poor housing, and general public indifference. Much of what is regarded as senile degenerative disease is actually emotionally induced illness, in which STH factors are prominent.

If you are young, prepare for age by developing emotional stasis, that is to say, a happy disposition—NOW. Plan future finances and a place to live when you are old. Develop new active interests, against the time when your job runs out.

If you are already aged, you can produce contentment inside, even if there isn't any reason for it outside. Cooperate with the inevitable; find a new friend when an old one leaves. Stay flexible and adaptable in your thinking. Do not criticize youth. Dress neatly. Keep that disposition pleasant; greet people with a smile. Sit down when you must, but don't let yourself know how tired you are. And as for death—didn't everyone before you stand it?

14.

THE FULFILLMENT OF
YOUR SIX BASIC NEEDS

There are some people with E. I. I. who are unaware of any emotions that might be responsible for their illness. These people frequently have fundamental emotions of a wrong variety because their *basic psychological needs* are not being filled.

The ordinary human being, like you and me, has six basic instinctive needs—six psychological WANTS—things that he feels deeply inside himself he must have. If one of these needs is not filled, a deep-seated restlessness is produced, a vague unrequited longing, and an undercurrent of disappointment that colors every minute of the day and night.

Such an individual may be adapting himself very well, otherwise, to his environment, managing to put up a cheerful pleasant front; but deep down inside, there is a great gnawing longing because one or more of his psychological needs is only an empty yawning sore of misery.

1. THE FIRST OF THESE BASIC NEEDS IS THE NEED FOR LOVE

Everyone (even the person who seems to hate everybody else) has an inner desire and need for love—he wants to receive the affection and high regard of at least one other human being. Receiving such affection makes us feel important and valuable; it makes us feel that we have a place in the order of people and things.

The proper fulfillment of this need adds a glow of warmth, richness, and beauty to what is otherwise very dull living. If there is no love from anyone, no high regard from a single other soul, a deep vacuum is made in a person into which are sucked the emotions of distress, longing, lonesomeness, and, eventually, social hostility. And these unhealthy emotions are present constantly, day and night, tainting the fundamental background of living.

This lack may begin in childhood. There are many unfortunate people who feel the sting of the lack of affection from early childhood on, because they have the bad luck to have been born into a family where real affection simply does not exist. Mother and father wage a continual cold war against each other, with periods when the war gets pretty hot and the air is filled with angry words, with, perhaps, a dish or two for punctuation. What they can't take out on each other, the parents take out on the children.

The children, learning by imitation, imagine that constant bickering, quarreling, spite, and hatred are the stuff that all life is made of; so sisters and brothers return blow for blow. Everyone feels alone, hunted, exploited, uncomfortable, and on the defensive. These boys and girls may get quite old, or may go all the way through life, without ever getting the idea that there is such a thing as affection, or that there are human beings capable of it. But the psychological need for it is present, and these people have a restlessness, and a yearning, for something they haven't got. Basically, they are very unhappy.

The odd and tragic thing is that they don't consciously realize it and, of course, they don't know that it is lack of affection that underlies their restlessness.

This sort of thing isn't at all uncommon. It often shows its effects (which are functional disease and gross unhappiness) in some of the best families.

Verna was a beautiful girl whose mother died when she was a baby. Her father, who showed very little affection for her at any time, put the girl in an orphanage where she found more abuse and psychological torment than affection. At the age of 15, she met Eugene, an only child and a wealthy boy, with a very protective and selfish mother.

Eugene was captivated more by Verna's sexual attractiveness than anything else, and for the first (and only) time in his life, he did something his mother did not want him to do —he eloped with Verna. Verna had received no affection in the orphanage and she received less as the wife of Eugene. Eugene was too selfish, too self-centered and dependent on his mother to be capable of affection for Verna. Eugene's mother, who always lived just a few blocks away, resented Verna's position with her son and did her best to hold Eugene and turn him against Verna in every way she could.

For years this went on. When children came, the mother worked on them to turn them against Verna; in this she succeeded to the point where a 16-year-old daughter repeatedly told Verna, "I hate you!" The need for affection wasn't the only need that went empty in Verna; some of the others that we are going to talk about, likewise, were empty gulfs of despair. Verna experienced years of functional disease which grew gradually to the point of complete disability. When the cause of her illness was explained to a much-doubting husband and mother-in-law, they went through the outward appearance of affection. But wise Verna sensed this as a sham. The only thing that could have altered the situation would have been for Verna to start life all over. It was only with great difficulty and self-discipline that Verna began to feel a sense of value in the returned good-will of other people when she went into Red Cross work on an all-out scale.

Even worse than Verna's situation is the situation of a girl who has been brought up in an affectionate family atmosphere and then finds herself married to a man who is capable of about as much affection as a cold blob of cottage cheese. These husbands (and there are a lot of them) forget their wives are human beings with human wants and feelings.

These chaps have little idea that there are such things as human wants and feelings—outside their own. They have a childhood arrest in certain essential compartments of their personalities. If they are capable of any affection, they never show their wives the capacity. After all, it would be easy for the big lugs to show the little woman some affection in many little ways every day. A hug, a kiss, a pleasantry, a compliment on her appearance, or an appreciation of a meal, would put a few blooms in the arid desert that such a woman, unfortunately, inhabits.

It finally serves the big fool right when he has to pay a long, hard medical bill for functional illness of which he is the cause. But this, too, he turns against the wife, blaming her for the sickness his immature stupidity produced. Men like this are one of the big reasons for functional illness in married women.

Sexual love is basically important. The thing we call love, the kind of thing we mean by affection, is a complex thing composed of various parts, and part of this basic need for love is the basic need for sexual love. In any marriage, conjugal affection is intimately bound with sexual affection. A marriage can seldom be unified, affectionate, and mutually satisfactory if the sexual experience between the partners is not unified, affectionate, and mutually satisfactory.

If, for one reason or another, sexual love never develops in a marriage, or fades away and disappears, one or both of the married couple becomes restless, dissatisfied, grumbly, irritable, and complaining. The functional disease produced by this kind of a situation is often hard to treat because the patient would rather not tell about the trouble; consequently it can never be remedied. Sometimes this kind of trouble is hard to remedy anyway. But this type of trouble produces some very odd results.

For instance, Mrs. T——— had a severe fibrositis of the lower back, to severe that she went to many clinics and many hospitals. The usual treatment did her very little good.

Mrs. T——— was a career woman. Both she and her husband held important and responsible positions that took precedence over their home life. After their day's work, they came to a home (managed by a housekeeper) used only for meals or for social entertainment. Their sexual life gradually grew thinner and more disinterested, partly because of Mrs. T———'s tendency to deprecate sexuality in favor of her career, and finally because Mr. T——— found more satisfaction in a secret mistress.

At first the decreasing sexual atmosphere of their marriage was welcomed by Mrs. T———. Then she developed fibrositis, which on the surface had nothing to do with Mrs. T———'s womanliness. But then she, too, was catapulted into the arms of a lover, and for the first time in her life experienced sexual satisfaction. The remarkable thing was that her fibrositis disappeared *at once*.

Because of her career position, and also because of a profound feeling of guilt, Mrs. T——— periodically tried to deny herself to her lover. With each of these episodes, the fibrositis returned, only to disappear when this illicit love was allowed again into her life.

In many other ways, sexual incompatibility or unhappiness in marriage is the primary cause of functional disease in husband or wife, or both.

The old people must be loved, too. A group of people who commonly suffer from the need of love and affection are the aged, who must walk more and more alone as those whom they loved, and those who loved them, are taken away by the robber, death. An old man loses his wife, the only person who showed him affection, and finds in her place a daughter-in-law, who shows him in many little open or half-hidden ways that he belongs in the category of a "necessary-care which-we-will-have-to-tolerate." And so the last of life, for which the first was made, becomes a toasting on a spit turned by a mean wench, assisted by her children, silently aided by the unfeeling attitude of the man's own son. A great deal of what in older people appears superficially to be degenerative disease characteristic of old age is in fact functional disease, the result of the lonesomeness, futility, despair, and sadness that have become the closest companions of their nights and days.

2. YOUR SECOND BASIC NEED IS THE NEED FOR SECURITY

Freud said that man wants most of all to be loved. Adler, that he wants most of all to be significant. Jung, that he wants security. All three are valid; man is complex and needs many things.

You feel secure if—and only if—there is enough income to buy at least the necessities of life now and in years to come, if your right to life is protected from irresponsible fiends and egomaniacal tyrants by a just government, if you are relatively sure that you will not be struck down by a devastating disease or catastrophe, if you have about you people you know will help you through a deal of trouble.

Because *complete* security is an impossible thing, many worry warts defeat an otherwise secure state by worrying over the insecurity of security. They worry about cancer, and experience, thereby, more agony than death, again and again. To them, government policies spell their certain ruin 30 years hence. They are sure that disaster, in one of its endless forms, is always around the corner.

Such people, of course, never know a feeling of security. Because of continual insecurity, they lead miserable lives, mentally and physically. They became racked with functional disease. The trouble with people like these is obvious; they are always worrying right out in plain sight before the entire world.

But many people who *are* in insecure positions never show it outwardly, and very often even minimize their insecurity to themselves. Yet down beneath the surface of moment-to-moment emotions, they have a deep feeling of insecurity, felt through its physical manifestations.

An executive may feel an insecurity in regard to his position because capable younger men are coming up and pushing at his heels. A man may feel insecure about life itself— the boy in battle, the Jew in Nazi Germany, the anti-communist in Soviet Russia. There may be the insecurity felt by a woman whose husband wants a divorce. There may be the insecurity felt by the boy who is the target of bullies in a boarding school. There is the insecurity felt by a man in any kind of a serious jam.

There are hundreds or, perhaps, thousands of varieties of insecurity this world can concoct for those who live in it. Even though we keep them in the background of our thinking, these insecurities can become the type of monotonous repetitions of unpleasant emotions that lead to functional disease.

One of the common ingredients that people discover in old age is a feeling of insecurity. They need to fear ill health, particularly disabling illness. Many need to fear financial insecurity. Many feel insecure as to what the end of life may bring them. There is the inevitable feeling of insecurity at losing loved ones whom they depended upon for certain assistance and qualities of life.

So, to a lack of affection many aged people must add lack of security. At the time when life should be gentle and kind, it becomes cruel and forbidding. When the race is nearing the end and a fellow is coming down the homestretch, there should be the cheering of the audience along the way; instead there is the jeering of the insensitive, and the interrogation of the welfare department.

The types of emotion that these situations saddle upon the elderly persons are those emotions that stress the pituitary production of STH. The chronic STH effects are essentially those of degeneration of the kidneys, the arteries, and the organs, in general, as you saw in Chapter 4. Thus it is that degenerative changes are accelerated by the old person's adverse situations. If the type of emotion in such individuals is changed by fulfilling the basic needs in which they have been deficient, such as the needs for love and security, the processes of degeneration are reversed to such a degree that the individual seems to become years younger.

Many families are made to feel the pangs of insecurity because of a nonsupporting husband; whether the lack of support stems from alcoholism, laziness, or bad luck alters only the intensity of the emotions, not their essential color. The impending loss of home, property, and prestige adds up to headaches, disturbances of the gastrointestinal system, and a host of other functional effects.

3. THE THIRD BASIC NEED IS THE NEED FOR CREATIVE EXPRESSION

The child building with blocks, the housewife making a set of curtains, the financier planning a new holding corporation, the girl writing poetry, the carpenter building a house —all have the very satisfying feeling that out of raw materials they are creating something new.

No one, including you and me, has fundamental happiness if he is not being constructive either in his leisure hours or in his work. It is natural for everyone to identify himself with the world of human beings and to feel that he is assuming a part in that world. The universal urge toward creative expression is a vague kind of restlessness that becomes more and more unpleasant and disturbing if it is not put into action. But when it is put into action, there is the accompanying thrill—a sort of mental breathlessness, and an inward joy of *doing* and *creating*.

Creative activity must not be thwarted. There is probably no frustration greater than a thwarted person with an intense desire for major creation. There was Ethel, for instance, whom I saw because of a functional illness she developed because her desire for creation was nipped in the bud by an unthinking family.

Ethel married Roger. They were both fine people with excellent families behind them. Through high school and college, Ethel had built up plans of the kind of home and the kind of family she wanted to raise. At the time of their marriage, economic conditions in the country were bad, and Roger's parents invited the newlyweds to live on the first floor of their own home. They moved to the second floor. Ethel's mother-in-law was a considerate, kind individual who wished to be tactful and kind to Ethel. She cautiously and carefully suggested to Ethel that she might do a certain thing in such and such a way. Ethel was truly grateful for the tip and followed the suggestion. The mother-in-law was encouraged, by Ethel's enthusiasm, to make more suggestions.

As Ethel's children came, the mother-in-law took a more and more active hand. Ethel had an inner, unexpressed feeling that she had in fact become a member of Roger's family and was rearing no new family, was creating no home of her own. Her dreams were dissolving into nothing. Worse still, she couldn't get out of her predicament without being rude in the extreme and making life miserable for all of them. Ethel grew gradually more frustrated and began more and more to suffer ill health. This was an additional indication to the mother-in-law that her help was needed. The mother-in-law was, in fact, the mother of both families; Ethel was a dependent child. And Ethel became quite ill.

Because Roger and his parents were intelligent people, the

doctor could at last make them see Ethel's predicament; they could be shown that Ethel needed above all to be the Ethel she had always hoped to be; she needed to be allowed to create her own home and her own family. Ethel and Roger moved away by themselves in a new home they planned together. Ethel recovered.

There are many people just as deeply upset, just as frustrated as Ethel, because they have been unable to follow an urge to do or to create certain things, an urge they may have felt since childhood. These people may appear to be cheerful people on the surface, but the deeper color of their emotions is anything but happy—their thwarted drives end in restless, unrequited yearning, anxiety, discouragement, and finally, perhaps, a loss of self-esteem.

4. THE FOURTH NEED IS THE NEED FOR RECOGNITION

There is in everyone the need to feel that he and his efforts are being appreciated—appreciated by those for whom we strive.

Everyone needs to be regarded by *someone* as being of *some* importance, and doing *something* that is of *some* good.

It often happens that a man may leave a perfectly good position because he feels that his efforts are not being properly appreciated. He resents the fact that although he worked above the call of duty and did an extraordinarily good job, none of his superiors or equals showed any indication of having recognized it. His need for recognition is given a severe blow. He leaves.

The unthanked home-maker. But consider the housewife. Actually, from a standpoint of sheer dreariness and the amount of time spent on the job, she has the toughest job there is. But most of our housewives never receive a word of recognition from one year's end to the other. They, and their washing and ironing, come to be taken as a matter of course by their husbands and children. The meals are accepted in the same silent air of "after all, we have this coming." Everyone assumes that the house cleans itself, that the things they drop pick themselves up, that clean clothes get into the closets automatically, that the comforts of home just naturally exist without anyone's skillful touch.

This lack of recognition for a difficult job, this thanklessness, goes a long way to make homemaking the world's toughest job. The husband quits his job because of lack of recognition, but the housewife doesn't quit hers. But she feels all the more keenly the disappointment at the lack of recognition. Much of the tiredness that goes with constant housework rises directly out of the lack of recognition the housewife receives. Her tiredness is the tiredness of a human being who is being relegated to the position of a lifeless, meaningless drudge.

The unthanked oldster. Again in old age, there is this matter of lack of recognition.

Most of the recognition for his work, or recognition of him as an individual, goes out of an older person's life with the death of his friends. An important element in what we mean by friendship is the trading of mutual recognition. A man who has no friends can fill his need for recognition only by sheer capacity, and that avenue is no longer open to the elder who is denied a job at his old trade. The people who remain surrounding the elder regard age as incapacity, and generally do not regard the old as worthy of respect because they are old. Especially when he is poor, the elder is regarded as a social inconvenience. If he is rich, he becomes an exploitable opportunity. In place of recognition, the aged person is treated as a failure, a burned-out being who is about to be flicked away. A person who lived courageously and well, whose earlier actions benefited the younger generation who are now critical, is often ushered out coldly and unsympathetically, under a hail of spiritual, if not physical, stones. Gone the recognition; gone the acclaim; just an old man no one really wants. Such a crying need of recognition brings emotions that hasten the end.

Appreciate your child, but don't spoil him. At the beginning of life, too, recognition is important—just as important as love. The intelligent, advanced child is apt to be showered with too much recognition—he may be buried in it so that he can never get his head out into the clear and really evaluate himself for what he is, and forever after he lives under the handicap of too high an opinion of himself.

On the other hand, the slow and awkward child's feeling of recognition may be very negligible. He tries in his halting imperfect way to do something that might bring a bit of the recognition which he, like everyone else, longs for. But instead, the reactions of those around him make him feel that his efforts belong in the failure class. He feels that he does not measure up to his brothers or sisters. All the attention he receives is on the disciplinary level. Compliments rarely come his way. He develops an increasing sense of incompetence. The important element of self-esteem gradually leaves him, perhaps never to return. He is always miserable and restless. He may seek even the kind of recognition that the doer of bad deeds receives. He becomes a lost cause because his need for recognition is a lost cause.

5. The Fifth Need Is the Need for New Experiences

A human being cannot be kept in a dull monotonous routine without developing a monotonous repetition of unpleasant emotions, and functional disease with it. Any kind of a job, long continued, carries with it a certain amount of monotony. But the most monotonous job can be made bearable by the thought of a new experience that lies ahead. As one housewife said, "I'd scream if I didn't have that trip to the Black Hills next month to look forward to."

It's an emotionally bad day that starts without the hope or expectancy of a single lift. Even a trip to the meat market might be called a lift; so might an airy conversation, or an interesting person.

Here again the housewife is decidedly in a more unfortunate position. The average day offers more variations and opportunities for new experiences for the male of the species. He goes outside the house and outside the neighborhood to work, meets and talks to people, and his work itself may hold interesting variations. These ready opportunities for new experiences are not available to his wife.

Probably the best example I have seen of how a dearth of new experiences can produce severe functional disease was Mrs. S———. She was only 26 when I first saw her. She was staying with her mother because she had been sick abed almost three months. Whenever Mrs. S——— tried to get up, she became so dizzy and faint she had to go back to bed. She was obviously hyperventilating. I remember when the call first came to see her. I was occupied, and I sent a fourth-year medical student who was a preceptee in my office.

He returned all aglow. "Oh, boy, do I have a dandy hyperventilator for your clinic!" The lad was a smart student. The several doctors, who up to that time had cared for Mrs. S———, had labeled her illness variously as "anemia," "female trouble," and even "heart disease," so that, in addition to being discouraged, she was also confused.

Since childhood, Mrs. S——— had been an eminently normal sort of person—which means also that she had the normal fulfillment of her basic needs. She married during World War II and soon had two children. When her husband left the Army, he took a job trucking bread from a central distributing station to outlying towns. He left home at two o'clock in the morning and got back at noon. Houses were at a premium but they finally found one that had the advantage of a low rent. The house was six miles from the nearest town, a desolate, dull-green house, set on a desolate, rocky, treeless hilltop. There, in that dismally awful setting, with no neighbors, with only shabby, poorly furnished rooms, Mrs. S——— tried hard and desperately to make a livable home and bring up the children in a happy frame of mind.

Because of the husband's need for sleep, and because of the small children, the couple found it impossible to go out evenings. Besides, there was nothing convenient to go to. After her husband left in the wee early hours, Mrs. S——— felt afraid to be alone with the children in that desolate place. A restless, questionable watch dog offered poor solace. The brown, weathered rocks outside added a dismal dreary note during the day.

Had the husband had a dime's worth of understanding, five cents' worth of sympathy, and two cents' worth of good intentions, he might have sensed what the situation meant for his wife. He made *his* bread rounds, joked with the other truckers and workmen, *saw* things and *did* things. Mrs. S——— couldn't even leave the place because Mr. S——— had to take the car to work.

He was surprised and disgruntled as his wife became increasingly more complaining and sick. Her increasingly long stays with her mother he regarded as depriving him of a home he was rightfully entitled to. He criticized her for the medical expense she was creating. Finally, after the medical student had discovered Mrs. S———'s true illness, Mr. S——— thought the doctor's explanation was an unrealistic figment of the imagination.

But later on, Mr. S——— did develop more of an appreciation for his wife's needs when he found that after treatment she was again a functionally valuable housewife who could get his meals and wash his clothes. She improved even more after he had moved her to a nice little place in an attractive little town where she had a tree in the yard, pleasant neighbors, and a sandbox for the children. It was little enough.

But, as I said, Mrs. S——— was a normal person—she had a good power of adjustment. It had been the utter impossibility of new experiences (which a sensitive, life-

172

loving girl like Mrs. S——— needs) plus, of course, the lack of security, the absence of affection, and the depressing effects of that awful environment, that had tossed her into bed for three long months. But now she is doing fine.

6. THE SIXTH BASIC NEED IS SELF-ESTEEM

In spite of disappointments, in spite of the little or big personal failures that a person experiences through life, most everyone, nevertheless, manages to think sufficiently well of himself to be encouraged to go ahead. His actual capacities may be ever so minute, his deficiencies may (to others) far overshadow his insignificant good qualities, but he himself is able to find some field for personal satisfaction—at least a rebuttal against criticism, supporting it with an injustice complex.

A person who is fired from a job he thought he was holding down well, or a person who is "told off" by someone whose good will he assumed, or a person who loses, by some catastrophe, all he has been working for, feels afterward as though there were nothing left, he feels the utter emptiness of failure; he is done up. But after a little time, his assurance, his feeling that he is worth something after all, gradually returns, and though it may be nicked and chipped a bit, his self-esteem is back. He hardly notices the nicks.

But there are many people who lose *every* vestige of self-esteem; they look upon themselves as failures in every respect; there is nothing more to do or to try. They feel they have no place in the world, no worth, no importance, no ability, no judgment, no future, no past except guilt and failure. There is no bottom to the despair these people feel. They are the most miserable, the sickest, and the most deplorable of all human beings. Such a condition in which *all* self-esteem is gone is called a depressive state. The sheer hopelessness of it all, hour after hour, may finally bring a fling of desperate bravado; this is known as a *manic-depressive state*.

Two types of person prone to depression. Two types of people are most apt to lose their self-esteem and have depressive states. One type is the person with a great abundance of self-confidence and esteem without much in the way of abilities to back it up. The other is the person who starts out with a strong inferiority complex in youth, never rises above it, and finally succumbs to a series of failures.

Depressions can occur anytime during life, but are most

common after middle life, about the time when one looks back and recoils from the obvious fact that one's accomplishments and achievements have nowhere measured up to early plans and hopes. This alone will not bring on the depression, but if there is added a set-back or two, preventable or unpreventable, what is left of self-esteem begins to vaporize.

John Doe was always a confident fellow who bragged rather easily. He was always ready to criticize the other fellow's political or religious views and "set him straight." This made him somewhat of an irritation in any office, particularly to the boss whose abilities John Doe regarded as far lower than his. At forty, John Doe stormed out of the office one day. He had quit! What was more, he had put the boss in his place. Work at that time was easy to get, and J. D. joined a much larger company where he figured his abilities would be recognized and amply rewarded.

But he was never advanced. His politics grew very nasty. He began to be sharp to everyone and anyone. And one day, when he was 56, he was calmly told his services were no longer necessary. This time a job was much harder to find, and before he found one, he became truly alarmed that possibly another job was not to be had. He was on his new job only two months when he was laid off. His wife, who had never been too easy to live with, berated him day and night.

John was at last completely flattened out. All that he thought he was, he now recognized as a mistake; everything he had prided himself on was now a delusion; the things he had always dreamed of being and doing had melted away. The only future lay with the welfare department. John Doe went into a severe depression and was institutionalized at the expense of the state.

There are all sorts of variations on that theme. Sometimes the failure of the individual is unquestionable, but sometimes the failure is not nearly so great as the victim imagines it is.

What happens in either case is that the person does not have enough self-confidence to go on or to do anything. He is in a state of being personally whipped.

The loss of this sixth psychological need has more immediate and apparent effects than does the lack of any of the other basic needs. The others lead eventually to an agitated feeling of vague anxiety and unrest. The loss of self-esteem is characterized by the depressive state.

Gradually the feeling of complete failure wears off, and

after months or years, the person again acquires enough self-esteem to become useful to himself and others.

If a person who is developing a depression can put into action the program of conscious thought-control, which we are outlining in these chapters, he can avert his depression. Once a classical depression has developed, there are only two things that can be done to help the patient: take care of him and wait until the depression wears off naturally, or give the patient electroshock therapy, which snaps him out of it in two or three weeks. The alternative to this is, of course, to exercise conscious thought-control and keep yourself out of a dangerous depression.

What to Do About Your Basic Needs

Review for yourself the presence or absence in your life of these six basic psychological needs. Ask yourself: *Do I in my private world:*

1. *Receive the* love *of others, or am I a lone, unwanted individual;*

2. *Have* security, *or am I afraid of my finances, my job, my social status, my legal status;*

3. *Exercise* creative expression *in my work, in my hobbies, or in any other way;*

4. *Receive the* recognition *of any of my fellow men;*

5. *Have the possibility of* new experiences, *or am I an old fossil in a deep rut;*

6. *Have my own* self-esteem, *or am I going down in my own estimation?*

You might as well be frank, candid, and objective in your answers—it is yourself you are dealing with.

1. If you are situated somewhat like Verna, and there is no one in your world who really cares a penny's worth about you, the best compensation is to give *your love* to those about you, and do for them as you would like to be done by. Part of maturity, you will remember, is to have the giving rather than the receiving attitude. It becomes a great satisfaction to love and do good for the people around you who do not deserve or expect it.

175

2. If it's *security* you lack, decide what you are going to do about it and then quit turning it over and over in your mind. If you cannot do anything to increase your security, there is no use adding worry to it; it's already bad enough. Remember how William, King of Living, handled insecurity? You might re-read Chapter 8.

3. If it's *creative expression* you lack; if you feel you are not making or creating *anything*, that you are just a machine for menial chores, get busy and don't let it eat you any longer. Try doing something you have always hankered to do; try it on your own; or go to the nearest vocational school and pick up a creative art. You might as well start to live!

4. If it's *recognition* that you yearn for, quit yearning; accept the compensation of knowing that you are doing as good a job *for other people* as you possibly can. Give them the recognition instead.

It could be, madam, that if your husband reads this the big goof might give you a little recognition tomorrow by saying, "It is a wonderfully good dinner, my darling!" It would feel good, wouldn't it? But even if you get no recognition from him, you tell him, "You look fine and nice this morning, Fred! I've got a swell-looking man!" He'll like that, and your recognition of him will help you almost as much. Maybe someday he'll give some of it back.

5. If you've become a drudge, caught tight in dull routine, by all means, bust out into some *new experience*. You should be looking ahead and *planning a new experience all the time*. Buy something; do something, something exciting; join something; go somewhere. Off with you, this minute, into planning a new experience!

6. If your *self-esteem* has been jolted lately, smooth yourself with humility. Don't try to be, don't think yourself as being, too much. Just an ordinary person. There have been lots of them—many more of that kind than any other. Lincoln was a plain person, with humility, just like you. Then smile! Put conscious thought control into action to substitute equanimity, courage, determination, and cheerfulness for those stress emotions of failure, disappointment, futility. You are just as good as I am; and we are just as good as they are, God bless them!

There are six basic psychological needs in every person. If a person lacks any one of them in his life, he will be basically unhappy, tense, and restless without knowing why. These needs are the need for *affection, security, creative expression, recognition, new experiences,* and *self-esteem.*

If you lack love and affection from others—
Give more than your share of love and affection to others.

If you lack security—
There is no use adding worry to a bad situation; run the emotionally healthy flags up on your masthead.

If you lack creative expression—
Go to it, nothing is holding you.

If you lack recognition—
Give recognition to other people instead; some of it will come back.

If you lack new experiences—
Go out and get them; be planning something all the time.

If you have lost your self-esteem—
Remember this: you are just as good as I am, you and I are just as good as they are, God bless them.

HERE IS YOUR
FINAL BLUEPRINT

THE CHOICE IS YOURS

Practice thought control. When you catch yourself starting a thought that will produce a stressing emotion like worry, anxiety, fear, apprehension, discouragement, or the like, STOP IT, and substitute thinking that brings a healthy emotion, like equanimity, resignation, courage, determination, and cheerfulness.

KEEP THIS ALWAYS IN MIND:

The key thought: Carry this idea every minute of every day: *I am going to keep my attitude and thinking calm and cheerful*—RIGHT NOW.

HANDLE LIFE THIS WAY:

When the going is good: Tell yourself life is good, and allow yourself the delightful feeling of being happy.

When the going gets rough: 1. Stay outwardly as cheerful and as pleasant as you possibly can. Lighten an awkward situation with a lift of humor, with kindness, or a bit of a smile.

2. Avoid running your misfortune through your mind like a repeating phonograph record. Above all, do not let yourself get irritated, upset, hysterical, or self-pitying.

3. Try to turn every defeat into a moral victory.

4. Run these flags up on your masthead and *keep them flying:*

> *Equanimity ("Let's stay calm.")*
> *Resignation ("Let's accept this setback gracefully.")*
> *Courage ("I can take all this and more.")*
> *Determination ("I'll turn this defeat into victory.")*
> *Cheerfulness ("See, I'm coming up.")*

(2)

Pleasantness ("I still have good will toward men.")

IMPORTANT AREAS IN LIVING TO WATCH
Keep life simple.
Avoid watching for a knock in your motor.
Like work.
Have a good hobby.
Learn to be satisfied.
Like people.
Say the cheerful, pleasant thing.
Turn the defeats of adversity into victory.
Meet your problems with decision.
Concentrate on making the present moment an emotional success.
Always be planning something.
Say "Nuts" to irritations.

MAKE YOUR FAMILY AN ASSET RATHER THAN A LIABILITY
Put These Things into the Family:
Simplicity in living, and simplicity in enjoyment.
The idea of the family enterprise.
The idea that the family is part of the human enterprise.
The attitude of turning defeat into victory.
An atmosphere of affection, mutual respect and regard.
A general tone of kindly cheerfulness.
Reasonable, firm, yet pleasant discipline.
A feeling of mutual confidence and security.
An atmosphere of enjoyment—right now.

CONTROL YOUR SEX URGE RATHER THAN HAVING IT CONTROL YOU

If you are unmarried: Sublimate your energies into interesting, absorbing, and vigorous activities, and develop your general maturity.

If you are married: Every relation between you and your wife, or husband, and this includes the sexual relation, needs to be mature, that is to say, sympathetic, understanding, unselfish, cooperative, and affectionate.

In any case: Be content to keep sexuality within the accepted bounds. It is easier to stay out of trouble than to get out of it once you get into it.

FILL UP YOUR OWN UNFULFILLED BASIC NEEDS
Here Is How:
If you lack love and affection from others—

Give more than your share of love and affection to other human beings.
If you lack security—
There is no use adding worry to a bad situation; run the emotionally healthy flags up on your masthead.
If you lack creative expression—
Go to it, nothing is holding you.
If you lack recognition—
Give recognition to other people instead; some of it will come back.
If you need new experiences—
Go and get them; be planning something all the time.
If you have lost your self-esteem—
Remember this: you are just as good as I am; you and I are just as good as they are, God bless them.

THIS BLUEPRINT LEADS TO MATURITY

By following the blueprint (and the choice is yours) you will be developing maturity and emotional basis.
Maturity Is This:

Responsibility and independence, instead of dependence.

A giving rather than a receiving attitude.

Cooperativeness and a feeling for the human enterprise, instead of egoism and competitiveness.

Gentleness, kindliness, and good-will, instead of hostile aggressiveness, anger, hate, cruelty, and belligerence.

The ability to distinguish fact from fancy.

Flexibility and adaptability, instead of awkward and stubborn resistance to changes dictated by fate, fortune, and intelligence.

GOOD LIVING IS YOURS

If you are going to limp through year after year of anxious, troubled misery, 100 years, or 75, or even 50, is an interminable hell on earth; the shorter life is, under such conditions, the better; none at all would be best.

But once you learn the trick of striding along, eyes calm with equanimity; head up with determination; chest out with courage; a pleasant word for fellow-travelers, and resignation on meeting rocky rough roads, your years will beg repetition, and your living will be a fascinating enterprise that you would welcome for a hundred years.

The choice of whether to limp or to stride is yours— RIGHT NOW.

A WORD TO THE PROFESSIONAL READER

The physician who prescribes this book for his patient, or the teacher who is interested in "total" education, may wish to know more about the psychological concepts underlying my method of treating emotionally induced illness.

THE BASIC PSYCHOLOGICAL CONCEPT IN THE METHOD

The basic psychological concept of the method of treatment presented in this book is the *learning-maturity concept*. Simply stated, this means that emotional stress is the result of miseducation, or lack of proper education, and that emotional stasis can be achieved by *learning* the qualities that comprise *maturity*. Stress is bound to arise in an immature person because he is trying to handle adult situations and problems with primitive and childish techniques. The learning-maturity concept has gradually been emerging from the constantly boiling cauldron of psychiatric and psychological thinking. This concept is the direct antithesis of Freudian psychiatry, which has been oriented by the concept that emotional stress is conditioned early in life by an unacceptable experience that is relegated to the dusky murkiness of the subconscious, where it preys on the host forevermore.

The learning-maturity concept further implies that the treatment of emotional stress consists in showing the patient precisely what maturity means in the handling of everyday living, and then showing him a practical discipline for carrying on his living with a passable degree of maturity.

In contrast, the therapy of traditional psychiatry consists quite largely of digging into the personal history and the half-buried past, a very interesting though, in my opinion, not a very fruitful method of treatment. It does afford the therapist an excellent idea of the particular variety of immaturity a patient has, but this is a matter which can be determined fairly readily, without hours spent on a psychiatric couch. Being interested mainly in the past, the traditional psychiatrist often prefers to do very little about the present or the future.

The learning-maturity concept, on the other hand, insists that, regardless of the omissions and commissions of the past, a person has to *start in the present* to acquire some maturity so that the future may be better than the past. The present and the future depend on learning new habits and new ways of looking at old problems. There simply isn't any future in digging continually into the past.

Instead of recreating the past, as does the conditioning concept, the learning-maturity concept emphasizes an improved approach for the present and future.

THE COMMON DENOMINATOR IN EMOTIONALLY INDUCED ILLNESS

The starting point in the treatment of E. I. I. becomes simple and clear when one realizes that the underlying emotional problem has the same common denominator in every patient. This common denominator is that the patient has forgotten how, or probably never learned how, to control his *present* thinking to produce *enjoyment*. Constant fear, anxiety, apprehension, irritation, frustration, and discouragement absolutely preclude the possibility of enjoyment. Emotional stress can be helped *only by learning* to react to situations RIGHT NOW with equanimity, courage, determination, and cheerfulness. The person who learns to handle the majority of life situations with equanimity, courage, determination, and cheerfulness has taken a long step into maturity. Beyond this step there remains the development of unselfish cooperativeness and good judgment to make maturity fairly complete. My method of therapy places the patient on the enjoyment principle by a conditioned reflex through conscious thought control, by substituting equanimity, courage, determination, and cheerfulness, whenever anxiety, apprehension, and so on, begin to make their appearances. This substitution is done by conscious thought control until habit can eventually take over. Such substitution is what people with emotional stasis are doing habitually all the time.

THE PRACTICAL APPLICATION OF THE COMMON DENOMINATOR AND THE LEARNING-MATURITY CONCEPT

The point of greatest practical difference between the traditional adequate psychotherapy and the learning-maturity method is this: adequate psychotherapy requires hours and hours of the doctor's time and can, therefore, be used only on an extremely small fraction of patients who need therapy; the learning-maturity method can be applied in ways that require practically none of the doctor's time.

How can the learning-maturity method be applied without hours of the doctor's time?

First, because maturity in one person is the same thing as maturity in another person, and second, because there is the same common denominator in every person with emotionally induced illness, the course and procedure of therapy *is the same in every patient,* regardless of how their problems may differ in detail.

The essential thing to show patients is how they may henceforth meet the ordinary life situations with maturity and emotional stasis, and how they may introduce enjoyment into the present moment. This can be done in the same way for everyone. Therapy for emotionally induced illness can be standardized to a single pattern and yet help practically 100-per cent of the patients. If one can develop a system of instruction that will help *one* patient develop maturity and emotional stasis, the same system would work for almost any other patient. For the past 20 years I have tried various methods and various techniques, working always with this requirement in mind: *Because there are so many patients with E. I. I., the doctor must have a method that does not require much of his time.* I submit that *unless a method meets this criterion, it is useless in medical practice.*

One method that at first seemed to promise well was group therapy. Ten, 25, 50, even 75 patients would meet periodically for orientation lectures, followed by general group discussion. But this grew to a point where I was spending three hours every night with such groups. This was not saving the doctor's time and it was a grueling program!

The results of group therapy were encouraging, but not too satisfactory. Much still remained to be given the patient in private sessions. After several false starts with sound alone, I finally tried an audiovisual demonstration, using wire recordings, and later tape recordings, coupled with colored slides projected on a screen. Almost at once patient response indicated that this was it!

The method was perfected so that one patient, and his spouse, could receive instruction in private. What this method lacked by not having the doctor talking directly to the patient was more than compensated by the thoughtful care that could go into the preparation of a tape recording far superior to an off-the-cuff lecture, plus the additional interest of slides on a screen giving point and interest to the demonstration. The doctor saw the patient briefly before and after each audiovisual demonstration.

Here was a method which worked during the day while the doctor was attending his other patients. Bit by bit the audiovisual demonstrations were pieced together, changed here and altered there, until they developed a hitting power that far exceeded the group therapy sessions. The present demonstrations can admittedly be vastly improved upon, and, indeed, they are constantly being added to and changed.

The audiovisual sessions are attended by the patient and his spouse at weekly intervals. He sees the doctor for a period of five minutes before and after each session, so that the doctor may make certain that the patient is being suitably oriented. The tape recordings present essentially the same material contained in this book, greatly augmented by the visual aid of the screen projections.

During the past six years, thousands of patients have attended these therapeutic sessions. The majority have either been cured of their ailment, or have been shown how to tolerate their symptoms. Most of them have been shown how to live happily. The doctor, too, benefits by removing his greatest worry and care, which is "How can I possibly bring effective help to these scores of people with emotionally induced illness?" The layman cannot possibly appreciate what a tremendous burden functional disease produces for the doctor. The doctor needs a method of therapy as much as does the patient. Having seen what can be accomplished by audiovisual sessions utilizing the learning-maturity concept, and failing to see how the tremendous number of patients can be given the necessary therapy in any other way, I am of the opinion that eventually this system, or some modification of it, *must* become the universally accepted method of treating emotionally induced illness.

A COMPARISON OF THE LEARNING-MATURITY METHOD AND "ADEQUATE PSYCHOTHERAPY"

Adequate psychotherapy for E. I. I. consists of three distinct phases, the period of explanation, the period of ventilation, the period of education.

The emphasis is placed on the period of ventilation; the period of explanation is very sketchy and often unconvincing; the period of education varies in intensity with various psychiatrists. Some leave it out altogether.

Psychoanalysis consists only of the period of ventilation. The analyst considers a period of education entirely superfluous. The learning-maturity method by audiovisual presentation emphasizes the period of explanation and the period of education. The period of ventilation is turned into a period of demonstration.

The period of explanation. The initial step, in both adequate psychotherapy and in the learning-maturity method, is to explain to the patient that he has emotionally induced ill-ness, and to give him some idea of how E. I. I. works.

The adequate psychotherapist has considerable trouble in doing this because his explanations are exceedingly ephemeral, and leave the average patient completely unconvinced.

As an example: a patient of mine who was seen by a psychiatrist was given this explanation of his diarrhea: "You hate your mother-in-law, and you would like nothing better than to have her out of your life. Your diarrhea is your body's organ-language of that repressed desire." To the patient that sounded pretty weak. He was not convinced that his diarrhea had anything to do with his mother-in-law, especially when his diarrhea did not stop after his mother-in-law had been killed in an accident (with which the patient had nothing to do). Admittedly the man's mother-in-law had much to do with the emotional stress which was manifesting itself in his colon, but to give the explanation that the body is acting out a phrase of language, which the mind dare not express, is, in my opinion, just as silly as it sounds. It sounded silly to the patient. Another symbolic psychiatric explanation is, "You feel a lump in your throat because that is your body's expression of the fact that you have things in your life you can't swallow." There is, of course, a connection between the "things in your life" and the lump; but why can't the explanation be factual, that is to say, physiological, instead of merely figurative?

It is much easier to convince patients that they have E. I. I. if the explanation is physiological, as in the first part of this book. After the audiovisual sessions on explanation, the patient usually says, "Sure, you were describing me all the time. Why didn't someone tell me before how this worked?"

We know, today, what the mechanism of E. I. I. is. Why not use it? In fairness, it must be noted that psychiatrists are turning more and more to physiologic explanations of the emotion-symptom relationship. But many of them still rely on the hokus-pokus of symbolism.

The period of ventilation. Traditional psychiatrists, and especially psychoanalysts, place their main emphasis on the part of their therapy they term "ventilation," which consists in having the patient talk about himself.

The ventilative sessions of an hour each, at weekly intervals, extend from weeks to years, depending on how deeply buried the subconscious material happens to be.

From such ventilation, the psychiatrist hopes to have the patient uncover the mainspring of his illness, the theory being that emotional stress is due to repressed and buried complexes that tend to disappear as soon as the patient knows of their presence and significance. The main objection to this theory is that it does not often work; it does not often produce a cure of the patient's emotional stress.

In the audiovisual presentation of the learning-maturity method there is obviously no place for ventilation. Instead of listening to the patient ventilate, as in "adequate psychotherapy," the doctor ventilates for the patient. In the audiovisual sessions, as in this book, the patient is presented with the chief situational and personality factors that produce emotional stress. He has time to compare his own situation with the hypothetical ones presented during the sessions; he analyzes himself and realizes that perhaps what he has always considered normal for himself is, after all, abnormal.

Very often, a person who has attended several audiovisual sessions will voluntarily reveal a situation in his life that he had been hiding. If the patient doesn't voluntarily bring me an assay of himself after a reasonable number of sessions, I ask him, "Now that you have seen the kind of thing that produces E. I. I. in most people, what do you think is doing it in you?" If he doesn't have an immediate answer, I ask him to bring it with him before he attends the next session.

The period of education. After the explanatory and ventilative periods, the psychotherapist usually discusses, with the patient, ways and means of alleviating his difficulties. This period of education is by no means universally used by all psychiatrists. Many psychiatrists do not give the patient any directive program and believe educational efforts are useless. Their emphasis, of course, is on the cathartic effect of the ventilative period. The learning-maturity concept emphasizes the educative period. The main effort is *not* to dig up the past but to show the patient how he may go about acquiring the qualities that will make his present and future more endurable and satisfactory than his past.

A person is what he is because of the sum total of influences that he has met in the past. Whatever those influences were does not preclude the application of new influences and new learning patterns now or in the future. If a poor swimmer is shown how, the chances are he can be a better swimmer. Once in a great while, of course, there will be someone who just can't learn to swim, but the majority can be helped.

The *final* know-how for developing maturity and emotional stasis we do not yet have; it is something that will have to be acquired through trial and error. However, there is already quite a bit we do know; let us begin to apply that.

Wie interpretiert man ein Gedicht?

Von
Hans-Dieter Gelfert

Philipp Reclam jun. Stuttgart

RECLAMS UNIVERSAL-BIBLIOTHEK Nr. 15018
Alle Rechte vorbehalten
© 1990 Philipp Reclam jun. GmbH & Co., Stuttgart
Bibliographisch ergänzte Ausgabe 1994
Gesamtherstellung: Reclam, Ditzingen. Printed in Germany 2007
RECLAM, UNIVERSAL-BIBLIOTHEK und
RECLAMS UNIVERSAL-BIBLIOTHEK sind eingetragene Marken
der Philipp Reclam jun. GmbH & Co., Stuttgart
ISBN 978-3-15-015018-4

www.reclam.de

Inhalt

Vorwort

Das vorliegende Buch – oder, bescheidener, Büchlein – wendet sich an Schüler, Lehrer und Liebhaber der lyrischen Dichtung, um mitzuhelfen, daß aus ersteren letztere werden, wobei denen in der Mitte, den Lehrern, die mühevolle Aufgabe zufällt, dies Ziel in der alltäglichen Praxis des Deutsch- und Fremdsprachenunterrichts zu verwirklichen, was manchem von ihnen als die Quadratur des Kreises erscheinen mag. Der Verfasser ist sich darüber im klaren, daß er seinem Ziel nur näher kommt, wenn es ihm gelingt, sein Schifflein zwischen der Skylla des germanistischen Fachjargons und der Charybde des schöngeistigen Geschwätzes unversehrt hindurchzusteuern. Nichts ist für einen lyrikliebenden Literaturwissenschaftler deprimierender, als mit ansehen zu müssen, wie die Dichtung von einem Dschungel von Sekundärliteratur überwuchert wird, durch den sich der arme Student den Weg mit der Machete bahnen muß und den der literarische Laie vorsichtshalber gar nicht erst zur Kenntnis nimmt. Dies Buch versucht, dem interessierten Leser Lagepläne in die Hand zu geben und ihm Pfade durch besagten Dschungel aufzuzeigen, um ihn so zu einem zwar durchaus ernsthaften, aber dennoch lustvollen Umgang mit Lyrik anzuleiten. Da ein Gedicht zuallererst ein Gegenstand der ästhetischen Wahrnehmung ist, sollte es nicht ausschließlich als Reckstange für intellektuelle Klimmzüge mißbraucht werden. Auch wenn das angemessene Verstehen von Lyrik zweifellos ein beträchtliches Maß an literarischem Sachwissen und längere Übung in der methodischen Textanalyse erfordert, wird dieser Aufwand doch nur dann lohnen, wenn sich am Ende ein ästhetisches Lusterlebnis einstellt. Darum schließt unser Buch mit einem Kapitel »Über den Grund des Vergnügens beim Lesen eines Gedichts«, wobei die Anlehnung an Schillers bekannten Aufsatz »Über den Grund des Vergnügens an tragischen Gegenständen« nicht zufällig erfolgt; denn Schiller war es, der Lust und Spiel in den Mittelpunkt seiner Kunsttheorie gestellt hatte.

Allgemeiner Teil

Wozu überhaupt Interpretation?

Fragt man Studenten der Literaturwissenschaft, bei denen man doch wohl am ehesten ein überdurchschnittliches Interesse an Literatur vermuten darf, nach ihrer Einstellung zur Lyrik, so wird man mit Betrübnis feststellen, daß diese bei den meisten die am wenigsten geliebte der drei klassischen Gattungen ist. Noch betrüblicher, geradezu niederschmetternd ist es zu hören, daß ihnen Gedichte durch das Interpretieren im Deutschunterricht restlos verleidet worden seien. Gewiß gibt es auch solche, denen der Zugang dadurch erst richtig eröffnet wurde, doch ist die abschreckende Wirkung bei Schülern so weit verbreitet und scheint so lange Zeit anzuhalten, daß sich schon mancher Deutschlehrer gefragt haben mag, ob es dann nicht besser wäre, auf die Behandlung von Lyrik ganz zu verzichten. Eine so radikale Konsequenz würde freilich bedeuten, daß dann auch bei denen, die durch den Unterricht zum Lesen von Gedichten motiviert werden, das Interesse ungeweckt bliebe, so daß die ohnehin sehr kleine Insel der Lyrikleser bald ganz aus der kulturellen Landschaft verschwände. Dies wäre für die literarische Kultur einer Gesellschaft ein unersetzlicher Verlust; denn erst an der Lyrik erweist sich, ob Literatur für den Leser überhaupt noch den Status des Kunstwerks hat. Romane werden von den meisten nur als Lesefutter konsumiert, Theateraufführungen dienen der Unterhaltung, bestenfalls der Auseinandersetzung mit aktuellen Zeitproblemen. Der Kunstcharakter dieser Werke wird dabei vom Konsumenten oft gar nicht wahrgenommen. Nur in der Lyrik steht das Artefizielle so im Vordergrund, daß man sie gar nicht anders lesen kann als eben als Kunst. Ein Student der Germanistik, der vorgibt, sich für Literatur zu interessieren, aber bekennt, daß er für Lyrik keinen Nerv habe, ist wie ein Farbenblinder, der Malerei studiert. Gewiß ist niemand, der Gedichte langweilig findet, darum schon ein schlechterer oder weniger gebildeter Mensch. Aber eine Literatur, in der die Lyrik keinen zentralen Platz hat, wird sich fragen lassen müssen, ob sie dann überhaupt noch eine künstlerische und nicht nur eine kritische Widerspiegelung menschlichen Lebens wäre. Ein Verschwinden der Lyrik aus dem Deutschunterricht würde für die allgemeine Lesekultur bedeuten, daß die auch so schon schwach genug entwickelte ästhetische Sensibilität noch stärker verkümmert. Ehe man also durch einen gänzlichen Verzicht auf die Lyrikinterpretation das Kind mit dem Bade ausschüttet, sollte man lieber versuchen, das Bad für das Kind etwas lustvoller zu gestalten.

Damit sind wir am entscheidenden Punkt des Problems; denn die Ursache für die so oft eintretende kontraproduktive Wirkung der Interpretation liegt sicher nicht in der Inkompetenz der Lehrer, sondern in der Sache selbst. Gedichte wurden und werden geschrieben, um im Leser eine affektive Reaktion, ein ästhetisches Lusterlebnis, auszulösen; die landläufigen Interpretationsverfahren hingegen versuchen, den auslösenden Gegenstand auf kognitive Weise zu erfassen. Diese extreme Kognitivierung des Interpretationsbegriffs ist eine Eigentümlichkeit der Literaturwissenschaft, die es in den anderen beiden Künsten nicht gibt. In der Musik wird die Interpretation einer Beethoven-Sonate nicht von einem Wissenschaftler auf bedrucktem Papier, sondern von einem Pianisten am Klavier geleistet. In der bildenden Kunst ist der Kunsthistoriker, der eine kritische Bildbetrachtung vornimmt, zwar nicht ganz so nah am kreativen Schöpfungsakt wie der Musiker, aber auch seine kognitive Analyse des betrachteten Werks, für die der Begriff Interpretation im allgemeinen bewußt vermieden wird, ist nicht wie beim Literaturwissenschaftler auf bloßes Verstehen, sondern der Intention nach auf die Begründung eines Geschmacksurteils gerichtet. Er bleibt also wie der Musiker in der ästhetischen Sphäre, dem ureigensten Reich der Kunst. Nur die Literaturwissenschaft bewegt sich nahezu ausschließlich in der kognitiven Welt der Wissenschaft. Dieser Unterschied zeigt sich besonders deutlich in den jeweiligen Ausbildungsgängen der den drei Künsten zugeordneten Lehrberufe. Während Musiklehrer und Kunsterzieher die praktische Ausübung ihrer Kunst lernen, sind Deutschlehrer wissenschaftliche Germanisten, die während ihres Studiums nicht einmal lernen, wie man ein Gedicht vorträgt, geschweige denn, wie man eines macht.

Der ausschließlich kognitive Umgang mit Literatur hat in der Germanistik und den anderen Philologien dazu geführt, daß man – im mißverstandenen Sinn des Goetheworts von »der Dichtung Schleier aus der Hand der Wahrheit« – immer zuerst die verschleierte Wahrheit zu enthüllen sucht, statt die vollendete Machart des Schleiers genießend zu würdigen, durch den die Wahrheit ins Reich der Kunst überführt wurde. Selbst da, wo Literaturwissenschaftler die ästhetische Gestalt des Gedichts analysieren, tun sie es meist so, als handle es sich dabei um etwas Organisches, gleichsam Naturwüchsiges, das nur die sinnliche Außenseite jener Wahrheit ist. In Wirklichkeit aber ist ein Gedicht ein Gebilde von kalkulierter Künstlichkeit, und zwar auch dann noch, wenn es dem Dichter dank seiner Begabung in spontaner Intuition eingefallen ist. Statt Schüler dazu zu bewegen, sich in ein Gedicht mit Andacht zu versenken und seiner geheimnisvollen Offenbarung zu lauschen, sollte man ihren Blick viel eher auf die – meist sehr raffinierte – Machart des Textes lenken. Die Frage, die am Anfang jeder Interpretation stehen sollte, ist eine, die heute oft – in anderem Zusammenhang – mit einer englischen Redewendung ausgedrückt wird: What makes it tick? Was ist der Nerv, der bestimmte Gedichte über Jahrhunderte hinweg am Leben erhalten hat, während unzählige andere vollkommen vergessen sind? Was macht ihren Reiz, ihre besondere Finesse aus? Will man diese Frage beantworten, muß man versuchen, sich in den Dichter als Macher des Gedichts zu versetzen. Poiesis heißt im Griechischen »Machen«, »Verfertigen«. Wer die Qualität eines Stuhls beurteilen will, prüft nach, wie er gemacht ist. Ist der Prüfer mit Material und Verarbeitung zufrieden, wird er ihn sich vielleicht käuflich aneignen. Mit dem gleichen kritischen Blick sollte man an ein Gedicht herangehen. Auch hier sollte man fragen, ob es aus dauerhaftem Material gemacht, dicht gefugt und restlos durchgearbeitet ist. Fällt die Antwort positiv aus und findet man dann noch, daß es etwas vermittelt, das man auf diese ganz bestimmte Weise noch nicht erfahren hat, so wird man es sich aneignen und ihm in seinem geistigen Inventar einen Platz neben den vielen anderen dauerhaften Kunsterlebnissen einräumen, die man im Laufe seines Lebens hatte und denen die Kultur ihr Überleben verdankt. Wer freilich in einem Gedicht immer zuerst nach der tieferen Wahrheit schürft, der wird die hier befürwortete Haltung als eine bloß kulinarische abtun. Der Vorwurf wäre berechtigt, wenn der Leser sich das Gedicht nur wie eine Speise auf der Zunge zergehen ließe. Wenn er dabei aber mit Sachverstand bewundernd die Leistung des Kochs anerkennt, ist sein Urteil zweifellos angemessener als das des Lebensmittelchemikers, der die Bestandteile des Gerichts analysiert. Wenn Literaturwissenschaftler ein Gedicht interpretieren, dann übersetzen sie dessen affektiv wirksame Formensprache in eine kognitiv verstehbare Sprache. Das Ergebnis ist dann die Interpretation des Gedichts. Ein solcher verdinglichter Interpretationsbegriff verstellt aber eher den Blick für das Gedicht, als daß er ihn eröffnet. Will man das Gedicht in seiner ästhetischen Gestalt erfassen, muß man Interpretation verbal verstehen: sie ist ein Tun, nicht das Getane, sie ist das Übersetzen, nicht die Übersetzung. Insofern ist bereits das verständige, um Aneignung bemühte Lesen Interpretation; und der geschulte Sprecher, der die Lautgestalt des Gedichts zu voller Wirkung bringt, interpretiert es angemessener als der Literaturwissenschaftler, der diese Lautgestalt beschreibend analysiert. Dennoch ist dessen Analyse nicht wertlos; denn wenn es ihm gelingt, die subtile Machart des Gedichts freizulegen und in den dabei verwendeten Kunstgriffen das Wirken einer vielfältigen Tradition aufzuzeigen, wird der

9

Sprecher wie der Hörer plötzlich im Klang der Verse Akkorde hören, die dem einen wie dem andern ohne die Hilfestellung des Literaturwissenschaftlers verborgen geblieben wären. Hier erweist sich seine Daseinsberechtigung, indem er die Voraussetzungen dafür schafft, daß der Leser die Interpretationshandlung des verstehenden Lesens vornehmen kann. Allerdings wird er dieser Aufgabe nur dann gerecht, wenn er durch Bereitstellung seines Fachwissens den Zugang zum Gedicht wirklich öffnet und ihn nicht, wie dies leider allzuoft der Fall ist, mit einem Wust von Sekundärliteratur zuschüttet. Literaturwissenschaft ist, wie die Medizin, keine reine, nur um Erkenntnis bemühte Wissenschaft, sondern eine angewandte, und zwar eine didaktische. Ihre wesentliche Aufgabe besteht darin, dem Leser einen stetig wachsenden Bereich der Literatur so vollständig als möglich zu erschließen und für die Literatur ihrerseits eine stetig wachsende Leserschaft zu gewinnen.

Damit ist der Interpretation eine Richtung vorgezeichnet. Aber noch immer ist die Frage offen, weshalb man überhaupt interpretieren soll. Schüler haben oft eine instinktive Abneigung gegen das Reden über Gedichte. Sie empfinden es als ein Breittreten und Zerschwatzen von etwas, das man viel besser ohne Worte auf sich wirken lassen sollte. Deshalb weigern sich manche, ihre Lieblingsgedichte mit einer Interpretation zu besudeln. Nun ist sicher richtig, daß das Wesen eines Gedichts, seine spezifisch ästhetische Individualität, unaussprechlich ist. *Individuum est ineffabile*, lautet ein alter philosophischer Grundsatz: das Individuelle ist unaussprechlich. Es ist, da mit nichts anderem vergleichbar, auf keinen Begriff zu bringen. Man kann nur mit dem Finger darauf zeigen. Auch in der bildenden Kunst und der Musik ist das, was die Werke eines Leonardo oder Mozart so großartig macht, unaussprechlich. Aber soll man deshalb darüber schweigen? Der Mensch ist seinem Wesen nach rational, d. h., er nimmt die Welt nicht in einem blinden Reiz-Reaktions-Schema wahr, sondern in Begriffen, er will sie begreifen; und er begreift sie, indem er sie versprachlicht.

Alles, worüber Menschen reden, hört damit auf, bloß subjektiv zu sein. Sprache ist intersubjektiv, sie ist Kommunikation zwischen einzelnen Subjekten. So ist auch das Reden über Gedichte nicht nur erlaubt, sondern notwendig, weil dies die spezifisch menschliche Form der Aneignung ist. Es liegt die Wahrheit einer uralten Menschheitserfahrung darin, wenn in der Bibel das Essen vom Baum der Erkenntnis und das Erkennen im Geschlechtsakt mit einem Verlust der Unschuld gleichgesetzt wird. Auch das erkennende Versprachlichen eines intensiven ästhetischen Erlebnisses nimmt diesem etwas von seinem Glanz und seiner Unschuld. Doch dieser Verlust an undifferenzierter Spontaneität wird mehr als aufgewogen durch den Gewinn an differenzierter Wahrnehmung. Differenzierung macht aus Intensität nuancenreiche Fülle. Das jederzeit wiederholbare und immer weiter vertiefbare Durchschauen der Kunstfertigkeit eines Gedichts verschafft auf die Dauer mehr intellektuelles Vergnügen als spontan überwältigende Ersterlebnisse, die mit der Zeit verblassen. Die nachfolgenden Kapitel wollen versuchen, den Weg zu diesem Vergnügen ein wenig zu ebnen und, wo es nottut, freizuschaufeln.

Was ist ein Gedicht?

Ein Gedicht, was immer es sonst noch sein mag, ist zuerst und vor allem Ausdruck eines Bewußtseinsinhalts in formalisierter Sprache. Dies klingt wie eine Definition aus dem Lexikon und mag auch getrost als solche genommen werden; denn der Satz enthält das, was nach Aristoteles jede Definition enthalten sollte: das *genus proximum*, also die nächsthöhere Klasse, der das zu Definierende angehört, und die *differentia specifica*, das gewisse Etwas, wodurch es sich als Teilmenge vom Rest der Klasse unterscheidet.

Als »Ausdruck von Bewußtseinsinhalten in Sprache« gehört das Gedicht zur Gesamtklasse sprachlicher Äußerungen. Es gehört, wie man heute sagt, zur Klasse der Texte. Aus dem schier unübersehbaren Meer der Texte ragt es aber als kleine, scharf abgegrenzte Insel heraus; denn während die übrigen Texte – z. B. Zeitungsartikel, Sachbücher, Kochrezepte – ohne Informationseinbuße umformuliert werden können, liegt das Gedicht in einer unveränderlichen, festen, gleichsam kristallinen Gestalt vor.

> Schöpft des Dichters reine Hand,
> Wasser wird sich ballen,

heißt es bei Goethe, und damit ist genau das beschrieben, was das Gedicht von allen anderen Texten unterscheidet. Wenn nun diese feste Form als die *differentia specifica*, als das Wesen des Gedichts oder zumindest als sein wesentliches Merkmal angesehen werden muß, so wird man, um Dichtung zu verstehen, zuallererst untersuchen müssen, wie und wodurch solch dauerhafte Formalisierung zustande kommt. Ein kleines Gedankenspiel soll uns helfen zu verstehen, was Formalisierung bewirkt. Gegeben sei die Zahlenfolge

$$2 \quad 19 \quad 28 \quad 32 \quad 34 \quad 37 \quad 44$$

Auf den ersten Blick scheint es sich um Lottozahlen zu handeln. Wäre dies so, dann hätten wir es mit dem genauen Gegenteil von Formalisierung zu tun, da ja im Zahlenlotto für jede Zahl die gleiche Wahrscheinlichkeit besteht, mithin die ausgeloste Zahlenfolge das Zufälligste und Ungeordnetste ist, das sich überhaupt denken läßt. Falls es sich aber nicht um Lottozahlen, sondern um einen Ausschnitt aus einer geordneten Zahlenfolge handelt, müßten wir versuchen, die verdeckte Ordnung freizulegen. Wir probieren es mit der Bildung von Differenzfolgen.

$$
\begin{array}{ccccccccccccc}
2 & & 19 & & 28 & & 32 & & 34 & & 37 & & 44 \\
& 17 & & 9 & & 4 & & 2 & & 3 & & 7 & \\
& & -8 & & -5 & & -2 & & +1 & & +4 & & \\
& & & 3 & & 3 & & 3 & & 3 & & &
\end{array}
$$

Während die erste Differenzenfolge noch ebenso ungeordnet erscheint wie die ursprüngliche Zahlenfolge, läßt die zweite bereits eine klare Ordnung erkennen, und die dritte ist konstant. Wir haben es also mit einer wohlgeordneten Zahlenfolge zu tun, die der Mathematiker als arithmetische Folge dritter Ordnung bezeichnen würde und die er leicht in eine handliche Formel fassen könnte. Sind z. B. von dieser Folge drei aufeinanderfolgende Elemente n_1, n_2, n_3 gegeben, so könnte man das nächstfolgende Element n_4 durch eine einfache Formel berechnen:

$$n_4 = 3(n_3 - n_2) + n_1 + 3$$

Was hat man dadurch gewonnen? Zweierlei: erstens eine schlagartige Vereinfachung, die es gestattet, eine unendliche Zahlenfolge durch eine knappe Formel zu ersetzen, und zweitens einen ebenso schlagartig eintretenden Machtgewinn, der uns erlaubt, über die zunächst ganz chaotisch erscheinende Zahlenfolge zu verfügen. Der Mathematiker könnte z. B. die Folge in eine arithmetische Reihe verwandeln, indem er die Zahlen addiert. Dann ließe sich durch eine einfache Formel die Summe zwischen zwei beliebig gewählten Gliedern der Reihe ermitteln. *Scientia est potentia*, Wissen ist Macht, sagte Francis Bacon, und genau diese Macht haben wir durch unser Beispiel illustriert.

Was hat nun dies alles mit Dichtung zu tun? Läßt man die frühesten Epochen der europäischen Literaturen Revue passieren, wird man auf zwei Klassen formalisierter Texte stoßen, die als das älteste poetische Urgestein in die geschichtliche Überlieferung hineinragen: Merkverse und Zaubersprüche. Von beiden Textklassen sind zwar nur wenige Beispiele erhalten geblieben, doch kann es gar keinen Zweifel geben, daß dies die Reste einer immensen Fülle sind. In Zeiten, als es noch keine schriftliche Überlieferung gab, mußte das gesamte Wissen eines Stammes, vor allem seine Geschichte und insbesondere die Genealogie des Fürstenhauses mündlich überliefert werden. Damit dies in unverstümmelter Form geschehen konnte, mußten so stark formalisierte Texte geschaffen werden, daß jede Abweichung von der ursprünglichen Form sofort als Fehler erkennbar war. Vor allem aber ermöglichte die strenge Form überhaupt erst das Memorieren der Texte, was bei der Fülle des zu Überliefernden von großer Wichtigkeit war. Noch heute findet man solche Merkverse in lateinischen Grammatiken und anderen Lehrbüchern, um Schülern das Behalten bestimmter Regeln und Fakten zu erleichtern.

Auch von der anderen Textklasse, den Zaubersprüchen, ist nur ein winziger Teil erhalten geblieben, z. B. in den bekannten Merseburger Zaubersprüchen. Da es sich um heidnisches Kulturgut handelte, wurden sie von den christlichen Mönchen, die als einzige solche Verse hätten aufschreiben können, entweder bewußt unterdrückt oder zumindest des Aufschreibens nicht für wert befunden. Während im Merkvers das Moment der Vereinfachung wirksam ist, schöpft der Zauberspruch seine Wirkung aus der bannenden Kraft, die die Menschen seit je in formalisierten sprachlichen Äußerungen gefühlt haben. Das Magische solcher Formeln ist heute nur noch als schwacher Abglanz in volkstümlichen Sprüchen erkennbar wie dem bekannten »Heile, heile Gänschen ...« Die »bannende Kraft« aber wird von Reklamesprüchen weidlich ausgenutzt.

Dichtung und Werbung haben manches miteinander gemein. Beide appellieren nicht kognitiv, sondern ästhetisch und damit affektiv an den Adressaten. Beide gehen von dem Prinzip aus, daß das Produkt, wie gut es auch sein mag, ohne eine entsprechend gute Verpackung keinen Marktwert hat. Dem Verhältnis von Produkt und Verpackung entspricht in der Dichtung das Verhältnis von Inhalt und Form. Diese beiden lange Zeit geläufigen Begriffe werden inzwischen nicht mehr gern verwendet, da sie zu implizieren scheinen, daß man die Form, also die Verpackung, vom Inhalt trennen und womöglich durch eine andere ersetzen kann. Mit dem Aufkommen der methodischen Werkinterpretation begann man deshalb, von Gehalt und Gestalt zu sprechen, womit deren untrennbare Einheit zum Ausdruck gebracht werden sollte, da eine Gestalt immer nur an einem Gestalteten ablesbar ist und umgekehrt ein Gehalt immer nur in einer bestimmten Gestalt vorliegen kann. Inzwischen sind auch diese Begriffe z. T. schon wieder aus dem Verkehr, und man spricht jetzt oft nur noch von Text, den man als ein System von Zeichen definiert, die etwas bezeichnen, wodurch ebenfalls die Einheit von Form und Inhalt bzw. von Zeichen und Bezeichnetem ausgedrückt wird. Nun wird jeder zugestehen, daß schon die geringfügigste Veränderung der Form eines Gedichts Auswirkungen auf dessen inhaltliche Substanz hat und diese um eine Nuance verändert. Dennoch lassen sich Form und Inhalt an einem Gedicht getrennt beobachten und beschreiben. Sie lassen sich sogar, wenn auch nur mit beträchtlichen Einbußen, voneinander trennen. Dies geschieht z. B. bei der Übersetzung des Gedichts in eine andere Sprache. An dieser Stelle muß der Einwand kommen, daß Gedichte unübersetzbar seien; und dem wird jeder zustimmen. Dennoch werden seit Jahrhunderten immer wieder Gedichte übersetzt. Offenbar sind sie nicht schlechthin und prinzipiell unübersetzbar, sondern nur nicht so übersetzbar, daß die Übersetzung mit dem Original in allen wesentlichen Aspekten übereinstimmt. Die Behauptung von der Untrennbarkeit von Form und Inhalt wird man darum ein wenig einschränken müssen. Die Form eines Gedichts ist ein rein ästhetisches Phänomen, der Inhalt dagegen hat eine kognitive und eine ästhetische Dimension. Die kognitive Substanz ist so übersetzbar wie die jeder anderen sprachlichen Äußerung, zwar mit gewissen Einbußen, die unvermeidlich sind, die aber doch als quantité négligeable angesehen werden dürfen. Die ästhetische Form läßt sich so nachbilden, daß sie mit der des Originals zwar nicht identisch ist, aber ihr in glücklichen Fällen in der Wirkung doch sehr nahe kommt. Am größten ist der Verlust beim Zusammenpassen von Form und Inhalt. Nicht einmal in den seltenen Glücksfällen, in denen die Übersetzung ein ästhetisch genauso befriedigendes Gedicht darstellt wie das Original, wird die übersetzte Substanz sich in ihrem neuen formalen Kleid so frei und anmutig bewegen, wie sie dies in ihrer ursprünglichen Sprachhaut tut. Form und Inhalt ergeben also nur in ihrer originalen Abstimmung aufeinander ein Höchstmaß an dichterischer Vollkommenheit, aber trennbar sind sie durchaus, sowohl zum Zwecke der getrennten Analyse als auch – mit den genannten Einbußen – bei der Übersetzung. Deshalb wollen wir nun im folgenden erst einmal die Grundprinzipien der Formalisierung eines Gedichts betrachten.

Prinzipien sprachlicher Formalisierung

Wie schon das Beispiel unserer Zahlenreihe gezeigt hat, ist ein Text – oder irgendein System von Elementen – dann formalisiert, wenn wir mit einer größeren als der bloßen Zufallswahrscheinlichkeit vorausahnen können, was als nächstes folgt. Das aber können wir nur, wenn sich etwas wiederholt, das vorher schon dagewesen ist. Alle sprachlichen Formalisierungstechniken beruhen auf diesem Prinzip. Der Reim ist zweifellos das augenfälligste Beispiel dafür, aber er ist nur eines unter vielen. Shipleys englischsprachiges Sachwörterbuch *Dictionary of World Literature* zählt unter dem Stichwort *repetition* über vierzig griechische Begriffe auf, die alle eine jeweils besondere, auf Wiederholung beruhende Figur bezeichnen:

– Wenn zwei Sätze (oder Verszeilen) mit dem gleichen Wort beginnen, spricht man von *Anapher*;
– wenn sie mit dem gleichen Wort enden, von *Epipher*.
– Wiederholt sich das Wort unmittelbar, nennt man dies *Epanalepse*.
– Endet ein Satz (oder Vers) mit dem Anfangswort, so ist es ein *Kyklos*.

Die Liste dieser Zungenbrecher könnte man noch um rund vierzig weitere verlängern. Damit dürfte hinreichend deutlich sein, wie fundamental das Prinzip der Wiederholung für die sprachliche Formalisierung ist. Dabei beschränkt es sich keineswegs auf bloße Wortwiederholungen. Auch die Wiederholung von Versfüßen, gleichen Lauten, rhythmischen Abfolgen und syntaktischen Anordnungen (z. B. Parallelismus) gehört hierher. Bei Gedichten wiederholt sich oft eine Strophenform oder ein Refrain. Selbst moderne Dichter, die auf alle traditionellen Formen verzichten, brechen ihre Texte gewöhnlich so in Zeilen, daß sich eine charakteristische Form der Kurzzeile ständig wiederholt. Wäre nun aber Wiederholung das einzige Prinzip sprachlicher Formalisierung, dann wäre die Zeile

das Haus, das Haus, das Haus, das Haus, das Haus

bereits ein Gedicht oder zumindest im weitesten Sinne poetisch. Sie ist aber nach allgemeiner Erfahrung nicht poetisch, sondern – wie jede bloße Wiederholung – monoton und langweilig. Poetisch wird ein Text dadurch, daß er die Monotonie der Wiederholung aufbricht, indem er die Elemente nicht identisch wiederholt, sondern in größtmöglicher Vielfalt variiert. Das Wechselspiel von Wiederholung und Variation ist das allgemeinste Bauprinzip, das der Formalisierung poetischer Texte zugrunde liegt. Auch hierfür ist der *Endreim* das augenfälligste Beispiel; denn er wiederholt eben nicht die ganze Reimsilbe, sondern diese vom reimenden Vokal an, während der Anfangskonsonant variiert wird: S-*onne*, W-*onne*; St-*ein*, P-*ein*. Umgekehrt wiederholt der *Stabreim* den Anfangskonsonanten und variiert statt dessen den Rest der Silbe: *W*interstürme *w*ichen dem *W*onnemond (R. Wagner). Hier noch einige weitere Beispiele:

- Wortwiederholungen können dadurch variiert werden, daß man das Wort in verschiedenen Flexionsformen wiederholt: Laufen, lief, gelaufen. Dies nennt man ein *Polyptoton* (Vielfallfigur).
- Man kann aber auch die Wortwurzel in verschiedenen Wortarten wiederholen: Der Läufer lief den schnellsten Lauf. Hier spricht man von *figura etymologica*.
- Wiederholungen des Satzmusters variiert man, indem man

zwei parallel gebaute Sätze gegeneinander kehrt: Die Kunst ist lang, und kurz ist unser Leben. Dies nennt man Kreuzstellung oder *Chiasmus*.

– Schließlich bleibt auf der semantischen Ebene noch das weite Feld der Metaphorik, die es ermöglicht, eine bestimmte Bedeutung vermittels einer Analogie auf die verschiedensten Bilder zu übertragen und so den Ausdruck der intendierten Bedeutung zu variieren.

Formalisierung ist der Aspekt eines Gedichts, der sich auch dann beobachten läßt, wenn die semantische Dimension dem Leser verschlossen ist. Am Beispiel eines Gedichts von Luis de Góngora sei dies verdeutlicht:

> Mientras por competir con tu cabello
> oro bruñido al Sol relumbra en vano,
> mientras con menosprecio en medio el llano
> mira tu blanca frente el lilio bello;
>
> mientras a cada labio, por cogello,
> siguen más ojos que al clavel temprano,
> y mientras triunfa con desdén lozano
> del luciente cristal tu gentil cuello;
>
> goza cuello, cabello, labio y frente,
> antes que lo que fué en tu edad dorada
> oro, lilio, clavel, cristal luciente,
>
> no sólo en plata o víola troncada
> se vuelva, mas tú y ello juntamente
> en tierra, en humo, en polvo, en sombra, en nada.

Wer kein Spanisch versteht, wird mit dem Gedicht wenig anfangen können. Dennoch wird er auf den ersten Blick erkennen, daß es sich um ein Gedicht handelt. Es besteht aus je zwei gleich gebauten Quartetten und Terzetten mit dem Reimschema abba abba cdc dcd, kann also von jedem, der diese Form kennt, als Sonett identifiziert werden. Wer

18

außerdem aus dem Latein- oder Französischunterricht weiß, daß auslautende Vokale mit unmittelbar folgenden Vokalen an Wortanfängen zusammengezogen werden, wird auch bereits die Silben der einzelnen Zeilen zählen können und dabei feststellen, daß sich in jeder Zeile ein Elfsilbenschema wiederholt. Desgleichen wiederholen sich eine Reihe von Wörtern, so bereits das erste, das am Anfang der dritten, der fünften und der siebten Zeile wiederkehrt. Im ersten Terzett werden in der ersten und dritten Zeile je vier Wörter wiederholt, die in den vorangegangenen Quartetten erwähnt wurden, und zwar so, daß man annehmen darf, daß sie paarweise zusammengehören.

2 cabello	–	oro
4 frente	–	lilio
3 labio	–	clavel
1 cuello	–	cristal

In der aufgelisteten Reihenfolge treten sie in den Quartetten auf, während die Zahlen angeben, in welcher Abfolge sie im Terzett wiederholt werden. Wieder erkennen wir das Prinzip von Wiederholung und Variation. Schlagen wir nun in einem Wörterbuch nach, so finden wir für die acht Begriffe die folgenden Bedeutungen:

Haar	–	Gold
Stirn	–	Lilie
Lippe	–	Nelke
Nacken	–	Kristall

Wir werden vermuten, daß hier die Schönheit einer Frau gerühmt wird, indem vier körperliche Attribute mit Bildern von erlesener Kostbarkeit verglichen werden. Die Körperattribute werden in ihrer natürlichen Reihenfolge vom Haar abwärts aufgeführt. Auch die vier anderen Bilder lassen so etwas wie ein System erkennen. Zwei Blumen mit den Farbqualitäten Weiß und Rot werden von zwei Bildern aus dem Mineralreich eingerahmt, wobei die eigentümliche Farbe des Goldes erst im darauffallenden Licht durch seinen Glanz entsteht, während der Kristall sich im durchscheinenden Licht als rein und farblos erweist. Alles dies könnte symbolisch bedeutsam sein, aber zunächst einmal gibt es der Bildkonfiguration eine gewisse Ordnung. Versucht man, das Gedicht weiter zu übersetzen, so stößt man auf die Begriffe »plata« (Silber) und »viola troncada« (gepflücktes Veilchen), die zu den vorausgegangenen in einer gewissen Beziehung stehen, da sie die Qualität von Gold bzw. Lilie / Nelke auf einer niedrigeren Wertstufe wiederholen. Versucht man nun den Inhalt des Gedichts mit Hilfe eines Wörterbuchs zu erschließen, so wird man zu folgender Rohübersetzung kommen:

> Während, um mit deinem Haar zu wetteifern,
> das getriebene Gold vergeblich in der Sonne leuchtet,
> während deine weiße Stirn mitten in der Ebene
> mit Geringschätzung auf die schöne Lilie schaut;
>
> während jeder deiner Lippen, um sie zu erhaschen,
> mehr Augen folgen als der frühen Nelke,
> und während mit kecker Verachtung dein edler
>   Nacken
> über den leuchtenden Kristall triumphiert;
>
> genieße Nacken, Haar, Lippen und Stirn,
> bevor das, was in deiner goldenen Zeit
> Gold, Lilie, Nelke und leuchtender Kristall war,
>
> sich nicht nur in Silber und gepflücktes Veilchen
> verwandelt, sondern mit dir zusammen
> in Erde, Rauch, Staub, Schatten, Nichts.

Die Aussage dieses syntaktisch sehr elaborierten Gedichts erweist sich als höchst einfach. Es ist eine der typischen barocken Variationen über das *Carpe diem*-Motiv: Alles ist vergänglich, darum genieße den Tag. Die Kunst des Gedichts liegt nicht in seinem formulierten Gehalt, sondern in seiner formalisierten Gestalt. In vier parallel gebauten temporalen Nebensätzen, von denen jeder mit »mientras« beginnt, werden Haar, Stirn, Lippen und Nacken einer angeredeten Frau mit vier Gegenständen von exquisiter Schönheit verglichen, danach wird der Vergleich noch einmal in kunstvoll variierter Form zusammengefaßt, und über die Zwischenstufe einer verminderten Wiederholung des Vergleichs werden sie der Vergänglichkeit überantwortet. Die letzte Zeile ist von besonderer Finesse. Die asyndetische, d. h. nicht durch »und« verbundene Reihung der fünf Begriffe, die den Vorgang der Vernichtung ausdrücken soll, tut dies nicht nur durch ihren harten, unerbittlichen Staccato-Ton, sondern auch durch die Art, wie die Bilder aufeinander folgen. Am Anfang steht etwas Dreidimensionales und Festes, die Erde, dann schwindet mit jedem neuen Bild eine Dimension: In »humo« (Rauch) schwindet die Festigkeit, in »polvo«, dem auf der Erde abgelagerten Staub, die Dimension des Raumes, in »sombra« (Schatten) schwindet das Stoffliche, so daß am Ende nur noch das leere Nichts übrigbleibt. Eine solche semantische Steigerung, bei der eine Bedeutung, in diesem Fall die Nichtigkeit, von Mal zu Mal zunimmt, heißt in der Rhetorik eine *Klimax*. Sieht man allerdings im Vordergrund die Abnahme der Stofflichkeit, so würde man die Figur als *Antiklimax* bezeichnen. Beide Figuren sind gleichermaßen Beispiele für das Prinzip des Zusammenspiels von Wiederholung und Variation.

Wir werden in unserer Schlußbetrachtung noch einmal auf den Aspekt der Formalisierung eingehen und ihn als Quelle der ästhetischen Lust zu deuten versuchen. Eine kurze Vorüberlegung zu dem dort entwickelten Gedankengang sei aber schon hier vorausgeschickt. Wir sagten bereits, daß zuviel Wiederholung im Leser oder – falls es sich um ein Werk in einer der beiden anderen Künste handelt – im Hörer bzw. Betrachter Langeweile hervorruft. Zuviel Variation wiederum bewirkt, daß man das Werk als formlos, unschön und künstlerisch unbefriedigend empfindet. Der geheimnisvolle Punkt ästhetischer Vollkommenheit scheint irgendwo zwischen den beiden Polen des einheitstiftenden Prinzips der Wiederholung auf der einen Seite und des die Wahrnehmung immer neu stimulierenden Prinzips der Variation auf der anderen Seite zu liegen, wobei dieser Punkt in klassisch orientierten Stilepochen wie der Antike, der Renaissance oder dem Klassizismus mehr zur Einheit hin tendierte, während er in Epochen wie der Gotik, dem Barock oder der Romantik näher am Prinzip der Variation gesehen wurde.

Ausdrucksmittel

Nun mag ein Text noch so variationsreich formalisiert sein, ein gutes Gedicht ist er darum noch längst nicht; denn dieses, so definierten wir eingangs, ist »*Ausdruck* eines Bewußtseinsinhalts in formalisierter Sprache«.
Formalisierung ist nur das handwerkliche Grundgewebe, ohne das der Dichter seinen kunstvollen Sprachteppich nicht knüpfen kann. Das eigentlich Dichterische aber sind die Ausdrucksmittel, durch die – um im Bilde zu bleiben – der Teppich erst gestalterische Kontur, bildhafte Fülle, Beziehungsreichtum der Motive und gedankliche Tiefe erhält. Dabei lassen sich verschiedene Wirkungsebenen unterscheiden. Jedes gesprochene Wort ist zunächst einmal eine Sequenz von Lauten und hat als solche bereits einen sinnlichen und damit ästhetischen Reiz. Sprachlicher Wohlklang, aber auch harte Fügungen und Dissonanzen können als dichterische Ausdrucksmittel wirkungsvoll eingesetzt werden. Wörter sind aber nicht nur Laute, sondern vor allem Zeichen, die für Bedeutungen stehen. Dies ist die semantische Dimension der Sprache. Das Wort »Baum« bezeichnet etwas, das in allen Bäumen identisch ist, also den Begriff »Baum«. Dennoch denken wir, wenn wir das Wort hören, nicht an diesen abstrakten Begriff. Viel eher werden wir uns

einen Baum vorstellen, keinen bestimmten, aber auch nicht irgendeinen beliebigen. Wie die Vorstellung im einzelnen aussieht, wird bei jedem Hörer verschieden sein, aber immer wird sie konkret und bildhaft sein: ein mächtiger Stamm, eine dichte Krone, rauschende Blätter und viele andere Details. Ein Autor, der über das Hörspiel schrieb, hat das Wort einmal als »Werdebefehl« charakterisiert. Dies ist es in der Tat; denn bevor es uns einen abstrakten Begriff vermittelt, ruft es erst einmal eine Vorstellung vor unser inneres Auge. Dieser Bereich der sinnlichen Vorstellung ist die wichtigste Schicht in jedem Gedicht. Auf klanglichem Gebiet ist die Dichtung der Musik unterlegt, auf begrifflichem der Philosophie, aber auf dem Gebiet der sinnlichen Vorstellung erreicht sie eine von den physikalischen Bedingungen der raumzeitlichen Welt völlig losgelöste Freiheit der Evokation einer fiktiven Welt, neben der die Möglichkeiten der Malerei und des Films als geradezu arm erscheinen; denn diese sind auf die Sinneswahrnehmungen des Auges und beim Film auch noch des Ohrs eingeschränkt, während die vorgestellte Welt der Dichtung in der Fiktion von allen Sinnen wahrgenommen wird. Die dritte Wirkungsebene der Sprache ist, wie schon angedeutet, die begriffliche. Auch wenn Dichtung nicht abstrakt argumentiert und reflektiert wie Wissenschaft und Philosophie, ist abstraktes Denken dennoch Bestandteil der Innenwelt eines Gedichts. Große Dichtung beschränkt sich nie auf das Beschwören einer vorgestellten Bilderwelt, sondern läßt in dieser immer auch Bedeutungen erkennen, die Teil einer implizierten Argumentationskette sind. Ezra Pound, der große amerikanische Dichter und Anreger der Moderne, hat für die drei hier aufgeführten Wirkungsebenen der Sprache die Begriffe *Melopoeia*, *Phanopoeia* und *Logopoeia* geprägt. Da sie den Sachverhalt sehr treffend bezeichnen, wollen wir sie im folgenden als Termini übernehmen.

Neben den drei genannten hauptsächlichen Wirkungsebenen der dichterischen Sprache darf eine vierte nicht ganz übersehen werden, die *graphische*. Seit Erfindung der Schrift hat es bis auf den heutigen Tag immer wieder Dichter gegeben, die auch das Schriftbild ihrer Gedichte als Ausdrucksmittel eingesetzt haben. Im europäischen Kulturraum lag die Kunst der Kalligraphie zwar weitgehend in den Händen der Buchdrucker und professionellen Graphiker, aber auch hier haben Dichter, so z. B. manche im Barock oder noch in diesem Jahrhundert Stefan George, auf die graphische Gestalt ihrer Gedichte großen Nachdruck gelegt. In den ostasiatischen Literaturen dagegen, wie z. B. in der japanischen Haiku-Dichtung, galt der kalligraphische Schreibakt jahrhundertelang als fester Bestandteil des dichterischen Schaffensprozesses. Auf eine ganz andere Weise haben in diesem Jahrhundert die Vertreter der konkreten Poesie das Druckbild als Ausdrucksmittel eingesetzt. Hier ist die graphische Anordnung des Textes weder kalligraphische Einkleidung noch bildhafte Umsetzung des semantisch Gesagten, sie will vielmehr ganz konkret als die eigentliche Aussage genommen werden. Im zweiten Teil des Buches werden wir dies an zwei Beispielen vorführen.

Melopoeia: das Wort als Klang

Auf dem Gebiet der lautlichen Ausdrucksmittel hat die Lyrik viel mit der Musik gemein. Wie diese kennt sie Rhythmus, Klangfarbe und Melodie. Nur die Dimension der Harmonik ist ihr verschlossen, da Sprachlaute Geräusche und keine reinen Töne sind und da ein Sprecher nicht mehrstimmig sprechen kann. Dennoch haben es manche Dichter verstanden, in einigen besonders klangwirksamen Gedichten so kunstvolle Vokalfolgen zu gestalten, daß diese sich beim Lesen wie aufgelöste Akkorde anhören, so daß in der Tat eine Art von Harmonik zur Wirkung gelangt. Im folgenden wollen wir die drei obengenannten melopoetischen Ausdrucksmittel etwas näher betrachten. Es muß aber schon hier vorausgeschickt werden, daß dieser Wirkungsbereich der Sprache in der gegenwärtigen Lyrik nur noch eine sehr geringe Rolle spielt. Dies rührt z. T. daher, daß Gedichte heute meist nur noch gelesen und nicht mehr rezitiert werden. Der Hauptgrund dürfte wohl aber darin zu suchen sein, daß die Dichtung ebenso wie die Musik und die bildende Kunst alles meidet, was in der unmittelbaren sinnlichen Wahrnehmung ästhetische Lust erregt. Das sinnlich Schöne scheint durch seine Vermarktung so entwertet worden zu sein, daß seine nackte Unmittelbarkeit bei Künstlern wie beim Publikum inzwischen als etwas geradezu Obszönes empfunden wird. Schönheit im traditionellen Sinn ist in der Kunst offenbar nur noch in einer durch Reflexion gebrochenen Form zu ertragen. Deshalb ist sprachlicher Wohlklang aus der Dichtung fast ebenso verschwunden wie der Belcanto aus der Musik. Das heißt aber nicht, daß der moderne Dichter der Lautgestalt seines Gedichts gegenüber völlig gleichgültig ist. Das konsequente Vermeiden des sprachlichen Wohlklangs erfordert die gleiche Kunstfertigkeit wie das planvolle Anstreben desselben. Übrigens gab es auch früher schon Dichtung, die einen spröden, ganz unmelodiösen Sprechduktus wirkungsvoll einsetzte. Der Engländer John Donne, ein jüngerer Zeitgenosse Shakespeares, wird nicht zuletzt deswegen heute so hoch geschätzt.

Takt / Rhythmus

Gesprochene Sprache besteht aus gegliederten Folgen von Sprechlauten. In ungebundener Sprache, also in der Prosa, wird die Gliederung durch die geltenden Konventionen der Wortbetonung und der Satzintonation bestimmt. Das läßt dem Sprecher die Freiheit, in ein und demselben Satz je nach seiner Kommunikationsabsicht den Hauptton ganz unterschiedlich zu setzen. In der gebundenen Sprache der Lyrik dagegen wird die Gliederung des Sprachflusses vom Dichter weitgehend festgelegt. Die vertrauteste Form solcher Festlegung ist ein sich regelmäßig wiederholender Takt (= *Metrum*). In der Musik ist ein Takt der in seiner zeitlichen Länge festgelegte Zwischenraum zwischen zwei Betonungen. Dieser kann auf die verschiedenste Weise gefüllt werden. Eine halbe Note ergibt ebenso einen vollen ¾-Takt wie sechzehn Zweiunddreißigstel. Das *quantitierende* Prinzip, das die Lautfolge in gleich lange Zeiteinheiten gliedert, galt auch in der griechischen und lateinischen Lyrik, was daher rührt, daß Gedichte in der Antike in einer Art Sprechgesang rezitiert wurden. Allerdings gab es dabei nur zwei verschiedene Notenlängen, nämlich lange und kurze Silben, wobei zwei kurze einer langen entsprachen und oft durch diese ersetzt werden konnten. So hat z. B. der *Hexameter* (Sechsfüßler), der klassische Vers des antiken Epos, das Schema (— = Länge, ∪ = Kürze):

‒́ ∪∪ / ‒́ ∪∪ / ‒́ ∪∪ / ‒́ ∪∪ / ‒́ ∪∪ / ‒́ ∪

Der zweitwichtigste Vers der Antike, der *Pentameter* (Fünffüßler), hat das Schema:

‒́ ∪∪ / ‒́ ∪∪ / ‒́ // ‒́ ∪∪ / ‒́ ∪∪ / ‒́⌣

(// markiert einen Einschnitt, Diärese genannt).

Auch dieser Vers scheint aus sechs Füßen zu bestehen. Da aber der dritte und der sechste Versfuß nur die halbe Länge haben, ergibt sich insgesamt ein Vers von fünf Zeiteinheiten. In der deutschen Lyrik kennen wir das quantitierende Prinzip nicht. Wir gliedern den Vers nicht in Längen und Kürzen, sondern in betonte und unbetonte Silben. Zwei Takte, die beide dem Schema Hebung–Senkung folgen, werden auch dann als gleichartig empfunden, wenn einer davon beim Sprechen auf eine vielfache Länge des anderen gedehnt wird. Wenn wir heute lateinische Verse lesen oder lateinische Versmaße im Deutschen verwenden, ersetzen wir automatisch Längen durch (betonte) Hebungen und Kürzen durch (unbetonte) Senkungen. Deshalb gibt es für den antiken *Spondeus*, einen aus zwei Längen bestehenden Versfuß, keine deutsche Entsprechung, da zwei aufeinanderfolgende betonte Silben immer so gelesen werden, daß eine davon etwas stärker betont wird, so daß die andere infolgedessen als Senkung erscheint. Die vier übrigen klassischen Versmaße haben dagegen alle ihre deutsche Entsprechung:

Jambus	=	steigender Zweier:	x x́
Trochäus	=	fallender Zweier:	x́ x
Daktylus	=	fallender Dreier:	x́ x x
Anapäst	=	steigender Dreier:	x x x́

Ursprünglich kannten die germanischen Sprachen nur das reine *akzentuierende* Prinzip der Metrik. Sie gliederten eine Verszeile in eine feste Anzahl von Hebungen, deren Zwischenräume mit einer unregelmäßigen Anzahl von Senkungen gefüllt werden konnten. Dieses Prinzip kennen wir noch heute als sogenannten *Knittelvers*. Unter dem Einfluß der romanischen Dichtung, die für die Verszeilen feste Silbenzahlen und für die Betonung das *alternierende* Prinzip des regelmäßigen Wechsels von Hebung und Senkung eingeführt hatten, setzte sich auch in der deutschen Dichtung das Prinzip der regelmäßigen Wiederholung eines festen Taktschemas durch. Während im Französischen aber die Alternation von Hebung und Senkung gegen den Wortakzent verstoßen kann, hat dieser im Deutschen den Vorrang. Das akzentuierende Prinzip erscheint uns so natürlich, daß wir den Knittelversen, mit denen Faust in seinem berühmten Eingangsmonolog auftritt, durchaus die unregelmäßige Füllung der Senkungen zwischen den Hebungen verzeihen, während wir sofort ins Stolpern kommen und es als Kunstfehler empfinden, wenn ein festes Metrum gegen den natürlichen Wortakzent verstößt.

Ein festes Metrum, das früher in der Lyrik die Regel war, ist heute die Ausnahme. Deshalb sind viele oft kaum noch in der Lage, beim Lesen eines älteren Gedichts den Takt zu halten. Sie kommen aus dem Tritt. Als Eselsbrücke empfiehlt sich am Anfang das, was früher an Schulen verpönt war, das leiernde Lesen. Sobald man aber das Metrum erkannt und Tritt gefaßt hat, sollte man das Leiern wieder

aufgeben und zu einer sinngemäßen Betonung zurückkehren, doch so, daß die metrische Formalisierung als ästhetischer Ordnungswert weiterhin spürbar bleibt.

Strenggenommen hätte der Takt unter der Rubrik Formalisierung abgehandelt werden müssen, da seine Hauptfunk-
tion darin besteht, einen Text zu »binden«. Erst der *Rhythmus* macht aus der taktmäßigen Gliederung ein Ausdrucksmittel. Man kann ihn definieren als die sinnunterstützende
Akzentuierung des Sprachflusses, die das feste Metrum frei
umspielt. Goethes berühmte Zeile

> Kennst du das Land, wo die Zitronen blühn?

ist metrisch ein fünfhebiger Jambus. Lesen wir sie aber
sinnbetont, so sieht das rhythmische Schema ganz anders
aus:

> Kénnst du das Lánd, wo die Zitrónen blühn?

Statt der fünf Hebungen sind jetzt nur noch drei zu hören,
von denen die erste noch dazu auf eine Silbe fällt, die vom
Metrum her eigentlich unbetont sein müßte; dennoch kommen wir beim Lesen nicht ins Stolpern. Die Betonung einer
metrisch unbetonten Silbe ist am Anfang eines Verses gestattet, da sie mit keiner vorausgehenden Betonung zusammen-
stoßen kann und da das metrische Schema für das Ohr des
Zuhörers noch nicht fest etabliert ist. Im Versinnern würde
man dagegen eine solche Verschiebung als Kunstfehler empfinden. Läßt man z. B. den Artikel vor »Zitronen« weg, so
ist nicht nur das metrische Schema, sondern auch der rhythmische Fluß unterbrochen.

> Kennst du das Land, wo Zitronen blühn?

Daran erkennt man, daß der Rhythmus dem Metrum zwar
nicht sklavisch folgen muß, aber auch nicht dagegen verstoßen darf.
Gute Gedichte haben selten mehr als zwei oder drei Be-
tonungsgipfel in einer metrisch fünfhebigen Zeile. Die
schlechteren erkennt man daran, daß sie in leierndem Auf
und Ab dem Metrum folgen, so daß keine ausgreifende

rhythmische Geste und damit auch kein freier Flug des Gedankens zustande kommt. Andererseits hat das Metrum aber auch eine positive, disziplinierende Wirkung. Nur große Dichter wie Goethe haben in freien Rhythmen ohne metrische Bindung Gedichte von höchster Konzentration geschaffen, während geringere Dichter sich durch freie Rhythmen oft zu geschwätzigem Psalmodieren verführen lassen. Wer ein empfindliches Ohr für Rhythmus hat, dem wird schon aufgefallen sein, daß jeder Dichter seinen eigenen, ganz persönlichen Sprechgestus hat. Allerdings haben Versuche, wie E. Sievers sie mit seiner Schallanalyse unternahm, um gleichsam die akustischen Fingerabdrücke der Dichter am Lautbild ihrer Gedichte abzulesen, zu keinen überzeugenden Ergebnissen geführt.

Was der Rhythmus im Gedicht zu leisten vermag, sollen nun zwei Beispiele demonstrieren. Zuerst Goethes bekanntes Gedicht

Auf dem See

Und frische Nahrung, neues Blut
Saug ich aus freier Welt;
Wie ist Natur so hold und gut,
Die mich am Busen hält!
Die Welle wieget unsern Kahn
Im Rudertakt hinauf,
Und Berge, wolkig himmelan,
Begegnen unserm Lauf.

Aug, mein Aug, was sinkst du nieder?
Goldne Träume, kommt ihr wieder?
Weg, du Traum! so gold du bist;
Hier auch Lieb und Leben ist.

Auf der Welle blinken
Tausend schwebende Sterne,
Weiche Nebel trinken
Rings die türmende Ferne;

> Morgenwind umflügelt
> die beschattete Bucht,
> Und im See bespiegelt
> Sich die reifende Frucht.

Hier werden drei unterschiedliche Gemütsverfassungen durch drei verschiedene Rhythmen zum Ausdruck gebracht. Die steigenden Jamben der ersten Strophe vermitteln den Eindruck von Optimismus und Tatendrang, von Überschwang und jugendlichem Weltvertrauen. In der zweiten Strophe tritt an die Stelle des Jambus der fallende Trochäus. Schlagartig verdüstert sich die Stimmung, und es kommt ein Gefühl von Betrübtheit auf, gegen das der Dichter sich zur Wehr setzt. In der dritten Strophe hat er sein inneres Gleichgewicht wiedergefunden. Jetzt pendelt der Rhythmus wie ein schwankendes Boot zwischen dem langsam fallenden Trochäus und dem ebenfalls fallenden Daktylus, der aber im Unterschied zu ersterem einen leichtfüßig beschwingten Charakter hat.

Ein Meisterstück rhythmischer Gestaltung ist das folgende Gedicht von Robert Browning:

After

> Take the cloak from his face, and at first
> > Let the corpse do its worst.
>
> How he lies in his rights of a man!
> > Death has done all death can.
> And absorbed in the new life he leads,
> > He recks not, he heeds
> Nor his wrong nor my vengeance – both strike
> > On his senses alike,
> And are lost in the solemn and strange
> > Surprise of the change.

> Ha, what avails death to erase
> > His offence, my disgrace?
> I would we were boys as of old
> > In the field, by the fold –
> His outrage, God's patience, man's scorn
> > Were so easily borne.
>
> I stand here now, he lies in his place –
> > Cover the face.

Es handelt sich hier um ein Rollengedicht, in dem ein Sprecher fingiert wird, der vor dem Leichnam eines von ihm im Duell getöteten Mannes steht. Das Gedicht beginnt in regelmäßigen Anapästen, die den Eindruck vermitteln, als versuche der Sprecher ganz bewußt, sich zusammenzureißen. (Nicht ohne Grund haben die Griechen den Anapäst für Marsch- und Kampflieder verwendet.) In der Zeile aber, in der zum erstenmal vom Tod die Rede ist, hört die Regelmäßigkeit auf.

> Death has done all death can.

In dieser Zeile müßte eigentlich jedes Wort außer »has« mehr oder weniger gleich stark betont werden. Danach findet der Sprecher zurück zum regelmäßigen Anapäst bis zu der Zeile, in der der Tod zum zweiten Mal genannt wird:

> Há, whát aváils déath to eráse

Man wird die Zeile kaum anders lesen können als so, daß zweimal zwei Hebungen hart aufeinanderstoßen und die regelmäßige Ordnung erneut ins Wanken gerät. Noch einmal gelingt es dem Sprecher, die Fassade des kontrollierten Anapäst wiederherzustellen, doch in der Zeile

> His oútrage, Gòd's pátience, màn's scórn

fällt es ihm sichtlich schwer, das Schema einzuhalten. »God's« und »man's« tragen einen fast ebenso starken Akzent wie die unmittelbar folgenden Hebungen. In der vorletzten Zeile schließlich verliert er vollends die Fassung.

> I stand here now, he lies in his place –

Wie in der vierten Zeile müßte man auch hier jedes Wort mit Ausnahme von »in« gleich stark betonen. Dadurch entsteht eine stockende, fast schluchzende Bewegung. Die Schlußzeile wird der Leser danach wohl kaum mehr als metrisch gegliedert empfinden, sondern als schlichte Prosa. Das Gedicht hat damit in seiner rhythmischen Lautgestalt sinnfällig zum Ausdruck gebracht, wie der Sprecher angesichts des getöteten Gegners zunächst versucht, sich kühl und überlegen ins Recht zu setzen, und wie er dann doch mehr und mehr und zuletzt vollends die Fassung verliert.

Klangfarbe

Wenn wir a, o, u als dunkle und e, i, ü als helle Vokale bezeichnen, beschreiben wir eine akustische Wahrnehmung so, als sähen wir sie. Wir schreiben den Vokalen Farbqualitäten zu. Ähnliches tun wir, wenn wir m, n, l als weiche und p, t, k als harte Konsonanten bezeichnen. Nur sind es jetzt keine visuellen, sondern taktile Eindrücke, die uns die Konsonanten vermitteln. Weiterhin pflegen wir dunkle Vokale eher als warm, helle eher als kühl zu empfinden, womit ein weiterer Sinnesbereich angesprochen ist. Alle diese mit dem Sprachlaut assoziierten Sinnesqualitäten sollen hier unter dem Begriff Klangfarbe zusammengefaßt werden. Der Gebrauch dieses Ausdrucksmittels ist keineswegs der Dichtung allein vorbehalten. Schon die natürlichen Sprachen haben zahlreiche Wörter dadurch gebildet, daß sie die zu bezeichnende Sache lautmalerisch nachzuahmen suchten. Solche Lautmalerei (*Onomatopoesie*) ist in vielen Wörtern zu erkennen, z. B. in »zischen«, »klirren«, »schwirren«, »krachen«. Im Barock wurde sogar die Ansicht vertreten, daß ursprünglich alle Wörter einer Sprache so entstanden seien. Deshalb machten die Barockdichter z. T. exzessiven Gebrauch vom Mittel der Lautmalerei, da sie glaubten, auf diese Weise dem Ursprung der Sprache besonders nahe zu sein. Hier als Beispiel eine Strophe aus einem Gedicht von

Johann Klaj, worin dieser ein Freudenfeuerwerk nicht nur beschreibt, sondern mit lautmalerischen Mitteln nachzuahmen versucht:

> So reißet, zerschmeißet kein Hagel die Blätter,
> So rasselt, so prasselt kein donnerndes Wetter,
> So prallet, so knallet kein fallend Gemäuer,
> als knicket und knacket das knisternde Feuer.

Während die Barockdichter vor allem den Reiz rasselnder, polternder und scheppernder Konsonantenfolgen auskosteten, hatten es den Romantikern die Vokale und die weichen Nasale und Liquide angetan. Als ein Musterbeispiel romantischer Lautmalerei gilt das folgende Gedicht von Clemens Brentano:

> Hör, es klagt die Flöte wieder,
> Und die kühlen Brunnen rauschen.
> Golden wehn die Töne nieder,
> Stille, stille, laß uns lauschen!
>
> Holdes Bitten, mild Verlangen,
> Wie es süß zum Herzen spricht!
> Durch die Nacht, die mich umfangen,
> Blickt zu mir der Töne Licht.

Die ö-Laute der ersten Zeile bilden die Flötentöne nach, die aus dem Nachtdunkel der u- und au-Laute der zweiten Zeile emporsteigen. Das Brunnengeplätscher wird durch die Zischlaute in »rauschen« und »lauschen« für das Ohr vergegenwärtigt, und die hellen i- und ö-Laute, mit denen das Gedicht in der letzten Zeile ausklingt, wecken die Vorstellung von Sternenlicht.

Gleichzeitig ist dieses Gedicht aber noch ein Musterbeispiel für ein zweites Ausdrucksmittel, das bei den Romantikern sehr beliebt war: die *Synästhesie*. Man versteht darunter das Ineinanderübergehen verschiedener Sinnesbereiche. So werden z. B. in der Zeile

> Golden wehn die Töne nieder

ein visueller (»golden«), ein taktiler (»wehn«) und ein akustischer Sinneseindruck verschmolzen. Das gleiche gilt für die Schlußzeile, wo ebenfalls eine akustische (»Töne«) mit einer visuellen (»Licht«) Sinneswahrnehmung zusammengebracht und beide zusammen durch das »blickt« noch personifiziert werden. Die Synästhesie gehört eigentlich in den Bereich der Bildersprache, sie tritt aber oft, wie unser Beispiel zeigt, zusammen mit Lautmalerei auf.

In der nachromantischen Lyrik kamen dann wieder die Konsonanten zu Ehren. Niemand hat sie im 19. Jahrhundert wirkungsvoller eingesetzt als Annette von Droste-Hülshoff. Mit unnachahmlicher Meisterschaft gelingt es ihr, westfälische Heidelandschaft so zu beschreiben, daß man in den Konsonanten den stachligen Ginster förmlich knistern und knacken hört.

> Dunkel, Dunkel im Moor,
> Über der Heide Nacht,
> Nur das rieselnde Rohr
> Neben der Mühle wacht,
> Und an des Rades Speichen
> Schwellende Tropfen schleichen.
>
> Unke kauert im Sumpf,
> Igel im Grase duckt,
> In dem modernden Stumpf
> Schlafend die Kröte zuckt,
> Und am sandigen Hange
> Rollt sich fester die Schlange.

(Aus: »Das Hirtenfeuer«)

Hier wird ein Bild so beschrieben, daß der Leser das, was die Wörter semantisch sagen, gleichzeitig mit den Ohren wahrnehmen kann. Das Dumpfe des Sumpfes, das Stachlige des Igels, die weiche Bewegung der Schlange: alles wird durch Lautmalerei intensiviert, wobei die Konsonanten noch wirksamer sind als die Vokale. Ein Bravourstück der

Lautmalerei ist »Der Knabe im Moor«, ein Gedicht, das selbst erwachsenen Lesern eine Gänsehaut über den Rücken jagt.

Meist dient die Lautmalerei der wirkungsvollen Unterstreichung des jeweiligen Wortsinns. Sie hat dann punktuell eine illustrierende Funktion. Manchmal aber kann auf solche Weise ein ganzer Ablauf dem Leser sinnfällig vor Augen geführt werden. Angenommen, ein Dichter wollte mit onomatopoetischen Mitteln einen Sonnenaufgang darstellen. Wie könnte er es tun? Er würde wahrscheinlich mit einer Folge sehr dunkler Vokale beginnen, diese dann langsam heller werden lassen und das Hervorbrechen des Lichts mit dem hellsten, strahlendsten Vokal, dem i, zum Ausdruck bringen. Um das Eindrucksvolle, Eruptive des Naturvorgangs hervorzuheben, könnte er beim Übergang vom Dunkel zum Licht zusätzlich eine Folge rasselnder Konsonanten einfügen. Das würde den Eindruck vermitteln, als sprengte der Tag die Tore der Nacht und marschierte mit lärmenden Truppen ein. Genau so hat Goethe am Anfang von *Faust II* einen Sonnenaufgang beschrieben:

> Horchet! horcht dem Sturm der Horen!
> Tönend wird für Geistesohren
> Schon der neue Tag geboren.
> Felsentore knarren rasselnd,
> Phöbus' Räder rollen prasselnd,
> Welch Getöse bringt das Licht!

(Vers 4666–71)

Da Lyrik-Interpretationen meist allzu direkt auf Tiefsinn aus sind und den Kunstgriffcharakter der Dichtung dabei ganz übersehen, wollen wir ein weiteres Beispiel anfügen. Angenommen, ein Dichter wollte ein Gedicht über eine Katze schreiben und dabei deren taktile Qualitäten, das weiche Fell und die scharfen Krallen, lautmalerisch zum Ausdruck bringen. Er könnte versuchen, durch gehäufte Verwendung von Nasalen und Liquiden, also von m, n, ng, l und r, einen weichen, samtigen Untergrund zu schaffen, in den dann scharfe, stimmlose Explosivlaute wie p, t, k eingestreut werden. Ebendies hat John Keats, ein für die Sinnlichkeit seiner Sprachgebung besonders berühmter englischer Dichter, mit spielerischer Virtuosität in dem folgenden Gedicht getan, das hier im Original ohne Übersetzung abgedruckt werden kann, da sein Inhalt fast vollständig an seiner Oberfläche abzulesen ist:

> Cat, who hast passed thy grand climacteric,
>   How many mice and rats hast in thy days
>   Destroyed? How many titbits stolen? Gaze
> With those bright languid segments green, and prick
> Those velvet ears – but prithee do not stick
>   Thy latent talons in me, and upraise
>   Thy gentle mew, and tell me all thy frays
> Of fish and mice, and rats and tender chick.
> Nay, look not down, nor lick thy dainty wrists –
>   For all the wheezy asthma, and for all
> Thy tail's tip is nicked off, and though the fists
>   Of many a maid have given thee many a maul,
> Still is that fur as soft as when the lists
>   In youth thou enter'dst on glass-bottled wall.

Melodie

Die Melodie eines Verses ist dessen am schwersten zu beschreibende lautliche Qualität; denn sie entsteht erst aus dem Zusammenwirken von Klangfarben, Tonfolgen, metrischem Grundmuster und rhythmischem Fluß. Da dunkle Vokale tief und helle hoch artikuliert werden, lassen sich durch gut gewählte Vokalfolgen weit ausschwingende Melodiebögen gestalten, die durch Explosivlaute oder syntaktische Fugen so interpunktiert werden können, daß sich eine ausdrucksvolle, reich gegliederte Melodielinie ergibt. Durch

36

das Kontrastieren von Zeilen mit hellen und solchen mit dunklen Vokalen lassen sich darüber hinaus regelrechte Klangterrassen anlegen, die der Klanggestalt eines Gedichts einen weiten Tonraum eröffnen. Bei den besten Werken klangbewußter Dichter hat man als Leser das Gefühl, daß die Verse ruhig und tief atmen wie die Stimme eines ausgebildeten Sängers, während die weniger guten Gedichte einen kurzen, flachen Atem haben. Einige Beispiele mögen dies verdeutlichen.

Hölderlin: Mit gelben Birnen hänget
             und voll mit wilden Rosen
             das Land in den See.

(Aus: »Hälfte des Lebens«)

Um sich die klangliche Kunstfertigkeit dieser Zeilen klarzumachen, braucht man nur einmal einige geringfügige Veränderungen vorzunehmen, und man wird sehen, wie sich der poetische Zauber sogleich verflüchtigt:

             Mit gelben Äpfeln hänget
             und voll mit roten Rosen
             das Land in den See.

Die Finesse des Originals liegt darin, daß die Melodie zweimal zum hellsten Vokal, dem i, hinauf- und wieder hinabschwingt, wobei sie in der ersten Zeile von der neutralen e-Terrasse und in der zweiten von der tiefen o-Terrasse ausgeht, bevor sie in der dritten Zeile über das a zur Mittellage des e zurückschwingt. In der veränderten Fassung sind die beiden Melodiebögen eingeebnet. Jetzt haben wir eine e- und eine o-Terrasse parallel nacheinander, ohne daß irgendeine Melodiebewegung stattfindet. Die Verse sind klanglich tot. Leser, deren Ohr für Sprachmelodien noch wenig geschult ist, sollten immer wieder dieses Experiment einer geringfügigen Veränderung machen, und sie werden bald voller Hochachtung für die subtile Sprachkunst der großen Dichter sein.

Sprachmelodie von betörendem Wohlklang war zwar eine Domäne der klassisch-romantischen Lyrik, aber auch bei der verhalteneren, spröderen Sprache der Moderne führt unser Test zu den gleichen Ergebnissen. Brecht, der einen neuen, kargen, fast prosaischen Ton in die Lyrik eingeführt hat, fängt seine berühmte »Legende von der Entstehung des Buches Taoteking« so an:

> Als er Siebzig war und war gebrechlich
> Drängte es den Lehrer doch nach Ruh

Hier die veränderte Fassung:

> Als er Achtzig war und grau und faltig
> Drängte es den Lehrer doch nach Frieden

Wieder ist der klangliche Reiz der Zeilen vollkommen zerstört. Im Original schwingt die Melodie zuerst zum hohen i hinauf (»Siebzig«), sinkt auf das a zurück, hält sich dann in »gebrechlich / Drängte es den Lehrer« gleichmäßig auf dem e und führt schließlich über o und a zum tiefen dunklen u. Das ist der melodische Gestus eines alten Mannes, der sich aufrichtet, sich mühsam auf den Beinen hält, sich dann aber doch niederlassen muß, um zu verschnaufen. Diese innere Bewegung der beiden Zeilen ist aus der veränderten Fassung verschwunden. Jetzt haben wir eine flache, monotone Zeile auf a und eine zweite, die über a und o zum i hinaufführt, was dem Inhalt des Satzes völlig zuwiderläuft.
Selbst da, wo moderne Dichter es bewußt darauf anlegen, das Gedicht auf der Sensibilität des Lesers wie Schmirgelpapier knirschen zu lassen, tun sie es mit Sätzen von höchst wirkungsvoller Sprachmelodie.

Enzensberger: Reffen wir ruhig die Regenschirme,
die nächste Sintflut wird seicht sein.

Wenn ein Gedicht so anfängt, weiß der Leser, daß er kein poetisches Belcanto zu erwarten hat. Und doch beziehen diese Zeilen ihre Wirkung nicht aus der bewußten Unpoesie

ihres Inhalts, sondern aus der kunstvollen Rhetorik ihres
Sprachflusses. Der dreimalige Stabreim gibt beiden Zeilen
die Stoßkraft, der Wechsel vom fallenden zum steigenden
Metrum unterstreicht die Vorstellung von steigender Flut,
und die beiden ei-Laute, die am Ende der zwischen i und u
hin und her pendelnden Vokalfolge stehen, wecken die
Vorstellung von etwas Weichem, Breiigen.

Die wohlklingenden Versmelodien eines Claudius, Eichendorff und Heine, die sich wie Volkslieder ins Gedächtnis des
Lyriklesers eingegraben haben, begegnen uns heute nur
noch da, wo sie zu satirischem, parodistischem oder sprach-
spielerischem Zweck verwendet werden. Der unübertrof-
fene Virtuose in der verfremdenden Adaption solcher lyrischen Ohrwürmer ist Peter Rühmkorf. Ihm gelingt es, die
bizarrsten Metaphern in Verse von betörendem Wohlklang
zu gießen. Hier zwei Beispiele:

> Sommer, und die Schwalbe piepste
> Monde zwischen Dach und Tür –
> Dumm wie Dotter meine Liebste,
> weich wie Melde unter mir.

> (Aus: »Das Zeitvertu-Lied«)

Dies ist die Melodie, die wir aus vielen romantischen
Gedichten kennen, z. B. aus Storms »Schon ins Land der
Pyramiden . . .«.
Ähnlich das zweite Beispiel:

> Spiel mit dem Lämmersterz
> tändelnde Agnes –
> ich hab ein rohes Herz,
> du ein gebacknes.

> (Aus: »Auf ein rohes Herz«)

Auch diese Melodie, eine Abwandlung des Adonischen
Verses aus der Antike, kennt man, u. a. aus Rilkes Sonett an
Orpheus »Nur wer die Leier schon hob«. So amüsant

Rühmkorfs Kunststücke zweifellos sind, wird man doch kaum verhehlen können, daß sie bedenklich nahe am bloßen Kunstgewerbe liegen. Trotzdem möchte man seine Stimme im Konzert der zeitgenössischen Lyrik nicht missen.

Phanopoeia: das Wort als Bild

Jeder sprachliche Text, der etwas Konkretes beschreibt, ruft in uns eine Vorstellung des Beschriebenen wach. Das bedeutet, daß der Dichter mit Worten Bilder und Bildsequenzen malen kann. Während aber der Maler auf die visuellen Sinneswahrnehmungen und die zweidimensionale Fläche seiner Leinwand eingeschränkt ist, hat der Dichter die Freiheit, eine dreidimensionale Vorstellung mit den Wahrnehmungen aller fünf Sinne zu evozieren und diese obendrein noch so zu verdichten, daß sie an Intensität der sinnlichen Präsenz jede reale Wirklichkeit übertrifft. Da aber in unserem Bewußtsein hinter der Vorstellung einer Sache immer schon deren Begriff steht, hat auch die in einem Gedicht evozierte Bilderwelt eine natürliche Affinität zum Begrifflichen. Je nachdem, ob ein Bild mehr Bild oder mehr Zeichen für eine Bedeutung sein will, lassen sich verschiedene Arten von Bildlichkeit unterscheiden.

Darstellende Bildlichkeit

Wenn man den Begriff »Bild« auf den Gesamtbereich konkreter Vorstellungen anwendet, so wird man diejenige Form von Bildlichkeit, die nichts weiter bedeutet als das, was sie darstellt, als *einfaches Bild* bezeichnen müssen. Hier ein Beispiel:

Richard Dehmel

Manche Nacht

Wenn die Felder sich verdunkeln,
Fühl ich, wird mein Auge heller;
Schon versucht ein Stern zu funkeln,
Und die Grillen wispern schneller.

Jeder Laut wird bilderreicher,
Das Gewohnte sonderbarer,
Hinterm Wald der Himmel bleicher,
Jeder Wipfel hebt sich klarer.

Und du merkst es nicht im Schreiten,
Wie das Licht verhundertfältigt
Sich entringt den Dunkelheiten.
Plötzlich stehst du überwältigt.

Das Gedicht beschreibt mit großer Anschaulichkeit das
Hereinbrechen der Nacht, wie es vor allem in nördlichen
Breiten an klaren Sommerabenden zu beobachten ist. Ehe
der Himmel sich verdunkelt, wird er erst einmal blaß und
sehr hell, während die Silhouette des Waldes sich scharf und
dunkel von ihm abhebt. Es ist eine kurze Zeitspanne von
eigentümlicher Paradoxie, da die Dunkelheit zunächst mit
zunehmender Helligkeit und das Verstummen der Welt mit
einer zunehmenden Deutlichkeit der noch hörbaren Geräusche beginnt. Dehmel gestaltet dieses Phänomen mit großer
Eindringlichkeit und läßt es in ein Erlebnis subjektiven
Überwältigtseins münden. Man könnte dabei zwar an einen
seelischen Zustand plötzlicher Hellsichtigkeit denken, aber
das Gedicht enthält nichts, was auf eine weitergehende
symbolische Bedeutung verweist. Es scheint nichts weiter
darstellen zu wollen als das präzise Abbild eines subjektiv
erfahrenen atmosphärischen Vorgangs.
Anders verhält es sich bei Goethes berühmtem Gedicht

Wanderers Nachtlied

Über allen Gipfeln
Ist Ruh,
In allen Wipfeln
Spürest du
Kaum einen Hauch;
Die Vögelein schweigen im Walde.
Warte nur, balde
Ruhest du auch.

Auch dieses Gedicht evoziert ein Bild von großer Anschaulichkeit. Aber die Art, wie es aufgebaut wird, zwingt den Leser förmlich, es als Ausdruck einer tieferen Bedeutung zu verstehen. Die Beschreibung beginnt bei den Gipfeln, verengt sich auf die Wipfel und führt schließlich mit der Erwähnung der Vögelein in die Wipfel hinein. Parallel zu der Bildverengung erfolgt eine zunehmende Belebung. Die Gipfel gehören noch zur unbelebten Natur, die Wipfel bereits zum Pflanzenreich, die Vögelein zum Reich der Tiere. Damit ist in dem Gedicht eine Bewegung angelegt, die der Leser intuitiv fortsetzt. Als nächsten Schritt erwartet man den Eintritt in die Menschenwelt und eine noch stärkere Verengung des Bildes. Die lautliche Härte des »Warte« markiert akustisch den Drehpunkt, an dem sich das Gedicht von der Außenwelt in die Innenwelt wendet. Damit hört das äußere Bild auf, nur ein einfaches Bild zu sein. Es wird zur symbolischen Vergegenständlichung dessen, was als innere Erfahrung gemeint ist. Trotzdem bleibt es für den Leser konkret und real. Es ist keineswegs eine bloße bildhafte Einkleidung der intendierten Bedeutung. In dieser Doppelheit von gegenständlicher Realität und implizierter abstrakter Bedeutung entspricht das Bild genau der Definition, die Goethe vom *Symbol* gegeben hat: »Es ist die Sache, ohne die Sache zu sein, und doch die Sache; ein im geistigen Spiegel zusammengezogenes Bild, und doch mit dem Gegenstand identisch.« Das Symbol enthält eine Analogie, die nicht expliziert wird, sondern darauf angelegt ist, vom Leser spontan und intuitiv erfaßt zu werden. Wird die Analogie rational in ihre Bedeutung übersetzt, so haben wir es mit einem *Vergleich* zu tun, der, wenn er als längere Sequenz ausgeführt wird, sich zum *Gleichnis* erweitert. Auch dafür ein Beispiel:

Joseph von Eichendorff

Die Nachtblume

Nacht ist wie ein stilles Meer,
Lust und Leid und Liebesklagen
Kommen so verworren her
In dem linden Wellenschlagen.

Wünsche wie die Wolken sind,
Schiffen durch die stillen Räume,
Wer erkennt im lauen Wind,
Ob's Gedanken oder Träume?

Schließ ich nun auch Herz und Mund,
Die so gern den Sternen klagen:
Leise doch im Herzensgrund
Bleibt das linde Wellenschlagen.

Das Gedicht gibt bereits in der ersten Zeile zu verstehen, daß es keine reale Nacht beschreiben will. Durch einen Vergleich wird die Nacht in das Bild des Meeres übersetzt und erscheint nun als ein »lindes Wellenschlagen«. Die zweite Strophe geht von etwas Innerem, den »Wünschen«, aus und übersetzt sie in das Bild der Wolken, die ihrerseits mit Schiffen verglichen werden, worauf sich die Vergleiche beider Strophen in dem Bild des Meeres treffen. Dieses, ursprünglich nur zum Zwecke des Vergleichs herbeizitiert, erscheint nun in der dritten Strophe als die bildhafte Veranschaulichung eines inneren Zustands.

Es gibt aber auch die Möglichkeit, daß Inneres zur Besee-

lung von Äußerem herangezogen wird. Dies ist in allen
Formen von *Personifizierung* der Fall. Statt z. B. die Nacht
zur Verbildlichung eines Seelenzustands heranzuziehen,
kann ein Dichter umgekehrt die reale Nacht darstellen,
indem er sie mit seelischen Attributen versieht. Dies tut
Mörike in dem folgenden Gedicht:

Um Mitternacht

Gelassen stieg die Nacht ans Land,
Lehnt träumend an der Berge Wand,
Ihr Auge sieht die goldne Waage nun
Der Zeit in gleichen Schalen stille ruhn;
    Und kecker rauschen die Quellen hervor,
    Sie singen der Mutter, der Nacht, ins Ohr
        Vom Tage,
Vom heute gewesenen Tage.

Das uralt alte Schlummerlied,
Sie achtet's nicht, sie ist es müd;
Ihr klingt des Himmels Bläue süßer noch,
Der flüchtgen Stunden gleichgeschwungnes Joch.
    Doch immer behalten die Quellen das Wort,
    Es singen die Wasser im Schlafe noch fort
        Vom Tage,
Vom heute gewesenen Tage.

Mörike will den atmosphärischen Zustand der irdischen
Nacht so intensivieren, daß er als Teil einer kosmischen
Polarität erscheint. Er tut es, indem er die Nacht personifiziert, ihr seelische Qualitäten zuschreibt und sie so als die
große Weltenmutter erscheinen läßt, aus der alles hervorgeht
und in die alles zurückkehrt. Auf diese Weise wird die
Nacht ins Mythische überhöht. Mythos ist ein Begriff, der
hier durchaus paßt; denn das Wesen des Mythos ist, daß er
kosmische Kräfte nicht als Einkleidung abstrakter Sachver-
halte, sondern als konkrete Personifizierung darstellt.

Fällt das Moment des Konkreten in der Personifizierung weg, ist also das Bild nur Veranschaulichung des gemeinten Abstrakten, dann haben wir es mit einer *Allegorie* zu tun. Auch dafür ein Beispiel:

Andreas Gryphius

Über die Geburt Jesu

Nacht, mehr denn lichte Nacht! Nacht, lichter als der Tag!
Nacht, heller als die Sonn, in der das Licht geboren,
Das Gott, der Licht in Licht wahrhaftig, ihm erkoren!
O Nacht, die alle Nächt und Tage trotzen mag!

O freudenreiche Nacht, in welcher Ach und Klag
Und Finsternis und was sich auf die Welt verschworen
Und Furcht und Höllenangst und Schrecken war verloren!
Der Himmel bricht; doch fällt nunmehr kein Donnerschlag.

Der Zeit und Nächte schuf, ist diese Nacht ankommen
Und hat das Recht der Zeit und Fleisch an sich genommen
Und unser Fleisch und Zeit der Ewigkeit vermacht.

Die jammertrübe Nacht, die schwarze Nacht der Sünden,
Des Grabes Dunkelheit muß durch die Nacht
                                        verschwinden.
Nacht, lichter als der Tag! Nacht, mehr denn lichte Nacht!

Auch hier ist die Nacht das zentrale Bild. Aber es ist von Anfang an klar, daß nicht das atmosphärische Phänomen gemeint ist. Die reale Nacht, in der Jesus geboren wurde, ist nur der bildhafte Anlaß, um allegorisch von der Nacht der unerlösten Menschheit, der Nacht der Sünde und des Todes zu reden und um die Paradoxie auszusprechen, daß die Nacht von Jesu Geburt heller als die hellste Sonne erstrahlt und daß diese Nacht aller Nacht ein Ende bereitet hat.

Metaphorik

Die zuvor betrachteten Formen von Bildlichkeit – also einfaches Bild, Symbol, Gleichnis, Personifizierung und Allegorie – stellen alle an den Leser den Anspruch, sich in ihrer bildhaften Realität vorzustellen. Anders verhält es sich bei der Metapher. Sie ist eine rhetorische Figur, die das Bild nur als Vehikel benutzt, ohne für dieses die Vorstellung von Realität zu beanspruchen. Man spricht deshalb von »uneigentlicher« Bildlichkeit. Meist werden alle Formen uneigentlicher Bildlichkeit unter den Terminus Metapher subsumiert. Bei größerer begrifflicher Strenge lassen sich aber zwei Klassen unterscheiden: Bilder, bei denen innerhalb ihres materiellen Bereichs die Bedeutung »verschoben« wird (*Metonymie*), und die eigentliche *Metapher*, bei der die Bedeutung vermittels einer Analogie »übertragen« wird (griech. metaphorein, »übertragen«). In beiden Fällen ist das Ziel, eine Sache interessanter, ungewohnter und damit poetischer auszudrücken, indem man sie bei einem anderen Namen nennt.

Zuerst ein Beispiel für Metonymie:

> Auch so das Glück
> Tappt unter die Menge,
> Faßt bald des Knaben
> Lockige Unschuld,
> Bald auch den kahlen
> Schuldigen Scheitel.

> (Aus: Goethe, »Das Göttliche«)

Dies ist ein typisches Beispiel dafür, wie der Dichter die sinnliche Dichte des Textes dadurch erhöht, daß er das Allgemeine auf das Besondere zurückführt und anstelle des Ganzen einen anschaulichen Teil davon nennt. Statt also von jungen und alten Menschen zu reden, spricht er von »des Knaben lockiger Unschuld« und dem »kahlen schuldigen Scheitel«. Der lockige und der kahle Kopf stehen als pars pro toto für den Jüngling und den Greis. Umgekehrt wird durch die Begriffe »Unschuld« und »schuldig« als totum pro parte die ganze Welt der unschuldigen Kindheit bzw. des schuldbeladenen Alters genannt, um je einen Vertreter der beiden Welten zu bezeichnen. Solche Verschiebungen vom Teil zum Ganzen und vom Ganzen zum Teil sind in der Dichtersprache gang und gäbe.

Die häufigste Form uneigentlicher Bildersprache ist zweifellos die Metapher im engeren Sinne. In ihrer klassischen, schon von Aristoteles definierten Form beruht sie auf einer Proportionsgleichung: A verhält sich zu B wie C zu X, wobei X dasjenige ist, das durch die Metapher umschrieben werden soll. Ein Beispiel: das Meer verhält sich zum Schiff, wie die Wüste zum Kamel; also kann man das Kamel als »Wüstenschiff« bezeichnen. Unzählige Wörter unserer Alltagssprache sind auf diese Weise entstanden: »Stuhlbein«, »Tonarm«, »Buchrücken«, »Tochterunternehmen«, »Straßenkreuzer« usw. Die Analogie, die der Metapher zugrunde liegt, kann auch ohne vollständige Proportionsgleichung wirksam werden, sofern nur irgendeine strukturelle Ähnlichkeit vorliegt, z. B. in »Augapfel«, »Menschenkette«, »Wolkenwand«. Die Metapher hat sich im Laufe der Sprachgeschichte als eine unerschöpfliche und immer noch sprudelnde Quelle neuer Wortprägungen erwiesen. Kein Wunder, daß alle Dichter sich ihrer bedient haben und noch immer bedienen, um alte, abgegriffene Wörter durch Neuprägungen zu ersetzen.

> Zedernhäuser trägt der Atlas
> Auf den Riesenschultern,

heißt es bei Goethe in »Mahomets Gesang«; gemeint sind die Schiffe, die der mit Atlas verglichene Fluß trägt. In dem gleichen Gedicht heißt es an anderer Stelle:

> Drunten werden in dem Tal
> Unter seinem Fußtritt Blumen,
> Und die Wiese
> Lebt von seinem Hauch.

> Doch ihn hält kein Schattental,
> Keine Blumen,
> Die ihm seine Knie umschlingen,
> Ihm mit Liebesaugen schmeicheln:
> Nach der Ebene dringt sein Lauf
> Schlangenwandelnd.

Hier wird der Fluß zunächst personifiziert, worauf ihm dann Fußtritte und Knie zugeschrieben werden können, was der Leser sich aber nicht bildhaft vorstellen wird, da es sich dabei um uneigentliche, bloß über das Analogieprinzip vermittelte Bilder handelt. Wie der Musiker im tonalen Raum durch Modulation von einer Tonart in eine andere hinüberwechseln kann, so hat der Dichter durch das Analogieprinzip die Möglichkeit der semantischen Modulation. Er kann ein und dieselbe Sache auf verschiedenen Bildebenen wiederholen, ohne daß die Melodie der gemeinten Bedeutung verloren geht.

Eine der geläufigsten Metaphernformen ist die Genitivmetapher, die mit der Zeit zu einem so konfektionierten und abgedroschenen Versatzstück wurde, daß sie inzwischen bei Dichtern verpönt ist.

> Der liebliche Korall der Lippen wird verbleichen,
> Der Schultern warmer Schnee wird werden kalter Sand.

> (Aus: Hofmann von Hofmannswaldau, »Vergänglichkeit der
> Schönheit«)

Der nicht unpoetische Grand Old Man der amerikanischen Country-music Johnny Cash hat ein Lied in seinem Programm, das aus einer einzigen Aneinanderreihung von Genitivmetaphern besteht. Hier die erste Strophe:

> From the backdoor of your life you swept me out, dear,
> In the bread-line of your dreams I lost my place.
> At the table of your love I got the brush-off,
> At the Indianapolis of your heart I lost the race.

Im 19. Jahrhundert kam im französischen Symbolismus eine neue Form der Metapher auf, die nicht mehr wie die klassisch-aristotelische durch eine Analogie entschlüsselt werden konnte. Jetzt fügten Dichter weit auseinander liegende Bilder zusammen und zogen gerade aus der Spannung der disparaten Teile den poetischen Reiz. Diese Form der Metapherndichtung war bis in die 60er Jahre unseres Jahrhunderts die charakteristische Ausdrucksweise moderner Lyrik. Bei Paul Celan, ihrem bedeutendsten Vertreter in deutscher Sprache, stehen solche Metaphern bereits im Titel seiner Gedichtbände: »Die Niemandsrose«, »Fadensonnen«. In Celans Gedichten finden sich zahlreiche Metaphern von irritierender und zugleich faszinierender Ausdruckskraft. Bei seinen Epigonen aber zeigt sich das Bedenkliche dieser Metapherndichtung, nämlich die extreme Beliebigkeit der Bildkombinationen. Manche Gedichte lesen sich, als hätte sie ein Computer über einen Zufallsgenerator erzeugt, und selbst einige der schwächeren Gedichte Celans kranken an dieser Beliebigkeit ihrer weithergeholten Bildverknüpfungen. Deshalb begann das Pendel schon in den 60er Jahren wieder zurückzuschwingen. Die gegenwärtige Lyrik ist nicht nur äußerst sparsam im Gebrauch der Metapher, in ihr treten auch die anderen phanopoetischen Ausdrucksmittel ganz in den Hintergrund. Den heutigen Dichtern geht es nicht um symbolisch aufgeladene Bilder oder um hermetisch-evokative Chiffren, sondern um einen spröden, sehr persönlichen, oft geradezu privatistischen Ton. Sie wollen nicht mehr allgemeine Wahrheiten einer allgemeinen Leserschaft mitteilen, sondern mit größtmöglicher Authentizität die modernen Lebensverhältnisse artikulieren, so wie sie sich bruchstückhaft in ihrem ganz privaten Bewußtsein reflektieren. Symbolische Dichtung setzt ein Vertrauen in allgemeine Bedeutungen voraus. Dieses scheint aus der zeitgenössischen Lyrik gänzlich verschwunden zu sein. Der vorerst letzte Vertreter der traditionellen, sinnvermittelnden Bildersprache ist mit Peter Huchel dahingegangen, den man neben Celan wohl als den bedeutendsten deutschen Lyriker der zweiten Jahrhunderthälfte ansehen darf. Wie Celan hatte auch er einen eigenen Bildwortschatz, nur war der seine nicht hermetisch chiffriert, sondern noch an der klassischen Tradition der symbolischen Verdichtung orientiert. Im folgenden Gedicht werden, ähnlich wie in Goethes *Faust II*, zwei Kultur- und Lebensräume, der klassisch mediterrane und der nordisch-deutsche, miteinander kontrastiert, wobei der nordische deutlich die Züge von Huchels brandenburgischer Heimat trägt.

Ölbaum und Weide

Im schroffen Anstieg brüchiger Terrassen
dort oben der Ölbaum,
am Mauerrand
der Geist der Steine,
noch immer
die leichte Brandung
von grauem Silber in der Luft,
wenn Wind die blasse Unterseite
des Laubs nach oben kehrt.

Der Abend wirft sein Fangnetz ins Gezweig.
Die Urne aus Licht
versinkt im Meer.
Es ankern Schatten in der Bucht.

Sie kommen wieder, verschwimmend im Nebel,
durchtränkt
vom Schilfdunst märkischer Wiesen,
die wendischen Weidenmütter,
die warzigen Alten
mit klaffender Brust,
am Rand der Teiche,
der dunkeläugig verschlossenen Wasser,
die Füße in die Erde grabend,
die mein Gedächtnis ist.

Unendlich viel größer als der lautliche und der bildhaft-
evokative Bereich der Sprache ist die in ihr sich ausdrük-
kende Gedankenwelt. Angefangen mit dem Regelsystem der
Grammatik über die Denkgesetze der Logik bis hin zu den
abstrakten Begriffsinhalten tut sich ein weiter Bereich einer
nichtsinnlich wahrnehmbaren Wirklichkeit auf, der mit der
Sprache untrennbar verbunden ist und deshalb genauso in
ein Gedicht eingearbeitet wird wie die sinnlichen Reize des
Klangs und der vorgestellten Bilderwelt. Von den Aus-
drucksmitteln dieses Bereichs können hier nur solche
betrachtet werden, die zum Standardrepertoire der Dichtkunst gehören.

Das elementarste logopoetische Ausdrucksmittel ist die Syntax, die Anordnung der Wörter im Satz gemäß den gramma-
tischen Regeln. Da diese Regeln ein hohes Maß an Variation
zulassen, hat der Dichter die Möglichkeit, den Satzbau auch
zum Vehikel einer Aussage zu machen. Nur dies wollen wir
hier als Ausdrucksmittel gelten lassen und die vielen rhetorischen Kunstgriffe, die nur der Dekoration oder der Ver-
lebendigung des Textes dienen, als Formalisierungsmittel
außer acht lassen. Dazu gehören Figuren mit exotischen
Namen wie Ellipse, Syllepse, Zeugma, Anakoluth, Apo-
koinu, Enallage und Hyperbaton. In der Syntax lassen sich
zwei Stiltendenzen unterscheiden, der *parataktische* Stil, der
einfache, nebengeordnete Sätze bevorzugt, und der *hypo-
taktische* Stil, der aus über- und untergeordneten Sätzen
spannungsreiche, oft schwer zu verstehende, aber eben
darum besonders ausdrucksvolle Satzgefüge baut. Wie wirkungsvoll karge, parataktische Sätze sein können, hat
Hemingway mit seinem oft kopierten Stil bewiesen, während die Möglichkeiten des hypotaktischen Stils niemand
besser genutzt hat als Heinrich von Kleist. Ihm gelingt es
oft, das, was er auf der semantischen Ebene sagt, noch ein
zweites Mal auf der Ebene der Syntax abzubilden. In dem
folgenden Beispiel kann der Leser am Fluß des Satzes genau

ablesen, wie Kohlhaas zunächst wutentbrannt losreitet, dann langsamer wird, zu überlegen beginnt, schließlich kehrtmacht und nun in erneuter Steigerung einen sich immer mehr verfestigenden Entschluß faßt:

> Spornstreichs auf dem Wege nach Dresden war er schon, als er, bei dem Gedanken an den Knecht, und an die Klage, die man auf der Burg gegen ihn führte, schrittweis zu reiten anfing, sein Pferd, ehe er noch tausend Schritte gemacht hatte, wieder wandte, und zur vorgängigen Vernehmung des Knechts, wie es ihm klug und gerecht schien, nach Kohlhaasenbrück einbog. Denn ein richtiges, mit der gebrechlichen Einrichtung der Welt schon bekanntes Gefühl machte ihn, trotz der erlittenen Beleidigungen, geneigt, falls nur wirklich dem Knecht, wie der Schloßvogt behauptete, eine Art von Schuld beizumessen sei, den Verlust der Pferde, als eine gerechte Folge davon, zu verschmerzen. Dagegen sagte ihm ein ebenso vortreffliches Gefühl, und dies Gefühl faßte tiefere und tiefere Wurzeln, in dem Maße, als er weiter ritt, und überall, wo er einkehrte, von den Ungerechtigkeiten hörte, die täglich auf der Tronkenburg gegen die Reisenden verübt wurden: daß wenn der ganze Vorfall, wie es allen Anschein habe, bloß abgekartet sein sollte, er mit seinen Kräften der Welt in der Pflicht verfallen sei, sich Genugtuung für die erlittene Kränkung, und Sicherheit für zukünftige seinen Mitbürgern zu verschaffen.

Ein anderer Geniestreich hypotaktischen Stils ist Kafkas nur aus zwei Sätzen bestehendes Prosastück »Auf der Galerie«. Solche stilistischen Kunststücke sind in der Lyrik sehr viel schwieriger, da die Syntax mit der Klang- und Bildebene des Gedichts in Einklang gebracht und meist noch ein Metrum und ein Reimschema berücksichtigt werden muß. Aber das Shakespeare-Sonett, das wir im zweiten Teil dieses Buches (S. 141–145) betrachten werden, zeigt, wie auch hier die Syntax als Ausdrucksmittel eingesetzt werden kann.
Ein anderes logopoetisches Ausdrucksmittel ist das der Stei-

gerung (Klimax), das wir bereits in der letzten Zeile von Góngoras Sonett (S. 18) kennengelernt haben. Auch größere thematische Einheiten können so angeordnet werden, daß das Gedicht in einer stetigen Crescendo-Bewegung auf einen Höhepunkt zustrebt. In Shelleys »Ode an den Westwind«, die wir ebenfalls im zweiten Teil (S. 104–112) untersuchen werden, finden wir ein eindrucksvolles Beispiel dafür. Desgleichen werden wir bei der noch zu betrachtenden Form des Sonetts sehen, wie die Antithese zwischen Aufgesang und Abgesang zu einem logopoetischen Ausdrucksmittel werden kann. In einem der schönsten philosophischen Gedichte in deutscher Sprache, in Schillers »Das Ideal und das Leben«, folgt auf eine Exposition des Problems eine Sequenz von Strophen, von denen die eine immer mit »wenn«, die andere mit »aber« beginnt, bis am Schluß eine mit »bis« eingeleitete Strophe die Synthese des dialektisch entfalteten Problems verkündet.

Alle rhetorischen Kunstgriffe, die für den geschickten Aufbau eines Arguments in einer Rede oder einem Essay verwendet werden können, eignen sich grundsätzlich auch im Gedicht dazu, einen Gedanken wirkungsvoll auszudrücken oder der Entwicklung eines Arguments eine ästhetisch reizvolle *Struktur* zu geben. Die melo- und phanopoetischen Ausdrucksmittel dienen vor allem dazu, das Gedicht im Detail mit einer lebendigen *Textur* von großer Dichte zu versehen. Deshalb lassen sie sich auch eher zu einem Repertoire standardisierter Kunstgriffe zusammenfassen. Die logopoetischen Ausdrucksmittel dagegen werden meist zum Aufbau der größeren Strukturen eingesetzt. Da jedes Gedicht entsprechend seiner Thematik eine eigene logische Struktur verlangt, lassen sich die dafür bereitstehenden Ausdrucksmittel nicht so leicht systematisieren. Textur und Struktur sind zwei Begriffe, die sich für die Gedichtinterpretation als nützlich erweisen, da der eine den Blick auf die Durchformung im Detail und der andere ihn auf die Makrostruktur des ganzen Gedichts lenkt. Beide Aspekte werden wir im zweiten Teil des Buches an Beispielen untersuchen.

Gedichtformen

Germanische Formen

In einer Anthologie moderner Lyrik sind Gedichte, die eine der strengen traditionellen Formen erkennen lassen, die Ausnahme. Bis in die erste Hälfte dieses Jahrhunderts dagegen war es genau umgekehrt. Von der Antike bis zum Ausklang der Romantik hatte sich ein Repertoire an festen Gedichtformen herausgebildet, denen zu folgen für die Dichter fast eine Selbstverständlichkeit war. Nach ihrer Herkunft lassen sich diese Formen in drei Gruppen zusammenfassen: die germanischen, die klassischen und die romanischen Formen.

Von den *germanischen* Formen haben sich drei bis heute erhalten: der Spruch, das Lied und die Ballade. Der *Spruch* ist ein knappes Gedicht, das höchste Prägnanz und Dichte anstrebt. Dabei kann es sich um eine enigmatische Beschwörungsformel wie im Falle der Zaubersprüche handeln, es kann aber auch eine präzise didaktische Aussage sein, die an den Verstand appelliert. Da der Spruch nur durch seine Kürze und ansonsten durch keine feste Form charakterisiert ist, brauchen wir ihn nicht im einzelnen zu betrachten. Es sei aber daran erinnert, daß er unter dem Einfluß Brechts und seiner Nachfolger zu einer der wichtigsten Formen der politischen Lyrik wurde. Erich Frieds Gedichte stehen formal fast alle in der Tradition der Spruchdichtung.

Die meistgebrauchte Gedichtform in der deutschen Lyrik ist ohne Zweifel das *Lied*. Sein charakteristisches Merkmal ist seine Gliederung in eine beliebige Anzahl gleichgebauter Strophen. Die Zeilenzahl der einzelnen Strophentypen reicht von zwei bis neun und darüber. Die Dichter der barocken Kirchenlieder liebten vor allem die sechszeilige Strophe wie in Paul Gerhardts »Nun ruhen alle Wälder«, dessen Form noch Mathias Claudius in seinem Abendlied übernimmt. Aber auch die achtzeilige Strophe wie in Gerhardts »O Haupt voll Blut und Wunden« und die neunzeilige in Luthers »Ein feste Burg ist unser Gott« sind öfters anzutreffen. In der Romantik setzte sich dann die vierzeilige Volksliedstrophe als die Standardstrophe der deutschen Lyrik durch. Ihre Zeilen sind vierhebig, dreihebig oder alternierend vier- und dreihebig. Das Reimschema ist gewöhnlich abab oder abcb. Der große Vorzug des Liedes ist seine formale Flexibilität. Es zwängt das Gedicht nicht in das Korsett einer fest vorgeschriebenen Zeilenzahl und bewirkt dennoch eine sehr feste, auf den ersten Blick erkennbare Formalisierung, die vor allem bei Gesangstexten das Auswendiglernen sehr leicht macht. Sein Nachteil ist das bloß additive Prinzip der Aneinanderreihung von Strophen. Darin liegt für den Dichter die Versuchung, seinem Pegasus allzusehr die Zügel schießen zu lassen, so daß sein Gedicht, das großartig begonnen haben mag, mit jeder weiteren über-flüssigen Strophe an Kraft verliert. Paul Gerhardts bekanntes Lied »Geh aus mein Herz und suche Freud« ist als Ausdruck naiver Freude an der Schönheit der Schöpfung ein sehr anschauliches Gedicht, das den Duft einer taufrischen Sommerlandschaft vermittelt; und doch wäre die Essenz dieses Duftes sicher noch stärker, wenn sie nicht über 15 Strophen gestreckt würde. Manche Dichter, so z. B. Eichendorff, hatten ein untrügliches Gefühl dafür, wie weit der Liedton eine poetische Empfindung tragen konnte, und so sind sie selten über eine Strophenzahl von sechs bis acht hinausgegangen. Andere, z. B. Brentano, haben oft einen großartigen Anfang durch viele Strophen hindurch so sehr verdünnt, daß in der Erinnerung des Lesers dann nur noch der Titel zurückbleibt (Beispiel: Brentanos »Frühlingsschrei eines Knechtes aus der Tiefe«). Es hat sicher auch etwas mit der Länge zu tun, daß Heines »Loreley« mit ihren sechs Strophen in alle Anthologien eingegangen ist, während man von den 26 Strophen der »Lureley« Brentanos nur noch den Titel kennt. Allerdings darf hier nicht verschwiegen werden, daß Brentanos Gedicht schon der nächsten, hier zu betrachtenden Form, der Ballade, angehört und damit anderen formalen Gesetzen folgt.

Die *Ballade* nimmt eine Zwischenstellung zwischen Lyrik und Epik ein. Einerseits bedient sie sich der gleichen Formalisierungs- und Ausdrucksmittel wie die Lyrik, andererseits drückt sie keine subjektiven Bewußtseinsinhalte aus, sondern erzählt in gedrängter Form eine Geschichte. Wie in der Liedform die Tradition des Volksliedes weiterwirkt, so in der Balladenform die der Volksballade. Obwohl Schiller eine von dieser Tradition unabhängige Form der Kunstballade geschaffen hat, folgt die Mehrzahl der in den Anthologien vertretenen Balladen dem Muster der Volksballade. Zur Entdeckung der Volksdichtung als einer ernstzunehmenden Kunst kam es zuerst in England im 18. Jahrhundert. Deshalb wurde die Standardstrophe der englisch-schottischen Volksballade, die nach einer der bekanntesten Balladen so benannte *Chevy-Chase-Strophe*, auch von deutschen Dichtern übernommen. Fontane verwendet sie z. B. in »Archibald Douglas«:

> Ich hab es getragen sieben Jahr,
> Und ich kann es nicht tragen mehr!
> Wo immer die Welt am schönsten war,
> Da war sie öd und leer.

Als dann im 19. Jahrhundert die Ballade zur beliebtesten Form für vaterländische, entweder historisierende oder patriotisch motivierende Inhalte wurde, griff man in Ermangelung einer echtdeutschen Balladenstrophe auch auf die *Nibelungenstrophe* zurück, wie z. B. Uhland in »Des Sängers Fluch«:

> Es stand in alten Zeiten ein Schloß, so hoch und hehr,
> Weit glänzt' es über die Lande bis an das blaue Meer,
> Und rings von duftgen Gärten ein blütenreicher Kranz,
> Drin sprangen frische Brunnen in Regenbogenglanz.

Nach Inhalt und Grundton lassen sich die Balladen grob in vier Klassen einteilen:
1. die Schauerballade, die das Übernatürliche und Numi-

56

nose beschwört (Bürgers »Lenore« und Goethes »Erlkönig«)
2. die Ideenballade, die ein moralisches oder metaphysi-
sches Problem exemplifiziert (Schillers »Die Kraniche
des Ibykus« und Goethes »Der Gott und die Bajadere«)
3. die Geschichtsballade, die einen historischen oder sagen-
haften Stoff gestaltet (Chamissos »Die Weiber von Wins-
perg«)
4. die realistisch-naturalistische Ballade, die ein Ereignis aus
der Gegenwart moralisierend oder sozialkritisch darstellt
(Fonantes »John Maynard«).

Obwohl die Ballade wegen ihrer moralisierenden Tendenz
und ihrem Hang zur patriotischen Deutschtümelei die vermutlich am häufigsten parodierte lyrische Form ist, hat sie
bis heute nichts von ihrer Beliebtheit verloren. Nach dem
Vorbild Brechts wurde sie nach dem Kriege von Stephan
Hermlin, Volker von Törne und vielen anderen verwendet,
allerdings nur in der vierten Variante als Gefäß bitter-
sarkastischer oder satirisch-ironischer Zeitkritik.

Antike Formen

Auch von den Gedichtformen der klassischen Antike haben
sich nur drei bis in die neuere Zeit erhalten: das Epigramm,
die Ode und die Elegie.
Das *Epigramm* ist das antike Gegenstück zum germanischen
Spruch. Seine standardisierte Form ist die des Distichons:
ein Zweizeiler, bestehend aus einem Hexameter und einem
Pentameter. Goethe und Schiller haben die Form in den
»Xenien« verwendet. Eins davon dient oft als Merkvers für
die beiden Versformen:

Im Hexameter steigt des Springquells flüssige Säule,
Im Pentameter drauf fällt sie melodisch herab.

Die *Ode* ist ein ernstes, weihevolles Gedicht, das gewöhnlich an einen Adressaten – einen Helden, einen Gott, das Vaterland oder die Vaterstadt – gerichtet war und sich in strenger Form mit allgemeinmenschlichen Dingen auseinandersetzte. In späterer Zeit wurde von der antiken Ode oft nur der feierliche Ton übernommen. Klopstock, Hölderlin und andere haben aber auch ihre strengen Strophenformen wiederbelebt. Die drei Hauptformen sollen hier kurz vorgestellt werden, obwohl es nicht sonderlich wichtig ist, sie unterscheiden zu können:

1. die alkäische Ode

> Nur Einen Sommer gönnt, ihr Gewaltigen!
> Und einen Herbst zu reifem Gesange mir,
> Daß williger mein Herz, vom süßen
> Spiele gesättiget, dann mir sterbe.

> (Aus: Hölderlin, »An die Parzen«)

2. die asklepiadeische Ode

> Schön ist, Mutter Natur, deiner Erfindung Pracht
> Auf die Fluren verstreut, schöner ein froh Gesicht,
> Das den großen Gedanken
> Deiner Schöpfung noch *einmal* denkt.

> (Aus: Klopstock, »Der Zürchersee«)

3. die sapphische Ode

> Heilige Unschuld, du der Menschen und der
> Götter liebste, vertrauteste! du magst im
> Hause oder draußen ihnen zu Füßen
> Sitzen, den Alten;

> (Aus: Hölderlin, »Unter den Alpen gesungen«)

Während in den ersten beiden Beispielen die deutsche Sprache sich noch einigermaßen willig in das formale Prokrustesbett schmiegt, zeigt das dritte Beispiel, daß der poetische Reiz eines Gedichts durch die allzu gewaltsame Formalisierung eher zerstört als bestärkt wird.

Auch von der *Elegie*, der antiken Form des Trauer- und Klagegedichts, wurde später meist nur der klagende Ton übernommen. Nur wenige haben, wie Schiller in »Nänie«, auch das elegische Metrum, das schon erwähnte Distichon, nachgebildet. Die berühmtesten Beispiele aus diesem Jahrhundert sind Rilkes »Duineser Elegien«, die die Grundhaltung der Klage zu der einer allgemeinen meditativen Inbrunst ausweiten.

Als vierte antike Form wäre noch die *Hymne* zu nennen. Da sie aber in keiner festen Form überliefert ist, haben spätere Dichter auch von ihr nur den hymnischen Ton übernommen, wie er uns aus Goethes frühen Hymnen vertraut ist. Dieser Ton ist freilich so universal, daß er sich auch ohne antiken Einfluß hätte ausbilden können, wie sich übrigens auch der elegische Ton in den altenglischen Elegien ohne jenen Einfluß ausgebildet hat.

Romanische Formen

Da in den romanischen Sprachen die Reimfindung besonders leicht ist, konnten sich dort Gedichtformen mit sehr komplizierten Reimschemata entwickeln. Viele dieser Formen sind auch im Deutschen nachgebildet worden, aber es blieb doch meist bei kunstfertigen Fingerübungen. Rondeau, Rondel, Triolett, Villanella und Sestine sind in deutschen Anthologien so selten vertreten, daß man sich ihre Formen kaum merken muß. Die Sestine ist vermutlich die schwierigste Form überhaupt, da sie aus sechs sechszeiligen Strophen besteht, in denen die Reimwörter der ersten Strophe nach einem strengen Permutationssystem fünfmal identisch wiederholt werden. Das Gedicht schließt mit einer dreizeiligen siebten Strophe, die die Reimwörter ein letztes Mal wiederholt, drei davon in der Mitte und drei am Ende der Zeilen. Bei barocken Dichtern wie Opitz und Weckherlin, die die spielerische Seite der Dichtkunst besonders betonten, und auch bei formbewußten Spätromantikern wie Friedrich Rückert findet man Beispiele für die Sestine. Aber der Aufwand an Kunstfertigkeit entspricht dabei selten dem dichterischen Ertrag.

Nur zwei romanische Gedichtformen spielen in der deutschen Lyrik eine Rolle: die Romanze und das Sonett. Die spanische *Romanze* wurde schon im 18. Jahrhundert durch Gleim in die deutsche Dichtung eingeführt. Herder verhalf ihr durch seine Übersetzung des spanischen *Cid* zu weiterer Verbreitung, und die Romantiker machten regen Gebrauch von ihr. Wirklich populär aber wurde sie erst, als Heine ihr den satirisch-parodistischen Ton gab, den wohl die meisten Lyrikleser seitdem mit dieser Gedichtform verbinden. Hier ein Beispiel aus dem »Atta Troll«:

> Mancher tugendhafte Bürger
> Duftet schlecht auf Erden, während
> Fürstenknechte mit Lavendel
> Oder Ambra parfümiert sind.
>
> Jungfräuliche Seelen gibt es,
> Die nach grüner Seife riechen,
> Und das Laster hat zuweilen
> Sich mit Rosenöl gewaschen.
>
> Darum rümpfet nicht die Nase,
> Teurer Leser, wenn die Höhle
> Atta Trolls dich nicht erinnert
> An Arabiens Spezereien.

Der charakteristische Effekt dieser Strophenform beruht darauf, daß einerseits das trochäische Metrum der vierhebigen Zeilen extrem glatt und regelmäßig ist, während andererseits durch das Fehlen des Reims eine penetrante Überformalisierung vermieden wird. An die Stelle des Reims tritt in der Romanze gewöhnlich die Assonanz, d. h. der bloß vokalische Gleichklang der Versenden von der letzten Hebung an, und zwar in der zweiten und vierten Zeile. Die Assonanz kann aber auch fehlen oder durch einen echten Reim ersetzt werden. Bei Heine findet man alle drei Möglichkeiten. In den drei zitierten Strophen verwendet er weder Reim noch Assonanz, und doch wirken sie so fest formalisiert, daß der Leser nach der Lektüre in der Erinnerung vermutlich das Gefühl haben wird, ein gereimtes Gedicht gelesen zu haben.

Ehe wir uns dem Sonett zuwenden, sollte als dritte romanische Form vielleicht noch das *Madrigal* kurz erwähnt werden. Es entstand als Hirtenlied in Italien, wo es sich bereits im 14. Jahrhundert zu einem Kunstlied entwickelte. Im Barock, in der Zeit der Anakreontik und noch in der Romantik war es auch in der deutschen Lyrik weitverbreitet. Da man über seine Form aber kaum mehr sagen kann, als daß sie zwischen 4 und ca. 20 Zeilen von unterschiedlichem Metrum und wechselnder Länge umfaßt, läßt sich fast jedes locker gefügte, nicht strophisch gegliederte Gedicht als Madrigal bezeichnen, womit der Name als Formbegriff wertlos wird.

Das Sonett

Die mit Abstand wichtigste romanische Gedichtform ist das Sonett. Entstanden in Sizilien im 13. Jahrhundert, durch Petrarca zu höchster Vollkommenheit gebracht, verbreitete es sich im 16. Jahrhundert über ganz Europa und ist bis heute die meistgebrauchte der strengen Gedichtformen geblieben. Das italienische Sonett besteht aus 14 Zeilen vom Typ des *endecasillabo* (Elfsilber), der im Deutschen und Englischen gewöhnlich durch einen fünfhebigen Jambus ersetzt wird. Die 14 Zeilen gliedern sich in zwei Quartette, den sog. Aufgesang, und zwei Terzette, den Abgesang. Das Reimschema in der strengen italienischen Form ist

abba   abba   cdc   dcd

Das bedeutet, daß im Aufgesang zweimal je vier und im Abgesang zweimal je drei Wörter auf einen Reim gefunden werden mußten. Im Italienischen mit seinen vielen Endungen auf -ano, -ato, -ino usw. stellte das kein Problem dar, in den germanischen Sprachen dagegen war dies sehr viel schwerer. Deshalb haben die Engländer das Reimschema schon sehr früh vereinfacht. Shakespeare und seine Zeitgenossen entwickelten eine Sonettform mit folgendem Reimschema:

abab   cdcd   efef   gg

Dadurch veränderte sich die gesamte Struktur des Sonetts. Statt einer Oktave (zwei Quartette) als Aufgesang und einem Sextett (zwei Terzette) als Abgesang hat das *Shakespearean sonnet* drei Quartette und ein abschließendes Reimpaar, das sog. *couplet*.

Die Bezeichnungen Aufgesang und Abgesang legen bereits nahe, daß sich die beiden Teile des Sonetts in einem Spannungsverhältnis befinden. In vielen Sonetten stellt sich diese Spannung als klare Antithese dar, z. B. so, daß der Aufgesang ein Argument entwickelt, das im Abgesang attackiert und widerlegt wird. Das Verhältnis kann aber auch so aussehen, daß die These des Aufgesangs nicht widerlegt, sondern nur erläutert und kommentiert wird; oder der Aufgesang stellt einen komplizierten Vergleich an, der im Abgesang explizit gedeutet wird. Wie immer das Verhältnis der beiden Teile inhaltlich begründet sein mag, stets ist zwischen beiden eine deutliche Zäsur spürbar. Dieser Drehpunkt macht den intellektuellen Reiz des Sonetts aus; denn er zwingt den Dichter, ein Argument, ein Bild oder einen Vergleich so zuzuspitzen, daß der Gedankenstrom über die Zäsur hinweggeführt wird und dabei dennoch eine andere Richtung erhält. Im englischen Sonett ist die Hauptzäsur ans Ende des dritten Quartetts verlegt. Aber die meisten Sonette, zumal die von Shakespeare, weisen auch da, wo das italienische Sonett die Zäsur hat, eine deutlich spürbare Schwelle auf, was oft schon daran zu erkennen ist, daß das dritte Quartett mit einem »but«, »yet« oder einer anderen entgegensetzenden Konjunktion beginnt. Diese Form erhält dadurch eine dreigliedrige Struktur, die von den Dichtern in der Regel auch voll zur Wirkung gebracht wird, z. B. so, daß die beiden ersten Quartette eine These entwickeln, das dritte eine Gegenthese aufstellt und das *couplet* ein abschließendes Fazit zieht.

Die deutsche Lyrik, die zur Blütezeit des Sonetts um 1600 selber nicht in Blüte stand, hat zunächst die französische Form des italienischen Sonetts übernommen, die das strenge Reimschema beibehielt. Zugleich aber übernahm sie das französische Versmaß des Alexandriners. Darunter versteht man einen sechshebigen Jambus mit einer scharfen Zäsur nach der dritten Hebung. Die Übernahme dieses Verses war ein folgenschwerer Mißgriff der deutschen Barockdichter. Im Französischen ist der Alexandriner ein sehr klangvoller, schön ausschwingender Vers. Da französische Wörter am Ende betont werden, stellte die Zäsur in der Mitte der Zeile keinen trennenden Graben, sondern nur eine kleine Schwelle dar, die ein kurzes *ritardando* des Sprachflusses bewirkte. Im Deutschen dagegen werden die Wörter auf der Anfangssilbe betont. Wenn also die Zäsur nach der dritten Hebung liegen soll, muß diese in der Regel ein einsilbiges Wort sein, und es muß, damit es auch wirklich betont wird, vom folgenden klar abgetrennt sein. Dieser Sachverhalt bewirkt, daß die deutsche Alexandrinerdichtung auf eine störende Weise kurzatmig ist. Jede Zeile wird in zwei dreihebige Hälften zerhackt, und wenn man 28 solcher Hälften hintereinander gelesen hat, sehnt man sich nach einem langen Satz, der über das Zeilenende hinausschwingt und durch Enjambement in die nächste Zeile hinübergeführt wird. Die eindrucksvollsten, sprachlich schönsten Sonette von Andreas Gryphius, dem bedeutendsten deutschen Barockdichter, werden oft durch das monotone Stakkato des Alexandriners um ihre Wirkung gebracht. Eines dieser Sonette wollen wir in der zweiten Hälfte dieses Buches mit einem englischen vergleichen (S. 121–126). Um das Manko des deutschen Alexandriners zu zeigen, wählen wir hier eine Strophe aus einem von Martin Opitz übersetzten Sonett des berühmtesten französischen Dichters seiner Zeit, Pierre de Ronsard. Der Vergleich mit dem Original wird zeigen, wie der weiche Fluß des französischen Alexandriners im Deutschen zu einem harten, sehr unmelodiösen Rattern wird.

Pierre de Ronsard

Chacun me dit, Ronsard, ta maistresse n'est telle
Comme tu la descris. Certes je n'en sçay rien:
Je suis devenu fol, mon esprit n'est plus mien,
Je ne puis discerner la laide de la belle.

Martin Opitz

Ein jeder spricht zu mir, dein Lieb ist nicht dergleichen,
Wie du sie zwar beschreibst: ich weiß es wahrlich nicht,
Ich bin fast nicht mehr klug; der scharffen Sinnen Liecht
Vermag gar kaum was weiß und schwartz ist zu erreichen.

Ronsard, der den Alexandriner zum Standardvers des französischen Sonetts machte, hat auch Sonette in dem früher üblichen Zehnsilber geschrieben, dessen deutsche Entsprechung der fünfhebige Jambus gewesen wäre. Dennoch hat Opitz auch diese Sonette im Alexandriner übersetzt. Die Vorliebe der deutschen Barockdichter für diesen Vers ist dadurch zu erklären, daß die Zweigliedrigkeit mit der Zäsur in der Mitte sich in besonderem Maß dazu eignete, die charakteristische Denkfigur des Barock, die Antithese, zum Ausdruck zu bringen. Diese Figur, die in der dualistischen Philosophie Descartes' ihre metaphysische Ausformung erfuhr, hat das Denken des Barock so sehr beherrscht, daß die Dichter ihr nicht nur den sprachlichen Wohlklang opferten, sondern sich auch der Möglichkeit des Ausdrucks komplexer gedanklicher Strukturen begaben, wie sie der größte *metaphysical poet* der Engländer, John Donne, den man im europäischen Kontext als Barockdichter bezeichnen darf, so meisterhaft gestaltet hat. Ein Vergleich mit Gryphius wird dies später noch zeigen.

Das Sonett hat bis heute nichts von seinem Reiz verloren, der in seiner charakteristischen Verbindung des Sinnlich-Poetischen mit dem Gedanklich-Reflektierenden liegt. Zwar wird es inzwischen seltener und oft in sehr freier, z. T. reimloser Form gebraucht, aber noch Josef Weinheber, der Hauptvertreter des lyrischen Neuklassizismus in diesem Jahrhundert, schrieb in altmeisterlicher Manier ganze Sonettenkränze, das sind Folgen von 15 Sonetten, von denen jedes folgende mit der Schlußzeile des vorhergehenden beginnt, während das 15. Sonett alle Anfangszeilen noch einmal nacheinander wiederholt.

Sprachliche Komik

Unzählige Gedichte wurden und werden zu keinem anderen Zweck geschrieben, als den Leser für einen Augenblick zum Schmunzeln, Lächeln oder Lachen zu bringen. Da diese Wirkung nur dann eintritt, wenn der Leser spontan auf die Komik des Textes reagiert, bedürfen solche Gedichte keiner Interpretation. Im Gegenteil, diese würde die komische Wirkung viel eher verhindern, so wie jeder Witz aufhört, witzig zu sein, wenn jemand anfängt, ihn zu erklären. Dennoch ist es für den neugierigen Leser von intellektuellem Reiz, die Machart eines komischen Textes zu durchschauen.

Kant definierte das Lachen als »die Auflösung einer gespannten Erwartung in nichts«. Dies ist immer noch die kürzeste und treffendste Beschreibung dessen, was physiologisch den Ablauf unserer Reaktion auf Komik ausmacht. Sie beginnt damit, daß sich in uns eine psychische Spannung aufbaut, wenn wir auf das Eintreten eines ungewissen, aber doch irgendwie vermuteten Ereignisses warten. Wird diese Erwartung dann auf eine unerwartete Weise erfüllt, entlädt sich die Spannung in befreiendem Gelächter. Voraussetzung ist allerdings, daß sich die Spannung »in nichts« auflöst, d. h., es darf weder Schmerz noch Trauer, noch eine den Geist erhebende Erkenntnis übrigbleiben. Nur dann werden wir vom Gipfel der Spannung auf die Nullebene der völligen Entspannung zurückfallen und den Lachreiz verspüren. Dieser psychische Mechanismus, der in der Komödie kunstvoll in Handlung umgesetzt wird, liegt auch allen komischen Effekten auf der sprachlichen Ebene zugrunde.

Die einfachste Form, eine gespannte Erwartung zu erzeugen und sie auf unerwartete Weise zu lösen, ist das Wortspiel. Ein Wort, das zwei oder mehr Bedeutungen hat, kann so verwendet werden, daß der Leser zunächst eine Bedeutung erwartet, die die nächstliegende zu sein scheint. Wenn er dann merkt, daß eine andere gemeint ist, reagiert er je nach dem Grad der Überraschung mit Schmunzeln oder Gelächter. Diese Reaktion tritt aber nur dann ein, wenn der Leser durch einen Kunstgriff des Textes und nicht durch ein eigenes Mißverständnis auf die falsche Fährte gelockt wurde, da er sich sonst seines Mangels an Bildung oder an Geistesgegenwart schämen müßte. Am spontansten ist die Reaktion, das Lachen, in der Regel dann, wenn das Durchschauen unmittelbar auf die Täuschung folgt, weil der Leser dann die zusätzliche Befriedigung hat, daß er sich nicht hat hinters Licht führen lassen. Im Deutschen sind Wortspiele verhältnismäßig selten, da es nicht allzu viele mehrdeutige Wörter gibt. Im Englischen dagegen ist das *punning* ein nationaler Volkssport; denn hier gibt es unzählige, meist einsilbige Wörter, in denen mehrere, ursprünglich ganz verschiedene Wörter durch den sprachgeschichtlichen Wegfall der Endsilben zusammengefallen sind. So kann z. B. das Wort, das soul gesprochen wird, *soul* »Seele«, *sole* »Sohle«, *sole* »Seezunge«, *sole* »einzig« bedeuten. Daraus kann sich leicht ein Wortwechsel wie dieser ergeben:

»You have no soul.« – »I've got two soles ... under my feet.«
»That's the sole sort of soul you've got.«

Ein besonders geistreicher Gesprächspartner könnte sicher auch noch die Seezunge in dem Dialog unterbringen. In der englischen Dichtung von Shakespeare bis zur Gegenwart begegnet man solchen *puns* auf Schritt und Tritt, ebenso in Zeitungen und politischen Reden. Ein englischer Politiker sagte einmal: »Nato reminds me of the Venus of Milo: much SHAPE, but no arms.« SHAPE ist die Abkürzung für das Nato-Hauptquartier in Paris, bedeutet aber zugleich soviel wie »gute Figur« und *arms* heißt sowohl »Arme« wie auch »Waffen«. Unseren deutschen Politikern verwehrt es die Sprache, sich auf so geistreiche Weise zu profilieren.

Limerick

Als Inbegriff sprachlicher Komik gilt allgemein der englische Limerick. Seine Mechanik läßt sich in den meisten Fällen einem der folgenden Typen zuordnen, die wir gleich mit je einem Beispiel illustrieren wollen:

1. Die überraschende Situation:

> There was a young man of Bengal
> Who went to a fancy-dress ball.
>   He went just for fun
>   Dressed up as a bun,
> And a dog ate him up in the hall.

Hier wird nur sprachlich ausgedrückt, was der Leser sich als szenische Situationskomik vorstellen soll, wobei die Sprache den Vorzug hat, daß sie auch unmögliche Situationen evozieren kann.

2. Die überraschende Bedeutung:

> There was a young girl of West Ham,
> Who smiled as she jumped on a tram;
>   As she quickly embarked
>   The conductor remarked,
> »Your fare, Miss.« She said, »Yes, I am.«

Das Mädchen wird aufgefordert, den Fahrpreis zu entrichten: »Your fare«. Sie reagiert aber auf den lautlich identischen Satz: »You're fair« = Du bist hübsch (oder blond oder fair). Es handelt sich also um den schon besprochenen Mechanismus des Wortspiels.

3. Die überraschende grammatische Verknüpfung:

> There was a young lady from Riga
> Who smiled as she rode on a tiger,
>   But after the ride
>   Her place was inside
> And the smile on the face of the tiger.

Die Komik dieses wohl bekanntesten englischen Limericks beruht darauf, daß ein makabres Geschehen in die witzige Form des Zeugmas gekleidet wird. Das ist eine rhetorische Figur, bei der zwei Objekte oder, wie in unserem Fall, Subjekte auf das gleiche Prädikat bezogen werden, obwohl sie zu diesem eine unterschiedliche semantische Beziehung haben. Ein anderes Beispiel: »Erst schlug er alle Fensterscheiben und dann den Weg zum Bahnhof ein.«

4. Der überraschende Absturz vom Erhabenen ins Lächerliche:

Curt Peiser:
> Ein Knabe aus Tehuantepec,
> Der lief auf der Bahn seiner Tante weg,
>   Sie lief hinterher,
>   Denn sie liebte ihn sehr,
> Und außerdem trug er ihr Handgepäck.

Im Englischen wird dieser plötzliche Absturz ins Banale, der unfreiwillige ebenso wie der geplante, mit dem von Alexander Pope geprägten Begriff *Bathos* bezeichnet. Das griechische Wort bedeutet Höhe oder Tiefe. Entscheidend für die Wahl des Wortes war aber wohl der lautliche Kontrast zu Pathos, dessen negatives Pendant der Begriff bezeichnet. Seine Übernahme in die deutsche Fachterminologie wäre sicher ein Gewinn.

5. Der überraschende Reim:

> There was a young lady of Tottenham,
> Who'd no manners, or else she'd forgottn'em;
> At tea at the vicar's
> She tore off her knickers
> Because, she explained, she felt 'ot in 'em
> (= hot in them).

Reime von so verwegener Art sind im Deutschen kaum möglich. Der »Knabe aus Tehuantepec« ist so ungefähr das Äußerste, was sich in unserer Sprache machen läßt. Charakteristisch an diesem Limerick ist noch etwas anderes, die Pikanterie. Von der versteckten Anzüglichkeit bis hin zur Obszönität sind im Limerick alle Spielarten des Frivolen vertreten.

6. Das überraschende Schriftbild:

Ogden Nash:
> There was a brave girl of Connecticut
> Who flagged the express with her pecticut
> (= petticoat)
> Which critics defined
> As presence of mind,
> But deplorable absence of ecticut
> (= etiquette).

Diese Technik sprachlicher Komik ist natürlich nur in einer Sprache wie dem Englischen möglich, wo die Wörter anders geschrieben als gesprochen werden.

Die sechs hier unterschiedenen Techniken sprachlicher Komik, denen sich der größte Teil aller Limericks zuordnen läßt, beruhen allesamt auf einem Überraschungseffekt, also auf der unerwarteten Auflösung einer gespannten Erwartung. Daneben gibt es aber komische Techniken, die ihre Wirkung nicht aus der Auflösung, sondern aus der Aufrechterhaltung einer Spannung ziehen. Im Limerick, der ja auf eine Pointe und somit auf Auflösung hin angelegt ist, sind sie nur selten anzutreffen, ansonsten aber in der heiteren Muse weit verbreitet. Die allgemeinste von ihnen ist die Technik der Überformalisierung. Jeder weiß, daß man den banalsten Dingen eine komische Wendung geben kann, wenn man sie gespreizt und hochgestochen ausspricht. Voraussetzung ist allerdings ein so hohes Stilniveau, daß niemand auf die Idee kommt, es könnte ernsthaft gemeint sein. Dadurch entsteht eine Spannung zwischen dem Anspruch des Stilniveaus und der Banalität der Sache, die nicht durch eine überraschende Pointe, sondern durch die Einsicht in den Unernst des stilistischen Anspruchs aufgelöst wird. Da etwas vorgetäuscht wird, handelt es sich hier um eine Form der Ironie. Häufig wird aber die Überformalisierung von vornherein so überdreht, daß der Schein des Ernstes, den Ironie immer voraussetzt, gar nicht erst aufkommt. In solchen Fällen ist eher von Clownerie und Sprachgroteske zu sprechen. Hier ein Beispiel (die erste von drei Strophen):

Hanns von Gumppenberg

Sommermädchenküssetauschelächelbeichte

An der Murmelrieselplauderplätscherquelle
Saß ich sehnsuchtstränentröpfeltrauerbang:
Trat herzu ein Augenblinzeljunggeselle
In verwegnem Hüfteschwingeschlendergang,
Zog mit Schäkerehrfurchtsbittegrußverbeugung
Seinen Federbaumelriesenkrämpenhut –
Gleich verspür' ich Liebeszauberkeimeneigung,
War ihm zitterjubelschauderherzensgut!

Der unbefangene Leser wird dieses Gedicht als reine, spielerisch überdrehte Sprachgroteske lesen. Erst aus einer Anmerkung des Dichters »Nach O. J. Bierbaum und anderen Wortkopplern« erfährt er, daß dahinter eine parodistische Absicht steht. Damit wären wir bei einer weiteren, sehr beliebten Spezialform komischer Gedichte.

Parodie

Auch die Parodie zieht ihre Wirkung aus der entlarvenden Diskrepanz zwischen einer anspruchsvollen Form und einem banalen Inhalt. Ihr Ziel ist aber nicht das befreiende Lachen, das durch die Wahrnehmung des bewußten Unernstes der Diskrepanz ausgelöst wird, sondern das Lächerlichmachen einer von einem anderen Dichter übernommenen Form, die zu diesem Zweck mit einem banalen Inhalt gefüllt wird. Die Parodie kann sich auf ein einzelnes Gedicht, auf den persönlichen Stil eines Dichters oder auf die typischen Gattungsmerkmale einer ganzen Textklasse beziehen. Am häufigsten ist zweifellos die erste Variante. Während bei den beiden anderen Varianten der Parodist seine Absicht irgendwie ankündigen muß, da er sonst Gefahr läuft, für einen Imitator gehalten zu werden, ist die Parodie eines bestimmten Gedichts für jeden, der die Vorlage kennt, als solche erkennbar. Das folgende Beispiel ist ein virtuoses Kabinettstück, das ein bestimmtes Gedicht, nämlich Schillers »Lied von der Glocke«, parodiert und dabei die Mechanik der Überformalisierung auf die Spitze treibt, indem es außerdem noch statt einfacher Reime Schüttelreime verwendet. Noch interessanter als die Frage nach der parodistischen Technik wäre allerdings die nach der Parodierbarkeit einzelner Dichter, der hier leider nicht nachgegangen werden kann. Ganz offensichtlich gibt es Dichter, z. B. Shakespeare, die kaum zu parodieren sind, während andere wie Schiller zur Parodie förmlich einladen.

Sita Steen

Ein Glied von Schillers Locke

Und drinnen waltet die putzsüchtge Hausfrau:
Sie füttert im Stalle die hochfrüchtge Haussau,
die Mutter der Vierpfünder,
mit Futter für vier Münder,
und lebet weise
und webet leise
und lehret die Mädchen
und mehret die Lädchen
und strickelt und webet
und wickelt und strebet,
Gewinne zu mehren,
der Minne zu wehren,
und müht sich ohn' Ende, mit Fleiße zu sticken,
die Strümpfe zu stopfen, die Steiße zu flicken,
und füllet mit Schätzen und hehren Laken
die Schreine, die Truhen, die leeren Haken
und spinnet zum Faden die schimmernde Wolle
und findet zum Spaten die wimmernde Scholle
und nutzet die Kräfte und ganze Glut
und zeigt sich im festlichen Glanze gut –
trotz scheußlichem Harm –
mit häuslichem Charme!

Nonsense-Dichtung

Das Lösen einer gespannten Erwartung – sei es durch einen
Überraschungseffekt, sei es durch Einsicht in eine Inkon-
gruenz – ist gewissermaßen das klassische Reaktionsschema,
das allen traditionellen Formen des Komischen – also der
Komödie, dem Schwank, der Anekdote, dem Witz usw. –
zugrunde liegt. In neuerer Zeit hat sich daneben eine zweite
Form des Komischen etabliert, die Nonsense-Dichtung. Ihr

72

Mechanismus funktioniert in entgegengesetzter Richtung. Anstelle einer gespannten Erwartung wird hier gerade deren Ausbleiben als Quelle von Komik genutzt. Sie spielt mit dem Leser, indem sie ihn darauf warten läßt, daß seine Erwartung endlich in eine bestimmte Richtung gespannt werde. Diese »ungespannte« Erwartung wird durch eine unsinnige, ganz und gar unlogische Schlußfolgerung enttäuscht, wobei gerade das Ausbleiben der Pointe den Lachreiz bewirkt. Der Leser hat das Gefühl, auf eine verschlossene Tür zuzugehen: doch ehe noch seine Neugier recht geweckt ist, öffnet sich die Tür, und dahinter ist – nichts. Da Nonsense semantische Leere bedeutet, genügt bereits eine »ungespannte« Erwartung, um mit der Auflösung in ein absolutes Nichts einen komischen Effekt zu erzielen. Dazu zwei Beispiele:

Günter Grass

Vergleichsweise

Eine Katze liegt in der Wiese.
Die Wiese ist hundertzehn
mal neunzig Meter groß;
die Katze dagegen ist noch sehr jung.

Gerhard Rühm

wer doch wer

Wer in der sahara
miete zahlt
beweist mut

doch wer mit tomaten
tennis spielt
beschwört sodom

Während der erste Text seine komische Wirkung ganz aus dem Ins-Leere-Laufen der ungespannten Erwartung zieht, funktioniert der zweite nur an der Oberfläche nach diesem Schema. Der Leser wird unschwer erkennen, daß das Gedicht einen doppelten Boden hat. Nach der Logik des gesunden Menschenverstandes müßte die letzte Zeile beider Strophen lauten

... ist dumm.

Wenn es statt dessen aber heißt

beweist mut

bzw. beschwört sodom,

wird beides, heroischer Mut und sittenlose Libertinage, als Dummheit entlarvt. Das Gedicht hat also hinter seiner vermeintlichen Nonsensefassade eine satirisch-moralisierende Tendenz.

Es ist betrüblich, daß der Deutschunterricht an den Schulen immer noch so sehr auf die ernsthafte Lyrik fixiert ist. Dabei eignen sich komische Verse oft viel besser dazu, Kunst als Kunstgriff zu durchschauen. Außerdem eröffnet sich hier ein Feld, auf dem der Schüler selber kreativ werden kann, und zwar mit weitaus befriedigenderen Ergebnissen als auf dem ernsthaft-lyrischen Felde, wo Schülergedichte sehr häufig epigonal oder kitschig sind. Es ist zwar richtig, daß man, um ein Gedicht kritisch beurteilen zu können, nicht unbedingt selber ein Dichter sein muß. Aber ebenso richtig ist, daß die beste Einübung in das Verstehen von Gedichten darin besteht, daß man sich selber einmal im Handwerk des Dichtens übt, und sei es auch nur durch den Versuch, ein paar kunstgerechte Limericks zu verfassen.

Zum Herstellen eines Gedichtes
bedarf's keines geistigen Lichtes,
zum Limerick reicht es
bei jedem. Auch Leichtes
entbehrt manchmal nicht des Gewichtes.

Was man wissen muß,
um ein Gedicht interpretieren zu können

Gedichte sind gemalte Fensterscheiben!
Sieht man vom Markt in die Kirche hinein,
Da ist alles dunkel und düster;
Und so sieht's auch der Herr Philister:
Der mag denn wohl verdrießlich sein
Und lebenslang verdrießlich bleiben.

Kommt aber nur einmal herein!
Begrüßt die heilige Kapelle;
Da ist's auf einmal farbig helle,
Geschicht' und Zierat glänzt in Schnelle,
Bedeutend wirkt ein edler Schein;
Dies wird euch Kindern Gottes taugen,
Erbaut euch und ergetzt die Augen!

(Goethe)

In den 50er Jahren geisterte der Begriff der werkimmanenten Interpretation durch den Deutschunterricht und durch die germanistischen Seminare der Universitäten. In seiner radikalsten Variante besagte er, daß jedes Gedicht ein autonomes Kunstwerk sei, das allein aus sich selbst heraus verstanden werden müsse. So sei es beispielsweise falsch, nach der Intention des Autors zu fragen; denn nicht auf diese komme es an, sondern auf die Intention des Werkes. Die gemäßigtere Variante, die allgemein akzeptiert war, betonte nur den absoluten Vorrang des Werkes, was dann eine entsprechende Vernachlässigung aller anderen, werkfremden Aspekte zur Folge hatte. In der Praxis bewirkte dieser Ansatz eine deutliche Verfeinerung der Interpretationsmethoden, in der Theorie aber war er völlig unhaltbar. Schon bei der allerersten Annäherung an ein Gedicht muß man etwas kennen, das außerhalb des Werkes liegt: die Sprache. Da Sprache das symbolische Zeichensystem ist, in dem sich für uns die Welt abbildet, ist in ihr die Welt ständig gegenwärtig. Lesen wir z. B. ein Gedicht des 18. Jahrhunderts, so müssen wir, um seine Sprache zu verstehen, erst einmal die Welt kennen, die in sie eingegangen ist. Gewiß sind viele Gedichte so allgemeinverständlich, daß man sie ohne irgendwelche Information über den Autor, die Zeit und den literarhistorischen Kontext hinreichend verstehen kann, um an ihnen Freude zu haben. Aber der Leser wird dann immer nur das aus ihnen herauslesen können, was sich mit seinen eigenen Erfahrungen deckt. Gedichte sind für ihn Spiegel, nicht die »gemalten Fensterscheiben«, von denen Goethe spricht. Will man durch die Fensterscheiben sehen, muß man in die Gedichte eintreten. Dazu braucht man einen Schlüssel. Je älter, je komplexer, je schwieriger ein Gedicht ist, um so mehr Schlösser muß man öffnen, ehe man durch die »gemalten Fensterscheiben« sehen kann. Auf der Suche nach den Schlüsseln und Schlössern wollen wir uns erst einmal einen Lageplan des zu Entschlüsselnden verschaffen. Die folgende Skizze soll uns dabei helfen:

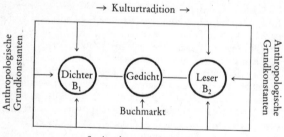

Ein gedrucktes Gedicht ist zunächst nichts weiter als eine bestimmte Anzahl schwarzer Zeichen auf einem weißen Blatt Papier. In diese Zeichen wurde von einem Dichter ein Bewußtseinsinhalt (B_1) enkodiert, der durch einen Leser dekodiert und wieder in einen Bewußtseinsinhalt (B_2)

zurückverwandelt wird. Im Idealfall sollten B_1 und B_2 identisch sein. Dies ist aber nicht nur praktisch, sondern auch theoretisch unmöglich, da das Bewußtsein eines Menschen, sein Ich, das schlechthin Individuelle an ihm ist, das nicht einmal bei eineiigen Zwillingen identisch ist. Das Ziel kann also nur eine größtmögliche Annäherung von B_2 an B_1 sein.

Der erste Schritt der Annäherung ist das Lesen, das Dekodieren, des Gedichts. Wenn es in unserer eigenen Sprache vorliegt, erscheint uns dieser Schritt problemlos. Aber auch dann kann der Sprachcode des Gedichts durchaus von unserem verschieden sein. Wenn es sich z. B. um ein älteres oder ein dialektal gefärbtes Gedicht handelt, müssen wir erst die historische bzw. regionale Sprachvariante lernen, um den Text zu verstehen. Der gewöhnliche Leser wird nach diesem Schritt bereits glauben, er habe das Gedicht verstanden. In Wirklichkeit aber weiß er nur, was in dem Gedicht gestanden hätte, wenn er selbst es in der vorliegenden Form geschrieben hätte. Da es aber von einem anderen gschrieben wurde, muß er nun versuchen, den kodierten Bewußtseinsinhalt dorthin zurückzuverfolgen, wo er herstammt: ins Bewußtsein des Dichters. Dies wäre aber nicht einmal dann zugänglich, wenn der Dichter noch lebte und man ihn fragen könnte. Es ist für jeden Außenstehenden etwas, das behaviouristische Psychologen als *black box* bezeichnen, eine schwarze Kiste, in die man nicht hineinschauen kann, deren Inhalt sich deshalb nur aus dem erschließen läßt, was in sie hineingegangen und was aus ihr herausgekommen ist. Herausgekommen ist aus dem Bewußtsein des Dichters sein Gesamtwerk, hineingegangen ist die Gesamtheit seiner Lebenserfahrung. In dieser lassen sich grob vier Schichten unterscheiden: erstens die aus lauter Zufällen zusammengesetzte persönliche Biographie, zweitens die inhaltliche Prägung der Wert- und Geschmacksnormen durch die umgebende Kultur (Enkulturation), drittens die Konditionierung des Bewußtseins durch die gesellschaftlichen Verhältnisse (marxistisch: Klassenlage) und viertens die allgemeine Determinierung durch anthropologische Grundkonstanten, die geographisch, klimatisch oder rassisch verschieden sein mögen, aber gesellschaftlich und kulturell invariant sind. Dies ist die archäologische Schichtung im Bewußtsein des Autors. Die gleiche Schichtung findet sich aber auch im Bewußtsein des Lesers, nur mit dem Unterschied, daß er eine andere persönliche Biographie hat und daß er anderen gesellschaftlichen und kulturellen Determinanten ausgesetzt war. Die anthropologischen Grundkonstanten dürften die gleichen sein.

Will man als Leser die verstehende Aneignung eines Gedichts bis an die Grenzen des Möglichen treiben, so müßte man in diesem Bezugsrahmen alle Wege bis zu Ende gehen, d. h., man müßte das Gesamtwerk des Dichters lesen, seine Biographie studieren, die Kultur und Gesellschaft seiner Zeit und sein Verhältnis zu beiden untersuchen und die anthropologischen Bedingungen aufklären, unter denen das Werk entstanden ist. Doch nicht genug damit, der Leser müßte die gleiche Untersuchung an sich selber vornehmen, da er B_2, den dekodierten Bewußtseinsinhalt des Gedichts, ja nur als Teil seines eigenen Bewußtseins erfahren kann. Ein Leser, der sich ein so gewaltiges Programm vornähme, würde wohl bald wie die bekannten Ameisen von Ringelnatz handeln, die von Hamburg nach Australien aufbrachen; doch

> Bei Altona auf der Chaussee
> Da taten ihnen die Füße weh,
> Und da verzichteten sie weise
> Dann auf den letzten Teil der Reise.

Zum Glück ist das hermeneutische Problem, um das es hier geht, nur für den Philosophen so schwierig, für den Leser stellt es sich keineswegs so entmutigend bodenlos dar. Da Leser und Dichter selbst dann, wenn sie durch viele Jahrhunderte voneinander getrennt sind, wie zwei kommunizierende Röhren durch die gemeinsame anthropologische Grundausstattung und durch den Strom einer gemeinsamen

Kulturtradition verbunden sind, kann jener schon auf introspektivem Wege vieles nachvollziehen, was dieser in seinem Gedicht artikuliert hat. Vor allem aber – und dies ist der entscheidende Punkt – ist ein Gedicht, das als solches für Leser geschrieben wurde, keine private Äußerung. Es spricht mit einer öffentlichen Stimme und will, bei aller Subjektivität der hineingegangenen Erfahrung, als etwas aus dem Bewußtsein des Dichters Herausgestelltes, Objektiviertes verstanden werden. Selbst da, wo es mit allen Sprach- und Formkonventionen bricht, will es dennoch dem Leser etwas mitteilen, setzt also voraus, daß er den Code des Textes verstehen wird, wenn er sich entsprechend darum bemüht. Dieser objektive, vom privaten Subjekt des Dichters abgenabelte Teil des Gedichts ist das, was der Leser verstehen soll; und da es objektiv geworden ist, steht es dem Leser im Prinzip nicht fremder gegenüber als dem Dichter selbst. Zwar läßt sich dies Objektive besser und vollständiger verstehen, wenn man es aus seiner subjektiven Genese heraus rekonstruiert; aber alles das, was man über die biographischen, gesellschaftlichen, psychologischen, womöglich gar tiefenpsychologischen Voraussetzungen seiner Entstehung in Erfahrung bringen kann, ist bestenfalls ein Hilfsmittel zum Verstehen des Gedichts, aber kein Bestandteil desselben. Die Aufgabe der Literaturwissenschaft ist es, solche Hilfsmittel zur Verfügung zu stellen, und für den Leser ist es von Gewinn, sie zu benutzen. Worauf es aber ankommt, ist nicht, daß der Leser die subjektiven Wurzeln, die das Gedicht im Dichter hatte, nun in sich selber wiederbelebt, sondern daß er sich das objektiv gewordene Gedicht verstehend aneignet, indem er es für sich selber zu einer eigenen subjektiven Erfahrung macht.

Um von diesen komplizierten hermeneutischen Gedankengängen wieder auf den Boden des Allgemeinverständlichen zurückzukehren, sei noch einmal mit aller Entschiedenheit gesagt: Gedichte sind verstehbar, weil sie von ihrer Intention her verstanden werden wollen. Für schwerverständliche braucht man einen Schlüssel, oder mehrere; hat man aber die

Schlösser geöffnet, dann zählt nur das, was tatsächlich im Safe ist, und nicht ein von Soziologen attestierter, psychoanalytisch beglaubigter Gutschein, der durch das Werk nicht eingelöst wird.

Zur Frage der Intention

Wo immer der Leser unsicher ist, wie ein Gedicht oder eine bestimmte Stelle darin zu verstehen sei, stellt sich ihm die Frage, was der Dichter wohl intendiert haben mag. Die Intention, die vor dem Schreiben des Gedichts da war, scheint die letzte Instanz zu sein, bis zu der man beim Interpretieren zurückfragen kann. Und doch hat es in der Literaturwissenschaft eine lange Debatte darüber gegeben, ob diese Frage überhaupt zulässig sei. Der Streit darüber ist nicht ganz unbegründet. Wie will man die Intention des Autors überhaupt erkennen, wenn sie sich nicht schon deutlich genug im Gedicht ausdrückt? Und wenn sich aus anderen biographischen Quellen eine Intention erschließen ließe, die im Gedicht gar nicht zu erkennen ist, von diesem womöglich konterkariert wird, was gilt dann: das Werk oder die ursprüngliche Intention?

Zunächst einmal sollte man sich darüber klarwerden, was unter Intention überhaupt zu verstehen ist. Eine Fußballmannschaft hat die Intention, das Spiel zu gewinnen. Das Publikum möchte teils die eine, teils die andere Mannschaft gewinnen sehen. Was aber beide Mannschaften und das Publikum zuerst und vor allem wünschen, ist ein gutes Spiel. Ganz ähnlich verhält es sich bei einem Gedicht. Der Dichter mag die Intention gehabt haben, eine bestimmte Aussage, also eine Botschaft, zu verkünden. Der eine Leser, dem diese Botschaft aus dem Herzen gesprochen ist, fühlt sich bestätigt, ein anderer fühlt sich zum Widerspruch herausgefordert, und der dritte glaubt, aus dem Gedicht eine ganz andere Botschaft herauslesen zu können. Die Botschaft samt allen möglichen oder für möglich gehaltenen Lesarten ist untrennbar mit dem Gedicht verbunden, hat aber nichts mit dessen dichterischem Wesen zu tun; denn sie hätte ja ebensogut auf eine undichterische Weise ausgesagt werden können. Intention hat immer eine finale Ausrichtung, sie zielt auf einen ganz bestimmten Endpunkt; ist dieser erreicht, hat sich die Intention realisiert und ist im Werk aufgehoben, und zwar in dem doppelten Sinn des Wortes, nämlich aufgelöst und aufbewahrt. Kunst aber führt nicht finale Handlungen aus, sondern schafft Objekte, in denen Handlung aus der Zeit herausgehoben und stillgestellt ist. Deshalb ist das Entscheidende an einem Gedicht nicht sein Zielpunkt, sondern das, was in seinem Inneren geschieht. Von einer intendierten Aussage erwarten wir, daß sie erstens eindeutig, zweitens wahrhaftig und drittens ethisch vertretbar sei. Ein Gedicht hingegen kann uns gerade wegen seiner irritierenden Mehrdeutigkeit reizen, es kann unser Denken mit einer absurden Scheinlogik beschäftigen, und es kann uns mit einer moralisch verwerflichen These positiv bewegen. Haß, Obszönität, Menschenverachtung, selbst eine Hymne auf Satan verzeihen wir einem Gedicht, wenn es gut ist. Aber wir dürften nichts der Intention verzeihen, die dahintersteht. Würde man z. B. Goethes Ballade »Die wandelnde Glocke« intentional verstehen, müßte man den Dichter einen Heuchler nennen; denn als erklärter Gegner alles Kirchlichen schreibt er hier ein Gedicht ganz im Sinne pietistischer Frömmelei, die den versäumten Kirchgang als sündhafte Verfehlung ansieht. Man wird dem Gedicht aber wohl eher gerecht, wenn man annimmt, daß Goethe hier fiktional verfährt und in die Psyche eines Kindes schlüpft, um auf diese Weise den Schwebezustand zwischen kindlicher Angst und kindischem Aberglauben darzustellen, womit er dann indirekt zugleich eine Kritik an letzterem ausdrückt.

Im Begriff der Intention stecken noch viele literaturtheoretische und philosophische Probleme, die hier nicht erörtert werden können. Zusammenfassend läßt sich in unserem

Kontext vielleicht soviel sagen: Zum bestmöglichen Verständnis eines Gedichts sollte man sich, wenn irgend möglich, auch dessen vergewissern, was als Absicht des Dichters in das Werk eingegangen sein könnte. Wesentlich für das Gedicht ist aber nicht seine finale Intention, sondern das, was real in ihm geschieht.

Orpheus, Daedalus, das Weltkind und Villon

Es scheint in der Natur des menschlichen Denkens zu liegen, die Gegenstände der Erfahrung nach einem möglichst einfachen System zu ordnen. Am einfachsten ist ohne Zweifel ein binäres (oder dichotomisches) System, das alle Gegenstände nach dem Entweder-Oder-Prinzip in zwei Klassen und jede Klasse wiederum paarweise in Subklassen unterteilt. Da Kulturphänomene schwer zu fassen sind, erfreut sich die binäre Klassifizierung gerade in diesem Bereich besonderer Beliebtheit. So glaubte Schelling, in der menschlichen Schöpferkraft zwei Grundorientierungen unterscheiden zu können, die er mit den Begriffen »apollinisch« und »dionysisch« bezeichnete. Durch Nietzsche wurde dieses Begriffspaar zur gängigen Münze und gehört seitdem zum Wortschatz aller Gebildeten. Wölfflin sah eine ähnliche Dichotomie in der bildenden Kunst und definierte Renaissance und Barock als typische Ausdrucksformen zweier konträrer Künstlertemperamente. Diese typologische Unterscheidung übertrug Fritz Strich analog auf die Literatur und bezeichnete sie mit dem Begriffspaar »klassisch« und »romantisch«. Bei aller Fragwürdigkeit solcher Klassifizierungen ist doch nicht zu bestreiten, daß im Kulturschaffen der Menschen tatsächlich eine Tendenz zur Polarisierung zu beobachten ist. Das ist auch nicht weiter verwunderlich; denn wo Menschen etwas schaffen, das nicht durch praktische Zwecke bestimmt ist, sondern sich an rein ideellen Wertvorstellungen orientiert, werden sie bestrebt sein, ihre Wertnormen möglichst deutlich von solchen abzusetzen, die von den eigenen abweichen.

Läßt man einmal die lyrische Dichtung des Abendlandes von den alten Griechen bis zur Gegenwart Revue passieren, so wird man darin immer wieder zwei gegensätzliche Künstlertemperamente antreffen. Da ist auf der einen Seite der inspirierte Dichter, der »mit Zungen redende« *vates*, der in trancehafter Entrücktheit göttliche Weisheit verkündet. Orpheus ist seine mythologische Verkörperung. Ihm steht als Gegentyp der dichtende *artifex* gegenüber, der kunstfertige Handwerker, der das Unnennbare – das Göttliche, Dämonische oder Numinose – in ein raffiniert angelegtes Labyrinth einsperrt, so wie Daedalus, das mythologische Urbild des artifex, auf Kreta das Labyrinth baute, in dem der blutrünstige Minotaurus gefangengehalten wurde. Orpheus und Daedalus sind archetypische Verkörperungen zweier gegensätzlicher Haltungen, die uns in der Dichtung immer wieder begegnen. Dichter wie Hölderlin, Rilke, Trakl und Walt Whitman scheinen reine Vertreter des orphischen Typs zu sein, während Dante, Edmund Spenser, E. A. Poe, Ezra Pound und Gottfried Benn dem Daedalus-Typ angehören. James Joyce, einer der größten Labyrinthbauer aller Zeiten, hat sogar seinem *alter ego* Stephen, dem Helden seines ersten Romans *Portrait of the Artist as a Young Man*, der als eine der drei Hauptfiguren in *Ulysses* wiederkehrt, den Nachnamen Dedalus gegeben und sich selbst damit auf das zutreffendste charakterisiert. Versucht man nun aber, alle Dichter in das Prokrustesbett dieser Typologie zu pressen, so wird man rasch merken, daß viele, darunter einige der größten, nicht in das Schema passen. Homer, Shakespeare und Goethe gehören keinem der beiden Typen oder beiden gleichermaßen an. Statt sie als Mischtypen zu klassifizieren, könnte man versuchen, einen dritten Typ zu definieren: den Dichter als die Stimme des Menschen schlechthin. Goethe hat in einem frühen Albumvers für diese von ihm selbst so empfundene Mittelposition eine Formel gefunden, die seitdem zu einem geflügelten Wort geworden ist:

Und, wie nach Emmaus, weiter ging's
Mit Sturm- und Feuerschritten:
Prophete rechts, Prophete links,
Das Weltkind in der Mitten.

Mit den beiden Propheten meinte Goethe die theoretischen
Eiferer Lavater und Basedow, mit denen er sich gerade auf
einer gemeinsamen Fußreise befand. Das »Weltkind« ist er
selber, wobei er wohl weniger auf Jesus, den Erlöser, als auf
dessen Selbstdefinition als des Menschen Sohn anspielt. Der
Dichter wird in dieser Vorstellung zur Inkarnation des
Menschlichen schlechthin. Er ist das ewige Kind, das aus
einem Zustand nichtentfremdeter Menschlichkeit heraus
auch dort noch das Menschliche aussprechen kann, wo der
gewöhnliche Mensch »in seiner Qual verstummt«, wie es im
Tasso heißt.
Aber auch mit diesem dritten Typ reicht unsere Typologie
noch nicht aus, um alle großen Dichter einigermaßen zutref-
fend zu klassifizieren. Es fehlt noch der Typus des frechen,
vollkommen respektlosen Dichters, der sich außerhalb der
bürgerlichen Wertewelt stellt und gerade deshalb den Menschen in wertneutraler Kreatürlichkeit, unverhüllt und
ungeschönt sieht. Die reinste Verkörperung dieses Typs in
der europäischen Tradition ist wahrscheinlich der Franzose
Villon, aber auch die spätmittelalterlichen Vaganten, Heinrich Heine, Wedekind und der junge Brecht gehören
hierher.
Vierertypologien sind ebenso beliebt wie triadische oder
binäre und nicht minder fragwürdig. Natürlich hat es nur
geringen Erkenntniswert, wenn man Dichter in diese vier
Schubfächer einsortieren kann. Dennoch sollte man solche
Ordnungsraster nicht von vornherein verwerfen; denn
erstens erleichtern sie den Überblick über ein komplexes
Datenmaterial, und zweitens beziehen sie sich in aller Regel
auf einen tatsächlich gegebenen Sachverhalt. Vieles spricht
dafür, daß die Kunst in der Innenwelt der menschlichen
Gesellschaft die gleiche Funktion erfüllt wie die kindliche

Spielphase in der Entwicklung des Individuums. Im Spiel werden Verhaltensmuster für den Ernstfall des Lebens geprobt. Da der Mensch sich seit altersher in drei Sphären bewegt – der religiös-transzendenten, der kulturell-menschlichen und der vital-animalischen – wird auch der Dichter, das spielende Kind der Gesellschaft, sich vorwiegend in einer dieser Sphären aufhalten. Entweder verkündet er Visionen des Göttlichen oder zeigt Möglichkeiten des Menschlichen auf oder stellt die menschliche Kreatur in ihrer Fleischlichkeit dar, oder aber er konzentriert sich ganz auf das Spielen des Spiels. Wir wollen diesen kurzen Denkanstoß nicht zu einer anthropologischen Fundierung der Kunst ausbauen. Wichtig ist in unserem Zusammenhang, zu wissen, daß man, um ein Gedicht richtig zu verstehen, auch die Grundhaltung des Dichters kennen muß. So wie z. B. Eifersucht sowohl Quelle von Komik wie auch Anlaß von Tragik sein kann, so gewinnt jeder Sachverhalt einen anderen Status, je nachdem, ob Orpheus, Daedalus, das Weltkind oder Villon ihn besingt.

Über die Schwierigkeit, dichterische Qualität zu erkennen

Als 1952 unter dem Titel *Ich schreibe mein Herz in den Staub der Straßen* Gedichte eines angeblich in Indochina verschollenen Fremdenlegionärs mit Namen George Forestier erschienen, war die Kritik des Lobes voll: endlich eine neue Stimme, die den Nerv der Zeit traf, romantisch und zynisch, süß und bitter zugleich. Selbst Dichter wie Gottfried Benn und Karl Krolow sparten nicht mit anerkennenden Worten. Das Bändchen erreichte in kurzer Zeit sensationelle Auflagenzahlen. Drei Jahre später kam heraus, daß ein George Forestier nie existiert hatte. Die Gedichte waren von Karl Emerich Krämer, einem Lektor des Diederichs Verlags, für eine von ihm erspähte Marktlücke nach Maß zurechtgeschneidert worden. Das Rezept war denkbar simpel: Exotik plus Weltschmerz plus Volksliedton und das ganze pseudomodern »angeschrägt«, wie man es aus der Unterhaltungsmusik kennt, wo Bach, Vivaldi und Mozart immer wieder zu gefällig modernisierter Geräuschkulisse verhackstückt werden. Als die Täuschung aufgeflogen war, stand die Kritik, wie so oft, wieder einmal blamiert da und hielt es für das beste, den Namen Forestier nie wieder zu erwähnen. Zur Illustration erst einmal eine Kostprobe:

> Rot sind die Nächte über den Inseln,
> O Purea, o Purea!
>
> Wenn die Lotosknospe springt,
> Knallt im Dorf die Handgranate,
> Wenn der junge Bambus blüht,
> Werden die Kanonen reden.
>
> Kinder wälzen sich im Sande,
> Hingekrümmt zur Feuerblume.
> Über ihre kleinen Leiber
> Schrillt der Blutgeruch der Kugeln.
>
> Wer wird unsre Fraun beschlafen,
> Wer aus unsern Näpfen essen?
> Welcher Priester wird jetzt kommen,
> Um die Toten zu besprechen?
>
> Wenn wir jetzt in dieser Stunde
> Aufstehn, um zurückzukehren
> Mit dem weichen Licht der Sonne
> Über den zerfransten Schädeln,
>
> Wer wird uns die Tore öffnen,
> Wer wird uns die Decken breiten?
> Wer wird uns die Kürbisflasche
> Mit dem süßen Saki reichen?

O Purea, o Purea,
Auf der Scheide des Gebirges
Blühen feuerfarbne Lilien,
Wuchert wilder Rhododendron.

O Purea, o Purea,
Wenn die Knospen wieder springen,
Hat der Wind uns schon vergessen.

Aus heutiger Sicht ist schwer zu begreifen, daß diese süßliche Limonade jemals von ernsthaften Kritikern für dichterischen Wein gehalten werden konnte. Und doch findet sich ähnlich gefälliges Wortgeklingel allenthalben in der Lyrik dieses Jahrhunderts, und manches davon von Dichtern mit großen Namen. Gerade die virtuosen Sprachbeherrscher wie Rilke oder Gottfried Benn waren immer in Gefahr, von einer leerlaufenden Sprachwoge davongetragen zu werden. In ihren Werken findet sich manches, das man als glänzend gemachte Parodie lesen würde, wenn man nicht wüßte, daß es von den Dichtern selbst stammt.

Je größer die historische Distanz zu einem Gedicht ist, um so stärker hat sich gewöhnlich das ästhetische Urteil verfestigt. Bei zeitgenössischer Lyrik aber steht sicher noch manchem Kritiker, der seine Favoriten in den Himmel hebt, eine Blamage bevor. Heutzutage ist die Unsicherheit des ästhetischen Urteils wahrscheinlich noch weit größer als in früheren Zeiten, da es keine verbindlichen Stilkonventionen mehr gibt und auf dem literarischen Markt unterschiedlichste Ausdruckshaltungen, Sprachregister und natürlich auch gimmickhafte Mätzchen miteinander konkurrieren. Der dadurch verunsicherte Leser läßt sich dann vielleicht durch ein bei Kritikern beliebtes Argument trösten, das die ständige Beckmesserei und das Erstellen von Rangordnungen als Unfug abtut und meint, ein Gedicht dürfe nur an sich selbst und nicht an der Konkurrenz gemessen werden. Das Argument klingt stichhaltiger als es ist. Dichtung verdankt ja ihre öffentliche Existenz zunächst einmal der Tatsache, daß sie vor dem Urteil eines Verlagslektors oder Zeitschriftenredakteurs Gnade gefunden und damit alle nichtpublizierten Gedichte ausgestochen hat. Dieses Urteil bedarf einer fortwährenden Revision, da sonst alle Dichtung, der von den Türhütern des Literaturbetriebs der Zutritt verwehrt wird, nie die Chance bekäme, doch noch publiziert zu werden. Das heißt aber, daß auch der Leser bei dem Versuch, ein Gedicht zu verstehen, sich immer zugleich auch ein Urteil über dessen Qualität bilden muß. Der Verzicht auf diese Urteilsbildung degradiert das Gedicht zum sentimentalen Konsumgegenstand.

Damit stellt sich für den Leser die Frage, nach welchen Kriterien dichterische Qualität überhaupt zu beurteilen ist. Manche Menschen haben einen nahezu untrüglichen Instinkt für künstlerischen Wert, nur leider stellt sich erst nach Jahrzehnten endgültig heraus, daß sie recht hatten. Andere wiederum, darunter solche, die selber große Dichter sein mögen, zeigen sich merkwürdig blind in ihrem Urteil. Goethe lag als Kritiker mit vielen seiner Urteile daneben. Einige der größten seiner Zeitgenossen – Hölderlin, Kleist, Jean Paul – hat er völlig verkannt. Noch schiefer waren seine Urteile auf dem Gebiet der Musik. Hier sparte er nicht mit Lob für die uninspirierten Kompositionen seines Freundes Zelter, während er Schubert, der ihm die Vertonung des »Erlkönig« zugeschickt hatte, nicht einmal einer Antwort würdigte. Wenn nicht einmal Goethe die Qualität seiner Dichterkollegen richtig einschätzen konnte, wie soll dann ein Durchschnittsleser die Spreu vom Weizen trennen? Zunächst einmal sollte er sich das Recht auf ein gefühlsmäßiges Urteil nicht beschneiden lassen. Wenn ihm ein Gedicht nach wiederholtem Lesen in größeren Abständen immer noch gefällt, spricht die Wahrscheinlichkeit dafür, daß es Qualität hat. Manche Gedichte gefallen auf Anhieb, mit der Zeit aber läßt die Wirkung nach, und der Leser merkt, daß der Reiz, durch den er sich hatte verführen lassen, in einer virtuosen Sprachgestalt lag, die sich auf die Dauer als allzu glatt und gefällig erweist. Andere Gedichte werden am

Anfang als reizlos und spröde empfunden und entfalten ihre Wirkung erst, wenn man in langem Umgang mit ihnen ihre Komplexität aufdeckt. Auch wenn es bisher noch niemandem gelungen ist, objektive Maßstäbe des ästhetischen Urteils nachzuweisen, gibt es doch einige Kriterien, die durch die Praxis der kritischen Rezeption bestätigt werden. *Originalität* ist sicher eines davon. Von einem guten Gedicht erwarten wir, daß es uns etwas auf eine neue Weise sehen und erfahren läßt. Ein weiteres Kriterium ist *Dichte*. In einem guten Gedicht sollten die wirksamen Elemente der Klang-, Bild- und Sinnschicht so dicht gepackt sein, daß dazwischen keine Hohlräume, keine überstehenden Enden und kein sprachlicher Leerlauf zu spüren ist. Ein anderes oft postuliertes Kriterium ist das der inneren *Stimmigkeit*. Dabei ist allerdings Vorsicht geboten. Zwar dürfen wir von einem Gedicht erwarten, daß es durchgängig kristallin ist und keine amorphen Stellen hat. Aber die Kristallstruktur kann durchaus Brüche, Reibungen und Verschiebungen aufweisen. Als inhaltliches Kriterium könnte man den leider sehr mißbrauchten und stark vorbelasteten Begriff der *Tiefe* nennen. Wir erwarten von einem Gedicht, daß es keine Platitüden ausspricht, sondern unsern Blick in tiefere Schichten menschlicher Erfahrung öffnet. Allerdings würden wir wohl die Waffen strecken müssen, wenn wir entscheiden sollten, ob Mörikes »Septembermorgen« tiefer ist als C. F. Meyers »Römischer Brunnen«. Wenn mit *Tiefe* ein Maß für die inhaltliche Substanz eines Gedichts gemeint ist, dann müßte man den Begriff wohl durch Kriterien wie *Fülle*, *Intensität* und *Authentizität* erweitern. Eines der geläufigsten Kriterien für den Wert eines Gedichts ist das der *Übereinstimmung von Form und Inhalt*. Auch dies ist mit dem gewissen Körnchen Salz zu genießen. Zwar erreicht ein Gedicht nicht die geforderte Dichte und Stimmigkeit, wenn nicht das Inhaltliche restlos in der Form aufgeht. Aber ein kitschiger Inhalt wird nicht schon dadurch Kunst, daß er eine kitschige, also adäquate Form erhält. Damit sind wir bei einem der schwierigsten Begriffe der Literaturkritik überhaupt.

Was ist Kitsch?

Auf jeden Fall ist es etwas anderes als bloß schlechte Kunst. Dichter, Maler und Musiker, die nicht die Schöpferkraft der großen Genies hatten, waren Künstler zweiter oder dritter Ordnung, aber was sie schufen, war deswegen noch längst nicht Kitsch. Kitsch ist nicht unzulängliche, sondern unehrliche Kunst. Er ist auf dem Gebiet der Ästhetik, was die Lüge auf dem Gebiet der Ethik ist. Kitsch verhält sich zur Kunst wie das Kindische zum Kindlichen, wie das Geschönte zum Schönen. Die beiden Hauptformen des Kitsches sind der ästhetische und der sentimentale. *Ästhetischer* Kitsch ist die Verselbständigung der schönen Form, die mit diktatorischem Anspruch über alles Inhaltliche triumphiert. Da im Inhaltlichen eines Gedichts (bzw. Bildes oder Musikstücks) ein Bewußtseinsinhalt, also ein Stück Menschlichkeit, ausgedrückt ist, ist es unethisch, wenn die Differenziertheit des Menschlichen der selbstherrlich ästhetisierten Form geopfert wird. Umgekehrt besteht *sentimentaler* Kitsch darin, daß sich Inhaltliches verselbständigt, daß bestimmte Gefühle und Wertvorstellungen (z. B. Liebe, Patriotismus, Heimatgefühl usw.) kritiklos, d. h. ohne formale Kontrolle ausgedrückt werden.

Damit das, was wir hier theoretisch anzudeuten versucht haben, auf etwas Konkretes bezogen werden kann, wollen wir zwei Beispiele folgen lassen. Zunächst eine Illustration des ästhetischen Kitsches:

Otto Julius Bierbaum

Abendlied

Die Nacht ist niedergangen;
die schwarzen Schleier hangen
nun über Busch und Haus.
Leis rauscht es in den Buchen,
die letzten Winde suchen
die vollsten Wipfel sich zum Neste aus.

Noch einmal leis ein Wehen;
dann bleibt der Atem stehen
der müden, müden Welt.
Nur noch ein zages Beben
fühl' durch die Nacht ich schweben,
auf die der Friede seine Hände hält.

Schon beim ersten Lesen merkt man, daß Bierbaum versucht, die beiden berühmtesten deutschen Abendgedichte,
nämlich das »Abendlied« von Claudius und »Wanderers
Nachtlied« von Goethe so zu verschmelzen, daß sein eigenes
Gedicht die Vorbilder an Dichte und sprachlichem Wohllaut
noch übertrifft. Tatsächlich aber gelingt ihm weder die
Ausweitung des Bildes zu einer moralischen Weltsicht wie
bei Claudius noch die symbolische Verdichtung wie bei
Goethe. Statt dessen schafft er eine weiche, samtige Sprach-
hülse, deren einziger Inhalt die Aussage ist, daß der Wind
immer leiser und leiser wird. Das Stillstehen des Atems kann
sich gar nicht in symbolische Bedeutung umsetzen, da diese
dann der Tod sein müßte, was gewiß nicht intendiert ist. So
ist das Gedicht nichts weiter als die mit beträchtlichem
sprachlichem Aufwand dargebotene Wiedergabe einer
meteorologischen Allerweltsimpression: eine schöne, aber
leere Hülse.
Nun ein Beispiel für sentimentalen Kitsch:

Carl Busse

Ich möchte sterben ...

Ich möchte sterben, wenn in Stadt und Hag
Zu Ende geht ein lieber Frühlingstag.
   Die jungen Mädchen stehn vor Tür und Tor,
Die Gärten blühn, die Kinder spielen munter,
Groß und verleuchtend geht die Sonne unter
Und Mütterchen nimmt sich die Bibel vor.
Die Welt so still; so still mein graues Haus,
Kaum daß im Zug sich die Gardinen regen,

Und meine Sehnsucht auf verklärten Wegen
Mit starken Schwingen schwebt sie mir voraus.
Und dunkler wird's, die ganze Welt schläft ein,
Ich aber geh auf eine weite Reise,
Und eine Stimme, eine tiefe, leise,
Sagt mir ins Ohr: »Bald wirst du bei mir sein.«

Todessehnsucht ist ein in der Romantik weitverbreitetes und oft gestaltetes Motiv. So aber, wie es hier in einen biedermeierlich frömmelnden Kontext eingebettet ist, wird es zur verlogenen Attitüde. Ein Dichter hat durchaus das Recht, den Tod als Befreier oder Erlöser zu feiern; denn das impliziert eine Kritik an der Unerträglichkeit des Lebens. Aber einen Anfall von Frühjahrsmüdigkeit zum Anlaß zu nehmen, um sich in einer Todesphantasie zu suhlen, ist unerträgliches Gesülze. Wie man sieht, geht auch in diesem Gedicht der Geist von »Wanderers Nachtlied« um, der das Hausgespenst des deutschen Lyrikkitsches zu sein scheint.

Neben diesen beiden Populärformen des Kitsches gibt es noch eine dritte Variante, den *ambitionierten* Kitsch. Herman Broch hat in einem scharfsinnigen Aufsatz »Zum Problem des Kitsches« das ganze 19. Jahrhundert als ein Treibhaus dieser Kitschvariante beschrieben, deren höchste, geniale Ausprägung er in der Kunst Richard Wagners sah. Wagnerverehrer werden über dieses Urteil entsetzt sein. Und doch wird niemand bestreiten können, daß sich im 19. Jahrhundert in der Tat überall in den innersten Bezirken der Kunst verführerisch schillernde Blüten öffneten, von denen ein betäubender, aber schon etwas angegangener Geruch ausgeht. Es war das Jahrhundert, in dem die Kunst die Rolle einer Ersatzreligion zu spielen begann. Damit überschritt sie ihre Grenzen und verstieg sich zu hochgestochenen Attitüden, die etwas Verlogenes und Unechtes haben mußten. Je virtuoser die Künstler, um so mehr waren sie in Gefahr, sich zu solchen Gespreiztheiten verführen zu lassen. In der Lyrik ist Rilke das prominenteste Beispiel. Er ist vielleicht der bedeutendste deutsche Dichter unseres Jahrhunderts, und doch begegnet man in seinen Werken immer wieder Gedichten, die sich wie unfreiwillige Selbstparodien lesen. So findet man im ersten Teil der *Neuen Gedichte* das wunderbare, in seiner Komprimiertheit unübertreffliche Gedicht »Der Panther«, das mit Recht in alle Anthologien aufgenommen wird. Dem folgt in *Neue Gedichte. Anderer Teil* dieses Gedicht:

Schwarze Katze

Ein Gespenst ist noch wie eine Stelle,
dran dein Blick mit einem Klange stößt;
aber da, an diesem schwarzen Felle
wird dein stärkstes Schauen aufgelöst:

wie ein Tobender, wenn er in vollster
Raserei ins Schwarze stampft,
jählings am benehmenden Gepolster
einer Zelle aufhört und verdampft.

Alle Blicke, die sie jemals trafen,
scheint sie also an sich zu verhehlen,
um darüber drohend und verdrossen
zuzuschauern und damit zu schlafen.
Doch auf einmal kehrt sie, wie geweckt,
ihr Gesicht und mitten in das deine:
und da triffst du deinen Blick im geelen
Amber ihrer runden Augensteine
unerwartet wieder: eingeschlossen
wie ein ausgestorbenes Insekt.

Die virtuose Sprachkunst des großen Dichters ist auch hier unverkennbar, und das Schlußbild verrät in seiner eindrucksvollen Dichte die Pranke des Löwen. Der Rest aber ist von einer so manierierten Gespreiztheit, zeugt von einer so geschwätzig leerlaufenden Sprache, daß kein Parodist die

befindlichen Schalen, aus deren oberster ein Wasserstrahl hervorschießt. Dieser fällt aus der Höhe zurück in die Schale, fließt über deren Rand in die zweite und dann in die dritte und wird von dort erneut nach oben gepumpt. Wenn das Gedicht nichts als den reinen Bewegungsablauf des Brunnens und dessen gleichnishafte Implikationen ausdrücken soll, dann müßte es folgende Phasen sprachlich nachvollziehen:

(1) das abrupte, mit einem zischenden Geräusch verbundene Hervorschießen des Strahls,

(2) den Übergang vom Zischen zum weichen, schleierartigen Herabfallen des Wassers,

(3) das erneute Zischen, wenn das Wasser sich in die Schalen ergießt,

(4) das dreimalige Fallen, Stauen und wieder Fallen,

(5) die zyklische Wiederholung des immergleichen Vorgangs.

(1) Das Abrupte ließe sich dadurch ausdrücken, daß man einen Satz nicht in gewohnter Weise mit dem Subjekt, sondern mit dem Verb beginnt: Inversion nennt es der Philologe. Das Zischen könnte man lautmalerisch durch Zischlaute realisieren, während (2) sich für das weiche, schleierartige Herabwallen des Wassers sog. Flüssiglaute, Liquide, anbieten, vor allem das l. (3) Mit den gleichen lautlichen Mitteln ließe sich nachzeichnen, wie sich das fallende Wasser in das ruhende ergießt und danach weich über den Rand der Schale wallt. Nur müßte das zischende Geräusch kürzer sein, da der vorherrschende Eindruck jetzt der des ruhenden Wassers ist. (4) Das Fallen, Stauen und erneute Fallen ließe sich wohl nur syntaktisch abbilden, indem man den Satzfluß durch einen Einschub unterbricht und dadurch die Stauungsphase aus der Bewegung des Herabfallens heraushebt. (5) Die zyklische Wiederholung des immergleichen Vorgangs könnte man in ihrer Monotonie durch eine Aneinanderreihung von mit »und« verbundenen Satzteilen ausdrücken, wie Schiller es z. B. im »Taucher« tut:

Und es wallet und siedet und brauset und zischt.

Polysyndeton heißt dieser Kunstgriff in der Fachsprache der Rhetorik.

Die hier ausgewählten Wirkungsmomente, die den Brunnen auf seine Minimalstruktur reduzieren, sollen nun in ein Gedicht eingehen, und zwar so, daß diese Minimalstruktur darin mit äußerster Prägnanz und Intensität zum Ausdruck kommt, damit das ganze Bild für den Leser so mit Bedeutung aufgeladen wird, daß dieser darin ein Symbol für die lebendige Einheit von Bewegung und Ruhe erkennt. Hier ist das Gedicht, das genau dieses Programm erfüllt:

Der römische Brunnen

Aufsteigt der Strahl	– Inversion, Zischlaute
und fallend gießt	– weiches ll zwischen f und zischendem ß
er voll der Marmorschale Rund,	– Zischen von v, sch mit Nasalen und Liquiden
die, sich verschleiernd, überfließt	– Einschub, Stauung, s, v, sch bzw. ß außen, innen l, n, fl
in einer zweiten Schale Grund;	– zwei Zischlaute mit Nasalen und Liquid
die zweite gibt, sie wird zu reich,	– Einschub, Stauung, drei Zischlaute
der dritten wallend ihre Flut	– ll, n; f, schwaches Zischen; dann l
und jede nimmt und gibt zugleich	– Polysyndeton: monotone Bewegung, die
und strömt und ruht.	in sich selber kreist; Nasale und Liquide mit zwei Zischlauten

Das Gedicht ist von C. F. Meyer und gehört mit Recht zu seinen bekanntesten und beliebtesten. Mit bewundernswerter Kunstfertigkeit hat er das Bild des Brunnens in das

Medium der Sprache übersetzt. Es wäre töricht, diese Kunstfertigkeit als bloße Virtuosität abzutun. Beherrschung des Handwerks gehört zu den Grundvoraussetzungen eines großen Dichters. Erst durch die Vollendung im Handwerklichen gewinnt das Gedicht seine unvergleichliche Prägnanz und Dichte, die den Leser förmlich zwingen, darin eine gleichnishafte Bedeutung zu sehen. In der drittletzten Zeile setzt der Dichter in der handwerklichen Durchführung noch das Tüpfelchen aufs i, indem er jetzt beim dritten Niederwallen des Wassers den Zischlaut durch das schwächere f ersetzt. Beim zweiten Becken verteilt sich die Wassermenge bereits auf einen so großen Schalenumfang, daß sie als weicher Schleier fast lautlos in die dritte Schale fällt.

Das Gedicht redet nicht, es drängt dem Leser keine Botschaft auf, es stellt nur dar; aber es tut dies mit solcher formalen Präzision, daß sich die Botschaft um so eindringlicher mitteilt. Dies bedeutet nun freilich nicht, daß jedes Gedicht bestrebt sein müsse, seinen Gegenstand auf solche Weise lautmalerisch und syntaktisch nachzubilden. Es gibt andere Brunnen-Gedichte, darunter ein nicht minder berühmtes von Rilke, die ganz andere Wirkungsmomente des Brunnens zum Ausdruck bringen wollen und darum ganz andere Mittel der Darstellung wählen. In Rilkes Gedicht »O Brunnen-Mund« aus den »Sonetten an Orpheus« ist die zentrale Vorstellung nicht das unaufhörliche Kreisen, sondern das unerschöpfliche Hervorquellen. Deshalb stehen im Mittelpunkt Bilder, die eine Öffnung bzw. ein schöpfendes Gefäß darstellen, nämlich Mund, Ohr und Krug. Aber auch hier beruht die Wirkung des Gedichts nicht auf dem, was es redet, sondern auf dem, was es zeigt. Das darf allerdings nicht so mißverstanden werden, als sei über die Lyrik ein generelles Redeverbot verhängt. Es gibt große Gedichte, die explizit sagen, was sie meinen, aber sie sagen es in einer Weise, daß nicht nur der Intellekt Stoff zum Nachdenken empfängt, sondern auch die ästhetische Wahrnehmung eine Kette reich abgestufter Vorstellungen nachvollzieht.

Wenn Schüler aufgefordert werden, ein Gedicht zu interpretieren, stehen sie gewöhnlich erst einmal ratlos davor und wissen nicht recht, wo sie anfangen sollen. Gerade die vollendetsten Gedichte haben eine so makellose äußere Gestalt, daß jeder Versuch, in sie einzudringen, an der dichtgefügten, vollkommen glattgeschliffenen Oberfläche abgleitet. Deshalb behilft sich der ungeübte Interpret dann meist damit, daß er aus lauter Verlegenheit erst einmal das Evidente konstatiert. Er beginnt damit, daß er die Strophen und Zeilen zählt und das Reimschema und das Metrum angibt. Ein solcher Anfang braucht nicht falsch zu sein, wenn er danach zu einem wirklichen Einstieg führt. Oft aber wird dieser Einstieg gerade dadurch verstellt, daß man ganz auf das Regelmäßige, eben das Evidente fixiert bleibt. Deshalb hier der erste Ratschlag: Statt mit der Aufzählung der Regelmäßigkeiten zu beginnen, sollte man das Gedicht erst einmal gründlich daraufhin untersuchen, ob sich nicht an irgendeiner Stelle eine Unregelmäßigkeit feststellen läßt, die sich beim Lesen als Widerstand bemerkbar macht. Dabei kann es sich um eine bloße Härte im Klangfluß, um ein Stolpern im Metrum, einen Bruch in der Gedankenfolge, eine Abweichung vom Reimschema oder um irgendeine andere Bruchstelle handeln, die man bei genauem Lesen so deutlich fühlt, wie man mit dem Finger den Sprung in einem Porzellangefäß spürt. Da man grundsätzlich davon ausgehen muß, daß der Dichter das Gedicht bis ins kleinste Detail so haben wollte, wie es dem Leser vorliegt, ergibt sich bei einer plötzlich ins Auge springenden Unregelmäßigkeit zwangsläufig die Frage, was diese zu bedeuten habe. In dieser Frage liegt oft schon der Schlüssel zum Einstieg in das Gedicht. Ein Beispiel mag das verdeutlichen. Mit Absicht wählen wir ein englisches Gedicht, damit der Leser ganz auf die äußere Form konzentriert bleibt und nicht voreilig auf die schon vermutete Sinnaussage des Gedichts zustrebt.

Wystan Hugh Auden

Musée des Beaux Arts

About suffering they were never wrong,   a
The Old Masters: how well they understood   b
Its human position; how it takes place   c
While someone else is eating or opening a window
   or just walking dully along: a
How, when the aged are reverently, passionately
   waiting   d
For the miraculous birth, there always must be   e
Children who did not specially want it to happen,
   skating   d
On a pond at the edge of the wood: b
They never forgot   f
That even the dreadful martyrdom must run its course   g
Anyhow in a corner, some untidy spot   f
Where the dogs go on with their doggy life and the
   torturer's horse   g
Scratches its innocent behind on a tree.   e

In Brueghel's *Icarus*, for instance: how everything
   turns away   h
Quite leisurely from the disaster; the ploughman may   h
Have heard the splash, the forsaken cry,   i
But for him it was not an important failure: the sun
   shone   j
As it had to on the white legs disappearing into the
   green   k
Water; and the expensive delicate ship that must have
   seen   k
Something amazing, a boy falling out of the sky,   i j
Had somewhere to get to and sailed calmly on.   j

Übers Leiden wußten sie bestens Bescheid,
die Alten Meister; wie gut verstanden sie doch
seinen menschlichen Platz; wie es stattfindet, während ein andrer
gerade ißt, ein Fenster öffnet oder einfach spazierengeht just zu der Zeit;
wie, während die Alten ehrfürchtig, inbrünstig warten
auf die wunderbare Geburt, immer Kinder sind, denen es gleichgültig bleibt,
wenn es geschieht, die lieber draußen vorm Garten
Schlittschuh laufen auf einem Wasserloch.
Sie vergaßen nie:
auch das schreckliche Martyrium muß seinen Lauf nehmen, irgendwie,
in einem schmutzigen Winkel, links oder rechts,
wo die Hunde ihr Hundeleben führen und das Pferd des Folterknechts
seinen unschuldigen Hintern an einem Baumstamm reibt.

In Breughels Ikarus zum Beispiel: Wie gleichgültig sich alles
abwendet von dem Unglück. Der Pflüger, Zeuge des Falles,
muß das Klatschen gehört haben und den einsamen Schrei,
aber für ihn war es kein bedeutsames Scheitern. Die Sonne schien,
wie sich's gehörte, auf das grüne Wasser mit den weißen Beinen,
und das kostbare Schiff, das etwas Unerhörtes gesehen hatte – einen
Jungen, der aus dem Himmel fiel –, ignorierte ihn;
es hatte ein Ziel zu erreichen und segelte ruhig vorbei.

Auch wer nur wenig oder gar kein Englisch versteht, wird leicht erkennen, daß dies kein regelmäßig gebautes Gedicht in einer der traditionellen Formen ist. Es hat weder ein festes

Metrum noch ein gleichbleibendes Zeilenschema. Dennoch ist der Text so in Zeilen gebrochen, daß kein Zweifel daran bestehen kann, daß er als Gedicht gelesen werden soll. Die Gliederung in einen längeren Aufgesang und einen kürzeren Abgesang erinnert sogar ein wenig an die klassische Sonettform. Sieht man sich den Text nun genauer an, wird man verwundert feststellen, daß er durchgängig gereimt ist. Allerdings liegen die Reime bis zu sechs Zeilen auseinander, so daß man sie beim ersten Lesen gar nicht wahrnimmt, zumal die Zeilenenden durch Enjambement so in die jeweils folgende Zeile übergeleitet werden, daß das Reimwort ganz in dem fast prosaischen Satzfluß untergeht. Macht man sich nun die Mühe, das Reimschema zu markieren, so wird man mit erneuter Verwunderung feststellen, daß eine einzige Zeile ohne Reimpartner bleibt, nämlich die dritte. Damit stellt sich die Frage: Weshalb bleibt ausgerechnet diese Zeile ungereimt? Ist es Zufall, Schlamperei oder künstlerische Absicht? Bei einem Dichter vom Range Audens kann es gar keinen Zweifel daran geben, daß er es mit Absicht tat. Wenn wir nun plausibel machen können, welche Absicht dahintersteckt, halten wir möglicherweise bereits den Schlüssel zu seiner zentralen Aussage in der Hand.

Auden sagt in dem Gedicht, und er sagt es in beiläufiglässigem Gesprächston, daß die alten Meister (gemeint sind die niederländischen Maler) genau wußten, daß auch das Leiden seinen festen Platz in der Weltordnung hat. Sie malten das Erhabenste neben dem Banalsten, das Martyrium eines Heiligen neben dem Pferdehintern, der sich an einem Pfahl scheuert. Und in der Tat vermitteln uns ihre Bilder oft den Eindruck, als sei für sie beides von gleicher Bedeutung. Breughels Bild vom Sturz des Ikarus, auf das sich das Gedicht bezieht, läßt nichts von der Tragik dieses Opfers menschlicher Hybris erkennen. Vielmehr sind die winzigen weißen Beine des in den Wellen Versinkenden nur ein kleines Ornament in einem wohlgeordneten, aus vielen Teilen zusammengefügten Bildteppich. Die Frage ist nun, ob Auden diese den alten Meistern unterstellte Weltdeutung wirklich teilt. Das Gedicht spricht so, als stimme es den Alten uneingeschränkt zu. Der lässige Gesprächston, der dem Ernst des Gesagten ein wenig die Spitze nimmt, läßt freilich auch an die Möglichkeit von Ironie denken. Es fehlt jedoch ein eindeutiges Ironiesignal. So bleibt der Leser weiterhin im ungewissen, ob Auden wirklich meint, daß das Leiden und die Sehnsucht nach Erlösung ein genauso natürlicher Bestandteil des menschlichen Lebens sei wie das alltägliche Treiben der Hunde oder das Spiel schlittschuhlaufender Kinder auf einem Teich. Es geht also darum, wie Auden den Platz (place) des Leidens im menschlichen Dasein bestimmt, »its human position«. Diese Schlüsselworte des Gedichts stehen nun aber genau in der Zeile, die keinen Reimpartner hat, die also selber im poetischen Gefüge des Gedichts keinen Platz findet. Auden gibt damit auf subtile Weise zu erkennen, daß er keineswegs der anfangs behaupteten Relativierung des Leidens zustimmt, daß er im Gegenteil das Leiden und das Martyrium als etwas Existentielles ansieht, das – im Wortsinn des lateinischen »ex-sistere« – aus dem Dasein »heraussteht«. Die Reimlosigkeit der Zeile ist das versteckte Ironiesignal, nach dem der Leser im übrigen Text vergeblich gesucht hat. Jetzt weiß er, daß Auden das genaue Gegenteil dessen meint, was er zunächst in lässigem Parlando-Ton zu behaupten schien. Leiden, Martyrium und tragisches Scheitern – so darf man den Dichter verstehen – sind für ihn eben nicht Bestandteile einer für den Menschen verstehbaren Ordnung, sondern existentielle Grenzüberschreitungen, die sich jeder Sinngebung widersetzen, auch wenn die alten Meister sie auf ihren Bildern gleichrangig neben den alltäglichsten Dingen dargestellt haben. Mit Bezug auf die Kunst kommt das Gedicht zu dem unausgesprochenen Fazit, daß das Leiden in seiner existentiellen Qualität nicht ästhetisierbar ist.

Jeder Versuch, ein Gedicht in allen seinen Wirkungsmomenten vollständig zu interpretieren, zwingt zur Betrachtung von so vielen Einzelheiten, daß der ungeübte Interpret dabei leicht den Überblick verliert und vor lauter Bäumen den Wald nicht mehr sieht. Deshalb ist es, zumal bei längeren Gedichten, ratsam, die Mikrostruktur (Textur) ganz beiseite zu lassen und erst einmal die Makrostruktur freizulegen. Dies soll im folgenden an einem Beispiel vorgeführt werden. Auch diesmal wählen wir mit Absicht kein deutsches Gedicht, sondern ein englisches in deutscher Übersetzung. Da ihm das originale Sprachkleid ausgezogen und durch ein gänzlich anderes ersetzt worden ist, erübrigt sich jede Frage nach der Textur; denn selbst wenn es der Übersetzung gelungen sein sollte, die texturalen Eigentümlichkeiten des Originals weitgehend nachzubilden, lassen sich doch nur Aussagen über die Mikrostruktur der Übersetzung machen, da die des Originals gar nicht vorliegt. Wir können uns darum ganz auf das Freilegen der Makrostruktur konzentrieren. Es darf allerdings nicht verschwiegen werden, daß unser Gedicht, das zu den berühmtesten und wohl auch besten der englischen Lyrik gehört, nicht nur eine höchst raffinierte Großstruktur aufweist, sondern diese auch durch eine nicht minder virtuos gestaltete Textur ausfüllt.

Percy Bysshe Shelley

Ode an den Westwind

I

O wilder Westwind, Herbstes Atem, du,
vor dem, wie vor des Zauberers Gebot,
die Blätter fliehn gleich Geistern ohne Ruh,

vergilbt und schwarz, blaß oder hektisch rot,
von Pest befallen, hingerafft in Scharen,
du trägst ins Winterbett, als wär'n sie tot,

die Samen, kalt und starr auf ihren Bahren,
bis deine blaue Schwester, Frühlingswind,
sie weckt mit einem Stoß ihrer Fanfaren

und füllt (als trieb' sie Knospenherden lind
und süß zu luft'ger Weide vor sich her)
mit Duft und Farbe Berg und Tal geschwind.

Du, wilder Geist, wehst über Land und Meer,
Zerstörer und Bewahrer: Hör, o hör!

II

Du, der auf seines wilden Stromes Tosen
die Wolken trägt, Gewitterengeln gleich,
geschüttelt aus dem Himmel wie die losen

Blattreste mächt'ger Kronen, überreich
weht um dein Antlitz regenschwere Fracht.
Mänadenhaar, in Strömen voll und weich,

treibt auf der blauen Woge hin mit Macht,
vom Horizont bis zum Zenit empor
weht hoch des nahen Sturmes Lockenpracht.

Du Requiem des Jahrs im dunklen Chor
des Doms, den diese Nacht jetzt ringsumher
zum Grabgewölbe macht. Dann bricht hervor

geballte Macht der Atmosphäre schwer
als schwarzer Regen, Feuer, Hagel: Hör!

III

Du, der du aus den sanften Sommerträumen
den Golf von Baia weckst, der schlafend ruht,
von Bildern eingelullt, die ihn umsäumen,

Turm, Schloß und Insel schwankend auf der Flut
im Spiel der Wellen, moosbewachsne Zinne,
schwach atmend in der trägen Mittagsglut.

Und alles schwer von Blüten, daß die Sinne
berauscht erschlaffen. – Da ertönt dein Mund,
und alles Leben hält erschauernd inne.

Und der Atlantik klafft, tief auf dem Grund
vernimmt der Schlammwald dich, und sein vom
                                    Meer
gebleichtes Laub erbebt, und ihm wird kund

die Stimme, die er kennt, und ringsumher
erzittert alles grau vor Angst: o hör.

                    IV

Wär’ ich das Blatt, das du ins Grab geleitest,
die Wolke, um mit dir davonzufliegen,
die Welle unter dir, auf der du reitest,

könnt’ ich, du Unbezähmbarer, mich schmiegen
in dich, dir gleich sein, wenn auch nicht so frei,
wär’ ich noch eimmal jung: dich einzukriegen

erschien mir damals in der Kindheit Mai
beinahe möglich, wenn ich mich nur spute,
ich schickte nicht zu dir hier diesen Schrei

aus tiefer Not mit allerletztem Mute.
O wär’ ich Welle, Wolke, Blatt – sieh hier:
des Lebens Dornen sind mein Bett, ich blute!

Schwer liegt der Jahre Kettenlast auf mir
und fesselt den, der, ach, zu ähnlich dir.

V

Mach mich, wie diesen Wald, zu deiner Leier,
daß ich wie er mein welkes Laub verschwende,
Nimm von uns beiden für die große Feier

des Herbstes einen dunklen Ton und wende
in süße Trauer ihn. In meinem Leibe
sei du mein Geist, nimm mich in deine Hände.

Die abgestorbenen Gedanken treibe
wie welkes Laub davon, daß Neues werde.
Von diesem meinem Vers beschworen, reibe

die Asche von der Glut im kalten Herde,
laß meine Worte wie die Funken streu'n
unter die ganze Menschheit. Laß der Erde

durch mich, o wilder Westwind, prophezein:
Kommt Winter jetzt, kann fern der Frühling sein?

Der Titel nimmt für das Gedicht die Bezeichnung Ode in
Anspruch und stellt es damit in eine formale Tradition, die
bis zu den alten Griechen zurückreicht. Dort war die Ode,
jedenfalls in ihrer hochentwickelten Form, eine feierliche
Dichtung, die sich in streng eingehaltener Strophenform an
einen Adressaten richtete und sich in einer eher gedanklich-
abstrakten als sinnlich-konkreten Weise mit einem erhabenen Gegenstand auseinandersetzte. Daß die vorliegende
Ode keine der antiken Strophenformen aufweist, ist für sich
allein noch kein Grund, ihr die Führung des Titels abzuspre-
chen. Aber auch im Ton weicht sie stark von der klassischen
Ode ab; er ist nicht feierlich-getragen, sondern emphatisch
drängend. Und auch das Gedanklich-Reflektierende tritt
ganz hinter die sinnliche Präsenz der dargestellten Natur-
phänomene zurück. Selbst bei sehr weitherzigem Gebrauch
des Begriffs kann man das Gedicht also kaum eine Ode
nennen. Vergißt man einmal ganz die literarische Tradition

und sucht nach einer überlieferten Form, die das Schema des Gedichts treffend beschreibt, so dürfte es kaum schwerfallen, eine solche zu finden: Es ist die klassische Form eines Beschwörungsrituals. Hier wird nach uraltem Brauch ein Geist beschworen. Dazu gehört zunächst einmal, daß man ihn *dreimal* ruft. Wenn er dann nach der dritten Anrufung erscheint, darf man ihn immer noch nicht gleich mit seiner Bitte überfallen, sondern muß sich ihm erst zu Füßen werfen und sich vor ihm demütigen. Erst dann wird man ohne Gefahr und mit der Hoffnung auf Erhörung seine Bitte vortragen dürfen. Dies fünfteilige Schema bestimmt die Grundstruktur des in fünf Strophen gegliederten Gedichts.

Die erste Strophe stellt den Westwind als »Atem des Herbstes« dar, der totes Laub von den Bäumen schüttelt, der zugleich aber auch die Samen für neues Wachstum in die Erde befördert. In dieser Rolle ist er »Zerstörer und Bewahrer« in einem. Im Zentrum des Bildes steht das Verhältnis Blatt–Erde, wobei Blatt den Samen einschließt. Noch weiß man nicht, was es mit dieser Relation auf sich hat. Aber schon in der nächsten Strophe wird der hellhörige Leser ahnen, worauf der Dichter hinauswill; denn jetzt erscheint der Westwind als eine tumultuarische Kraft, die die Wolken auf den blauen Himmelsstrom schleudert und sie zu dem düsteren »Grabgewölbe« (engl. »dome of a vast sepulchre«) eines spätherbstlichen Gewitterhimmels auftürmt. An die Stelle des Blattes tritt in dieser Strophe die Wolke, an die Stelle der Erde die Luft. Damit zeichnet sich bereits ab, daß hier eine bestimmte Bildkonfiguration durch die vier Elementarbereiche durchgespielt werden soll. Erwartungsgemäß wird in der dritten Strophe das Element des Wassers in den Mittelpunkt gerückt, und die Entsprechung zu Blatt und Wolke ist jetzt die Welle. In der Textur ist dies die kunstvollste der fünf Strophen. Hätten wir sie im Original vorliegen, könnten wir sehen, wie Shelley mit dichtgepackten Nasalen und Liquiden zunächst das Bild einer Meeres-bucht malt, die in heißer, bleierner Stille daliegt. Doch gleich darauf merken wir, daß es die Stille vor dem Sturm ist; denn plötzlich bricht der kunstvoll gestaute Sprachfluß los, und man hört in den schneidenden k-Lauten, mit denen der Sturm einsetzt, und in dem erregten Rhythmus der letzten Zeilen förmlich die See kochen.

In diesen drei ersten Strophen wurde das Verhältnis Blatt–Erde nacheinander in die Elementarbereiche der Luft und des Wassers übersetzt. Gleichzeitig wurde durch Bewegungen in drei unterschiedlichen Richtungen der sowohl kosmische wie magische Raum entfaltet. In der ersten Strophe fielen die Blätter von oben nach unten, in der zweiten wurden die Wolken von unten nach oben an den Himmel geworfen; in der dritten jagte der Wind die Wellen horizontal über das Meer. Jetzt wartet der Leser auf das vierte Element, das Feuer, und dieses müßte entsprechend dem angelegten Strukturplan vom Wind im dreidimensionalen Raum nach allen Richtungen verteilt werden. Da das Gedicht aber als Beschwörungsritual aufgebaut ist, muß der Beschwörende sich jetzt erst einmal dem Geist zu Füßen werfen und ihm seine Notlage bekennen. Diese vierte Strophe beginnt so, daß selbst der unaufmerksamste Leser den kunstvollen Plan nicht mehr übersehen kann; denn sie wiederholt in den ersten drei Zeilen noch einmal die zentralen Bilder der vorangegangenen Strophen, nämlich Blatt, Wolke und Welle, und nicht genug damit, sie wiederholt sie ein weiteres Mal am Schluß. Die Unterwerfungsphase des Rituals wirkt im Gedicht als retardierendes Moment und erhöht so die Spannung des Lesers auf das Erscheinen des noch ausstehenden Elements.

In der fünften und letzten Phase des Rituals darf der Beschwörende nun endlich seine Bitte vortragen. Er fleht den Westwind an, ihn zu seiner Leier zu machen, so wie der Wald die große Leier ist, auf der der Herbstwind seine wilden Lieder spielt. Noch einmal wird das Bild der fallenden Blätter aufgenommen. Aber jetzt will der Dichter nicht wie eben noch in der vierten Strophe ein Blatt sein, sondern er will dem Wald gleichen und wie dieser sein samentragendes Laub in die Welt verstreuen. Im nächsten Terzett geht er noch einen Schritt weiter und will wie der Westwind selber sein. Im dritten Terzett wird das Bild vom welken Laub erneut aufgenommen, jetzt aber mit einer eindeutigen Wendung ins Positive: Der Dichter bittet den Westwind, seine toten Gedanken über das ganze Universum zu verstreuen, um damit neues Leben hervorzurufen.

Im Original: Drive my dead thoughts over the universe
              Like withered leaves to quicken a new birth!

Jetzt endlich, nach diesem langen Anlauf, hat das Gedicht den Punkt erreicht, auf den es von Anfang an so kunstvoll und raffiniert zusteuerte. Im vierten und letzten Terzett, das wie der Schluß einer Beethovenschen Sinfonie zu einem grandiosen Finale anschwillt, spricht der Dichter die entscheidende Bitte aus, die nun endlich auch das langerwartete Bild des Feuers in Erscheinung treten läßt: Er, der Dichter, will, daß seine Worte wie die letzten Funken aus einem fast erloschenen Herd in die Welt verstreut werden, um dort ein neues Feuer des Geistes zu entfachen.

     Scatter, as from an unextinguished hearth
     Ashes and sparks, my words among mankind!

Dann mündet das Gedicht in die abschließende Bitte, der beschworene Geist möge ihn, den Dichter, zu seinem Sprachrohr machen und durch ihn der Welt mit einem Fanfarenstoß die Prophezeiung verkünden, daß auf den Winter ein neuer Frühling folgen werde.

Dieser Schluß wirkt nach dem Höhepunkt, den das Gedicht in den zuletzt zitierten Zeilen erreicht hat, merkwürdig schwach, fast ein wenig banal. In seiner thematischen Entwicklung war das Gedicht mit dem Erscheinen des Feuers abgeschlossen. Das Bild des Funkens enthält symbolisch die ganze prometheische Hoffnung, die der Dichter vermitteln wollte. Daß er diese nun zum Schluß explizit ausformuliert, nimmt ihr einen Teil ihrer Kraft. Würde das Gedicht mit der kühnen und zugleich frevelhaften Geste enden, mit der der Dichter für sich die Rolle eines neuen Prometheus oder eines ins Positive gewendeten Luzifer reklamiert, so wäre dies ein Finale von eindrucksvoller Kraft und irritierender Ambiguität. Da er aber der großen Geste noch die ausformulierte Prophezeiung folgen läßt, reduziert sich alles auf die abschließende Verkündigung, daß auf den Winter ein Frühling folgen werde. Das Platitüdenhafte dieser Prophezeiung ist die einzige schwache Stelle dieses großartigen Gedichts.

Unsere Strukturanalyse hat gezeigt, wie eine bestimmte motivische Grundfigur nacheinander durch die vier Elementarbereiche durchgespielt wird. Wie sich das Blatt zur Erde verhält, so verhält sich die Wolke zum Himmel, die Welle zum Meer, der Funke zum Feuer und der inspirierte Dichter zur Menschheit. Diese vierfach variierte Relation ist nichts anderes als eine bildhafte Formel für die Grundfigur des romantischen Denkens überhaupt: nämlich für das Verhältnis des Teils zum kosmischen Ganzen. In unzähligen Variationen haben die Dichter jener Epoche immer wieder das metaphysische Problem der Individuation, der Vereinzelung des Menschen und seiner Sehnsucht nach Rückkehr in die ursprüngliche Ganzheit gestaltet. Vom ersten Aufkommen des »unglücklichen Bewußtseins« bei Rousseau bis hin zur spekulativen Lösung des Problems in Hegels dialektischer Philosophie kreiste das Denken der romantischen Philosophen unablässig um dieses Problem. Shelley steht also mit seinem Gedicht in einer großen europäischen Geistesbewegung, obwohl bei ihm von spekulativer Philosphie nichts zu spüren ist. Während die deutschen Romantiker durch Kant, Fichte, Schelling und Hegel mit Philosophie förmlich überschwemmt waren, lebten die englischen Romantiker in einer philosophischen Wüste. Es gab nicht einen einzigen Denker in ihrem Lande, der sie intellektuell hätte inspirieren können. Das ist vielleicht der Grund dafür, daß Shelleys

Gedicht nicht die gedankliche Tiefe Hölderlins erreicht und ganz zum Schluß sogar auf ein merkwürdig banales Niveau absinkt. Andererseits erklärt es aber auch, weshalb die Dichtung der englischen Romantiker um so vieles vitaler, frischer und sinnlicher ist als die ihrer deutschen Kollegen. Auch dafür ist Shelleys Gedicht ein vorzügliches Beispiel.

Das Gedicht im Werkkontext (ohne Schlüssel)

Es gibt Gedichte, bei denen man als Leser jedes Wort und jeden Satz zu verstehen glaubt und dabei dennoch das Gefühl hat, daß einige Wörter etwas ganz anderes bedeuten, als die Sprachkonvention ihnen zuschreibt. In der Regel sind es Wörter, die konkrete Gegenstände oder Sinneseindrücke bezeichnen, dabei aber auf etwas anderes, Abstraktes, zu verweisen scheinen. Wenn diese Verweisung auf einer dem konkreten Bilde innewohnenden Analogie beruht, läßt sich das, worauf verwiesen wird, meist schon intuitiv erfassen. Werden aber die Bilder durch willkürliche Zuordnungen als Chiffren für bestimmte Bedeutungen verwendet, lassen sie sich nicht mehr über das Analogieprinzip entschlüsseln. Die Bilder mögen zwar die Richtung ihrer Verweisung erahnen lassen, so wie das Kind, das die Muttersprache erlernt, die Bedeutung der Wörter zunächst nur erahnt. Will man diese Bildersprache aber wirklich verstehen, so muß man sie durch intensive Beschäftigung mit dem Gesamtwerk des Dichters regelrecht lernen. Der literarische Laie, der Gedichte nur zum Vergnügen liest, wird freilich selten bereit und in der Lage sein, die Mühsal dieses Lernens auf sich zu nehmen. Hier bietet sich der Literaturwissenschaft eine Gelegenheit, ihre Daseinsberechtigung als Vermittlerin zu beweisen.

Am folgenden Beispiel soll einmal gezeigt werden, wie weit eine werkimmanente Interpretation vordringen kann und an welchem Punkt sie über die Grenzen des Einzelwerks hinaus auf das Gesamtwerk ausgreifen muß, um zu einem tieferen Verständnis des Gedichts zu gelangen.

Georg Trakl

In den Nachmittag geflüstert

Sonne, herbstlich dünn und zag,
Und das Obst fällt von den Bäumen.
Stille wohnt in blauen Räumen
Einen langen Nachmittag.

Sterbeklänge von Metall;
Und ein weißes Tier bricht nieder.
Brauner Mädchen rauhe Lieder
Sind verweht im Blätterfall.

Stirne Gottes Farben träumt,
Spürt des Wahnsinns sanfte Flügel.
Schatten drehen sich am Hügel
Von Verwesung schwarz umsäumt.

Dämmerung voll Ruh und Wein;
Traurige Guitarren rinnen.
Und zur milden Lampe drinnen
Kehrst du wie im Traume ein.

Die wirksamsten Sinnesqualitäten dieses Gedichts sind ganz offensichtlich die Farben. Blau, Weiß, Braun und Schwarz werden direkt genannt, die Sonne am Anfang und das milde Licht der Lampe am Schluß evozieren darüber hinaus die Vorstellung von Goldgelb. Rätselhaft bleibt, von welchen Farben Gottes die Stirne in der dritten Strophe träumt, aber sicher wird man sie sich als strahlend hell vorstellen müssen. Jede Strophe enthält zwei Farbelemente. Ordnet man sie so an, wie sie aufeinander folgen, so ergibt sich ein Schema, das man wohl kaum für bloßen Zufall halten wird.

1. Strophe:	(sonnengelb)	– blau	}
2. Strophe:	weiß	– braun	} außen
3. Strophe:	Gottes Farben	– schwarz	}

---

4. Strophe:	(goldener?) Wein –	Lampenlicht	innen

Das Gedicht beginnt mit dem Kontrast der Komplementär-farben Gelb und Blau und der Gegenüberstellung von Fülle (»Obst«) und Leere (»blaue Räume«). Dann folgt in der zweiten Strophe die Gegenüberstellung von Tod (»Sterbe-klänge«) und Erotik (»braune Mädchen«). Die nächste Bild-stufe ist der Gegensatz zwischen Gottes Farben, wahnhaft geträumt, und schwarzer Verwesung. An diesem Punkt des Auseinanderklaffens von erträumter Transzendenz und ver-wesender Immanenz verläßt das Gedicht die Außenwelt und tritt in einen Innenraum ein, der Ruhe und Frieden verheißt, wenngleich auch hier Trauer nachklingt (»traurige Guitar-ren«) und die Einkehr nur als etwas Traumhaftes beschrie-ben wird.

Das Ordnungsprinzip der Farben ist leicht erkennbar. Wäh-rend wir auf der linken Seite eine Farbreihe von zunehmen-der Helligkeit haben, die das Reich der sichtbaren Farben über das farblose Weiß hinaus transzendiert, haben wir auf der rechten Seite eine Reihe mit abnehmender Helligkeit, die in das farblose Schwarz mündet und damit ebenfalls aus dem Reich der Farbe hinaustritt. Weiß ist die Summe aller Far-ben, den Schritt darüber hinaus kann man sich dann nur noch als ein völlig entsinnlichtes reines Licht vorstellen. Schwarz hingegen ist die Abwesenheit aller Farben, für die sinnliche Wahrnehmung also das Nichts. An diesem Punkt des Gedichts, an dem die Polarität der beiden Farbreihen zum äußersten Extrem getrieben worden ist, löst sich die Spannung in der Schlußstrophe im Zusammenfall zweier identischer Farbwerte. »Wein« ist bei Trakl in aller Regel der Farbe Gold zugeordnet, er hat damit die gleiche Farbe wie das Licht der »milden Lampe«. Durch die Lösung der Farbspannung vermittelt das Gedicht die zweifellos intendierte Vorstellung von Erlösung in einem religiös-sakramentalen Sinne.

Kennt man von Trakl nur dies eine Gedicht, so wird man zögern, mehr als diesen vagen Umriß herauszulesen. Sobald man aber andere Gedichte heranzieht, wird man sehen, daß man es hier mit einem ganz bestimmten Bild-Wortschatz zu tun hat. Immer wieder verwendet Trakl Farben zur dichterischen Markierung bestimmter Zustände menschlicher Existenz, und immer wieder trifft man bei ihm auf die sakramentale Vorstellung der Einkehr und Erlösung. So endet das Gedicht »Ein Winterabend« mit der Strophe:

> Wanderer tritt still herein;
> Schmerz versteinerte die Schwelle.
> Da erglänzt in reiner Helle
> Auf dem Tische Brot und Wein.

Kennt man diese und ähnliche Stellen im Gesamtwerk, dann wird man auch aus der Schlußstrophe unseres Gedichts einen Hinweis auf das Abendmahl herauslesen, obwohl dort nur vom Wein die Rede ist. Auch die übrigen Bilder würden für uns an Aussagefülle gewinnen, wenn wir wüßten, in welchem Kontext die Farben Blau, Weiß, Braun und Schwarz in den übrigen Gedichten verwendet werden. Für eine solche statistische Fundierung unserer Interpretation fehlt hier der Raum. Aber es dürfte wohl klargeworden sein, daß man den ganz persönlichen Wortschatz eines Dichters nur aus seinem gesamten Werk und nicht aus einem einzigen Gedicht herauslesen kann. Daraus folgt, daß dieses ohne Kenntnis des Gesamtwerks nicht angemessen verstanden werden kann, obwohl unsere Interpretation andererseits gezeigt hat, daß man auch ohne solche Kenntnis recht tief in ein Gedicht eindringen kann.

Das Gedicht im Werkkontext (mit Schlüssel)

Johann Wolfgang Goethe

Dornburg, September 1828

Früh, wenn Tal, Gebirg und Garten
Nebelschleiern sich enthüllen,
Und dem sehnlichsten Erwarten
Blumenkelche bunt sich füllen,

Wenn der Äther, Wolken tragend,
Mit dem klaren Tage streitet,
Und ein Ostwind, sie verjagend,
Blaue Sonnenbahn bereitet,

Dankst du dann, am Blick dich weidend,
Reiner Brust der Großen, Holden,
Wird die Sonne, rötlich scheidend,
Rings den Horizont vergolden.

Das Gedicht scheint so einfach und sonnenklar zu sein, daß
eine Interpretation kaum mehr tun kann, als das Gesagte zu
paraphrasieren und die Machart zu kommentieren. Zunächst
wird das Bild einer Landschaft in der Morgendämmerung
entworfen. Daran schließt sich die Aussage, daß, wenn der
Betrachter beim Anblick dieses Bildes der Großen, Holden,
also der Natur, dankt, die Sonne am Abend den Horizont
vergolden wird. So jedenfalls wird das Gedicht von Walther
Killy in seinem Buch *Wandlungen des lyrischen Bildes* (Göttingen, 1956) gelesen. Die Botschaft, sofern man von einer
solchen überhaupt sprechen kann, scheint in der vagen und
recht biedermeierlich anmutenden These zu bestehen, daß
die Natur demjenigen am Ende ihren Segen gibt, der sich ihr
dankend anvertraut. Diese Deutung setzt freilich voraus,
daß mit »scheidend« und »vergolden« der Sonnenuntergang
gemeint ist. Wenn man aber das Inventar von Goethes

Bildersprache kennt, wird man einer solchen Deutung kaum zustimmen können.

Goethe hat in diesem Gedicht auf engstem Raum das Grundkonzept seiner *Farbenlehre* (= FL) entworfen. Farbe war für ihn keine Eigenschaft des Lichts, sondern dessen Erzeugnis. Sie entsteht, so meinte er, wenn das »höchst energische Licht«, das seinem Wesen nach farblos weiß ist, auf ein trübes Medium trifft und aus diesem die Farbe hervortreibt (FL 150, 151). »Die Farbe ist in ihrem lichtesten Zustand ein Dunkles, wird sie verdichtet, so muß sie dunkler werden, aber zugleich erhält sie einen Schein, den wir mit dem Wort rötlich bezeichnen« (FL 699). In unserm Gedicht fällt das weiße Licht der noch unterm Horizont stehenden Sonne auf die trübe Erdatmosphäre und verdichtet in dieser die Farbe, bis sie den »rötlichen« Schein annimmt. Dann geschieht die eigentliche Entstehung der Farbe. »Entstehen der Farbe und Sichentscheiden ist eins« (FL 695). Sichentscheiden ist aber für Goethe ein Scheiden. Er glaubte, daß unter dem Druck des anstürmenden Lichts die Farbe sich nach Plus und Minus, nämlich nach Gelb und Blau, polarisiert. Dies sind die beiden Extrempole, aus denen sich nach seiner Ansicht der ganze Farbkreis entwickelt. Sie sind damit für ihn Symbole einer den ganzen Kosmos durchwaltenden Polarität. Der Farbe Blau ordnete er die Begriffe »Beraubung, Schatten, Dunkel, Schwäche, Kälte, Ferne, Anziehen« zu, der Farbe Gelb die Begriffe »Wirkung, Licht, Hell, Kraft, Wärme, Nähe, Abstoßen« (FL 696). Von der gelben Farbe sagt er: »Das Gold in seinem ganz ungemischten Zustand gibt uns, besonders wenn der Glanz hinzukommt, einen neuen und hohen Begriff von dieser Farbe« (FL 767). Die Verdichtung der Farbe im Medium der trüben Morgendämmerung, ihre Steigerung ins »Rötliche« und schließlich ihre Polarisierung, ihr »Scheiden« in Blau (»blaue Sonnenbahn«) und Gelb (»vergolden«) ist der kosmische Vorgang, der in dem Gedicht dargestellt wird. Jetzt bleibt nur noch die Frage, wieso das Vergolden erst eintreten wird, wenn man vorher »der Großen, Holden« dankt. Die Antwort ist einfach: Der Satz »Dankst du dann ...« ist überhaupt kein Konditionalsatz, sondern ein Temporalsatz. Er will sagen: »Während du dann noch der Großen, Holden dankst (was bei Goethe nicht unbedingt ›Dank abstatten‹, sondern auch ›dankend eingedenk sein‹ heißen kann), wird die Sonne aufgehen und »rings den Horizont vergolden«. Wir haben es hier also nicht mit einer Vorausschau, einer biedermeierlichen Abendphantasie zu tun, sondern mit einem Sonnenaufgang, den Goethe als Symbol der Kosmogonie, des tagtäglichen Schöpfungsaktes gestaltet, weil jeden Morgen aufs neue von der Sonne die Farben erzeugt werden, die für ihn Symbol des Lebens und der Liebe sind. In einem seiner bekanntesten und tiefsinnigsten Gedichte aus dem Westöstlichen Divan hatte er den gleichen Gedanken schon einmal entwickelt:

Wiederfinden

Ist es möglich! Stern der Sterne,
Drück ich wieder dich ans Herz!
Ach, was ist die Nacht der Ferne
Für ein Abgrund, für ein Schmerz!
Ja du bist es! meiner Freuden
Süßer, lieber Widerpart;
Eingedenk vergangner Leiden
Schaudr ich vor der Gegenwart.

Als die Welt im tiefsten Grunde
Lag an Gottes ewger Brust,
Ordnet' er die erste Stunde
Mit erhabner Schöpfungslust,
Und er sprach das Wort: Es werde!
Da erklang ein schmerzlich Ach!
Als das All mit Machtgebärde
In die Wirklichkeiten brach.

Auf tat sich das Licht: so trennte
Scheu sich Finsternis von ihm,
Und sogleich die Elemente
Scheidend auseinander fliehn.
Rasch, in wilden wüsten Träumen
Jedes nach der Weite rang,
Starr, in ungemeßnen Räumen,
Ohne Sehnsucht, ohne Klang.

Stumm war alles, still und öde,
Einsam Gott zum erstenmal!
Da erschuf er Morgenröte,
Die erbarmte sich der Qual;
Sie entwickelte dem Trüben
Ein erklingend Farbenspiel,
Und nun konnte wieder lieben,
Was erst auseinander fiel.

Und mit eiligem Bestreben
Sucht sich, was sich angehört;
Und zu ungemeßnem Leben
Ist Gefühl und Blick gekehrt.
Sei's Ergreifen, sei es Raffen,
Wenn es nur sich faßt und hält!
Allah braucht nicht mehr zu schaffen,
Wir erschaffen seine Welt.

So, mit morgenroten Flügeln,
Riß es mich an deinen Mund,
Und die Nacht mit tausend Siegeln
Kräftigt sternenhell den Bund.
Beide sind wir auf der Erde
Musterhaft in Freud und Qual,
Und ein zweites Wort: Es werde!
Trennt uns nicht zum zweitenmal.

Shakespeare ist in der Schlegel-Tieckschen Übersetzung so in die deutsche Literatur eingegangen, daß er zeitweilig gar als ein Teil von ihr empfunden wurde. Dickens, Tolstoj, Flaubert oder Mark Twain werden in deutschen Übersetzungen so selbstverständlich angenommen, daß kaum ein Leser den Namen des Übersetzers auch nur eines Blickes würdigt. In der Prosa scheint die Sprache ein beliebig austauschbares Kleid zu sein, und auch im Drama haben Shakespeare, Molière und Calderón die Sprachgrenze mühelos passiert, von Pinter und Beckett ganz zu schweigen. Nur der Lyrik ist dieser Sprung nie gelungen. Kein Dichter einer fremden Sprache, mit Ausnahme vielleicht von Villon, ist bei uns heimisch geworden. Ein Gedicht ist mit seiner äußeren Sprachhaut so fest verwachsen, daß ein Austausch derselben durch Transplantation einer anderen so viele Narben hinterläßt, daß der Leser sich nicht dauerhaft in das Gedicht verliebt, mag dessen sonstige Gestalt noch so schön sein. Das Ausgesperrtsein der Lyrik anderer Sprachen aber bewirkt auch, daß dichterische Leistungen in der eigenen Sprache immer nur an der inländischen Konkurrenz gemessen werden. Während der anspruchsvolle Prosaleser eher zu Tolstoj als zu Gustav Freytag greifen wird, bleibt der Lyrikleser seinem Stefan George treu, da ihm Yeats und Mallarmé verschlossen sind. Das hat in der literarischen Urteilsbildung zu mancherlei Provinzialismen geführt, die in der deutschen Literatur besonders auffällig sind, da diese, anders als die französische oder die englische, einen sehr zerklüfteten Verlauf genommen hat. Während z. B. die englische Lyrik von Shakespeare bis zur Gegenwart sich als ein Hochplateau mit vielen gleichmäßig verteilten Gipfeln darstellt, hat die deutsche nach Walther von der Vogelweide erst wieder zur Goethezeit ein gewaltiges Massiv aufzuweisen, dem dann zwischen Heine und Rilke wieder eine eher bescheidene Hügellandschaft folgt. Am krassesten fällt die deutsche Lyrik gegenüber der europäischen im 16. Jahrhun-

dert ab, als sich überall in den Nachbarländern die Sonett-
dichtung zur vollen Blüte entwickelte. Gaspara Stampa,
Tasso, Ronsard, Góngora, Shakespeare: dies sind bestau-
nenswerte Gipfel, die auf eine deutsche Literaturlandschaft
herabsehen, die in der Versdichtung einzig durch Hans
Sachs vertreten wird, während die übrigen literarischen
Talente sich vorwiegend im Reformationsstreit verbrauch-
ten. Erst im Barock gewann die deutsche Lyrik allmählich
wieder Anschluß an die europäische Entwicklung. Es ist von
fast makabrer Ironie, daß sie sich ausgerechnet in der Zeit
des Dreißigjährigen Krieges von den Folgen der geistigen
Religionskriege des vorangegangenen Jahrhunderts zu erho-
len begann. Martin Opitz war es, der der deutschen Dichtung einen neuen Grund legte, und Andreas Gryphius schuf
auf diesem Grund das bedeutendste lyrische Werk der Epoche. In der literarischen Landschaft seiner Zeit ist er zweifellos eine herausragende Erscheinung, so wie der Harz im
norddeutschen Flachland ein beachtliches Gebirge ist. Erst
wenn man ihn mit Zeitgenossen in den Nachbarliteraturen
vergleicht, wird man seinen Rang gerechter und objektiver
beurteilen können. Einen solchen Vergleich wollen wir nun
durchführen, wobei der Engländer John Donne, obwohl 44
Jahre älter als Gryphius, der Vergleichsmaßstab sein soll.
England hatte keine wirkliche Barockkultur. In der bildenden Kunst hatte der Barockstil gegenüber dem Klassizismus,
der als Palladianismus schon früh im 17. Jahrhundert nach
England kam, keine Chance, da er als künstlerischer Ausdruck der Gegenreformation empfunden wurde und damit
für das protestantische England inakzeptabel war. In der
Literatur kommen nur die sog. *metaphysical poets* der deutschen Barockdichtung nahe. Ihr herausragender Vertreter,
wenngleich abseits von den übrigen stehend, ist John
Donne. Mit ihm verglichen zu werden gereicht Gryphius
zweifellos zur Ehre. Doch zuerst einmal die beiden zu
vergleichenden Sonette:

Andreas Gryphius

Es ist alles eitel

Du siehst, wohin du siehst, nur Eitelkeit auf Erden,
Was dieser heute baut, reißt jener morgen ein;
Wo jetzund Städte stehn, wird eine Wiese sein,
Auf der ein Schäferskind wird spielen mit den Herden.

Was jetzund prächtig blüht, soll bald zertreten werden.
Was jetzt so pocht und trotzt, ist morgen Asch und Bein;
Nichts ist, das ewig sei, kein Erz, kein Marmorstein.
Jetzt lacht das Glück uns an, bald donnern die Beschwerden.

Der hohen Taten Ruhm muß wie ein Traum vergehn.
Soll denn das Spiel der Zeit, der leichte Mensch, bestehn?
Ach, was ist alles dies, was wir vor köstlich achten,

Als schlechte Nichtigkeit, als Schatten, Staub und Wind,
Als eine Wiesenblum, die man nicht wiederfindt!
Noch will, was ewig ist, kein einig Mensch betrachten.

John Donne

Tod, sei nicht stolz. Zwar halten manche dich
für stark und furchtbar, du bist keins von beiden.
Die du hinwegzuraffen scheinst, erleiden
nicht dich, du tötest weder sie noch mich.

Aus Ruh und Schlaf, Abbildern deines Wesens,
fließt viel Erquickung, wieviel mehr aus dir.
Die besten unter uns, der Menschheit Zier,
finden durch dich das Ziel ihres Genesens.

Du dienst der Macht, dem Zufall, blinder Wut,
und lebst mit Gift und Krankheit, Krieg dazu.
Ein wenig Schlafmohn gibt uns bessre Ruh.
Was blähst du dich dann auf in stolzem Mut?

122

Nach kurzem Schlaf sind wir des Himmels Erben,
und Tod wird nicht mehr sein. Tod, du mußt sterben.

Gryphius' Sonett ist wahrscheinlich sein bekanntestes und sicher auch eins seiner schönsten. Dennoch merkt man bereits beim Lesen, daß es an etwas krankt, was wir schon bei der allgemeinen Betrachtung des Sonetts erwähnt haben: nämlich am Alexandriner. Da die starre Zäsur jeden Vers nach der dritten Hebung in zwei gleiche Hälften zerlegt, muß man beim Lesen 28 mal neu ansetzen. Allenfalls in Zeile 4 und 9 könnte man die Zäsur ein wenig einebnen, in den übrigen Zeilen wird sie durch trennende Satzzeichen eindeutig markiert. Nun ist aber gerade in diesem Sonett die Wirkung des Alexandriners durchaus nicht so restringierend wie in den meisten anderen jener Zeit. Da das Gedicht von der Vergänglichkeit alles Irdischen handelt und dies Memento Mori litaneihaft beschwörend vorträgt, passen die kurzatmigen, fast wie Seufzer klingenden Alexandrinerhälften recht gut zur zentralen Aussage. Dennoch bleibt der Vers eine Zwangsjacke, da er dem Dichter kaum eine Möglichkeit läßt, größere syntaktische Strukturen zu entwickeln. Wie kann er einen komplexen Gedanken entfalten, wenn er den Satz nach jeder sechsten Silbe durch eine gedankliche und meist auch syntaktische Zäsur unterbrechen muß? Es wundert deshalb nicht, daß Gryphius seine Bilder, Vergleiche und gedanklichen Aussagen nur additiv aneinanderreiht. Gerade diese Reihung drückt aber wiederum recht gut das gleichmäßige, unablässige und unaufhaltsame Hinschwinden alles Irdischen aus. Der Mangel an Komplexität wird also in diesem Fall durch eine glückliche und eher zufällige Übereinstimmung der Form mit dem Tenor der Aussage wieder wettgemacht. Inhaltlich enthält das Gedicht nichts, was einer Interpretation bedürfte. Der Grundgedanke ist einfach und von unmittelbarer Evidenz. Da er in jeder Zeile neu, wenn auch mit zunehmender Intensität, wiederholt wird, gibt es in dem Gedicht nichts, das den Geist des Lesers zum Widerspruch herausfordert, ihn zum Nachvollzug eines schwierigen Gedankens zwingt oder ihn in ein ausweglöses intellektuelles Dilemma verstrickt. Dafür aber hat es einen Ton von persönlicher Betroffenheit, es vermittelt ein Gefühl von großer Authentizität. Hier bahnt sich unter der einschnürenden Form bereits der schlichte, ergreifende Liedton an, der bei Paul Gerhardt, Claudius und dann bei den Romantikern zum deutschen Lyrikton schlechthin wird. (Heine hat einmal das Lied und die Philosophie als »die höchsten Blüten des deutschen Geistes« bezeichnet.)

Wie stellt sich nun gegenüber diesem lauteren, durch und durch authentischen, aber auch jeder Komplexität entbehrenden Memento mori das Sonett von John Donne dar? Obwohl es nicht in das Korsett des Alexandriners geschnürt ist, sondern sich in fünfhebigen Jamben frei bewegt und von dieser Freiheit tatsächlich so weiten Gebrauch macht, daß es stellenweise wie Prosa klingt, ist sein Ton dennoch härter und spröder als der liedhafte Ton bei Gryphius. Das liegt sicher nicht an der Übersetzung; denn das englische Original klingt eher noch spröder und unpoetischer. Donne gestaltet sein Gedicht wie ein kasuistisches Plädoyer. Er spricht den Tod an und bestreitet ihm das Recht, sich »mächtig und furchtbar« zu nennen. Dies ist seine *proposition*, die er – wie der Redner in einer *debating society* an einer englischen Universität – nun zu begründen versucht. Zuerst nimmt er sich das Argument »furchtbar« vor und weist nach, daß der Tod dies keineswegs ist. Wenn schon Ruhe und Schlaf, die doch nur Abbilder des Todes sind, uns so erquicken können, wie groß muß dann erst die Erquickung sein, die uns das Original, der Tod selber, bereitet. Die Edelsten der Menschheit folgen ihm und finden bei ihm die Ruhe ihrer Gebeine und die Erlösung ihrer Seelen. Damit erscheint der Tod als mächtiger Fürst, zu dem alles hinströmt, um ihm Tribut zu zollen und seine Gunst zu empfangen. Der Dichter wollte nachweisen, daß der Tod nicht furchtbar ist. Dies ist ihm vorzüglich gelungen, doch unversehens läßt er ihn damit als mächtigen Herrscher erscheinen. Die Macht aber hatte er ihm am Anfang ebenfalls abgesprochen. So muß er sich nun daranmachen, auch diesen Anspruch überzeugend zurückzuweisen. Er nennt den Tod einen Sklaven, der dem Zufall, der Willkür von Königen und wahnwitzigen Menschen gehorcht und sich mit Gift, Krankheit und Krieg verbündet. Eben hieß es noch, der Tod könne weit mehr Lust spenden als Ruhe und Schlaf. Jetzt sagt der Dichter, daß Schlafmohn und Zaubertränke weit besseren Schlaf bereiten könnten. Die Entmachtung des Todes ist ihm damit rhetorisch gelungen, doch hat er ihn nun zum Inbegriff des Schreckens gemacht. Also müßte er wieder von vorn anfangen mit seinem Beweis, daß der Tod nicht schrecklich sei, und er würde sich erneut in das gleiche Dilemma verstricken; denn in Wirklichkeit weiß er genau, daß der Tod mächtig und furchtbar ist und daß ihm alle kasuistischen Finten nicht helfen, diese Tatsache aus der Welt zu schaffen. So zerhaut er den gordischen Knoten und zieht sich auf eine Glaubensposition zurück. Da er an das ewige Leben glaubt, kann der Tod nicht mehr sein als ein kurzer Schlaf, der die Seele ins Jenseits hinübergeleitet. Für den glaubenden Menschen gibt es darum keinen Tod; der Tod selber ist es, der zu verschwinden, zu sterben hat. Und so spricht er am Ende seines Plädoyers über den Tod das Todesurteil:

Death thou shalt die.

Dieser Satz klingt nicht wie eine Tatsachenbehauptung, man spürt darin keine faktische Gewißheit. Er klingt viel eher wie ein Befehl, wie eine defensive Kampfhandlung, die das Gespenst des mächtigen, schrecklichen Todes bannen soll, mit dem der Dichter das ganze Gedicht hindurch gerungen hat. Anders als bei Gryphius, der eine Grundtatsache des menschlichen Daseins mit lyrisch eindrucksvollen Worten ausspricht, spüren wir bei Donne die intellektuelle Spannung eines Geistes, der ganz persönlich mit dem Problem ringt. Das Gedicht macht nicht wie bei Gryphius bloß eine Aussage, sondern es stellt den Verlauf einer geistigen Auseinandersetzung dar. Denkt man sich bei Gryphius einmal die schöne poetische Einkleidung weg, so bleibt am Ende nur ein Gemeinplatz übrig. Bei Donne hingegen bleibt das Problem in seiner ganzen inneren Widersprüchlichkeit zurück: Angst, Hoffnung, Erlösungssehnsucht, Glaubensgewißheit und nagender Zweifel, alles ist im Gedicht präsent und gibt ihm so viel Substanz, daß diese selbst nach der Einkleidung in eine andere Sprache für den Leser noch in ihrer ganzen Komplexität nachvollziehbar ist.

Vergleich zweier motivverwandter Gedichte

Es ist eine jedermann vertraute Tatsache, daß Unterschiedliches leichter wahrgenommen wird als Identisches. Wenn nun ein Gedicht so glatt und fugenlos ist, daß sich keine Bruchstelle finden läßt, an der die Interpretation ihr kritisches »Warum?« ansetzen kann, dann ist es manchmal hilfreich, den Anlaß zu dieser Frage künstlich zu schaffen, indem man das Gedicht mit einem motivverwandten vergleicht. Aus den Unterschieden zwischen den beiden Gedichten ergibt sich dann zwangsläufig die Frage, weshalb das eine etwas so und das andere es anders ausdrückt. Ist das Motiv in beiden identisch, z. B. eine Herbstlandschaft, so wird das Augenmerk des Interpreten vor allem auf die unterschiedliche formale Behandlung gerichtet sein. Weisen die Motive aber nur eine vage Ähnlichkeit auf, so hilft uns die vergleichende Interpretation auch, den jeweils spezifischen Gehalt besser zu verstehen. Ein solcher Vergleich soll am Beispiel der beiden folgenden Gedichte durchgeführt werden.

Joseph Freiherr von Eichendorff

Zwielicht

Dämmrung will die Flügel spreiten,
Schaurig rühren sich die Bäume,
Wolken ziehn wie schwere Träume –
Was will dieses Graun bedeuten?

Hast ein Reh du lieb vor andern,
Laß es nicht alleine grasen,
Jäger ziehn im Wald und blasen,
Stimmen hin und wieder wandern.

Hast du einen Freund hienieden,
Trau ihm nicht zu dieser Stunde,
Freundlich wohl mit Aug und Munde,
Sinnt er Krieg im tück'schen Frieden.

Was heut müde gehet unter,
Hebt sich morgen neugeboren.
Manches bleibt in Nacht verloren –
Hüte dich, bleib wach und munter!

Theodor Storm

Meeresstrand

Ans Haff nun fliegt die Möve,
und Dämmrung bricht herein;
Über die feuchten Watten
Spiegelt der Abendschein.

Graues Geflügel huschet
Neben dem Wasser her;
Wie Träume liegen die Inseln
Im Nebel auf dem Meer.

Ich höre des gärenden Schlammes
Geheimnisvollen Ton,
Einsames Vogelrufen –
So war es immer schon.

Noch einmal schauert leise
und schweiget dann der Wind;
Vernehmlich werden die Stimmen,
Die über der Tiefe sind.

Die Ähnlichkeit der beiden Gedichte liegt vor allem in ihrer gemeinsamen atmosphärischen Grundstimmung. Beide evozieren einen Dämmerzustand zwischen Tag und Nacht; beide beschreiben diesen Zustand als etwas, das das Vertraute fremd werden läßt, so daß ein Gefühl von Ungewißheit bei gleichzeitig geschärfter Wahrnehmung aufkommt. In der dichterischen Umsetzung aber schlagen sie beide entgegengesetzte Richtungen ein. Eichendorff bezieht sich zwar auf äußere Realität – Bäume, Reh, Jäger, Wald –, aber er fügt diese Bilder nicht zu einem kohärenten Landschaftsbild. Von der ersten Zeile an weiß der Leser, daß nicht eine äußere, sondern eine Seelenlandschaft beschrieben wird. Die Dämmerung wird mit einem geheimnisvollen Vogel verglichen, der seine Flügel ausbreitet, um seinen nächtlichen Flug anzutreten; die Bäume erscheinen als nach außen getretener Ausdruck eines inneren Schauders, und die Wolken werden, noch direkter, mit schweren Träumen verglichen. Bei der Erwähnung des Rehs weiß der Leser, daß kein wirkliches Reh gemeint sein kann; denn wie sollte man ein bestimmtes Reh mehr lieben als die anderen? Offensichtlich steht »Reh« hier für etwas Zartes, Gefährdetes, um das man sich in Liebe sorgt. Das heißt aber, daß auch die Jäger nur gleichnishaft zu verstehen sind. Ganz ins Innere der Seele geht dann die dritte Strophe. Hier wird der Zustand der Ungewißheit und Bedrohung sehr klar und sehr radikal ausgesprochen; denn es heißt dort, daß man nicht einmal einem Freunde trauen darf. Die vierte Strophe nimmt von dieser düsteren Warnung wieder etwas zurück, indem sie die Zeit der Gefahr auf jene zwielichtige Phase der Müdigkeit zwischen Nacht und Tag einschränkt. Bleibt man wach und munter, so ist man offenbar gegen den Trug des Zwielichts gefeit. Das Gedicht hebt also den atmosphärischen Zustand des Zwielichts in die ethische Dimension und spricht die Forderung aus, wach zu bleiben und nicht der Versuchung nachzugeben, die dann an den Menschen herantritt, wenn sein Blick durch das Zwielicht, also durch einen Mangel an Bewußtsein, getrübt ist. Dies ist eine Ethik aus dem Umkreis des Kantischen kategorischen Imperativs, die dem Menschen die permanente Willensbestimmung durch die wache Vernunft zur moralischen Pflicht macht. Allerdings ist bei Eichendorff das Wach-und-munter-Bleiben dem Tag und der Zeit des Zwielichts zugeordnet. Daneben gibt es aber noch die Nacht, in die der Mensch in Müdigkeit versinkt und der er dann ausgeliefert ist. Das Gedicht sagt inhaltlich nichts über sie aus, sondern stellt sie nur als Gegenpol zum Tag dar. Dies ist die spezifisch dichterische Weise, ein Problem zu entfalten. Während der Philosoph es diskursiv entwickeln und zu einer klaren Ja-nein-Entscheidung führen muß, kann der Dichter die im Problem offenbarwerdenden Antinomien, den Widerstreit der Wertpositionen, zeigen, ohne sie auflösen zu müssen. Ja, das Dichterische daran ist gerade, daß er sie nicht auflöst, daß er weder Erklärungen gibt noch Schlußfolgerungen zieht. Eichendorffs Gedicht stellt den Tag, auf den die Zeile

Hebt sich morgen neugeboren

verweist, als das Reich der Bewußtheit der Nacht als dem Reich der Bewußtlosigkeit gegenüber, ohne inhaltlich etwas über die beiden moralischen Sphären auszusagen. Die einzige moralische Aussage ist der Appell, sich im Zwielicht durch Wachbleiben gegen das Dunkel zu behaupten.

Nun zum Vergleich das Gedicht von Storm. Auch hier taucht gleich am Anfang das Wort »Dämmrung« auf, und Eichendorffs »schaurig« kehrt bei Storm in der vierten Strophe als »schauert« wieder. Desgleichen ist von Träumen die Rede, die bei Eichendorff mit Wolken, bei Storm mit Inseln verglichen werden. Während aber bei Eichendorff eine Seelenlandschaft beschworen wird, in die die reale Außenwelt in Gestalt von Bäumen, Wolken, dem Wald und dem Reh inselhaft hineinragt, wird bei Storm das Bild einer realen Küstenlandschaft entworfen, in das nun umgekehrt durch den Vergleich der Inseln mit Träumen etwas Seelisches hineinragt. Die Träume sind also selber wie Inseln der Innenwelt in einem Bild durchgängiger Außenwelt. Dieses reziproke Verhältnis der beiden Gedichte veranschaulicht sehr sinnfällig die unterschiedlichen literarhistorischen Epochen, denen die Dichter angehören. Eichendorff ist Spätromantiker; Storm, obwohl formal noch unter dem Einfluß der Romantik, ist Realist. Dieser Unterschied betrifft auch die gedankliche Substanz der Gedichte. Während Eichendorff das Naturbild in Seelenlandschaft verwandelt und damit ethisiert, beschreibt Storm es als etwas Objekthaftes. Aber auch bei ihm öffnet sich am Schluß das physisch-reale Bild und verweist auf etwas Immaterielles:

> Vernehmlich werden die Stimmen,
> Die über der Tiefe sind.

Dies klingt jedoch kaum wie eine Warnung, sondern eher wie das Offenbarwerden von etwas Verborgenem. Wie bei Eichendorff haben wir es mit drei Sphären zu tun: der dunklen Tiefe, der hellen Oberwelt und der Dämmerung dazwischen. Das Wort »Tiefe«, zumal im Kontext eines Bildes vom Meeresstrand, hat sicher etwas Bedrohliches, da es im Leser sogleich die Vorstellung von Ertrinken weckt, wobei durch das Bild des gärenden Schlammes noch die Vorstellung des Versinkens hinzukommt. Da das Gedicht die ganze Szenerie mit großer Intensität vergegenwärtigt, evoziert es im Leser Vorstellungen, die mit vagen, nicht genau definierbaren Bedeutungen aufgeladen sind. Aber unter diesen Bedeutungen wird wohl kaum eine Aufforderung zum Wachbleiben sein. Die »Tiefe« mag zwar etwas Bedrohliches haben, aber die Stimmen über ihr laden eher dazu ein, ihrem Geheimnis zu lauschen. Das Gedicht vermittelt nicht den Gestus des Auf-der-Hut-Seins, sondern den des lauschend hingeneigten Ohrs. Dieser Unterschied gegenüber Eichendorff ist literatur- und bewußtseinsgeschichtlich sehr aufschlußreich. Die Romantiker, die unter dem Einfluß des spekulativen Idealismus standen, strebten nach einer zunehmenden Vergeistigung des Materiellen. In der zweiten Hälfte des 19. Jahrhunderts macht sich dagegen schon die beginnende Geistmüdigkeit bemerkbar, die sich in der durch Schopenhauer, Nietzsche und Bergson vertretenen Lebensphilosophie ausdrückt und schließlich im Irrationalismus unseres Jahrhunderts kulminiert. Storms volksliedhaft schlichtes und in seiner Anschaulichkeit sehr poetisches Gedicht läßt an der Oberfläche nichts von irgendwelchen philosophischen Implikationen erkennen. Wenn man es aber mit Eichendorffs Gedicht vergleicht und nach den Gründen für die Unterschiede fragt, öffnet sich der Blick auf den bewußtseinsgeschichtlichen Kontext. Man spürt dann bereits die ersten Anklänge jenes Kokettierens mit der Tiefe, dem Dumpfen und Chthonischen, das im 20. Jahrhundert immer breiteren Raum einnimmt und im Blut-und-BodenKult des Nationalsozialismus seine fatalste Blüte treibt – mit dem Storm, dies sei mit Nachdruck gesagt, allerdings nicht das geringste zu tun hat.

Vergleich zweier gattungsverwandter Gedichte

Balladen gehören zu den am wenigsten interpretationsbedürftigen Gedichten. Da sie keine eigentlich lyrischen, sondern erzählende Texte sind, geht es bei ihnen nicht um den Aufbau komplexer Klang-, Bild- und Sinnstrukturen, sondern um die möglichst effektvolle Präsentation der erzählten Geschichte. Bereits aus diesem Grunde ist ihre Machart meist schon an der Oberfläche abzulesen. Außerdem stehen sie in der Tradition der Volksballade und bemühen sich deshalb um unmittelbare Verständlichkeit. Dies gilt auch für solche Balladen, die sich weit von Form und Ton der Volksballade entfernen. Die Interpretation einer einzelnen Ballade droht deshalb leicht zu einer bloßen Beschreibung dessen zu werden, was offen zutage liegt. Deshalb wollen wir im folgenden zwei Balladen miteinander vergleichen, um durch die Wahrnehmung der Unterschiede zu einem besseren Verständnis der Eigentümlichkeiten jeder einzelnen zu gelangen. Unsere Beispiele – Goethes »Erlkönig« und Schillers »Handschuh« – gehören zu den bekanntesten deutschen Balladen überhaupt. Beide Gedichte können als klassische

Beispiele für die beiden unterschiedlichen Balladentraditionen gelten. Während Goethe sich an die Tradition der Volksballade anlehnt, schreibt Schiller eine reine Kunstballade, die nichts mehr mit der volkstümlichen Form gemein hat.

Johann Wolfgang Goethe

Erlkönig

Wer reitet so spät durch Nacht und Wind?
Es ist der Vater mit seinem Kind;
Er hat den Knaben wohl in dem Arm,
Er faßt ihn sicher, er hält ihn warm.

Mein Sohn, was birgst du so bang dein Gesicht? –
Siehst, Vater, du den Erlkönig nicht?
Den Erlenkönig mit Kron und Schweif? –
Mein Sohn, es ist ein Nebelstreif. –

»Du liebes Kind, komm, geh mit mir!
Gar schöne Spiele spiel ich mit dir;
Manch bunte Blumen sind an dem Strand,
Meine Mutter hat manch gülden Gewand.«

Mein Vater, mein Vater, und hörest du nicht,
Was Erlenkönig mir leise verspricht? –
Sei ruhig, bleibe ruhig, mein Kind;
In dürren Blättern säuselt der Wind. –

»Willst, feiner Knabe, du mit mir gehn?
Meine Töchter sollen dich warten schön;
Meine Töchter führen den nächtlichen Reihn
Und wiegen und tanzen und singen dich ein.«

Mein Vater, mein Vater, und siehst du nicht dort
Erlkönigs Töchter am düstern Ort? –
Mein Sohn, mein Sohn, ich seh es genau:
Es scheinen die alten Weiden so grau. –

»Ich liebe dich, mich reizt deine schöne Gestalt;
Und bist du nicht willig, so brauch ich Gewalt.«
Mein Vater, mein Vater, jetzt faßt er mich an!
Erlkönig hat mir ein Leids getan! –

Dem Vater grauset's, er reitet geschwind,
Er hält in Armen das ächzende Kind,
Erreicht den Hof mit Mühe und Not;
In seinen Armen das Kind war tot.

Friedrich Schiller

Der Handschuh

Vor seinem Löwengarten,
Das Kampfspiel zu erwarten,
Saß König Franz
Und um ihn die Großen der Krone
Und rings auf hohem Balkone
Die Damen in schönem Kranz.

Und wie er winkt mit dem Finger,
Auf tut sich der weite Zwinger,
Und hinein mit bedächtigem Schritt
Ein Löwe tritt
Und sieht sich stumm
Rings um,
Mit langem Gähnen,
Und schüttelt die Mähnen
Und streckt die Glieder
Und legt sich nieder.

Und der König winkt wieder,
Da öffnet sich behend
Ein zweites Tor,
Daraus rennt
Mit wildem Sprunge
Ein Tiger hervor.

Wie der den Löwen erschaut,
Brüllt er laut,
Schlägt mit dem Schweif
Einen furchtbaren Reif
Und recket die Zunge,
Und im Kreise scheu
Umgeht er den Leu
Grimmig schnurrend:
Drauf streckt er sich murrend
Zur Seite nieder.

Und der König winkt wieder,
Da speit das doppelt geöffnete Haus
Zwei Leoparden auf einmal aus,
Die stürzen mit mutiger Kampfbegier
Auf das Tigertier,
Das packt sie mit seinen grimmigen Tatzen,
Und der Leu mit Gebrüll
Richtet sich auf, da wird's still,
Und herum im Kreis,
Von Mordsucht heiß,
Lagern die greulichen Katzen.

Da fällt von des Altans Rand
Ein Handschuh von schöner Hand
Zwischen den Tiger und den Leun
Mitten hinein.

Und zu Ritter Delorges spottenderweis
Wendet sich Fräulein Kunigund:
»Herr Ritter, ist Eure Lieb so heiß,
Wie Ihr mir's schwört zu jeder Stund,
Ei, so hebt mir den Handschuh auf.«
Und der Ritter in schnellem Lauf
Steigt hinab in den furchtbaren Zwinger
Mit festem Schritte,
Und aus der Ungeheuer Mitte
Nimmt er den Handschuh mit keckem Finger.

Und mit Erstaunen und mit Grauen
Sehen's die Ritter und Edelfrauen,
Und gelassen bringt er den Handschuh zurück.
Da schallt ihm sein Lob aus jedem Munde,
Aber mit zärtlichem Liebesblick –
Er verheißt ihm sein nahes Glück –
Empfängt ihn Fräulein Kunigunde.
Und er wirft ihr den Handschuh ins Gesicht:
»Den Dank, Dame, begehr ich nicht«,
Und verläßt sie zur selben Stunde.

Schon äußerlich zeigen die beiden Balladen auffällige Unterschiede: bei Goethe nach Art der Volksballade eine strophische Gliederung, bei Schiller eine Aufteilung in Sinnabschnitte, deren Länge, wie die der Verszeilen, stark variiert. Im »Handschuh« weiß der Leser von Anfang an, daß ihm eine Geschichte erzählt wird. Das Gedicht beginnt wie eine Erzählung im epischen Präteritum. Mit Beginn des zweiten Absatzes geht das Erzähltempus zwar ins Präsens über, was eine Art temporalen Zoom-Effekt bewirkt und das Geschehen näher an den Leser heranholt; dennoch weiß dieser, daß er alles durch das Kamera-Auge des Erzählers sieht. Alle qualifizierenden Adjektive – »weit«, »bedächtig«, »behend«, »wild«, »fruchtbar«, »mutig«, usw. – sprechen ein Urteil über die jeweils qualifizierte Sache und setzen damit einen Urteilenden voraus. Der Erzähler bleibt also in jeder Zeile präsent. Er steht wie ein unsichtbarer Dompteur im Löwenkäfig und führt nacheinander seine Raubkatzen vor, indem er jede mit einer detaillierten Beschreibung ihres Verhaltens präsentiert.
Ganz anders im »Erlkönig«. Hier steht am Anfang die rhetorische Frage »Wer reitet so spät durch Nacht und Wind?« Die Frage bewirkt, daß der Leser sich mit dem Fragenden identifiziert, und das Präsens signalisiert ihm, daß ihm keine Geschichte erzählt wird, sondern daß er Augenzeuge eines Geschehens werden soll. Das bedeutet, daß auch die Antwort auf die Frage nicht von einem Erzäh-

ler kommt, sondern aus dem Munde eines anonymen Prä-
sentators, der nur ausspricht, was der Leser in der Fiktion
selbst zu sehen glaubt. Danach verschwindet der Präsentator
aus dem Gedicht, und die nächsten sechs Strophen, die das
zentrale Geschehen darstellen, bestehen ausschließlich aus
Dialogen zwischen Vater, Sohn und dem Erlkönig. Erst in
der letzten Strophe kehrt der Präsentator wieder und
schließt das Gedicht ab, indem er mit knappen Worten den
Ausgang des Geschehens berichtet; und auch hier bleibt der
Leser innerhalb der Fiktion, daß er das, was dort in der
dritten Person beschrieben wird, selber sieht. Während
»Der Handschuh« ein durchgängig episches Gedicht ist, bei
dem ein dramatisch gespanntes Geschehen durch Beschreibung vergegenwärtigt wird, ist der »Erlkönig« eine
Art Miniaturdrama mit einem epischen Vor- und Nach-
spann. Dieser epische Rahmen stellt Vorgänge dar, aber er
enthält sich jeder Beschreibung. Die wenigen Adjektive
darin drücken objektive Qualitäten und keine subjektiven
Wertungen aus. Das, was sich dem Leser als szenische
Realität einprägt, sind nicht die mageren Angaben der ersten
und letzten Strophe, sondern es ist die phantastische Szenerie, die sich indirekt aus den Dialogen ergibt. Ohne daß
irgend etwas im eigentlichen Sinne beschrieben wird, sieht
der Leser dennoch vor sich eine nächtliche Landschaft mit
Weiden im Nebeldunst und die gespenstische Erscheinung
des Erlkönigs »mit Kron und Schweif«. Die großartige
Wirkung dieser nicht zu Unrecht so berühmten Ballade
beruht sicher zu einem großen Teil darauf, daß sie ohne jede
Beschreibung von außen auskommt und dennoch ein Sze-
nenbild von höchster Dichte beschwört. Dies ist die Technik der alten Volksballade, die ebenfalls weitgehend auf
Beschreibung verzichtet und das Geschehen durch knappe
Berichte und durch dramatische Wechselrede entfaltet.
Von ganz anderer Art ist die Wirkung des »Handschuh«.
Hier ist nichts Übernatürliches im Spiel, dem Leser läuft
kein Schauer über den Rücken, er verfolgt nur gespannt ein
kunstvoll präsentiertes Geschehen. Kunstvoll ist es in der

Tat. Mit großer sprachlicher Virtuosität gelingt es Schiller, die drei verschiedenen Raubkatzenarten so darzustellen, daß sich ihre unterschiedlichen Bewegungstypen beinahe lautmalerisch abbilden. Er erreicht dies durch geschickte Wahl der Klangqualitäten, vor allem aber durch das Metrum. So wird die träge, gelangweilt-bedächtige Gangart des Löwen zum einen durch sehr gedehnte Vokale – Gähnen, Mähnen – und zum anderen durch ein langsames Metrum zum Ausdruck gebracht. Das Gedicht arbeitet mit einem unregelmäßigen Wechsel von Zweier- und Dreiertakten, die steigend oder fallend sein können. Während steigende Metren die Bewegung eher stauen, wirken fallende beschleunigend. Diese unterschiedlichen Wirkungen werden von Schiller mit großer Kunstfertigkeit ausgenutzt. So läßt er den Auftritt des Löwen mit einer anapästischen Zeile beginnen, also einem steigenden Metrum, das die Bewegung staut:

> Und hinein mit bedächtigem Schritt
> Ein Löwe tritt

Nähme man vom ersten Anapäst eine Silbe weg, so würde sich das Tempo erheblich beschleunigen, da wir dann die unbetonte Anfangssilbe wahrscheinlich als Auftakt empfinden und die folgenden Versfüße als fallende Daktylen lesen würden. Das läßt sich leicht an der Zeile ablesen, mit der die Leoparden beschrieben werden:

> Die stürzen mit mutiger Kampfbegier
> Auf das Tigertier

Hier haben wir es nach dem Auftakt mit Daktylen zu tun, die der ganzen Bewegung einen raschen Hüpf- oder Sprungcharakter verleihen. In der zweiten Zeile geht der fallende Daktylus in den steigenden Anapäst über. Dadurch wird die Bewegung gestaut, was natürlich Absicht ist, da an dieser Stelle die Bewegung der Leoparden vom Tiger gestoppt wird. Der Daktylus als charakteristische Gangart der Leoparden war schon in den beiden vorangegangenen Zeilen vorbereitet worden:

> Da speit das doppelt geöffnete Haus
> Zwei Leoparden auf einmal aus

Ganz anders als das träge Schreiten des Löwen und die schnellen Sprünge der Leoparden ist die Bewegung des Tigers, der »mit wildem Sprunge« eintritt, dann aber sofort die Bewegung abstoppt und in ein lauerndes Kreisen von gestauter Kraft übergeht. Diese Mischung aus Schnelligkeit, Kraft und lauernder Zurückhaltung wird durch einen ständigen Wechsel von steigenden und fallenden, von zweiviertel- und dreivierteltaktigen Metren zum Ausdruck gebracht:

> Wie der den Löwen erschaut,
> Brüllt er laut,
> Schlägt mit dem Schweif
> Einen furchtbaren Reif
> Und recket die Zunge
> Und im Kreise scheu
> Umgeht er den Leu

Mit ähnlicher Raffinesse wird der weitere Verlauf des Balladengeschehens vorgeführt: Der Kampf des Tigers gegen die Leoparden; das Gebrüll des Löwen, der mit seiner Autorität Ruhe herstellt; die lauernde Stille; das Fallen des Handschuhs und der Gang des Ritters in den Zwinger. Es dürfte dem Leser nicht schwerfallen, dem Dichter dabei auf die Finger zu sehen.

Schiller zeigt seine Beherrschung des Handwerks ganz offen. Während im »Erlkönig« irrationales Dunkel herrscht, liegt im »Handschuh« alles in hellem Tageslicht. Goethes Gedicht vermittelt den Schauer des Numinosen, ohne jedoch darüber irgendeine Aussage zu machen. Die Botschaft ist weder eine Warnung vor dämonischen Kräften in der Natur noch umgekehrt eine Warnung vor Aberglauben. Wenn das Gedicht überhaupt eine Aussage hat, dann die, daß es »mehr Dinge zwischen Himmel und Erde gibt, als unsere Schulweisheit sich träumen läßt«, wie schon Shakespeares Hamlet sagte. Auch Schillers »Handschuh« hat

keine Botschaft im Sinne eines *fabula docet*, einer abschließenden »Moral von der Geschicht«. Er will weder junge
Männer zu mutigem Handeln animieren, noch rät er ihnen,
einer Dame, die nur männliches Imponiergehabe bewun-
dert, den Handschuh ins Gesicht zu werfen. Beide Gedichte
tun nichts weiter, als einen spannungsreichen Vorgang balla-
denhaft darzustellen. Aber sie tun es aus zwei entgegenge-
setzten Künstlertemperamenten heraus. Goethe schreibt ein
Gedicht, das in seiner Form so naturwüchsig erscheint wie
eine Volksballade und das inhaltlich die natürliche Außenwelt als eine dämonische Sphäre darstellt, die sich der rationalen und damit ethischen Kontrolle entzieht. Schiller
schreibt ein Gedicht, das in jedem Wort, in jeder Zeile die
handwerkliche Kunst des Dichters erkennen läßt und das
inhaltlich einen Vorgang darstellt, in dem es um ethisches,
um rationales Handeln geht. Die Raubkatzen haben nichts
Dämonisches an sich, sie sind nur gefährlich. Das Handeln
des Ritters Delorge folgt einem rationalen Kalkül. Um den
falschen, irrationalen Begriff von Männlichkeit zu entlarven,
mit dem die Dame sein Ehrgefühl verletzt, geht er ein
kalkuliertes Risiko ein, indem er die mutige, aber vollkommen irrationale, weil unvernünftige Tat vollbringt und sie
anschließend dadurch entwertet, daß er der Dame den
Handschuh ins Gesicht wirft und auf die Belohnung durch
ihre Gunst verzichtet. Schillers formal artifizielle und inhaltlich ethisierte Ballade wurde und wird von der Kritik bis
heute viel weniger geschätzt als Goethes Gedicht, das die
Naivität einer Volksballade ausstrahlt und vom Hauch des
Numinosen umweht ist. Diese unterschiedliche Beurteilung
hängt natürlich damit zusammen, daß wir in einer nachromantischen Zeit leben und daß alle unsere Urteile über
Dichtung noch immer durch die klassisch-romantische
Ästhetik geprägt sind. Schiller stand nicht in der klassisch-
romantischen, sondern in der barock-klassizistischen Tradition. Er zeigt sein Handwerk, so wie die barocken Dichter
es taten, und er spielt mit der Sprache und bedient sich der
formalen Ausdrucksmittel, um die behandelten Gegen-

stände in das hellste Licht der *ratio* zu rücken, so wie es die Franzosen Corneille und Racine oder – in satirischer Tonlage – der Engländer Alexander Pope taten. Faßt man die durch diese Namen repräsentierte Stilepoche als europäischen Klassizismus, wofür einiges spricht, so war Schiller der größte Klassizist in deutscher Sprache, während man Goethe, den wir als deutschen Klassiker zu sehen gewohnt sind, aus europäischer Sicht eigentlich den größten Romantiker nennen müßte, was die Franzosen auch tatsächlich tun.

Vorromantische Bildersprache

Seit Goethe sind wir daran gewöhnt, in Gedichten reale Bilder von solcher Prägnanz und Dichte zu erwarten, daß sie für uns jenen geheimnisvollen Verweisungscharakter annehmen, den Goethe als das Wesen des Symbols definiert hat. Gedichte, in denen die Bilder rational auflösbare Vergleiche darstellen, gelten demgegenüber als von minderem Rang. Dies ist eine sehr einseitige und ungerechte Wertung. Im 16. und 17. Jahrhundert haben große Dichter den Vergleich so kunstvoll eingesetzt, daß er dem Symbol an Ausdruckskraft keineswegs nachstand. Vor allem im Manierismus, jener schwer zu bestimmenden Stilepoche zwischen Renaissance und Barock, erfreute sich eine bestimmte Form des Vergleichs großer Beliebtheit, die in der Literaturwissenschaft mit dem italienischen Wort *concetto* oder auf englisch als *conceit* bezeichnet wird. Man versteht darunter einen extrem elaborierten Vergleich, der durch mehrere Vergleichsebenen durchgespielt wird und auf jeder Ebene eine neue Bedeutungsnuance erkennen läßt. Wenn es dem Dichter gelang, die aufeinanderfolgenden Vergleiche durch einen scheinbar logischen Zusammenhang miteinander zu verknüpfen, galt das *conceit* als besonders virtuos. Je weiter hergeholt und je verblüffender die Vergleiche waren, um so höherer Wertschätzung erfreuten sie sich. Shakespeare, John Donne und der Spanier Góngora haben dieses Kunstmittel mit großer Meisterschaft eingesetzt, was den beiden letztgenannten allerdings in der Zeit des Klassizismus und der Romantik den Ruf eingebracht hatte, gekünstelte Manieristen zu sein. Inzwischen hat sich die Einsicht durchgesetzt, daß man diese Dichter nicht an der klassisch-romantischen Poetik messen darf, sondern an der, die sie selber praktizierten, und an deren Leistungsfähigkeit. Seitdem gehören die genannten zu den Sternen erster Ordnung am Dichterhimmel Europas.

Was das *conceit* zu leisten vermag, soll nun an einem Beispiel demonstriert werden. Da die deutsche Dichtung in der Blütezeit des *concettismo*, also um 1600, keinen Dichter von Rang aufzuweisen hat, der es mit den obengenannten hätte aufnehmen können, wählen wir ein Sonett des größten englischen Meisters dieser Form, Shakespeare. Das Thema des Gedichts ist das wohl am häufigsten behandelte Motiv der gesamten Lyrik von der Renaissance bis zum Barock: die Vergänglichkeit. Bevor wir uns aber dem Gedicht selbst zuwenden, verdient die Aufgabe, die der Dichter sich darin gestellt hat, eine kurze Betrachtung. Wenn sein Sonett über den Zahn der Zeit nicht bloß die Wiederholung einer tausendmal breitgetretenen Platitüde werden soll, wird er das Vergehen der Zeit so darstellen müssen, daß der Leser auf dem engen Raum der 14 Zeilen durch die verschiedensten Aspekte und Dimensionen der Zeit hindurchgeführt wird. So könnte der Dichter z. B. versuchen, Gegenwart, Vergangenheit und Zukunft darzustellen; er könnte die physikalisch-objektive mit der subjektiv erlebten Zeit vergleichen oder dem unaufhaltsamen Zeitfluß die überwundene, stillgestellte Zeit, also die Ewigkeit, gegenüberstellen. Je mehr von diesen problematischen Facetten des Motivs in das Gedicht eingearbeitet werden, um so beziehungsreicher und um so weniger platitüdenhaft wird dann das fertige Werk sein. Hier nun das Sonett sowie der Versuch einer Nachdichtung:

Like as the waves make towards the pebbled shore,
So do our minutes hasten to their end;
Each changing place with that which goes before,
In sequent toil all forward do contend.
Nativity, once in the main of light,
Crawls to maturity, wherewith being crowned,
Crookèd eclipses 'gainst his glory fight,
And Time that gave doth now his gift confound.
Time doth transfix the flourish set on youth,
And delves the parallels in beauty's brow,
Feeds on the rarities of nature's truth,
And nothing stands but for his scythe to mow.
    And yet to times in hope my verse shall stand,
    Praising thy worth, despite his cruel hand.

So wie die Wellen hin zum Kieselstrand,
So hasten die Minuten unsres Lebens
Ans Ziel, und jede tauscht mit der, die schwand,
Und ist ein Teil des gleichen Vorwärtsstrebens.
Geburt, kaum in des Lebens hellem Glanz,
Kriecht hoch zur Reife, steht gekrönt im Lichte,
Schon droht Verfinstrung ihrem Strahlenkranz,
Und Zeit, die gab, macht ihr Geschenk zunichte.
Die Zeit kerbt in der Schönheit Stirn die Spur,
Durchbohrt die Jugend, blütenübersät,
Verzehrt die Kostbarkeiten der Natur,
Und alles steht nur, daß sie's niedermäht.
    Und doch, so hoff' ich, hat mein Vers Bestand
    Zu Deinem Lob, trotz ihrer harten Hand.

Shakespeare beginnt mit dem Bild der unablässig an den Strand rollenden Wellen, die er mit den Minuten unsres Lebens vergleicht. Zeit erscheint damit als etwas, das auf uns zukommt, als Zukunft; zugleich aber auch als etwas, das in zählbaren Einheiten eines periodischen Vorgangs gemessen werden kann. Die Wellen sind, wie Pendelschwünge oder die Schwingungen eines Quarzkristalls, diskrete Einheiten, die der Physiker als Maßeinheiten der objektiven Zeit verwenden kann. Es handelt sich hier also um einen Zeitbegriff, den man digital nennen könnte, da er Zeit durch zählbare *digits* darstellt.

Das zweite Quartett zeichnet die Lebenszeit des einzelnen nach: Geburt, Aufstieg, Kulmination, Abstieg, Untergang. Der astronomische Begriff *eclipse* signalisiert, daß der Leser hinter dieser Kurve des menschlichen Lebens den Sonnenlauf sehen soll. Zeit ist jetzt nicht mehr das unaufhörliche Auf-uns-Zukommen diskreter Einheiten, sondern eine einzige zugeteilte Einheit, die der Mensch von Punkt zu Punkt durchläuft, bis er ihr unabänderliches Ende erreicht. Diese Zeit wird an jedem Punkt anders erfahren, es ist erlebte Zeit. Während das erste Quartett Zeit digital darstellte, haben wir es jetzt mit einer Darstellung zu tun, wie wir sie von Analoguhren kennen, deren Kreisbewegung den Sonnenlauf nachahmt. Genaugenommen ist ja nur die Sonnenuhr eine echte Analoguhr, da nur sie die Zeit als fließendes Kontinuum abbildet und nicht aus diskreten *digits* zusammensetzt.

Das dritte Quartett bringt eine weitere Auffassung von Zeit ins Spiel. Jetzt erscheint sie personifiziert als die unerbittliche Zerstörerin von Jugend und Schönheit. Als solche arbeitet sie dem Tod in die Hände und wird zuletzt mit diesem identifiziert; die Zeit wird zum Sensenmann, der Zeitverlauf zu einem unablässigen Sterben.

Diesem auf drei Bedeutungsebenen entwickelten *conceit* auf die Zeit setzt der Dichter im abschließenden *couplet* einen ganz anderen Zeitbegriff entgegen, nämlich Zeit als ewige Dauer. Solche Ewigkeit will der Dichter durch die Kunst seines Verses schaffen und dem reißenden Zeitstrom entgegenstellen, und dadurch will er den nun zum erstenmal erwähnten Adressaten des Gedichts dem Zahn der Zeit entreißen. Mit der Jugend und der Schönheit, von denen im dritten Quartett die Rede war, waren offensichtlich Eigenschaften des Angeredeten gemeint, für die der Dichter mit seinen Versen ein unzerstörbares Gehäuse bauen will, damit sein Wert (»thy worth«) darin auf ewig überdauern kann.

Mit dem wortspielerischen Echo von *worth* auf *verse* sind wir bei einem weiteren Aspekt der handwerklichen Kunstfertigkeit des Gedichts. Was auf der Bedeutungsebene in den wechselnden Facetten des *conceits* zum Ausdruck kommt, wird auf der lautlichen Ebene durch virtuose Sprachkunst unterstützt. So wird z. B. der weiche Fluß der Wellen durch eine Folge von Wörtern mit Nasalen und Liquiden (minutes, end, toil, contend) zum Ausdruck gebracht, worin Wörter mit Zischlauten (hasten, changing, sequent) eingebettet sind, die das Rauschen der Wellen nachbilden. Im zweiten Quartett geht es darum, die aufsteigende, kulminierende und wieder absteigende Bewegung darzustellen. Shakespeare erreicht dies durch einen syntaktischen Kunstgriff. Indem er in den Hauptsatz zwei verkürzte Nebensätze einschiebt, zwingt er den Leser, der das Gedicht laut zu realisieren versucht, dazu, mit der Stimme nach oben zu gehen und dann wieder zur Stimmlage des Hauptsatzes zurückzukehren. So wird durch den Sprachfluß des Satzes das abgebildet, was der Satz selbst semantisch aussagt. Zur weiteren Intensivierung des Gesagten wird das Unerbittliche der Zeit durch eine Folge von Wörtern mit harten Explosivlauten unterstrichen (nativity, crawls, maturity, crowned, crooked, eclipses, confound). Die Härte der gehäuften t- und k-Laute wird keinem Leser entgehen.

Die vorliegende Übersetzung versucht, lautlich, syntaktisch und inhaltlich dem Original möglichst nahezukommen. Man könnte sich aber auch eine viel freiere Nachdichtung denken, z. B. die folgende für das zweite Quartett:

> Gebornes, kaum daß es ans Licht getreten,
> Müht sich zur Reife hoch, steht im Zenit,
> Und abwärts geht die Bahn seines Planeten.
> Schon mahnt die Zeit und kündigt den Kredit.

Diese Übersetzung bringt zwar die astronomische Anspielung deutlicher zum Ausdruck, fügt aber mit dem Bild des Kredits etwas völlig Neues hinzu, das im Original nicht einmal andeutungsweise erwähnt wird. Dennoch wäre denkbar, daß Shakespeare selber, wenn man ihn fragen könnte, dieser falschen Übersetzung den Vorzug geben würde, da sie das *conceit* um eine weitere Bedeutungsebene bereichert und damit noch effektvoller macht. Außerdem liebte Shakespeare besonders solche Vergleiche, die aus der Rechts- und Kaufmannssprache entlehnt waren. Die Klassizisten, die auf Einfachheit und elegante Präzision aus waren, und die Romantiker, die den naiven Ton des Volkslieds anstrebten, konnten solcher intellektualisierten und oft sehr scharfkantigen Lyrik wenig Geschmack abgewinnen. Leser aber, die mit der Lyrik unseres Jahrhunderts vertraut sind, werden Shakespeare, Donne und Góngora als viel moderner empfinden als Brentano oder Eichendorff.

Ironie im Gedicht

Ätzende Satire, parodistische Verhöhnung oder bitterer Sarkasmus sind in einem Gedicht leicht zu erkennen, da sie von der Intention her aggressive Stilhaltungen sind, die ganz bewußt erreichen wollen, daß der Leser den Angriff merkt. Viel schwieriger ist es dagegen, subtile Ironie zu erkennen. Wenn diese sich auf den inhaltlichen Gegenstand des Gedichts bezieht, ist sie meist noch als gezielter Stich wahrzunehmen. Wenn sie aber der eigenen Form gilt, wenn also der Dichter eine kunstvolle Sprachform schafft, ohne sie als Kunst völlig ernstzunehmen, entsteht ein ironischer Schwebezustand, der vom Leser oft nicht mit Sicherheit dingfest gemacht werden kann. Was der eine noch für bare Münze nimmt, mag dem anderen schon als subtile Selbstironie erscheinen. Der Großmeister dieser Technik der ironischen Brechung des eigenen Kunstanspruchs ist Heinrich Heine. Er trat als junger Dichter das Erbe der deutschen Romantik an, deren Sprache er virtuos beherrschte. Doch er merkte bald, daß diese Sprache verbraucht und ausgelaugt war. Eine neue Dichtersprache, wie sie in Frankreich später durch

Baudelaire und die Symbolisten und in Deutschland erst in diesem Jahrhundert durch Benn und Brecht geschaffen wurde, stand ihm noch nicht zur Verfügung. Er selbst war der Romantik viel zu nahe, als daß man von ihm die revolutionäre Erneuerung der deutschen Lyrik hätte erwarten können. So blieb ihm nichts weiter übrig, als diese Sprache, deren volksliedhaft eingängige Lyrismen er wie kein zweiter beherrschte, weiter zu benutzen. Da er aber ein großer und darum auch ehrlicher Dichter war, konnte er unmöglich mit vollem künstlerischen Anspruch die romantische Melodie singen. So entwickelte er jene unverkennbare Heinemelodie, die schlicht und naiv wie ein Volkslied anhebt, dann süß und betörend aufblüht, bis sie plötzlich einen zweifelhaften Glanz bekommt. An dieser Stelle gab er seinen schillernden Seifenblasen regelmäßig den ironischen Stich und ließ sie zerplatzen. Bei manchen Gedichten spürt man die ironische Nadel schon in der ersten Zeile, bei anderen erst in der letzten, und manchmal weiß man überhaupt nicht recht, ob sich der Dichter ironisch distanziert oder nicht. Ein typisches Beispiel der leicht zu erkennenden Art ist die folgende Strophe:

> Das Fräulein stand am Meere
> Und seufzte lang und bang,
> Es rührte sie so sehre
> Der Sonnenuntergang.

Wenn ein Gedicht so anfängt, weiß der Leser, daß es mit einer witzigen Pointe enden wird; dies ist sie:

> Mein Fräulein! Sei'n Sie munter,
> Das ist ein altes Stück;
> Hier vorne geht sie unter
> Und kehrt von hinten zurück.

Hier ist die ironische Desillusionierung der zunächst geweckten romantischen Erwartung unverkennbar. Anders sieht es dagegen in Heines berühmtestem Gedicht aus, der

»Loreley«. Im Ausland, zumal im englischsprachigen, wo Heine immer noch der populärste deutsche Dichter ist, wurde das Gedicht stets als ernsthafter Ausdruck eines romantischen Gefühls im Volksliedton gelesen, und wahrscheinlich verstehen auch die meisten deutschen Leser es immer noch so. Die Schlußstrophe wird dabei entweder ganz ignoriert oder so im Lichte der zuvor evozierten romantischen Stimmung gelesen, daß der ironische Bruch kaum bemerkt wird. Dabei ist die ironische Desillusionierung in dieser Strophe kaum zu überhören.

> Ich weiß nicht, was soll es bedeuten,
> Daß ich so traurig bin;
> Ein Märchen aus alten Zeiten,
> Das kommt mir nicht aus dem Sinn.
>
> Die Luft ist kühl und es dunkelt,
> Und ruhig fließt der Rhein;
> Der Gipfel des Berges funkelt
> Im Abendsonnenschein.
>
> Die schönste Jungfrau sitzet
> Dort oben wunderbar;
> Ihr goldnes Geschmeide blitzet,
> Sie kämmt ihr goldenes Haar.
>
> Sie kämmt es mit goldenem Kamme
> Und singt ein Lied dabei;
> Das hat eine wundersame,
> Gewaltige Melodei.
>
> Den Schiffer im kleinen Schiffe
> Ergreift es mit wildem Weh;
> Er schaut nicht die Felsenriffe,
> Er schaut nur hinauf in die Höh.

> Ich glaube, die Wellen verschlingen
> Am Ende Schiffer und Kahn;
> Und das hat mit ihrem Singen
> Die Lore-Ley getan.

Der Dichter beginnt mit der Fiktion, daß er sich an ein altes Märchen erinnert, und darauf beschreibt er dessen Inhalt sehr detailliert. Nur an den eigentlichen Höhepunkt, an die Katastrophe, kann er sich nicht mehr genau erinnern: »Ich glaube, die Wellen verschlingen ...« Mit der geläufigen Alltagsfloskel »Ich glaube« pflegt man eine Aussage einzuleiten, der man keine große Bedeutung beimißt, oder eine, die man bewußt herunterspielt, um sich von ihr zu distanzieren. Eben hatte der Dichter sich noch ganz mit dem bezauberten Schiffer identifiziert, der von »wildem Weh« ergriffen wird; jetzt tritt er ironisch zurück und beschließt die Erzählung mit der vagen Erinnerung, er glaube, die Wellen hätten Schiffer und Kahn verschlungen. Der Schlußkommentar macht die Ironie noch um eine Nuance deutlicher:

> Und das hat mit ihrem Singen
> die Lore-Ley getan.

Der bagatellisierende Ton, den wir heute aus der Wendung »mit ihrem Singen« heraushören, wurde wohl schon zu Heines Zeiten so empfunden. Auf der Skala zwischen »Gesang« und »Gesinge« liegt der Ausdruck »mit ihrem Singen« sicher näher an letzterem. »Und das hat mit ihrem Gesange ...« hätte zweifellos ernsthafter geklungen als »mit ihrem Singen«. Heine hat also auch in diesem Gedicht, das oft als Musterbeispiel eines Kunstvolksliedes angesehen wird, den allzu süß und schwermütig gewordenen Ton ironisch gebrochen, er hat, um es salopp zu sagen, die romantische Luft rausgelassen.

Um Ironie geht es auch in dem folgenden Beispiel:

Alfred Lichtenstein

Der Rauch auf dem Felde

Lene Levi lief am Abend
Trippelnd, mit gerafften Röcken,
Durch die langen, leeren Straßen
Einer Vorstadt.

Und sie sprach verweinte, wehe,
Wirre, wunderliche Worte,
Die der Wind warf, daß sie knallten
Wie die Schoten,

Sich an Bäumen blutig ritzten
Und verfetzt an Häusern hingen
Und in diesen tauben Straßen
Einsam starben.

Lene Levi lief, bis alle
Dächer schiefe Mäuler zogen,
Und die Fenster Fratzen schnitten
Und die Schatten

Ganz betrunkne Späße machten –
Bis die Häuser hilflos wurden
Und die stumme Stadt vergangen
War in weiten

Feldern, die der Mond beschmierte ...
Lenchen nahm aus ihrer Tasche
Eine Kiste mit Zigarren,
Zog sich weinend

Aus und rauchte ...

Der Titel läßt den Leser ein Gedicht erwarten, in dem eine
ländliche Idylle mit rauchenden Kartoffelfeuern oder ähnli-
chem beschrieben wird. Statt dessen haben wir es mit einem

149

Bild aus dem Umkreis der expressionistischen Großstadtmythologie zu tun. Die Stadt, wie sie hier erscheint, ist nicht der menschenverschlingende Moloch, den Georg Heym in »Der Gott der Stadt« beschwört, sie ist auch nicht das Vitalitätszentrum, das Döblin in *Berlin Alexanderplatz* oder der Amerikaner Carl Sandburg in seiner Hymne auf Chicago beschreibt, Lichtensteins Stadt ist ein Ort der Entfremdung, wo die stummen Häuserfronten groteske Grimassen schneiden, ansonsten aber jede Kommunikation verweigern. Die Straßen sind »leer«, »taub« und »stumm«. Lene Levis Worte, also ihre Kommunikationsversuche, prallen von den Häusern ab, werden zwischen ihnen hin und her geworfen, daß sie wie die Segelleinen (»Schoten«) knallten. Der Wind wirft sie wie hilflose Vögel in die Bäume und an die Häuser, bis sie zerfetzt zu Boden fallen und sterben. Als Lene endlich die stumme, teilnahmslose Stadt hinter sich gelassen hat und das offene Feld betritt, wird die Erwartung einer romantischen Idylle sogleich zerstört. Der Mond, seit Goethes Lied »Füllest wieder ...« Inbegriff der Wiederannäherung an eine entfremdete Natur, breitet nicht wie bei Goethe »lindernd seinen Blick« über die Felder aus, er beschmiert sie, ist also selber etwas Schmutziges. An dieser Stelle endet der trotz seiner surrealen Komik ernsthafte Teil des Gedichts, was durch drei Punkte deutlich gemacht wird. Der Ausbruch aus der entfremdeten Welt der Stadt in eine nicht-entfremdete Natursphäre erweist sich als Illusion. Jetzt erfolgt eine doppelte ironische Brechung. Mit dem Diminutiv »Lenchen« scheint sich eine Flucht in die verlogene Geborgenheit und Niedlichkeit des Kitsches anzubahnen, aber auch diese Illusion wird sogleich zerstört durch das grotesk-absurde Bild des Mädchens, das sich weinend auszieht und Zigarren raucht. Lichtensteins ironische Schlußpointe dient nicht wie bei Heine der Distanzierung von der eigenen, nicht mehr ernstgenommenen Dichtung, sondern der Durchbrechung einer falschen Dämonisierung. Während Georg Heym mit großem, ernstgemeintem Pathos den Dämon Stadt beschwört, ironisiert Lichtenstein dieses Pathos. Er läßt nicht die romantische, sondern die expressionistische Luft raus. In dieser ironisch gebrochenen Haltung wirkt er moderner als Heym, so wie Max Ernst moderner als Franz Marc und T. S. Eliot moderner als Rilke wirkt. In der modernen Kunst scheint es unmöglich zu sein, daß der Künstler sich noch ganz und ungebrochen in sein Werk entläßt. Heines ironische Brechung galt nur dem Anspruch eines als nicht mehr echt empfundenen Stils, im übrigen aber lebte er durchaus noch in der Gedanken- und Wertewelt der Spätromantik. Die moderne Form der Brechung ist radikaler. Sie gilt dem ganzen tradierten Wertbewußtsein und zerstört damit die unmittelbare Identifikationsmöglichkeit des Lesers, Hörers oder Betrachters des modernen Kunstwerks. James Joyce schuf im *Ulysses* ein Abbild dieser modernen gebrochenen Welt, während z. B. Thomas Manns Ironie der Heineschen noch nähersteht. Er ist insofern weniger modern als Joyce.

Hermetische Dichtung

Paul Celan

Sprachgitter

Augenrund zwischen den Stäben.

Flimmertier Lid
rudert nach oben,
gibt einen Blick frei.

Iris, Schwimmerin, traumlos und trüb:
der Himmel, herzgrau, muß nah sein.

Schräg, in der eisernen Tülle,
der blakende Span.
Am Lichtsinn
errätst du die Seele.

(Wär ich wie du. Wärst du wie ich.
Standen wir nicht
unter *einem* Passat?
Wir sind Fremde.)

Die Fliesen. Darauf,
dicht beieinander, die beiden
herzgrauen Lachen:
zwei
Mundvoll Schweigen.

Paul Celan ist wahrscheinlich der am schwersten zu interpretierende und eben darum der interpretationsbedürftigste Dichter in deutscher Sprache. Viele seiner Gedichte sind so hermetisch, daß selbst Kenner seines Gesamtwerks keinen Schlüssel finden, um in sie einzudringen. Ein Element von extremer Privatheit, das ihnen innewohnt, läßt vermuten, daß vielleicht ein enger Freund des Dichters den poetischen Assoziationsketten hätte folgen können, wenn er sie als chiffrierte Verweise auf ganz persönliche Erfahrungen gelesen hätte. Der normale Leser aber, dem dieses Privileg versagt ist, muß die Waffen strecken. Ihm bleibt nichts weiter übrig, als den poetischen Reiz der Gedichte auf seine Phantasie einwirken zu lassen. So ganz und gar unzugänglich sind aber längst nicht alle von Celans Gedichten. Sein bekanntestes, die berühmte »Todesfuge«, wird sicher vor allem deshalb so hoch geschätzt, weil es einen klar erkennbaren Realitätsbezug hat; auch ohne Interpretationshilfe sieht der Leser durch die gebrochenen Bildsplitter des Textes das Inferno von Auschwitz hindurchscheinen. Andere Gedichte, die keinen so konkreten Bezug erkennen lassen, öffnen sich dem Leser, wenn er sich mit der Bildersprache des Gesamtwerks vertraut macht. Mehr noch als bei Trakl muß man bei Celan wissen, welche Bedeutungsfelder durch Worte wie »Haar«, »Mohn«, »Urne«, »Stunde« etc. signalisiert werden. Da aber der gewöhnliche Leser selten bereit und in der Lage sein wird, sich einem einzigen Dichter mit solcher Gründlichkeit zu widmen, soll an diesem Beispiel noch einmal gezeigt werden, wie weit eine Interpretation auch ohne Rückgriff auf andere Werke in das Gedicht eindringen kann.

»Sprachgitter«, schon dieser Titel lenkt den Leser auf eine doppelte Spur. Einerseits kann man dabei an das Sprechgitter in der Tür eines Klosters oder eines Gefängnisses denken, durch das ein Eingeschlossener mit der Außenwelt kommuniziert, andererseits kann man das Wort aber auch als Metapher lesen und sich die Sprache selbst als ein begriffliches Gitterwerk vorstellen.

Augenrund zwischen den Stäben.

Auch diese Zeile läßt zwei Deutungen zu. Entweder man denkt an ein wirkliches Auge, das durch das Sprechgitter hindurch sichtbar ist, oder man versteht die Zeile so, daß eine runde vergitterte Öffnung metaphorisch als Augenrund bezeichnet wird. In beiden Fällen ist allerdings der gleiche poetisch wirksame Kontrast zwischen einer runden Öffnung und einem rechtwinkligen Gitterwerk festgelegt.

Flimmertier Lid
rudert nach oben,
gibt einen Blick frei.

»Flimmertier« ist offensichtlich eine Metapher für den unmittelbar folgenden Begriff »Lid«, der seinerseits an das Bild des Auges anknüpft. In Verbindung mit »rudert« könnte man aber auch an eines jener Wassertierchen aus der Gattung der Protozoen denken, die sich mit winzigen Flimmerhaaren fortbewegen. Allerdings wäre dann unklar, wieso ein nach oben ruderndes Flimmertier einen Blick freigeben sollte, während dies bei dem sich hebenden Lid selbstverständlich ist. Durch das neu hinzugetretene Bild des Wassers ändert sich nun aber auch der Assoziationsbereich von »Augenrund« und »Stäben«. Man könnte jetzt auch an eine vergitterte Brunnenöffnung oder etwas ähnliches denken.

> Iris, Schwimmerin, traumlos und trüb:
> der Himmel, herzgrau, muß nah sein.

»Iris« setzt das Bild des Auges fort, während »Schwimmerin« an »rudert« anknüpft und die Vorstellung von Wasser vertieft. Läge es nicht nahe, jetzt an das Spiegelbild des Himmels zu denken, der durch eine Öffnung auf eine Wasserfläche fällt?

> Schräg, in der eisernen Tülle,
> der blakende Span.

Unvermittelt öffnet sich ein völlig neuer Bildbereich. Wo soll man sich den blakenden Span vorstellen? In einem Gewölbe, das Wasser enthält und in das durch eine runde Öffnung in der Decke Licht fällt, also eine Art Zisterne? Die Vermutung läßt sich weder beweisen noch widerlegen.

> Am Lichtsinn
> errätst du die Seele.

Wieder wird auf das Auge Bezug genommen, aber man kann dabei ebenso gut an den Blick aus einem dunklen Raum zu einer lichtspendenden Öffnung hin denken.

> (Wär ich wie du. Wärst du wie ich.
> Standen wir nicht
> unter *einem* Passat?
> Wir sind Fremde.)

Abermals tritt etwas völlig Neues in das Gedicht ein. Wer ist das angeredete Du? Ist es ein geliebter Mensch? Und soll der Leser sich die Liebenden als zwei unter *einem* Passat nebeneinander segelnde Schiffe vorstellen?

> Die Fliesen. Darauf,
> dicht beieinander, die beiden
> herzgrauen Lachen:
> zwei
> Mundvoll Schweigen.

Was bedeuten die plötzlich ins Bild tretenden Fliesen? Auch sie stellen optisch ein rechtwinkliges Gitter dar. Sie würden außerdem zu der vermuteten Vorstellung einer Zisterne passen. Ist es Zufall, daß sich in Meyers Konversationslexikon (5. Aufl.) neben der Spalte, in der das Stichwort »Flimmer« erklärt wird, vier Abbildungen von Bodenfliesen befinden, in grauer Farbe und mit z. T. herzförmiger Ornamentik? Die »herzgrauen Lachen« knüpfen erneut an die Sequenz von Wasserbildern an. Das Wasser ist ein uraltes Symbol der Auflösung, Entgrenzung und Verschmelzung der Individualität. So wird z. B. durch das Eintauchen ins Wasser während des Taufaktes ein Ritual der Kommunion vollzogen. Hier aber bleiben selbst die beiden Wasserlachen noch voneinander getrennt. In jeder von ihnen, so scheint es, spiegelt sich der herzgraue Himmel. Da sie offenbar auf die beiden Liebenden Bezug nehmen, scheint ihr Getrenntsein die Unmöglichkeit jener Verschmelzung zu symbolisieren, die das utopische Ziel der traditionellen Liebesvorstellung ist. Von hier aus gewinnt nun rückblickend das Flimmertier eine weitere Bedeutung; denn falls damit wirklich auf ein Urtierchen von der Art der Infusorien angespielt wird, so wäre es wohl nicht ohne Bedeutung, daß diese Lebewesen ungeschlechtlich sind.

Was hat das alles nun mit dem Sprachgitter zu tun? Im ersten Teil des Gedichts scheint es um die Möglichkeit von Erkenntnis zu gehen. Die Seele blickt durch Gitterstäbe zum Licht. Das Gitter, das diesen Blick teils freigibt, teils versperrt, ist das kategoriale Raster der Sprache. Einerseits vermittelt es Erkenntnis, andererseits steht es der unmittelbaren Wahrnehmung des Lichtsinns im Wege. Ob der blakende Span in der schrägen Tülle als Symbol dieser durch die Sprache deformierten Wahrnehmung des Lichts gemeint ist? Im zweiten Teil des Gedichts tritt an die Stelle des Erkenntnisproblems das der Kommunikation, deren intimste Form im Liebesakt ja von der Bibel ebenfalls als Erkenntnis definiert wird. Auch hier scheint es, als symbolisierten die Fliesen mit ihrem rechteckigen Gradnetz die Sprache, durch die die Liebenden miteinander verbunden sind, ohne doch wirklich eins werden zu können. Wäre es eine Überinterpretation, wenn man sich bei dem Satz »Standen wir nicht unter *einem* Passat?« zwei nebeneinanderher segelnde Schiffe vorstellt, die durch das Gradnetz einer Seekarte verbunden sind? Wir hätten dann noch eine weitere Erscheinungsform des thematischen Gitterbildes.

Nichts von all dem, was wir hier an Vermutungen geäußert haben, ist beweisbar. Man kann kaum mehr sagen als dies, daß hier die Vorstellung eines Gitters beschworen wird, das sowohl verbindet als auch trennt. Es steht zwischen dem lichthungrigen Auge und dem Licht der zu erkennenden Wahrheit und ebenso zwischen den beiden Liebenden. Damit spitzt sich die Interpretation ganz auf das Wort zu, durch das die beiden Hälften des Gedichts verklammert werden: »herzgrau«. Grau ist auf der Skala des Lichts die Mitte zwischen völligem Dunkel und völliger Helle. Das Herz als Sitz der Seele steht nach alter Lehre auf ähnliche Weise in der Mitte zwischen der sinnlichen Wahrnehmung und dem begrifflichen Verstand. Ist dann die lichthungrige Seele als das herzgraue Abbild des Himmels im Menschen zu verstehen, so wie sich, wenn unsre Vermutung richtig ist, der durch einen Brunnenschacht fallende Himmel auf dem Wasser spiegelt? Die erste Hälfte des Gedichts scheint noch den Blick zum Licht für möglich zu halten, die zweite dagegen hält Kommunikation zwischen zwei Liebenden offenbar nur noch unter der irrealen Voraussetzung für möglich: »Wär ich wie du. Wärst du wie ich.«

Man könnte gewiß noch mancherlei Vermutungen anstellen und würde dem Gedicht dadurch vielleicht noch ein wenig näherkommen, aber verstehen im Sinne einer eindeutigen kognitiven Erkenntnis läßt es sich wohl kaum. Eine verdinglichende Interpretation, die vorgibt, das Gedicht erklären zu können, ist hier schlechterdings unmöglich. Celans Gedichte zwingen in ganz besonderer Weise zu der einzig angemessenen, nämlich verbal verstandenen Form der Interpretation. Man versteht sie immer nur in dem Maße, in dem man sie sich verstehend aneignet, aber man erreicht nie den Punkt, wo man sie verstanden hat.

Konkrete Poesie

Gerhard Rühm

sonett

erste strophe erste zeile
erste strophe zweite zeile
erste strophe dritte zeile
erste strophe vierte zeile

zweite strophe erste zeile
zweite strophe zweite zeile
zweite strophe dritte zeile
zweite strophe vierte zeile

dritte strophe erste zeile
dritte strophe zweite zeile
dritte strophe dritte zeile

vierte strophe erste zeile
vierte strophe zweite zeile
vierte strophe dritte zeile

Wer gewohnt ist, von Lyrik eine in kunstvoller Sprache artikulierte Sinnaussage zu erwarten, wird beim Lesen dieses Gedichts nicht nur erstaunt, sondern wohl auch ein wenig schockiert sein. Gehört so etwas überhaupt in eine Anthologie deutscher Dichtung, oder ist es nicht viel eher nur ein sprachlicher Jux, ein Gimmick? Rühms Sonett treibt eine uralte literarische Technik auf die äußerste Spitze, nämlich die der Parodie. Normalerweise funktioniert eine Parodie so, daß der Parodist aus den charakteristischen Stil- und Formeigentümlichkeiten des Parodierten eine scheinbar anspruchsvolle Form schafft, in die er dann einen so banalen Inhalt füllt, daß erstere dadurch als taube Nuß entlarvt und lächerlich gemacht wird. Rühm geht aber noch einen Schritt weiter. Er parodiert keinen bestimmten Dichter, sondern die Sonettform schlechthin, und er füllt sie mit einem Inhalt, dessen Banalität nicht mehr zu überbieten ist; denn jede Zeile seines Sonetts sagt semantisch nur das aus, was sie im graphischen Erscheinungsbild des Gedichts *ist*. Denkt man sich vor jeder Zeile die Worte »Dies ist die«, dann wird noch deutlicher, daß jeder Satz wie ein Zeigefinger auf sich selbst zeigt. Man könnte diese Beziehung mit dem Fachwort *deiktisch* (= hinweisend, auf etwas zeigend) bezeichnen. Und da die Sätze auf sich selber zeigen, könnte man sie deiktische Tautologien nennen.

Insofern das Gedicht als eine Radikalparodie auf die Sonettform gelesen wird, liegt es noch innerhalb der Kategorien, die wir auf traditionelle Lyrik anwenden, auch wenn der eigentliche Pfiff der Parodie, nämlich das Lächerlichmachen des Parodierten, ganz offensichtlich fehlt. Da das Gedicht aber semantisch nur das sagt, was es graphisch zeigt, und umgekehrt alles graphisch zeigt, was es semantisch sagt, gehört es zu einer Art von Texten, die mit traditioneller Lyrik nichts mehr gemein haben. Man nennt diese Textsorte konkrete Poesie, und zwar deshalb, weil das Semantische, also die abstrakte Bedeutung der sprachlichen Zeichen, konkret im Schriftbild dargestellt wird. Man wird sich fragen, ob man so etwas noch als Dichtkunst bezeichnen kann oder ob es nicht bloß eine geistreiche Spielerei ist. Und selbst wenn es Kunstcharakter hat, bleibt die Frage, ob es dann nicht eher in die Bildende Kunst als in die Literatur gehört. Bei den ersten Versuchen auf diesem Gebiet gehörte sicher eine geniale Frechheit dazu, alle gewohnten Normen auf den Kopf zu stellen, die Wörter aus dem Regelwerk der Grammatik herauszubrechen und sie völlig neu nach graphischen Gesichtspunkten zu ordnen. Die Semantik der Wortbedeutungen blieb zwar erhalten, aber ihre Anordnung gehorchte nicht mehr der vereinbarten Konvention eines symbolischen Zeichensystems, sondern erfolgte konkret auf dem Papier, buchstäblich schwarz auf weiß. Ohne Zweifel eröffneten sich dadurch ganz neue Möglichkeiten zur Herstellung ästhetisch reizvoller Gebilde. Das Problem ist nur, daß ein solcher revolutionärer Akt, der beim ersten Mal trotz seines destruktiven Charakters etwas Kreatives hatte, mit jeder weiteren Wiederholung zu billigem Kunstgewerbe degeneriert, so wie die Mobiles, die der Amerikaner Calder als phantasievolle Schwebeskulpturen erfand, später zu Kunstgewerbeartikeln wurden, die schließlich sogar schon in Kindergärten angefertigt wurden. Eine ähnliche Konfektionierung ist auch in der konkreten Poesie eingetreten. Dennoch gelingt es ihren Vertretern immer wieder, aus der Verbindung von semantischer Wortbedeutung und graphischer Grammatik verblüffende Wirkungen zu ziehen.

Um zu zeigen, was konkrete Poesie auf ihrem – zugegeben – sehr begrenzten Felde leisten kann, wollen wir uns einmal fragen, wie ein Dichter mit sprachlichen Mitteln das Schweigen darstellen kann. Die traditionelle Lyrik könnte nichts anderes tun als über das Schweigen zu reden. Je mehr aber darüber geredet wird, um so weniger ist das Schweigen selber in dem Gedicht präsent. Eugen Gomringer, ein Hauptvertreter der konkreten Poesie, drückt das Schweigen so aus:

> schweigen schweigen schweigen
> schweigen schweigen schweigen
> schweigen   schweigen
> schweigen schweigen schweigen
> schweigen schweigen schweigen

Hier dient das Reden über das Schweigen dazu, das Schweigen selber, nämlich das weiße Loch in der Mitte, zu definieren (= einzugrenzen). Damit ist das Schweigen rein logisch vermutlich überzeugender dargestellt als in Goethes berühmtem »Über allen Gipfeln ...«. Herwarth Walden, einer der theoretischen Wortführer des Expressionismus, hat sich über Goethes Gedicht mit ätzendem Spott hergemacht und vor allem die Zeile

> die Vögelein schweigen im Walde

aufgespießt. Er meinte, das Vokalgeklingel in dem Wort »Vögelein« vermittle das genaue Gegenteil von Schweigen, was kaum zu bestreiten ist. Schweigen ist mit den Mitteln

159

der klassisch-romantischen Poesie schlechterdings nicht dar-
stellbar, es kann nur als ein allmähliches Verstummen vorgeführt werden, was Goethe in seinem Gedicht auch tut. Trotz
dieses Mankos dürfte es aber wohl nur wenige Leser geben,
die Gomringers Gedicht dem Goetheschen vorziehen. Konkrete Poesie ist und bleibt ein experimenteller Seitenpfad der
modernen Dichtung, ein Weg, der aus der Sprache heraus in
sprachloses Neuland führt, ein Holzweg. Aber wie alle
Holzwege bereichert auch dieser die Erfahrung und die
ästhetische Wahrnehmungsfähigkeit.

»Formlose« Form

Alle Gedichte, an denen wir bisher unser interpretatorisches
Werkzeug angesetzt haben, erwiesen sich als kunstvoll
durchgeformte Texte, in denen jedes Element seinen not-
wendigen Platz in einem z. T. geradezu raffiniert angelegten
Gesamtplan einzunehmen schien. Sieht man sich aber die
Lyrik der jüngsten Zeit an, so wird man sich fragen, ob
dieser Begriff von Kunst als Kunstgriff auf sie noch anwend-
bar ist. Sind nicht die meisten modernen Gedichte so
spröde, so ablehnend gegenüber tradierten ästhetischen
Normen und so entschieden auf inhaltliche Authentizität
bedacht, daß es ganz unangemessen erscheint, in ihnen nach
einem spielerischen Formkalkül zu suchen? Viele von ihnen
lesen sich wie ein Stück Prosa, das nicht einmal besonders
kondensiert, sondern nur graphisch in ein eher zufällig
anmutendes Zeilenmuster gebrochen wurde. Wie soll man
als Leser eine Form beurteilen, bei der man einzelne Zeilen
und ganze Absätze beliebig umstellen kann, ohne daß ein
Bruch im Gedicht oder eine Einbuße an poetischer Wirkung
erkennbar würde? Diese Frage werden sich schon viele Leser
moderner Lyrik gestellt haben. Wir wollen nun an einem
Beispiel untersuchen, ob nicht auch in einem scheinbar
formlosen Gedicht ein verborgenes Organisationsprinzip zu
entdecken ist.

Hans Magnus Enzensberger

An alle Fernsprechteilnehmer

Etwas, das keine Farbe hat, etwas,
das nach nichts riecht, etwas Zähes,
trieft aus den Verstärkerämtern,
setzt sich fest in die Nähte der Zeit
und der Schuhe, etwas Gedunsenes,
kommt aus den Kokereien, bläht
wie eine fahle Brise die Dividenden
und die blutigen Segel der Hospitäler,
mischt sich klebrig in das Getuschel
um Professuren und Primgelder, rinnt,
etwas Zähes, davon der Salm stirbt,
in die Flüsse, und sickert, farblos,
und tötet den Butt auf den Bänken.

Die Minderzahl hat die Mehrheit,
die Toten sind überstimmt.

In den Staatsdruckereien
rüstet das tückische Blei auf,
die Ministerien mauscheln, nach Phlox
und erloschenen Resolutionen riecht
der August. Das Plenum ist leer.
An den Himmel darüber schreibt
die Radarspinne ihr zähes Netz.

Die Tanker auf ihren Helligen
wissen es schon, eh der Lotse kommt,
und der Embryo weiß es dunkel
in seinem warmen, zuckenden Sarg:

Es ist etwas in der Luft, klebrig
und zäh, etwas, das keine Farbe hat
(nur die jungen Aktien spüren es nicht):

Gegen uns geht es, gegen den Seestern
und das Getreide. Und wir essen davon
und verleiben uns ein etwas Zähes,
und schlafen im blühenden Boom,
im Fünfjahresplan, arglos
schlafend im brennenden Hemd,
wie Geiseln umzingelt von einem zähen,
farblosen, einem gedunsenen Schlund.

Das Gedicht ist weder gereimt, noch hat es eine feste
Strophenform. Auch ein metrisches Schema ist nicht zu
erkennen. Tauscht man den ersten und den letzten Absatz
gegeneinander aus, so scheint dies keinerlei Unterschied zu
machen. Auch die drei übrigen Abschnitte könnte man
untereinander austauschen, ohne daß sich am formalen
Gesamteindruck und an dem, was das Gedicht mitteilt,
Wesentliches ändern. Kann man dann überhaupt noch von
einer Form sprechen? Form ist etwas Einheitstiftendes, und
einheitlich ist das Gedicht zweifellos. Von der ersten bis zur
letzten Zeile hält es einen ganz bestimmten, unverwechsel-
baren Ton. Diese Technik, einen Text nicht durch eine
geregelte Form, sondern nur durch den einheitlichen Ton
zusammenzuhalten, gab es schon in Zeiten formstrenger
Dichtung. Es ist die Form der Rhapsodie. Während aber in
früheren Zeiten die rhapsodischen Gedichte durch einen
Ton emphatischer Begeisterung geprägt waren, weist unser
Gedicht einen Ton von galliger Bitterkeit auf, dem ein Schuß
Ekel beigemengt ist.
Enzensberger erreicht die Einheitlichkeit des Tons durch
einen kunstvollen Aufbau der Bildschicht, die sich aus zwei
ganz unterschiedlichen Bestandteilen zusammensetzt. Auf
der einen Seite stehen Bilder aus dem organischen Bereich:
Salm, Butt, Phlox, Embryo, Seestern, Getreide. Diesen
Bildern sind Adjektive und Verben zugeordnet, die die
Vorstellung von Auflösung und Verfall suggerieren: triefen,
gedunsen, klebrig, sickern usw. Eingebettet in diese klebrige
Schicht einer sich auflösenden organischen Welt sind Bilder

aus der ökonomisch-technischen Sphäre: Kokereien, Dividende, Primgelder, Radarspinne, junge Aktien usw. Diese Gegenstände sind nicht von der allgemeinen Auflösung erfaßt, im Gegenteil, sie verursachen diese, während sie selber offenbar recht gut gedeihen: »die Dividende« wird »gebläht«, »in den Staatsdruckereien rüstet das tückische Blei auf«, »die jungen Aktien spüren es nicht«, nämlich die klebrige Auflösung. Das Gedicht beschreibt offenbar einen Zustand, der aus dem Zusammenstoß der organischen mit der ökonomischen Welt resultiert. Für den heutigen Leser ist das ein vertrautes Szenario. Für 1960 aber, als das Gedicht in Enzensbergers Band *Landessprache* zum erstenmal erschien, war es eine hellsichtige Vision. Welcher Leser hätte wohl damals gedacht, daß dieses metaphorische Bild einer unaufhaltsamen Auflösung der Natur durch die kapitalistische Industriegesellschaft einmal als exakte Beschreibung der realen Welt gelesen werden könnte?

Beim ersten Lesen gewinnt man den Eindruck, als werde mit grobem Pinsel das vage Bild einer kaputten Zivilisation gemalt, die in unaufhaltsamer Auflösung begriffen ist. Bei näherem Zusehen aber wird man merken, daß das Gedicht seinen Gegenstand an einigen Punkten sehr präzise markiert. So steht z. B. genau in der Mitte eine Zeitangabe, nämlich August, und es folgt der Satz »Das Plenum ist leer«. Mit dieser Anspielung auf die Parlamentsferien wird der beschriebene Zustand als etwas charakterisiert, was ohne Kontrolle abläuft. Das Parlament als Vertreter des obersten Souveräns, des Volkes, ist auf Urlaub, es übt keine Kontrolle mehr aus; die »Minderheit hat die Mehrheit« und die großen Teilsysteme der modernen Zivilisation – die Industrie (»Kokereien«), Finanzwirtschaft (»Dividende«), Handel (»Primgelder«), Wissenschaft (»Professuren«), Medizin (»Hospitäler«) und Militär (»Radarspinne«) entfalten ihr destruktives Eigenleben. Die noch im Bau befindlichen »Tanker auf den Helligen« und der noch ungeborene Embryo wissen bereits »dunkel«, in was für ein System sie hineingestoßen werden. »Nur die jungen Aktien spüren es nicht«, d. h. diejenigen, die von dem Zustand profitieren, wollen nicht wahrhaben, daß die Entwicklung auf Untergang programmiert ist. Jetzt spricht das Gedicht zum erstenmal in der ersten Person, doch nicht in der Form eines lyrischen Ichs, sondern im Plural. »Und wir essen davon / und verleiben uns ein etwas Zähes, und schlafen im blühenden Boom.« »Wir« – das ist das Volk, das in dem leeren Plenum hätte vertreten sein müssen und das schlafend den Boom der Teilsysteme über sich ergehen läßt:

arglos / schlafend im brennenden Hemd.

Mit dieser Anspielung auf das Nessushemd, an dem Herakles zugrunde ging, wird eine neue Bildschicht in das Gedicht eingeführt. Herakles hatte den Kentauren Nessus mit einem vergifteten Pfeil getötet, als dieser sich an seiner Frau Deianeira vergehen wollte. Der sterbende Kentaur riet der Frau, sein Blut aufzubewahren, da es ein sicheres Mittel sei, ihr die Liebe ihres Gatten zu erhalten. Als Herakles ihr später zugunsten von Iole untreu wurde, tränkte sie ein Hemd mit dem Blut und gab es ihrem Gatten. Dieser zog es an und wurde durch das noch wirksame Pfeilgift qualvoll getötet. Man ginge sicher zu weit, würde man die Sage, auf die hier angespielt wird, bis in alle Einzelheiten als Allegorie aufschlüsseln. Aber daß hier das schlafende Volk mit Herakles verglichen wird, der ahnungslos an den Spätfolgen eines von ihm selbst abgeschossenen Giftpfeils zugrunde geht, dürfte wohl beabsichtigt sein; denn es entspricht der inneren Logik des Gedichts. Der moderne Mensch, der auf dem ökonomisch-technologischen Gebiet der Arbeit übermenschliche Taten vollbringt, die den zwölf Arbeiten des Herakles vergleichbar sind, wird eines Tages, wenn er nicht rechtzeitig aus seinem Schlaf erwacht, durch das von ihm selber verbreitete Gift vernichtet werden. In der vorletzten Zeile kommt als weiteres Bild das der »Geisel« hinzu. »Wir«, das Volk, sind nicht nur ein schlafender Herkules, wir sind zugleich auch »wie Geiseln«, denn wir haben uns einem selbstgeschaffenen System in die Hand gegeben, das uns zu verschlingen droht.

Damit zeigt sich nun aber, daß der letzte Absatz des Gedichts keineswegs gegen den ersten ausgetauscht werden kann, wie es anfangs schien; denn während im ersten nur der Zustand beschrieben wird, sagt der letzte etwas über die Ursache und die Folgen aus. Das Gedicht, das zunächst wie eine formlose Litanei über den beklagenswerten Zustand unserer Zivilisation anmutete, erweist sich nun als ein Text, der sehr bewußt auf seinen Schluß hin geplant wurde. Es mag Zufall oder ironische Absicht sein, daß ausgerechnet jener zitierten Textstelle, in der sich das Planvolle des Gedichts zeigt, wie ein Signal das Wort »Fünfjahresplan« vorausgeht. Interpreten entdecken manchmal Kunstgriffe in einem Gedicht, an die der Dichter nicht im entferntesten gedacht hat. Andererseits muß man sich darüber im klaren sein, daß der Dichter jedes einzelne Wort ganz bewußt an seinen Platz gestellt hat, so daß dem Interpreten wahrscheinlich weit mehr planvolle Kunstgriffe verborgen bleiben, als er möglicherweise ungerechtfertigt in das Gedicht hineininterpretiert.

Gedichte, die keiner Interpretation bedürfen

Seit das Interpretieren zur akademisch sanktionierten Normalform des Umgangs mit Lyrik geworden ist, hat sich die unausgesprochene, aber doch allgemein geteilte Ansicht durchgesetzt, daß Gedichte um so besser seien, je mehr sich durch Interpretation aus ihnen herausholen läßt. Umgekehrt werden solche, die alles sagen, was sie meinen, so daß es an ihnen nichts zu interpretieren gibt, gering geachtet. Dieser Geringschätzung fällt vor allem der ganze Bereich der didaktischen und der politischen Lyrik zum Opfer. In der Antike erfreute sich die didaktische Dichtung genauso hoher Wertschätzung wie die epische und lyrische. Über fast alle Bereiche des Wissens und der Praxis sind lehrhafte Darstellungen in Versform überliefert: über Astronomie, Geographie, Medizin, Ackerbau und Fischfang bis hin zur Kochkunst. Hesiods und Vergils Gedichte über den Ackerbau und Lukrez' naturphilosophische Abhandlung *De rerum natura* zählen zu den großen Werken antiker Verskunst. Bis ins 18. Jahrhundert hinein schrieben Dichter wie der Franzose Boileau oder der Engländer Pope Abhandlungen zur Poetik in Versform. Im 19. Jahrhundert trat an die Stelle der lehrhaft-didaktischen Dichtung die politisch-agitatorische. Die Dichter des Vormärz – Herwegh, Freiligrath, Hoffmann von Fallersleben u. a. – begründeten eine Tradition, die in unserem Jahrhundert von Tucholsky, Brecht und Kästner fortgesetzt wurde. Die letztgenannten werden wegen ihrer politischen Aktualität auch heute noch gelesen; die politische Dichtung des 19. Jahrhunderts aber tritt neben der lyrischen jener Zeit ganz in den Hintergrund. Ein Dichter wie Herwegh, der eine geschliffene Feder führte und einer der aufrechtesten Intellektuellen seiner Zeit war, ist heute fast vergessen. Aber auch Tucholsky und Kästner mögen zwar gelesen werden, doch zur Lyrik im eigentlichen Sinne zählt man ihre Gedichte nicht. Kaum ein Literaturwissenschaftler würde auf die Idee kommen, sie fachgerecht zu interpretieren. Man wüßte wohl auch gar nicht, was man darüber sagen sollte. Die Gedichte sind auf ihre Weise ausgezeichnet, sie haben Biß und agitatorische Durchschlagskraft. Aber alles, was sie sagen wollen, liegt – einschließlich der rhetorischen Mittel, die sie dafür verwenden – so offen zutage, daß eine Interpretation eigentlich nur noch wiederholen kann, was jeder Leser ohne weiteres sieht und versteht. Sie bedürfen keiner Interpretation. Muß man ihnen deshalb die höheren Weihen der Dichtkunst absprechen? Unser Urteil über Lyrik ist immer noch weitgehend durch die klassisch-romantische Poetik bestimmt. Wir erwarten von einem Gedicht, daß es wie ein Organismus aus Elementen besteht, die zueinander und zum Ganzen in vielfältigen, sehr komplexen Beziehungen stehen. Dieses charakteristische Phänomen der Selbstreferenz lyrischer Texte gilt als Qualitätsmerkmal eines Gedichts. Damit sind Gedichte, die direkt und unverhüllt sagen, was sie meinen, wie vor allem die didaktischen und politischen, als Lyrik minderen Ranges abgewertet, ja, strenggenommen sind sie gar keine Dichtung im akzeptierten Sinn, sondern nur versifizierte Formen von expositorischen Texten, was die übliche Bezeichnung aller nichtpoetischen Texte ist. Diese Abwertung ist zweifellos ungerecht. Manche der didaktischen und auch politischen Gedichte von der Antike bis zur Gegenwart stehen in ihrer intellektuellen Substanz und in der formalen Bewältigung ihres Stoffs hoch über dem Durchschnitt der anthologisierten reinen Lyrik. Dennoch hat das Dichterische bei ihnen einen anderen Status. Es ist angewandte Kunst so wie ein Werbeplakat oder das plastische Design eines Konsumgegenstands. Diese zielorientierten Gebrauchstexte, die kognitive Inhalte übermitteln oder zu politischem Handeln stimulieren wollen, entfalten ihre Wirkung nicht aus einer Selbstreferenz heraus, sondern aus dem Bezug auf etwas außerhalb des Textes. Wollte man sie interpretieren, müßte man die didaktischen in ihren kognitiven und die politischen in ihren Handlungskontext stellen. Auch dies wäre eine verstehende Aneignung und damit Interpretation im hermeneutischen Sinn. Aber das ästhetische Phänomen würde dabei nur eine untergeordnete Rolle spielen. Das Dichterische an ihnen wäre im Falle der didaktischen Gedichte nur eine ornamentale Beigabe und im Falle der politischen Lyrik eine rhetorische Unterstützung der beabsichtigten Wirkung. Man kann also sagen, daß manche didaktischen und politischen Gedichte im kulturellen Gesamtkontext durchaus einen höheren Wert haben können als ganze Bände landläufiger Lyrik, aber der »reinen« Kunstsphäre der ästhetischen Gegenstände gehören sie nicht an. Da sie immer schon kognitiv aufgeschlossen sind, bedürfen sie allenfalls eines Kommentars, aber nicht jener interpretierenden Übersetzung aus der ästhetischen in die kognitive Wahrnehmungsform, durch die wir uns lyrische Gedichte im engeren Sinne anzueignen suchen.

dies nicht getan, wäre sie längst aus ökonomischen Gründen abgestorben. Nur die Wissenschaft, die sich mit ihr befaßt, scheint sich für das Phänomen des Gefallens kaum mehr zu interessieren, obwohl es doch gerade das ist, was den ästhetischen Gegenstand von allen nichtästhetischen unterscheidet. Sollte dies womöglich daran liegen, daß etwas so Persönliches und Subjektives wie das ästhetische Lusterlebnis sich dem wissenschaftlichen Zugriff entzieht? Selbst wenn dem so wäre, müßte man doch zumindest die Frage stellen, weshalb bestimmte Kunstwerke mehr gefallen als andere, was also ihren besonderen ästhetischen Wert ausmacht. Diese Frage wollen wir nun zum Schluß im Hinblick auf die Lyrik aufwerfen.

Man wird sich wohl leicht darauf verständigen können, daß der Wert eines Gedichts nichts mit dem Gewicht und der Bedeutung seiner Aussage zu tun hat. Die große Masse aller Gedichte enthält nichts weiter als Meinungen und Gefühle, die jedermann vertraut sind und die man infolgedessen als Platitüden bezeichnen könnte. Gewiß gibt es Gedichte von Goethe, Hölderlin, Rilke und anderen, die so tiefsinnig sind, daß man sehr lange, vielleicht ein Leben lang darüber nachdenken kann, doch ist es nicht das, was sie am Leben erhalten hat; denn es gibt Bände von außerordentlich tiefsinniger Lyrik, die niemandem gefällt und darum vergessen ist. Umgekehrt wird sich ein Gedicht wie Mörikes »Septembermorgen« in den Anthologien halten, obwohl es nichts weiter ausdrückt als das, was wohl jeder Beobachter schon einmal empfunden hat, wenn er sah, wie eine Landschaft im Morgendunst langsam von der heraufsteigenden Sonne entschleiert wird. Was also ist der Grund des Vergnügens, das der Leser an einem Gedicht findet und das ihn veranlaßt, es immer und immer wieder zu lesen?

Um 1700 hätten die Kritiker in Europa auf diese Frage wohl noch mehr oder weniger einstimmig geantwortet: Der Grund liegt darin, daß das Gedicht nach den erprobten Regeln der Alten, also der Griechen und Römer, gemacht ist. Dichtung galt als Handwerk, das man lernen konnte, wenn auch der Lernerfolg im Einzelfall vom angeborenen Talent abhing. Hundert Jahre später wäre die Antwort ganz anders ausgefallen. Jetzt, auf dem Höhepunkt der Romantik, hätte man gesagt: Das Gedicht gefällt, weil es die originale, unverwechselbare Schöpfung eines vom göttlichen Funken inspirierten Genies ist. Weitere hundert Jahre später hätten die ersten wohlwollenden Leser Gottfried Benns 1912 beim Erscheinen von *Morgue* gesagt: Diese Gedichte gefallen, weil sie verlogene lyrische Klischees zerschlagen, weil sie unter die Haut gehen und authentisch sind. Ein halbes Jahrhundert später, als an Schulen und Universitäten die textnahe Werkinterpretation geübt wurde, erklärten die Lehrer ihren Schülern, das Kriterium eines guten Gedichts sei seine innere Stimmigkeit. Keines der genannten Kriterien kann erklären, weshalb das Gedicht ästhetische Lust hervorruft. Wenn der lustauslösende Reiz das Wesen des guten Gedichts ausmacht, dann muß seine Ursache in dem liegen, was das Gedicht von allen anderen nichtpoetischen Texten unterscheidet, also in der sprachlichen Formalisierung.

Von einem gelungenen Gedicht erwarten wir zunächst einmal vollständige Durchgeformtheit. Ein überstehender, formal nicht bewältigter Rest, ein stolperndes Metrum, eine ungrammatische Syntax, alles dies wird von uns als Kunstfehler empfunden, sofern es in keiner Beziehung zur Aussage steht. Gleichzeitig erwarten wir aber auch eine hohe semantische Dichte. Das Gedicht soll weder formal noch inhaltlich repetitiv sein. Einerseits soll es in seiner selbstgewählten Ordnung ohne Rest aufgehen, andererseits soll es innerhalb dieser Ordnung ein Höchstmaß an Vielfalt und Komplexität aufweisen, da wir auf eine allzu regelmäßige formale Ordnung mit Langeweile reagieren. Das Geheimnis großer Kunst scheint die goldene Mitte zwischen Ordnung und Komplexität zu sein. Schon die Ästhetiker des 18. Jahrhunderts haben dies immer wieder mit der Formel »Vielfalt in der Einheit« zu fassen versucht. Der englische Maler Hogarth schrieb ein Buch *The Analysis of Beauty*, in dem er die Sinuskurve, die er als *serpent line*, d. h. Schlangenlinie, bezeichnete, als Inbegriff der Schönheit, als *line of beauty*, beschrieb. Die Sinuskurve, deren trigonometrische Gesetzmäßigkeiten Hogarth gar nicht kannte, zeichnet sich gegenüber dem Kreis dadurch aus, daß sie zwar wie dieser an jedem Punkt eine andere Steigung hat, daß aber die Änderung der Steigung wiederum nach einer Sinusfunktion erfolgt, dem Kosinus. Wir haben es hier mit einem Musterbeispiel von Vielfalt in der Einheit zu tun. Ein anderes Beispiel ist der Goldene Schnitt, der schon bei den alten Griechen als die ästhetisch befriedigendste Teilung einer Strecke galt und dessen Proportionsgesetz sich überall in Architektur, Skulptur und Malerei nachweisen läßt. Ein Goldener Schnitt liegt vor, wenn eine Strecke so geteilt wird, daß sich die ganze Strecke zum größeren Teilstück wie das größere zum kleinen verhält. Klappt man nun aber das kleinere auf das größere um, so ist dieses wieder nach der gleichen Proportion geteilt und so fort. Im Goldenen Schnitt ist somit eine unendliche Wiederholung der ursprünglichen Proportion angelegt. Als drittes und letztes sei noch ein Beispiel aus der Musik genannt: die Obertonreihe. Alle Intervalle, die in der Harmonielehre der tonalen Musik eine Rolle spielen, sind bereits in den Obertönen jedes einzelnen natürlichen Tons angelegt; denn in jedem schwingt seine Oktave, Quinte, Quart, große Terz, kleine Terz usw. mit, so daß in jedem einzigen Ton die ganze Vielfalt musikalischer Harmonien gegenwärtig ist.

Wenn nun aber Vielfalt in der Einheit bzw. Komplexität in der Ordnung der Grund des Vergnügens an einem Kunstwerk ist, dann stellt sich die Frage, ob sich das Verhältnis der beiden Qualitäten nicht irgendwie messen läßt. Der amerikanische Mathematiker Birkhoff hat als erster versucht, den ästhetischen Wert zu quantifizieren, indem er das ästhetische Maß (M) als den Quotienten aus Ordnung (O) und Komplexität (C) definierte. Seine Formel lautet:

$$M = \frac{O}{C}$$

Obgleich die Vorstellung eines ausgewogenen Verhältnisses von Ordnung und Komplexität als Maß für den ästhetischen Wert zunächst eine gewisse Plausibilität hat, ist die Unhaltbarkeit der Formel leicht einzusehen; denn sie besagt ja, daß der ästhetische Wert sich proportional zur Ordnung und umgekehrt proportional zur Komplexität verhält. Von einem ausgewogenen Verhältnis, einer goldenen Mitte, kann keine Rede sein. Größte Ordnung bei geringster Komplexität ergäbe nach dieser Formel ein Höchstmaß an ästhetischer Wirkung, nach allgemeiner Lebenserfahrung aber ergibt es Langeweile. Birkhoffs Ansatz wurde von Max Bense und Rul Gunzenhäuser aufgegriffen und auf informationstheoretischer Basis zu einem mathematischen Kalkül weiterentwickelt. Auf die Ableitung dieses Kalküls müssen wir hier verzichten. Der Grundgedanke darin ist jedoch von genialer Einfachheit. Gunzenhäuser ersetzt in Birkhoffs Formel im Zähler des Bruchs die tatsächliche Ordnung durch den Ordnungsgewinn, der im Augenblick der ästhetischen Wahrnehmung eintritt. Der Betrachter eines Kunstwerks, bzw. der Leser eines Gedichts steht zunächst vor einer komplexen Vielfalt, deren Komplexität sich für ihn sogleich reduziert, sobald er die geheime Ordnung durchschaut hat. Die neue Formel lautet:

$$M = \frac{C_{(\text{vor Erkenntnis})} - C_{(\text{nach Erkenntnis})}}{C_{(\text{vor Erkenntnis})}}$$

Diese Formel wird dem tatsächlichen Vorgang der ästhetischen Wahrnehmung schon sehr viel eher gerecht als die von Birkhoff; denn sie besagt, daß der ästhetische Wert um so größer ist, je größer die Differenz zwischen Anfangskomplexität und Restkomplexität ist. Gunzenhäuser nennt diese Differenz »subjektive Redundanz«, weil informationstheoretisch Ordnung Redundanz bedeutet. Wenn wir auf Grund der erkannten Ordnung eines Systems das Eintreten eines bestimmten Zustands vorhersagen können, dann ist das tatsächliche Eintreten des Zustands redundant, d. h. überflüssig, da wir ja schon vorher wußten, daß er eintreten wird. Sein Eintreten hat für uns keinen Neuigkeitswert, es enthält keine Information. Die Komplexität des Anfangszustands, seine scheinbare Unordnung, bedeutet informationstheoretisch also seine Information. Das Erkennen der Ordnung ist in diesem Sinne eine Verminderung der Information des wahrgenommenen Zustands aus der Sicht des Erkennenden. Psychologisch könnte man diesen Erkenntnisvorgang als Informationsentnahme deuten. Damit hätten wir jetzt ein theoretisches Modell für die Erklärung des ästhetischen Lusterlebnisses. Wenn wir das zunächst noch sehr komplex erscheinende Kunstwerk zu erfassen versuchen, benötigen wir ein hohes Maß an psychischer Wahrnehmungsenergie. In dem Augenblick aber, in dem wir seine Ordnung durchschauen, also seine Information entnehmen und damit subjektiv für uns seine Komplexität drastisch senken, vermindert sich sogleich der erforderliche Aufwand an Wahrnehmungsenergie. Der freiwerdende Überschuß entlädt sich als ästhetische Lust, so wie sich beim Verstehen der Pointe eines Witzes der plötzliche Überschuß an psychischer Energie als Lachen entlädt. Nach unserem Modell wird die ästhetische Lust um so größer sein, je größer das Intervall zwischen Anfangskomplexität und Restkomplexität ist. Eine Vergrößerung dieses Intervalls ist auf zweierlei Weise möglich: zum einen durch vollständigere Durchformung des Gegenstands, wodurch die Restkomplexität vermindert wird, zum andern durch Erhöhung der Anfangskomplexität bei gleichbleibender Restkomplexität. Dies ist eine verblüffend plausible Erklärung dafür, daß sowohl höchst komplexe Kunstwerke wie die Gedichte Celans oder die Musik Schönbergs als auch sehr einfache, leicht faßliche Werke wie die Gedichte Eichendorffs oder Mozarts »Kleine Nachtmusik« ästhetisch befriedigen. Im zweiten Fall kommt die subjektive Redundanz mit der anschließenden lustvollen Freisetzung der überschüssigen Wahrnehmungsenergie dadurch zustande, daß wir an den Gegenstand zunächst mit der Erwartung einer durchschnittlichen Komplexität unseres mehr oder weniger ungeordneten Alltagslebens herangehen. Da der Gegenstand aber in so vollständig durchgeformter, unmittelbar faßlicher Gestalt vorliegt, daß er der Wahrnehmung keinerlei Widerstand entgegensetzt, erweist sich die bereitgestellte psychische Energie als überflüssig und entlädt sich als Lust.

Der zuletzt vorgeschlagene Erklärungsversuch berührt sich mit einem Gedanken, den schon Kant in seiner *Kritik der Urteilskraft* entwickelt hat. Seine Definition des ästhetischen Urteils läßt sich ungefähr so zusammenfassen: Schön ist, was ohne Hinzutun eines logischen Begriffs und ohne irgendein Interesse des sinnlichen oder sittlichen Begehrungsvermögens allein im Augenblick des Anschauens unmittelbar gefällt. Kant meinte, daß die Form eines schönen Gegenstands den Ordnungskategorien des Verstands so sehr entspreche, daß sie sich diesem gleichsam freiwillig unterwerfe, ohne von ihm unter das Joch eines Begriffs gezwungen werden zu müssen. In der Wahrnehmung des Schönen befänden sich die Sinneswahrnehmung und der begriffliche Verstand in so völliger Übereinstimmung, daß sich beide wie zwei Tänzer zu einem freien Spiel der Erkenntniskräfte verbänden. Auch wenn diese Beschreibung dem modernen Psychologen naiv erscheinen mag, läßt sich doch von hier eine Brücke zu unseren oben angestellten Überlegungen schlagen. Schöne Gegenstände scheinen wie Schlüssel in die Schlösser unserer Wahrnehmung zu passen. Der erforderliche Aufwand an psychischer Energie ist infolgedessen gering. Wir hatten ganz am Anfang einmal gesagt, daß das Gedicht eine kristalline Struktur habe. In der Chemie wird durch spontane Kristallisation eines vorher amorphen Stoffes Energie freigesetzt, weil die Atome, die sich vorher frei bewegten, plötzlich in eine feste Ordnung eingebunden werden, so daß die nicht mehr erforderliche Bewegungsenergie als Überschuß frei wird. Dieser Vorgang ist ein anschauliches Modell für das, was möglicherweise in unserem Gehirn bei der Wahrnehmung von etwas Schönem geschieht. Wäre nicht denkbar, daß es bei der Verarbeitung von Information auf ähnliche Weise verfährt, so daß beim Abspeichern eines schönen, d. h. vollständig durchgeformten, gleichsam kristallin gewordenen Gegenstands ein Überschuß an psychischer Energie frei wird, den wir als ästhetische Lust erleben?

Dem technisch versierten Leser wird schon an Gunzenhäusers Formel aufgefallen sein, daß sie exakt der physikalischen Formel für den Wirkungsgrad von Maschinen entspricht. Und in der Tat ist ja der ästhetische Reiz eines Kunstwerks nichts anderes als seine Wirkung. Bei einer Maschine ist der Wirkungsgrad um so größer, je mehr von der aufgenommenen Leistung sie wieder abgibt, d. h. je weniger Leistung sie durch Reibung oder andere Verluste für sich selbst verbraucht. Könnte man sich den Wirkungsgrad eines Kunstwerks nicht ähnlich vorstellen? Die in das Werk eingegangene Leistung ist die vom Künstler planvoll hergestellte Ordnung, die sich objektiv zunächst als Komplexität darstellt. Je mehr von dieser Komplexität wir als Ordnung durchschauen und dem Werk als Information entnehmen, um so größer ist die von ihm abgegebene Leistung und damit sein Wirkungsgrad. Der höchste theoretisch mögliche Wirkungsgrad einer Maschine hat den Wert eins. Er ist dann gegeben, wenn die aufgenommene Leistung ohne Verlust wieder abgegeben wird. Analog dazu läge im Kunstwerk der höchste Wirkungsgrad dann vor, wenn seine ganze Anfangskomplexität so vollständig in erkannte Ordnung umgesetzt wäre, daß keine Restkomplexität übrigbliebe. Man könnte diese Überlegung noch einen Schritt weitertreiben. Da die Komplexität eines Textes selbst dann, wenn sie vollständig auf erkannte Ordnung reduziert wird, nie unter die Restkomplexität einfachster Sprachmuster sinken kann, haben wir es hier mit einer Situation zu tun, die dem Wirkungsgrad von Wärmekraftmaschinen vergleichbar ist. Solche Maschinen, die ein Temperaturintervall ausnutzen, um Wärme in mechanische Arbeit umzuwandeln, könnten den theoretisch höchsten Wirkungsgrad eins nur dann erreichen, wenn die niedrigere Temperaturstufe unter dem absoluten Nullpunkt läge, was physikalisch unmöglich ist. Damit wären wir beim zweiten thermodynamischen Hauptsatz der Physik und bei dem schwierigen Begriff der Entropie, deren Formel nicht zufällig identisch ist mit dem informationstheoretischen Maß für die Information. Beide, Entropie und Information, sagen etwas über die Summe der Wahrscheinlichkeit bzw. Zufälligkeit aller Einzelzustände in einem geschlossenen System aus. Ein Text, dessen Buchstaben nacheinander ausgewürfelt werden, so daß für jedes Element die gleiche Zufallswahrscheinlichkeit besteht, hat informationstheoretisch die größtmögliche Information mit dem Wert eins. Er gleicht einem Gas in einem geschlossenen Gefäß, das bei gleichbleibender Temperatur den höchsten Entropiewert hat, da für den Zustand jedes einzelnen Atoms die gleiche Wahrscheinlichkeit besteht. Weil diese Information aber nicht auf eine erkennbare Ordnung reduziert und damit redundant gemacht werden kann, bleibt sie vollkommen wirkungslos, so wie bei gleichmäßiger Verteilung der Wärme in einem geschlossenen System keine Wärmekraftmaschine mehr funktionieren würde. Das System erliegt dem Wärmetod; und genauso erliegt der Zufallstext dem ästhetischen Wirkungstod.

An dieser Stelle wollen wir unseren spekulativen Denkanstoß abbrechen und an den Anfang zurückkehren, um die dort gemachte Grundannahme noch einmal in Frage zu stellen. Ist es wirklich sinnvoll und zulässig, dem Lusterlebnis bei der Wahrnehmung eines Kunstwerks so große Bedeutung beizumessen? Ist nicht der Nachvollzug der darin gestalteten menschlichen Erfahrung ungleich wichtiger? Als die erschütterndsten Beispiele solcher allgemeinmenschlichen Grunderfahrungen gelten gemeinhin die Werke der großen Tragiker. Aber gerade die Tragödie hat Aristoteles als die Nachahmung einer Handlung beschrieben, die durch Erregung von *phobos* (Schrecken) und *eleos* (Jammer) eine *katharsis* dieser Affekte bewirkt. Wir wissen heute, daß Aristoteles unter *katharsis* im medizinisch-physiologischen Sinne die lustvolle Abfuhr eines Affektstaus verstand. Durch *phobos* wird das Reizniveau des Zuschauers nach oben getrieben, und durch *eleos* wird es auf lustvoll orgastische Weise wieder abgesenkt, worauf der Zuschauer kathartisch befriedigt das Theater verläßt. So wird die weihevollste Literaturgattung vom ehrwürdigsten Ahnherrn literarischer Theorie als ein auf Lustgewinn hin angelegtes Unternehmen erklärt. Und doch werden wir zögern, die Kunst schlechthin als eine kulturell institutionalisierte Quelle hedonistischer Lust zu definieren; denn dann müßten wir den vordersten Rang in ihrem Bereich der Pornographie einräumen. Die scharfsinnigste Analyse des Phänomens hat auch hier Kant gegeben. Er hat überzeugend dargelegt, daß die Lust, auf die das Kunstwerk abzielt, etwas anderes ist als die physiologische Lust des Sinnengenusses einerseits und die moralische Lust am Guten andererseits. Von beiden unterscheidet sie sich durch ihre Interesselosigkeit. Sie ist frei von der physiologischen Determinierung unserer Triebausstattung, auf die z. B. die Pornographie spekuliert, und sie ist ebenso frei von unseren ethischen Normen, auf die die gutgemeinte Erbauungskunst abzielt, die in aller Regel Kitsch produziert. Das Schöne in der Kunst hat Schiller als »Freiheit in der Erscheinung« definiert. Diese aus Kantischem Geist stammende Definition ist wohl immer noch die zutreffendste allgemeine Beschreibung des Wesens der Kunst. Nichts unterscheidet den Menschen so sehr vom Tier wie seine Fähigkeit, sich selber frei in die Zukunft zu entwerfen, sich von sich selbst zu distanzieren, über sich selbst zu lachen und zu weinen und sich selbst in eine beliebige Wunschwelt hineinzuträumen. Die Kunst ist die Sphäre, in der der Mensch gänzlich frei ist von der Determinierung durch seine Natur und der Normierung durch die Moral. Darum ist der lustvolle Kunstgenuß kein platter Hedonismus, sondern die reinste, von allen Beimengungen befreite Erfahrung des Menschlichen schlechthin, nämlich die Erfahrung der nur dem Menschen eigenen Freiheit.

Statt eines Nachworts

mit Gruß an Morgenstern

Korf, wenn ihm der Hals verschleimt,
liest am liebsten, was sich reimt;
denn des Reimes Redundanz
senkt den Aufwand des Verstands.

Geisteskraft, die zum Verstehen
nicht gebraucht wird, geht in Wehen
durch die Glieder wie ein Kuß
und bewirkt den Kunstgenuß.

Doch als Korf bei Fachgelehrten
anfragt, wie sie dies erklärten,
waren selbige empört:
»Hat man so was schon gehört?

Wagt der Mensch sich zu erfrechen,
in der Kunst von Lust zu sprechen?
Kunst ist nichts, was amüsiert,
über Kunst wird promoviert!«

Korf, voll Wissenshunger, geht
an die Universität,
lernt dort in der Germanistik
Interpretationsartistik.

Dichtung ist, wie er erkennt,
metaphysisch-transzendent,
soziologisch relevant,
struktural signifikant.

Messerwerfend wie Artisten
definieren Linguisten
mit der Schärfe eines Dolches
das Gedicht schlechthin als solches.

Wörter sind fortan Sememe,
daraus bilden sich Texteme,
und aus Text um Text entsteht
Intertextualität.

Rekurrieren die Aktanten
wie bei einem Schiff die Spanten,
ist es fast schon Poesie
dank Partialisotopie.

Korf ist wie berauscht von diesen
bandwurmlangen Fachwortriesen,
und es wird ihm sonnenklar:
Nur was schwer ist, ist auch wahr.

Und so stemmt er jetzt Gedichte
wie der Heber die Gewichte
mit dem Stolz des Doktoranden.
Doch die Lust kam ihm abhanden.

Verfasser- und Quellenverzeichnis
der zitierten Texte

Auden, Wystan Hugh (1907–73)
Musée des Beaux Arts 100
Aus: Collected Shorter Poems 1927–1957. London: Faber 1966.

Brentano, Clemens (1778–1842)
Hör, es klagt die Flöte wieder 33
Aus: Werke. Hrsg. von F. Kemp. Bd. 1. München: Hanser 1963.

Bierbaum, Otto Julius (1865–1910)
Abendlied 90
Aus: Gesammelte Werke. Hrsg. von M. G. Conrad u. H. Brandenberg. Bd. 1. München: G. Müller o. J.

Browning, Robert (1812–89)
After 30
Aus: The Poems. Hrsg. von J. Pettigrew. Bd. 1. New Haven: Yale UP 1981.

Busse, Carl (1872–1918)
Ich möchte sterben... 91
Aus: Neuere deutsche Lyrik. Ausgew. u. hrsg. von C. Busse. Halle: Hendel 1895.

Celan, Paul (1920–70)
Sprachgitter 151
Aus: Sprachgitter. Frankfurt a. M.: S. Fischer 1959.

Dehmel, Richard (1863–1920)
Manche Nacht 41
Aus: Gesammelte Werke. Bd. 2. Berlin: S. Fischer 1913. © Tim Tügel, Hamburg.

Gomringer, Eugen (geb. 1925)

Aus: worte sind schatten. die konstellationen 1951–1968. Hrsg.
u. eingel. von H. Heißenbüttel. Reinbek bei Hamburg: Rowohlt
1969.

Góngora, Luis de (1561–1627)

Aus: Sonetos completos. Hrsg. von B. Ciplijauskaité. Madrid:
Clásicos Castalia 1969.

Grass, Günter (geb. 1927)

Aus: Deutsche Unsinnspoesie. Hrsg. von K. P. Dencker. Stuttgart:
Reclam 1978.

Gryphius, Andreas (1616–64)

Aus: Wir vergehn wie Rauch von starken Winden. Deutsche
Gedichte des 17. Jahrhunderts. Bd. 1. München: C. H. Beck 1985.

Gumppenberg, Hans von (1866–1928)

Aus: Das teutsche Dichterroß. In allen Gangarten vorgeritten von
Hans von Gumppenberg. 13. u. 14. erw. Aufl. München: Callwey
1929.

Heine, Heinrich (1797–1856)

Aus: Sämtliche Schriften. Hrsg. von K. Briegleb. Bd. 1 u. 4. München: Hanser 1976.

Hölderlin, Friedrich (1770–1843)

Aus: Sämtliche Werke. Kleine Stuttgarter Ausgabe. Hrsg. von F. Beißner. Bd. 1 u. 2. Stuttgart: Kohlhammer 1953.

Schiller, Friedrich (1759–1805)

Der Handschuh 133
Aus: Sämtliche Werke. Hrsg. von G. Fricke u. H. G. Göpfert.
Bd. 1. München: Hanser ³1962.

Shakespeare, William (1564–1616)

Sonett Nr. 60 142
Aus: Sonnets and A Lover's Complaint. Hrsg. von J. Kerrigan.
Harmondsworth: Penguin 1986.

Shelley, Percy Bysshe (1792–1822)

Ode an den Westwind (Ode to the West Wind) 104
Aus: The Complete Poetical Works. Hrsg. von Th. Hutchinson.
London: Oxford UP 1907.

Steen, Sita (geb. 1919)

Ein Glied von Schillers Locke 72
Aus: Mit dem Kopfe geschüttelt. Stuttgart: Deutsche Verlags-
Anstalt 1971.

Storm, Theodor (1817–1888)

Meeresstrand 127
Aus: Sämtliche Werke. Berlin: Aufbau-Verlag ⁴1978.

Trakl, Georg (1887–1914)

In den Nachmittag geflüstert 113
Aus: Dichtungen und Briefe. Histor.-krit. Ausg. Hrsg. von W.
Killy u. H. Szklenar. Bd. 1. Salzburg: O. Müller 1969.

Die vier anonymen Limericks Nr. 1, 2, 3 u. 5 (S. 67–69) finden sich
in älteren Fassungen in: The Complete Limerick Book. Hrsg. von
Langford Reed. London 1924. Die hier abgedruckten Fassungen
orientieren sich an der heute geläufigen mündlichen Überlieferung.

Alle Übersetzungen stammen, soweit nicht anders angegeben, vom
Verfasser.

Literaturempfehlungen

Zum Nachschlagen von Sachbegriffen

Gero von Wilpert: Sachwörterbuch der Literatur. Stuttgart: Kröner
⁷1989.
(Vorzügliches einbändiges Sachwörterbuch mit guten Bibliographien zu allen wichtigen Begriffen.)
Metzler Literatur Lexikon. Begriffe und Definitionen. Hrsg. von
Günther u. Irmgard Schweikle. 2., überarb. Aufl. Stuttgart: Metzler 1990.
(Ebenfalls vorzüglich; berücksichtigt die moderne Literaturtheorie
stärker als Wilpert.)

Als Lernhilfe

Ivo Braak: Poetik in Stichworten. Literaturwissenschaftliche Grundbegriffe. Eine Einführung. Kiel: Hirt ⁶1980.
(Sehr übersichtliche, didaktisch gut aufbereitete Darstellung des
literaturwissenschaftlichen Grundwissens.)

Zur Einführung in die Lyrik

a) Allgemeinverständlich

Walther Killy: Elemente der Lyrik. 2., durchges. Aufl. München: Beck
1972. München: Deutscher Taschenbuch Verlag 1983.

b) Stärker theoriebetont

Bernhard Asmuth: Aspekte der Lyrik. Mit einer Einführung in die
Verslehre. 7., erg. Aufl. Opladen: Westdeutscher Verlag 1984.
Dieter Lamping: Das lyrische Gedicht. Definitionen zur Theorie und
Geschichte der Gattung. Göttingen: Vandenhoeck & Ruprecht
1989.

Zur literaturwissenschaftlichen Interpretation

Wolfgang Kayser: Das sprachliche Kunstwerk. Eine Einführung in
die Literaturwissenschaft. Bern: Francke ¹⁹1983.
(Ein »Klassiker«, wie die Auflagenzahl beweist; als Einführung in

die Literaturwissenschaft etwas veraltet, aber als Anleitung zum Verstehen von Literatur immer noch vorzüglich.)

Jürgen Schutte: Einführung in die Literaturinterpretation. Korr. Nachdr. der 1. Aufl. Stuttgart: Metzler 1990. (Sammlung Metzler 17.)

Anleitung zum Verstehen und Interpretieren von Lyrik

Hans-Werner Ludwig: Arbeitsbuch Lyrikanalyse. Tübingen: Narr [2]1981.
(Geht von modernen literaturtheoretischen Ansätzen aus.)

Günter Waldmann: Produktiver Umgang mit Lyrik. Eine systematische Einführung in die Lyrik, ihre produktive Erfahrung und ihr Schreiben. Für Schule (Sekundarstufe I und II) und Hochschule sowie zum Selbststudium. 2., korrigierte Aufl. Baltmannsweiler: Schneider 1992.

Zu Verslehre und Metrik

Wolfgang Kayser: Kleine deutsche Versschule. Bern: Francke [20]1980.
(Sehr klare Darstellung der Vers-, Strophen- und Gedichtformen mit vielen Beispielen.)

Gerhard Storz: Der Vers in der neueren deutschen Dichtung. Stuttgart: Reclam 1970.
(Etwas weniger anschaulich, dafür stärker literarhistorisch ausgerichtet als Kayser.)

Christian Wagenknecht: Deutsche Metrik. Eine historische Einführung. München: Beck 1981. (Beck'sche Elementarbücher.)

Leif Ludwig Albertsen: Neuere deutsche Metrik. Bern u. Frankfurt a. M.: Lang 1984. (Germanistische Lehrbuchsammlung 55 b.)

Zur poetischen Bildersprache

Walther Killy: Wandlungen des lyrischen Bildes. Göttingen: Vandenhoeck & Ruprecht [7]1978. (Kleine Vandenhoeck-Reihe 1022.)

Anselm Haverkamp (Hrsg.): Theorie der Metapher. Darmstadt: Wissenschaftliche Buchgesellschaft 1983. (Wege der Forschung 389.)

Gerhard Kurz: Metapher, Allegorie, Symbol. 3., bibliogr. erg. Aufl. Göttingen: Vandenhoeck & Ruprecht 1993. (Kleine Vandenhoeck-Reihe 1486.)

Zur sprachlichen Komik

Erwin Rotermund: Die Parodie in der modernen deutschen Lyrik.
München: Eidos Verlag 1963.

Hermann Helmers: Lyrischer Humor. Strukturanalyse und Didaktik
der komischen Versliteratur. Stuttgart: Klett 1971.

Winfried Freund: Die literarische Parodie. Stuttgart: Metzler 1981.
(Sammlung Metzler 200.)

Klen: Schüttelreime selbst gemacht. Eine Einführung in die Theorie
und Praxis des Schüttelreims. Hildesheim: Lax 1987.

Zum Problem der literarischen Wertung

Jochen Schulte-Sasse: Literarische Wertung. 2., völlig neu bearbeitete
Aufl. Stuttgart: Metzler 1976. (Sammlung Metzler 98.)

Bernd Lenz u. Bernd Schulte-Middelich (Hrsg.): Beschreiben, Interpretieren, Werten. Das Wertungsproblem in der Literatur aus der
Sicht unterschiedlicher Methoden. München: Fink 1982. (Münch-
ner Universitätsschriften, Philosophische Fakultät 25.)

Interpretationsbeispiele

Die deutsche Lyrik. Form und Geschichte. 2 Bde. Hrsg. von Benno
von Wiese. Düsseldorf: Bagel 1956. Neuaufl. o. J.

Gedichte und Interpretationen. [Hrsg. von versch. Fachgelehrten.]
6 Bde. Stuttgart: Reclam 1982–84.

Zur Lyrik der Moderne

Hugo Friedrich: Die Struktur der modernen Lyrik von der Mitte des
neunzehnten bis zur Mitte des zwanzigsten Jahrhunderts. Erw.
Neuaufl. Reinbek bei Hamburg: Rowohlt 1985. (rde 420.)
(Seit seinem ersten Erscheinen 1956 in rowohlts deutscher enzy-
klopädie ist dieses Buch die fundierteste und theoretisch an-
spruchsvollste Einführung in die moderne Lyrik geblieben.)

Dieter Lamping: Moderne Lyrik. Eine Einführung. Göttingen: Vandenhoeck & Ruprecht 1991. (Kleine Vandenhoeck-Reihe 1557.)

Zur Konkreten Poesie

Thomas Kopfermann: Konkrete Poesie. Bern u. Frankfurt a. M.: Lang 1981.

Zur Gegenwartslyrik

Was alles hat Platz in einem Gedicht? Hrsg. von Hans Bender u. Michael Krüger. München: Hanser 1977.
(Enthält zahlreiche interessante Aussagen prominenter zeitgenössischer Lyriker aus der Sicht des Autors.)

Zur literaturtheoretischen Vertiefung

René Wellek u. Austin Warren: Theorie der Literatur. (Original: Theory of Literature. New York: Harcourt, Brace & Co. 1949.) Frankfurt a. M.: Athenäum Verlag 1985.
(Ein »Klassiker«. Obwohl schon vor mehreren Jahrzehnten erschienen und überwiegend auf die englischsprachige Literatur bezogen, ist dies wohl immer noch die beste Einführung in den Gesamtbereich der Literaturtheorie.)

Rolf Kloepfer u. Ursula Oomen: Sprachliche Konstituenten moderner Dichtung. Entwurf einer deskriptiven Poetik. Bad Homburg: Athenäum Verlag 1970.
(Am Beispiel der Lyrik Rimbauds.)

Rolf Kloepfer: Poetik und Linguistik. Semiotische Instrumente. München: Fink 1975. (UTB 366.)

Jurij N. Tynjanov: Das Problem der Verssprache. Zur Semantik des poetischen Textes. Aus dem Russischen übers., eingel. u. mit Registern vers. von Inge Paul. München: Fink 1977.

Zum informationstheoretischen Ansatz (vgl. Schlußkapitel)

Mathematik und Dichtung. Hrsg. von Helmut Kreuzer u. Rul Gunzenhäuser. München: Nymphenburger Verlagshandlung [4]1971.
(Die hier gesammelten, außerordentlich interessanten und stimulierenden Beiträge zu einer mathematisierten Poetik dürften zwar wenig hilfreich für die Interpretation sein, doch sind sie ein heilsames Korrektiv für das oft allzu subjektive, impressionistische ...den über Dichtung.)

Sachwortregister